The Supply and Demand
for Money

The Supply and Demand for Money

KEITH CUTHBERTSON

Basil Blackwell

First published 1985

Basil Blackwell Ltd
108 Cowley Road, Oxford OX4 1JF, UK

Basil Blackwell Inc.
432 Park Avenue South, Suite 1505,
New York, NY 10016, USA

British Library Cataloguing in Publication Data
Cuthbertson, Keith
   The supply and demand for money.
   1. Money
   I. Title
   332.4   HG221
   ISBN 0-631-14339-4

Library of Congress Cataloging-in-Publication Data
Cuthbertson, Keith
   The supply and demand for money.
   Bibliography: p.
   Includes indexes.
   1. Money supply.   I. Title.
   HG226.3.C87 1985   332.4'14   85-7524
   ISBN 0-631-14339-4

Typeset by Unicus Graphics, Horsham
Printed in Great Britain by TJ Press, Padstow

To Dot and Stan

Contents

Contents

Preface

This book is intended primarily for economists who have an interest in understanding the theory and empirics of the supply and demand for money although the role of the latter in the wider macroeconomic debate is also discussed. We hope to bridge the considerable gap between intermediate undergraduate texts and the material found in journal articles. It follows that the book is aimed at final year undergraduate and graduate students in economics and finance, as well as professional economists dealing with the financial sector.

The range of topics that come under the heading of 'monetary economics' is now so vast that one cannot hope to cover all aspects in reasonable depth, in one text. The material covered here is less than that found in a conventional text on monetary economics, as the title suggests. Some topics in monetary economics although ingenious and aesthetically pleasing are nevertheless about as much use as a chocolate teapot. I have therefore tried to concentrate on issues that yield practical insights and I think the book could provide a core text for a number of undergraduate and postgraduate courses in monetary economics that concentrate on analytic rather than institutional matters. However, I should welcome correspondence on how useful the book is for such courses: constructive criticism is always useful.

I am a great believer in the view that progress in economics requires an understanding of theoretical models and the empirical results from such models: naturally the content of the book reflects this. My first degree is not in economics and my postgraduate course in economics dealt only in theory: both econometric and economic theory. I remember leaving my MA course believing that the money supply could be (and ought to be) closely controlled and that the demand for money was a stable function of a few key variables. A few 'high-powered' regressions of my own would no doubt soon confirm these facts. This was in 1971 in the UK. It did not take me long to realize that academics do not have a monopoly of wisdom and truth in these matters and indeed that controversy abounds. Ever since, I have been sceptical of the pronouncements of economists. As a sceptic is what an idealist calls a realist, I accept the label with equanimity. However, I hope the book reflects problems that remain, as well as the intellectual advances in our understanding of particular areas of monetary economics.

Although the theory and empirics of the determination of the demand and supply of money provide the core elements in the book, I felt that I could not just present these issues in a vacuum. After all, monetary targets and 'monetarist policies' have been widely adopted by industrialized nations and the controversy surrounding alternative policies options continues apace. The supply and demand for money are central to an understanding of the impact of monetary and fiscal policy on the macroeconomy. I have tried, therefore, to place the detailed discussion on the supply and demand for money in the context of this general debate on macroeconomic policy. This has an advantage in that the reader can see how the detailed analysis of asset demands and supply may be used to build up alternative models of the financial sector and how the latter then react with the real sector in 'complete models'. Space constraints imply that this overview is somewhat sketchy but I hope it focuses on the main issues and above all is not misleading.

The overall framework of the book is as follows. In chapter 1 we provide an overview of alternative analytic models of the macroeconomy. In ensuing chapters we discuss the supply and demand for assets, particularly money, in detail. In the penultimate chapter we begin to bring the supply and demand sides of financial markets together when we discuss the term structure and this theme is reinforced in the final chapter where we provide practical illustrations of 'real world' financial and 'complete' models.

The variety of models discussed both for asset demand functions, and 'complete' models are numerous but the interconnections between issues discussed in individual chapters are continually stressed. The mathematical ability assumed is not high, elementary calculus being the main technique used and the emphasis is on the economics behind the results. Econometrics is a stumbling block for many students but an analysis of applied work is a necessary requirement for evaluating different theories. We have included an appendix where we discuss some recent issues in applied econometrics. This should enable the reader who has taken an introductory econometrics course to understand the empirical sections in the book and also to tackle some of the source material. Thus we hope to go some way towards dispelling the myth that an econometrician is the sort of person who goes into a revolving door behind you and comes out in front. Inevitably the level of difficulty and depth of coverage of topics varies somewhat but there is nothing in the text that goes beyond the abilities of a good final year student with reasonable mathematical ability. References are representative not exhaustive but enough are provided to enable the average 'economic sleuth' to pursue each 'case' in greater depth.

Acknowledgements

Completing the first draft of this book while a Hallsworth Fellow at the University of Manchester was most pleasurable, particularly discussions and help given by Mike Artis. James Foreman-Peck read large chunks of the first draft, Brian Tew made comments on the chapters on the money supply, David Hendry and Honor Stamler provided useful comments on the econometric sections. Charles Goodhart provided comments on articles which form the basis of some of the material in the book. Colleagues at the National Institute have provided much general encouragement over the years particularly Simon Brooks,

Steven Hall, Brian Henry, Gerry Kennally, David Mayes, Simon Wren-Lewis and Chris Johns. An anonymous referee provided numerous helpful points. Any remaining errors and omissions lie solely with the author. Unfortunately the 'literary slog' involved in producing the second draft of the book had to be done in my spare time – miraculously the family appears to have survived although I have the feeling that I have clocked up numerous 'penalty points' for which I hope to make amends in the future. Janet Sheppard and Anna Roberts helped with the typing although for typing most of the first draft my thanks go to the numerous typists in the department of economics at Manchester University and for the second draft, my home computer and my fingers – all ten (or is it eight?) of them.

1

An Overview

1.1 INTRODUCTION

There has been a great deal of controversy in macroeconomics over the past ten years or so. In retrospect the 1950s and the early 1960s appear to have been a period of consensus. The policy of 'fine tuning' using fiscal instruments to achieve full employment, was widely accepted over this period. The latter part of the 1960s and early 1970s saw the rise of monetarism and the view that 'money matters': control of inflation required control of the money supply. This approach was coupled with the view that uncertainties about the short-run impact of policy variables on the economy (but not their long-run impact) tilted the argument against the use of 'fine tuning' and in favour of setting policy instruments according to 'rules'. Those who favoured rules rather than discretion also accepted that the economy was self-correcting and that, in the long run, automatic full employment would ensue. In the early 1970s a number of countries abandoned the Bretton Woods 'fixed' exchange rate regime and allowed their currencies to float. It is probably true to say that subsequent movements in nominal and real exchange rates were more volatile than advocates of floating rates had anticipated. Large changes in real exchange rates caused fluctuations in real net trade and real output, and 'sound' monetary policies did not always appear to reduce inflation without also causing a substantial fall in real output. Just as the monetarist approach appeared to be losing credibility in practical terms, it received an academic boost from the so-called rational expectations–new classical (RE–NC) approach. Early versions of the new classical approach suggested that systematic attempts by the authorities to influence real output are futile. In particular, systematic monetary policy has no effect on output *even in the short run*, while unanticipated changes in the money approach supply exacerbate the economic cycle. Another powerful implication of the RE–NC approach is that it is impossible to assess alternative policy options using 'conventional' macroeconometric models. These NC propositions seemed to imply the demise of discretionary policy: at best it altered nothing, and at its worst it was likely to exacerbate the cycle.

Today, controversy still surrounds the relative impact of monetary and fiscal policy on the economy, the determinants of the exchange rate, the use of rules or discretion in the setting of policy instruments and whether the economy automatically moves to a full employment level of output. In a book which concentrates on the supply and demand for money, one could legitimately ignore these general issues. However, to put the detailed material of the rest of the book into perspective we present a brief overview of the main schools of thought, emphasizing the importance of the demand for money (and other assets) in the transmission mechanism of monetary and fiscal policy. In the final chapter we draw on this material and our detailed analysis of the supply and demand for money and present illustrative examples of 'complete real world' macromodels. Hence by the end of the book we hope the reader has a detailed knowledge of the building blocks of alternative 'financial models', together with some ideas on how these interact with the real sector.

1.2   ALTERNATIVE VIEWS ON THE MACROECONOMY

1.2.1   *Closed economy 'fix-price' models: monetarists and neo-Keynesians*

Much of the debate in the 1960s and early 1970s between monetarists and Keynesians about the determinants of aggregate demand was conducted in terms of the closed economy 'fix-price' IS-LM model which could be extended to include 'wealth effects' and a wider portfolio of assets (Levacic and Rebmann, 1982). In the simple IS-LM model the efficacy of monetary and fiscal policy ('financial crowding out') depends crucially on the size of the interest elasticity of the demand for money relative to that on expenditure (table 1.1). With the addition of 'wealth effects' working via the government budget constraint (Blinder and Solow, 1973) the time path to equilibrium is influenced by the size of the wealth elasticity of the demand for money (relative to that on real expenditure). Also, the 'wealth effects' literature indicates that it is possible for bond financed[1] or mixed money-bond financed fiscal deficits to be destabilizing. In this type of model the interdependence of monetary and fiscal policy is made explicit and this is examined in detail in chapters 7 and 8.

TABLE 1.1   Closed economy fix-price IS–LM model

Elasticities / Policy	$E_r^I = 0$	$E_r^m = \infty$	$E_r^I = \infty$	$E_r^m = 0$	Normal elasticities
Fiscal: $\Delta G > 0$	'full' Keynesian multiplier	'full' Keynesian multiplier	0	0	some crowding out, but $\Delta Y > 0$
Monetary: $\Delta M^s > 0$	0	0	'full' money multiplier	'full' money multiplier	$\Delta Y > 0$

E_r^I = interest elasticity of investment (absolute value).
E_r^m = interest elasticity of the demand for money (absolute value).

The temporal stability of the demand for money function is crucial in determining the predictability of monetary and fiscal policy. Also, the importance of lags in the demand for money function, whether these are due to adjustment or expectations formation is clearly demonstrated in 'dynamic' IS-LM models (Tucker, 1966; Laidler, 1966, 1973). These analytic 'fix-price' models therefore highlight the importance of the determinants of the demand for money in the transmission mechanism of monetary and fiscal policy. We discuss theoretical models of the demand for assets in chapters 2 and 3, the importance of lags and expectations are dealt with in chapter 4 and the size and stability of the parameters of the demand for money function are examined in chapters 5 and 6.

The portfolio adjustment process in the IS-LM model is very restrictive as substitution between only two assets, money and 'bonds', is allowed. In reality a whole range of assets, with varying degrees of substitutability, may provide substitutes for money. If so then a change in the money supply may involve a change in the yield on a wide range of financial and real assets, ranging from liquid assets to long term bonds, equity and capital goods. For example, Tobin (1980) stresses the possibility that the transmission mechanism of monetary policy may involve equities. After an increase in the money supply, interest rates fall and bond prices rise. The latter will lead to a rise in equity prices as agents switch out of low yielding bonds into equities. The market valuation of firms' real assets (the price of equities) now exceeds their costs of production and this provides an incentive for increased production of capital goods. Brunner and Meltzer (1972) extend the range of assets that may be substitutes for money and include real capital goods such as housing and consumer durables as well as 'fixed capital' (that is plant and machinery). An increase in the money supply yields diminishing utility at the margin, hence the higher (implicit) service yield of, say, durables encourages purchases of the latter, a rise in their demand price and an incentive to increase their supply.

Two important observations follow from this portfolio approach which are taken up in future chapters. First, the demand for money may depend on a *set* of interest rates (yields). Second, it may be necessary to model the demand for a whole range of financial assets if we are to understand fully the transmission mechanism of monetary policy. If the latter course is followed the resulting equations may be solved under the assumption of market clearing for the various 'short-term' and long-term interest rates. The relationship between long rates and short rates derived in this manner yield 'structural' term structure equations. An alternative to the above is to look at the relationship between short rates and long-term interest rates directly and apply a 'reduced form' (or 'unrestricted') term structure relationship. Both of these approaches are discussed in chapter 9 and provide the basis for our discussion of 'complete' models of the financial sector in chapter 10.

1.2.2 *The supply side and the neutrality debate*

Towards the end of the 1960s, in a number of industrialized nations, there was a simultaneous rise in both inflation and unemployment: stagflation had arrived and was to remain a major problem. It became increasingly recognized that changes in the money supply might have a powerful influence on inflation: a hypothesis which in its extreme version is summed up in Milton Friedman's assertion that 'inflation is always and everywhere a monetary phenomenon'. The Monetarist view relied on a *stable* demand function for money (with a unit price level elasticity) and a neo-classical view of the labour market and the 'supply side'.

The division of an increase in the money supply between a rise in the price level and a change in real output depends on the slope of the aggregate supply curve. In the neo-classical model of the labour market (which is consistent with the long-run vertical price expectations augmented Phillips curve, PEAPC) the long-run supply curve is vertical and unaffected by changes in the money supply or fiscal policy.[2] Money is 'neutral' in the long run, real output remains unchanged and the price level rises in proportion to the money supply. In the short run the aggregate supply curve is upward sloping because misperceptions about real wages on the part of workers (Friedman, 1968) lead to *temporary* changes in labour supply and output at a higher price level. (This provides an argument for the 'short-run' Phillips curve.) Monetarists tend to accept the neo-classical view of aggregate supply. On the other hand some neo-Keynesians would argue that the aggregate supply curve is upward sloping, even in the long run, because of rigidities in the labour market which prevent market clearing.[3] Monetary policy is therefore *non*-neutral in the long run as well as the short run.

With a neo-classical supply curve there is complete 'crowding out' of fiscal policy: we refer to this as 'physical' crowding out in contrast to 'financial' crowding out, discussed earlier, which operates on the demand side.

1.2.3 *Open economy aspects*

In the early part of the 1970s a number of industrialized nations abandoned the Bretton Woods 'fixed' exchange rate system, allowed their currencies to float and their exchange rates to be determined (largely) by market forces. It was widely thought at the time that nominal and real exchange rates would alter only slowly and that floating rates would allow 'small open economies' to have an independent monetary policy and hence to choose a rate of inflation independent of that in the rest of the world (Brooks et al., 1985).

International monetary models (IMM) came to prominence in academic and policy debates of the 1970s. However, an important precursor of these models is the so-called Mundell–Fleming (Mundell, 1960, 1963; Fleming, 1962) approach. The latter is a natural extension of the fix-price closed economy IS-LM model. Under floating exchange rates an additional transmission mechanism of monetary (and fiscal) policy is provided by the link between the interest rate, capital flows, the exchange rate and real net trade. In this model, monetary policy has an unambiguous effect on output but the efficacy of fiscal policy depends on the degree of capital mobility. With a high degree of capital mobility (that is horizontal BB curve (Artis, 1980)) fiscal policy is completely 'crowded out' by an induced fall in net trade whilst with a low degree of capital mobility (that is near vertical BB curve) there is 'crowding in' in the sense that the fiscal multiplier is higher than in the closed economy IS-LM model. In the model the efficacy of fiscal policy therefore depends on the substitutability between domestic and foreign assets. The latter is examined in chapter 5 for domestic and foreign money (that is currency substitution). Although space constraints prevent an empirical analysis of substitution between domestic and foreign non-money assets, nevertheless, some theories of the demand for assets discussed in chapters 2 and 3 may be usefully applied to this question.

In the 'current account monetary model' (CAM) under flexible exchange rates (Bilson, 1978), the rate of domestic monetary growth determines the domestic rate of inflation, and the rate of growth in the domestic relative to the foreign money supply determines the exchange rate. The basic assumptions of the model are stable domestic and 'foreign' demand for money functions with the exchange rate determined by purchasing power parity.

The CAM model was unable to account adequately for the volatile swings in real exchange rates that occurred in the floating rate period, and unless the model is extended it does not explain changes in real net trade and output consequent on these real exchange rate changes. The seminal article by Dornbusch (1976) provides a capital account monetary model (KAM) in which exchange rate 'overshooting' and changes in real output occur in the short run. The model is one of 'sticky' goods prices in the short run but the money and foreign exchange markets 'clear' in all periods. In addition, agents are assumed to form their expectations according to the rational expectations hypothesis, an issue we take up below. In the Dornbusch model, money is neutral in the long run (that is vertical long-run Phillips curve) and hence control of inflation requires control of the money supply and a stable demand for money function. However, it is explicitly recognized that a tight monetary policy may involve short-run costs in terms of lower output. The parameters of the demand for money function influence the path of output in the short run and, in particular, the size of the interest elasticity of the demand for money influences the degree of overshooting in the exchange rate (see also Frenkel and Rodriguez, 1982).

We may conclude this section by noting that in models of small open economies under flexible exchange rates the demand for money continues to play a key role in the transmission mechanism of monetary and fiscal policy and the money supply remains a key policy instrument.

1.2.4 *Rational expectations and the new classical school*

The rational expectations hypothesis (REH) has permeated all areas of macro-economics and may perhaps be considered as *the* major development in economics over the past fifteen years. It has influenced our views about individual behavioural functions and the scope and role for government policy (Begg, 1982; Minford and Peel, 1982; Sheffrin, 1983).

As we shall see in chapters 2 and 3, some theories imply that expectations variables, for example the expected capital gains on bonds, expected income, inflation and prices, influence the demand for assets and RE provides methods of modelling these (unobservable) expectations variables. We discuss this in chapters 4 and 5.

Throughout the 1970s the so-called new classical (NC) view was being developed, initially in the US but later by other economists. We may characterize the NC view as embodying two basic propositions: first, that all markets clear continuously and second, that agents form their expectations of economic variables (for example the rate of inflation) 'rationally': agents do not make systematic errors over a period of time, in their forecasts of the future course of economic variables. These two hypotheses are logically distinct and it is only when both are accepted that one may obtain the distinctive NC results. The major themes within the NC paradigm we discuss below include the policy ineffectiveness and policy evaluation propositions and the insights gained from partially rational models.

Policy ineffectiveness. In a wide variety of RE models it is possible to demonstrate that counter-cyclical monetary and fiscal policy is futile: the authorities cannot have a *systematic* effect on the mean level of output around its trend or natural rate. Indeed attempts at counter-cyclical policy may increase the variance of fluctuations in output, as compared with a policy whereby the money supply, for example, is fixed by a simple (non-contingent) rule. Thus the policy ineffectiveness debate also has implications for the rules versus discretion debate. It is the predictable part of the money supply that has no effect on output whereas unanticipated money supply changes do (temporarily) affect output. Clearly in such a model there is little or no rationale for any kind of monetary policy directed towards controlling output – announced targets for the money supply are used solely to achieve an inflation target (McCallum, 1980).

However, it is now clear that the policy ineffectiveness proposition and the claimed superiority of (non-contingent) rules in setting the money supply do not hold when some of the more restrictive assumptions of NC models are relaxed. Buiter (1980, 1981) provides a lucid account of the rules versus discretion debate in RE–NC models. The policy ineffectiveness proposition ceases to hold when, for example, (a) the authorities have access to information unknown to the private sector, (b) a subset of the private sector has an informational advantage (Weiss, 1980; King, 1981), (c) agents have access to some global information such as an economy-wide interest rate, (d) the authorities have a 'timing advantage' as in overlapping contract models (Taylor, 1979, 1980). In all of the above market clearing RE models the authorities can influence the variance of output around the natural rate but not the mean level of output. However, in non-market clearing RE models (Begg, 1982) the authorities can also influence the mean level of output.

Policy evaluation: Lucas critique. Lucas (1976) asserts that it is probably impossible to use existing econometric models to evaluate the consequences of alternative policy scenarios. This arises because the parameters of the model are likely to change under alternative policy regimes and it may not be possible to ascertain the new 'correct' values of the parameters at the time of the policy change. It also follows that the Lucas critique provides an explanation for the observed instability in coefficients of econometric models: different policy regimes give rise to 'shifts' in parameters.

The Lucas critique, if empirically important, is rather devasting. To see this, consider the way in which existing econometric models are used. After the model has been constructed on a particular data set, the model builder may use it to predict the consequences of, say, an increase in the money supply, on the assumption that the parameters of the model remain unchanged in the new environment. The model user then makes pronouncements that policy X rather than policy Y will produce a better outcome. Optimal control techniques provide a method of obtaining the optimal setting for the money supply given the preferences of the policy maker and have been fairly extensively used in policy analysis. These techniques also require an assumption that parameters are constant (or their probability distribution is known). Thus if the parameters of the model do not in fact remain constant under alternative regimes then the above policy scenarios are worthless. Parameter instability may arise whenever estimated coefficients are a convolution of expectations and 'structural' parameters, with the former altering under alternative regimes. We discuss this issue with respect to the demand for assets in section 4.4.

Partly rational models. It may be reasonable to consider some markets as clearing instantaneously and embodying RE and others where the converse applies. These partly rational models may be loosely described as New Keynesian. Asset markets, where homogeneous 'goods' are continuously sold in markets with low information and transactions costs, might provide good candidates for the assumption of Muth-RE. On the other hand the labour market (and to a lesser extent the goods market) which consists of largely heterogeneous 'units' with firm-specific skills that are traded relatively infrequently, may not conform to the RE hypothesis. The Dornbusch overshooting model discussed above provides one example of a partly rational model (see also Blanchard, 1981; Taylor, 1979; Fair, 1979).

In general terms, several characteristics of these partly rational models stand out. First, overshooting in the instantaneous market clearing variables may take place: the short-run response exceeds the long-run response. Second, and more important, the effects of anticipated and unanticipated changes in (policy) variables are very different over the path to the long-run equilibrium. Third, policy ineffectiveness may not apply and the authorities can influence the path of real output. Finally, these models usually allow 'persistence' effects: output can exhibit cyclical behaviour. In short, in partly rational models, the importance of the money supply as a policy instrument which influences both output and prices and the role of the demand for money function in the transmission mechanism are re-established.

1.2.5 *Summary*

All of the models discussed in this section treat the money supply as exogenous and under the control of the monetary authorities: this is a matter of analytic convenience. Clearly, if the money supply is to be an intermediate policy target the authorities must have a model of how the policy instruments that it does control, for example open market sales of government bonds, influence the behaviour of the private banks and hence the money supply. We discuss this matter in detail in the chapters on the analytic and practical problems of monetary control and also in the final chapter where we outline some properties of large scale 'real world' models, which incorporate an explicit account of the determination of the money supply. NC–RE models assume a stable demand for money function which forms part of the transmission mechanism of monetary policy. As we shall see, expectations play a major role in asset demand functions (for example expected income, expected capital gains and exchange rate changes) and the REH provides ways of modelling these expectations. Some of these methods use 'economically rational' expectations (Feige and Pierce, 1976) and therefore avoid the 'extreme' informational requirements of NC models where the whole structure of the model is assumed known. The NC approach, as expounded above, assumes (costless) instantaneous learning and our examination of other expectations mechanisms in chapter 4 provide a contrast to the RE approach.

In the non-RE models we have discussed, all schools (except the Keynesians) recognize the importance of the money supply in influencing real output in the short run (the monetarists) and, for some, in the long run (the neo-Keynesians). It is now widely accepted that the money supply may be a major cause of inflation and of changes in the exchange rate (the IMM models). Thus whether one wishes to control the money supply according to a rule or in a discretionary manner, a comprehensive model of the money supply process is required. We have also noted that the precise form of the demand for money function plays an important role in the transmission mechanism of monetary (and fiscal) policy. In particular wealth effects, the size of the interest elasticity of money demand and the presence of lagged responses all influence the time path of output and inflation.

1.3   OUTLINE OF THE BOOK

In the next two chapters we cover the main theoretical approaches to the demand for money (and other assets). There is an extensive discussion of recent developments in inventory and precautionary demand models and a detailed analysis of the mean-variance model. In chapter 4 we discuss the theoretical basis of lag responses and expectations determination as applied to asset demand functions. As well as the familiar partial adjustment and adaptive expectations models, we analyse the 'error feedback model', interdependent asset demands and compare the use of the rational expectations hypothesis with other expectations schemes. The reader is then in a position to examine empirical tests of the models.

Instead of the usual exhaustive and exhausting list of empirical studies, the latter are used to illustrate how the various models presented earlier may be tested. The emphasis is on recent advances in testing dynamic structure together with ('long-run') restrictions implied by theory. Systems of equations and associated cross equation restrictions are discussed. An appendix deals with recent econometric work on the evaluation of models: autocorrelation (common factors), reparameterization and the 'general to specific' modelling strategy. This material complements the empirical results discussed and provides a useful introduction to issues in the recent applied literature.

In chapter 6, after discussing some deficiencies in conventional demand for money functions, we analyse the theory and empirics of the 'buffer-stock' approach to the demand for money. We are able to integrate the buffer-stock approach with forward looking behaviour and the rational expectations hypothesis. Our analysis provides insights into possible causes of instability in 'conventional' demand for money functions and into the transmission mechanism of monetary policy.

Unlike other texts, 'conventional' monetary base and flow of funds approaches to modelling the money supply process, examined in chapter 7, are set firmly within the context of theories of the financial firm. Hence microeconomic issues such as real resource costs and the implications of alternative objective functions for the financial firm are examined. Our analysis of methods of monetary control in the UK and US in chapter 8 use the insights gained from the above theories and incorporate some of the empirical results on asset demands obtained in chapter 5. The implications for monetary targeting and monetary control of financial innovation in domestic and Euromarkets receive the prominence warranted in todays changing financial environment.

The term structure of interest rates is often treated in isolation from other areas of monetary economics. In chapter 9 we integrate theories of the term structure with the supply and demand for assets and the efficient markets rational expectations approach. Having looked in detail at the theory and empirics of asset demand and supply functions, we analyse in chapter 10 how these equations may be brought together to provide models of the financial sector and finally, how the financial sector and real sectors interact in 'complete' models. Fiscal and monetary policy are therefore examined in a more practical way than in chapter 1 and the reader is given some idea of the quantitative results obtained in different types of model. Again the empirical results quoted are used to illustrate the theoretical discussion in earlier chapters rather than providing an exhaustive account of competing models.

1.4 NOTATION

The notation used is fairly conventional. For example if we have a function of one variable, $U = U(W)$, the first and second derivatives may be written as $dU/dW = U'(W) = U_1$ and $d^2U/dW^2 = U'' = U_{11}$ respectively. For a function of two (or more) variables $U = U(x, y)$ we have $\partial U/\partial x = U_1 = U_x$ and similarly for the first derivative with respect to y. The expressions for the second derivatives are $\partial^2 U/\partial x^2 = U_{xx} = U_{11}$ (similarly for y) and $\partial^2 U/\partial x\,\partial y = U_{xy} = U_{12}$.

The absolute change in a variable S is given by $\Delta S = S - S_{-1}$ and the jth difference by $\Delta_j S = S - S_{-j}$. The proportionate change in the variable is given by $\dot{S} = (S - S_{-1})/S_{-1}$. The (natural) logarithm of a variable is usually (but not always) indicated by a lower case letter s and hence $\Delta s \approx \dot{S}$.

NOTES

1 The idea that government bonds are *not* net wealth arises because the (discounted present) value of future coupon receipts may be entirely offset by

higher expected tax liabilities. There is a thriving debate on this issue (Barro, 1974; Laidler, 1982; Buiter and Tobin, 1979).

2 This is true only under rather strong assumptions. If a change in the money supply affects the price level *and* the outstanding stock of bonds are considered as net wealth by the private sector, then changes in real wealth may shift the (neo-classical) labour supply curve and hence alter the supply of output. Thus money 'neutrality' also requires an assumption of debt neutrality. Similarly, fiscal changes (e.g. changes in tax rates) may influence the supply and demand for labour and 'shift' the vertical neo-classical supply curve. Neo-classical economists accept that fiscal changes might slowly alter the natural rate of output but usually argue in favour of debt neutrality.

3 There are a number of microtheoretic models that seek to explain 'sticky prices', for example Azariadis (1975), Akerlof (1970).

2

The Quantity Theory, Keynes and Inventory Models of the Demand for Money

2.1 INTRODUCTION

In the previous chapter we saw that the demand for money function plays an important role in the transmission mechanism of both monetary and fiscal policy. The temporal stability of the demand for money function is crucial if monetary and fiscal policy are to have a predictable effect on output and the price level. The size of the interest elasticity of the demand for money determines the size of the (short-run) money multiplier and the extent of financial crowding out in the simple IS–LM model. Wealth effects in the demand for money (and expenditure) function can substantially alter the long-run response and time profile of monetary and fiscal policy. In particular, a fixed rule for monetary growth may cause instability in real output when fiscal deficits are bond financed.

In the simple current account monetary model (CAM) the stability of the demand for money function is necessary in order to explain movements in the exchange rate and the price level. When rational expectations is applied to the foreign exchange market but goods market prices are 'sticky' we obtain the Dornbusch 'overshooting' result: the degree of overshooting in the exchange rate depends on the size of the interest elasticity of the demand for money. The transmission mechanism of monetary policy involves the interaction of a whole set of asset demand functions and it is therefore important to develop theories of the demand for assets in general as well as those that are specific to the demand for money.

The above arguments therefore provide convincing reasons for examining theories of the demand for assets in some considerable detail. In subsequent chapters we discuss empirical formulation and tests of these theories. It turns out that these theories may also be applied to the determination of the *supply* of assets, particularly the supply of money which we consider in chapters 7 and 8. However, in this chapter we begin our examination of theories of the demand for assets. We concentrate on the demand for money but a number of theories we discuss may be applied to financial assets (and liabilities) in general.

A number of the theories of the demand for money are based upon explicit motives for holding money: for transactions and speculative reasons for example.

This is in contrast to the theory of demand in consumer theory. According to neo-classical consumer theory, goods are held because the individual derives utility from them, but in applying the theory we do not analyse the motives for holding say a washing machine. This 'general utility' approach to the demand for goods may also be applied to the demand for assets and indeed this appears to be the basis of Friedman's restatement of the quantity theory of money.

Two general characteristics that encompass our models of the demand for money are, first, optimization is over a single period and, second, each model is a partial model in that only one motive for holding the asset is usually considered. However, this does not mean that the models are not applicable to real world circumstances. Each model may be usefully applied to particular agents, for example firms or persons, but may not be applicable for all agents and all circumstances. These single period optimization models are sometimes referred to as static equilibrium or long-run equilibrium models because they provide a solution for the demand for money at a point in time, but do not analyse how we move from one equilibrium to the next.

Two special characteristics of money that provide the starting point for a number of theories are its use as a universally acceptable means of exchange (at least in the domestic economy) and its role as a store of value. The former leads to 'transactions models' and the latter to 'portfolio models'. Money provides a capital certain asset in nominal terms. Ignoring default risk of private banks the value of money at the end of the accounting period is known with certainty in nominal terms. The above two characteristics may loosely be termed liquidity. Assets other than money possess liquidity to a greater or lesser extent. It is frequently argued that under conditions of perfect certainty people would not hold any zero yielding assets. They would merely meet their perfectly foreseen transactions needs by cashing earning assets at the time required. While it is true that money avoids barter and the necessity for the double coincidence of wants, nevertheless other assets could fulfil the same function. There is an extensive literature on why a particular financial asset might be useful in making transactions, the most obvious reason being the reduction in real resource costs (for example search time) in making transactions (Barro and Fischer, 1976). We do not discuss these microfoundations for holding money but simply accept the motives put forward for holding money as self-evident.

2.1.1   *Outline of the chapter*

We begin this chapter with a discussion of the quantity theory of money as put forward by the classical economists such as Irving Fisher and the Cambridge economists, Marshall and Pigou. For these economists money is viewed primarily as a means of payment, and therefore the main determinant of demand is the level of transactions. For the Cambridge economists other variables such as wealth and interest rates play a subordinate role.

After discussing these early theories of the transactions demand for money we turn to the restatement of the quantity theory as propounded by Friedman (1956). In a sense, Friedman emphasizes the elements in the quantity theory (of the Cambridge economists) that had been overlooked by later writers. He also put the quantity theory firmly in the tradition of the general utility approach to consumer demand theory and hence does not consider explicit motives for holding money. The budget constraint of the individual can be viewed as consisting of a whole host of real and financial assets and liabilities as well as human wealth in the form of future labour earnings. The rates of return on all such assets might therefore influence the demand for money while wealth, broadly defined to include human as well as financial wealth, should provide the scale variable rather than income.

Broadly speaking Keynes accepted the Cambridge view concerning the transactions demand for money and introduced two further motives for holding money. Money is held for precautionary reasons because the receipt and disbursement of funds is subject to a random element. The details of this relationship are not analysed by Keynes who tended to emphasize the speculative motive. In Keynes' speculative model, which we discuss in section 2.3, money is viewed as a store of value and, in choosing between money and 'bonds', individuals attempt to maximize their expected terminal wealth. Money is seen as an alternative to holdings bonds whose price is uncertain because capital gains and losses may be incurred. The speculative demand for money may therefore depend upon the *expected* capital gain on bonds as well as the running yield or interest rate. If a capital loss is widely expected then people might hold large quantities of money at the existing interest rate on bonds. This is the basis of the liquidity trap.

Inventory theoretic models are discussed in section 2.4 and are based on the transactions motive for holding money. In nearly all of these models the net inflow of receipts is assumed to be known with certainty. The individual tries to organize his money balances to minimize the cost of his known transactions. These comprise a brokerage fee in cashing the earning assets (bond) but a loss of interest if a high level of money balances are held. These inventory models result in the demand for money depending on the known levels of transactions and the known interest rate on bonds. We extend the simple inventory model to include interest payments on money.

Even if we accept the restrictive assumption that net receipts by firms are known with certainty, the simple inventory model may not adequately explain the demand for money by firms. We discuss Sprenkle's argument that with a low level of transactions it may not be worthwhile for firms to engage in optimal cash management at all and actual money balances may be determined by institutional arrangements rather than by income and interest rates as in the inventory model.

The inventory theoretic models outlined above assume that agents continuously adjust money balances in order to remain at their optimal level. This seems unlikely, particularly for persons. Akerlof and Milbourne (1980) make the more realistic assumption that individuals only actively adjust their money balances when they reach an upper or lower target level. In a simple version of this target-threshold model, discussed in section 2.5, receipts and disbursements are still assumed to be known with certainty and the model is broadly within the inventory theoretic framework. In an extension of the target-threshold model, Akerlof and Milbourne introduce an element of uncertainty concerning the timing of expenditures. In both versions of the model the income elasticity of th demand for money may be close to zero or even negative, in sharp contrast to results from the simple inventory model. We end the chapter with a brief overview of some other variants of the inventory model before presenting our summary and conclusions.

At this point it is worth noting that it is not until the next chapter that the impact of uncertainty on the demand for money is brought to the fore. Models of the precautionary demand for money assume that net receipts are uncertain. Thus generally speaking there are two broad approaches to modelling the demand for money based on the transactions motive: the inventory theoretic models (usually) assume receipts are certain, while precautionary models assume the opposite. In the next chapter we also discuss risk-aversion models where the only source of uncertainty concerns future asset (bond) prices. There are therefore some similarities between the risk-aversion model and Keynes' speculative demand model discussed in this chapter. However, we now begin our examination of theories of the demand for money starting with the transactions models of the 'classical' economists.

2.2   THE QUANTITY THEORY OF MONEY

The quantity theory of money has its genesis in the 'classical' economists, Irving Fisher, Marshall and Pigou. The latter two economists are associated with the so-called Cambridge view of the quantity theory. Both Fisher and the Cambridge economists are concerned primarily with money as a means of exchange and therefore provide models of the transactions demand for money. Fisher (1911) analyses the institutional details of the payments mechanism and therefore concentrates on the velocity of circulation of money. The Cambridge economists on the other hand are concerned with the determinants of the individual's desired demand for money.

Although the routes by which Fisher and the Cambridge economists reach their conclusions are different, nevertheless, both theories emphasize the proportionate relationship between the amount of money in circulation, the volume of transactions and the price level. In addition, the Cambridge economists also discussed the role of wealth and the rate of interest in determining the demand for money.

2.2.1   *Fisher's version of the quantity theory*

The basis of Fisher's theory is an identity linking the value of sales with the amount of money which 'changes hands'. If Y equals the number of transactions and P equals the average price level then $PY =$ the value of transactions undertaken. Each transaction involves an exchange of money. The number of times money changes hands, that is the velocity of circulation of money V multiplied by the fixed stock of money M, must be equal to the value of transactions. We therefore have the identity

$$MV \equiv PY \tag{2.1}$$

To give this identity some behavioural content, Fisher assumes that the payments mechanism is such that the velocity of circulation is constant in the short run and varies slowly and in a predictable way in the long run, as payments mechanisms in the economy change. Examples of changes in the payments mechanism are the introduction of credit cards, the move from payment in cash to payment by cheque and general improvements in the services offered by banks, such as automatic cash dispensers. Fisher's theory is a little like the input-output analysis of the theory of the firm. In Fisher's theory money is an input, velocity is the fixed input-output coefficient and the value of transactions is the output of the system. If we add a further assumption, namely that the money supply is exogenous and controlled by the authorities, then a 1 per cent change in the money supply leads to a 1 per cent change in the *value* of transactions. Further, if the volume of transactions is fixed at full employment equilibrium then any percentage change in the money supply will result in an equal percentage change in the price level. Fisher's theory, under these assumptions, implies that the money supply is the sole determinant of the price level.

2.2.2 *The Cambridge approach*

The Cambridge economists recognize that individuals may desire to hold money for the same general reasons as they desire to hold goods: both money and goods yield utility or satisfaction. When we consider the demand for goods we do not ask *why* particular goods such as a television set yield utility to the individual. However, the Cambridge economists did ask 'Why does money yield utility?' Not surprisingly, they believed that utility from money arises because it is accepted as a means of exchange. Thus, the transactions motive is the major determinant of desired money holdings. Assuming a proportionate relationship we may write

$$M^\mathrm{d} = KPY \tag{2.2}$$

However, the Cambridge economists were also aware that the more money the individual already holds then additional money balances yield less satisfaction. This is nothing more than the law of diminishing marginal utility. The Cambridge economists argue that one alternative to holding money is to hold an interest bearing asset which we will call a bond. The higher the rate of return on bonds, relative to the marginal (transactions) utility from money, the more individuals (who are utility maximizers) are encouraged to switch some of their money holdings into bonds. Hence, the Cambridge economists do not consider 'K' as a constant but are aware that K may depend upon the return to alternative assets, that is the (bond) interest rate and any expected capital gain, and also upon wealth. Naturally they also recognize, as did Fisher, that K would depend in part on the payments mechanism.

The velocity of circulation of money is not directly observable. A data series for the velocity of circulation may be obtained from the formula $V = PY/M^s$. If we assume money market equilibrium then $M^s = M^d = KPY$. Hence V equals $1/K$. Since K depends upon the interest rate and wealth, the Cambridge economists consider that the velocity of circulation is neither constant in the short run nor in the long run. The mechanical link between the exogenous money supply and the value of transactions has now been broken. An exogenous change in the money supply can influence not only the price level and the level of transactions but also the interest rate and possibly the level of wealth.

The main features of the Cambridge approach are therefore an emphasis on the individuals desire to hold money which in turn may depend upon a wide variety of factors such as the level of real transactions, the level of real wealth and the yield or return on alternative assets. Utility is determined by 'real' factors. The demand for money is a demand for real balances and therefore the demand for nominal money balances is proportional to the price level.

2.2.3   *The modern quantity theory*

The 'modern quantity theory' has its genesis in the work of Friedman (1956). Friedman does not ask what the motives for holding money are, but given that money yields utility, Friedman asks what factors determine *how much* money people desire to hold. However, in contrast to utility theory as usually applied to the demand for goods, Friedman applies utility theory to the demand for money in a rather loose fashion. No explicit utility function is posited and other possible variables in the utility function (for example expenditure on consumer goods) are not analysed. Although Friedman gives no detailed analysis of the motives for holding money, he does suggest that the services from money derive from the fact that money is a 'readily available source of purchasing power'. The transactions motive therefore plays a role in Friedman's demand for money.

Friedman discusses the utility function and the budget constraint in very general terms. He merely notes that there will be diminishing marginal utility from money and that a whole host of other financial assets, liabilities and *real* assets may provide alternatives to holding money (and thus appear as arguments in the utility function). As regards the budget constraint, the maximum amount an individual can convert into money consists of his net *financial* wealth (that is his gross financial wealth minus his financial liabilities, such as bank advances) and his *physical* wealth held in the stock of housing and consumer durables. In addition the individual has 'human wealth' in the form of the discounted present value of his future labour income. In principle, 'wealth' should include human wealth but social conventions and the existence of uncertainty concerning the future, limit the extent to which the individual may exchange future labour income for increased money holdings. Some substitution is possible, as the individual may use some of his non-human wealth to purchase education and increase his future human wealth. Friedman is able to circumvent the problem of the illiquidity of human wealth. He asserts that the demand for money should depend upon total wealth (that is non-human wealth plus human wealth) but because of the illiquidity of human wealth he also includes the ratio of human to non-human wealth h as a determinant of the demand for money. The higher the ratio of (illiquid) human wealth to non-human wealth (for a given level of total wealth) the higher we might expect the demand for money to be, *ceteris paribus*.

Having established wealth as the scale variable in the budget constraint Friedman then considers the yield on alternative assets. If money earns interest, this may influence the demand for money positively. In general terms the alternative to holding money consists of holding near-monies, such as building society deposits; long-term 'bonds', such as gilt-edged stock; equities, real assets, such as consumer durables and housing and, in the case of firms, capital equipment. For 'capital certain' assets such as building society deposits, the relevant yield is simply the current (after tax) interest rate. Long-term bonds if they are sold before their date of maturity, earn not only an interest rate or running yield but also capital gain or loss due to changes in bond prices. Similarly, equities earn a dividend which is uncertain ('income uncertainty') and the market price of equities may also vary. Finally, if the individual holds real assets, the rate of return on such assets is given by the expected rate of inflation over the holding period (less any depreciation and storage costs).

Since there is no formal maximization procedure in Friedman's quantity theory of money, it is difficult to do other than present a list of variables which may enter the demand for money function. The relationship between these variables and the demand for money is left to intuition. By analogy with utility theory as applied to the demand for *goods*, we may hypothesize that the demand for money depends positively on the scale variable, total wealth, and positively on the own rate of interest on money (assuming that the 'income effect' outweighs the 'substitution effect').

The rate of inflation will influence the demand for all *financial* assets in a similar fashion: the return on money, (most) bonds and near monies is in nominal terms. However, a higher rate of inflation increases the return to be obtained from holding real assets such as housing, consumer durables, stocks of finished goods and capital equipment. A higher rate of inflation encourages a substitution into real assets but it is by no means certain that there will be a substitution out of money: substitution could be from bonds to real assets, rather than from money to real assets. However, Friedman did assume a substitution from money to real assets at higher rates of inflation.

The quantitative significance of these potential variables in the demand for money is to be determined by empirical work. There is an analogy here with the usual demand theory for goods where income and price elasticities and the existence of substitutes and complements are left to be determined empirically.

Friedman recognized that yields on certain assets, namely those that are close substitutes for each other may well move together. In such a case the number of interest rates and yields in the demand for money function may be reduced somewhat. Again this is to be determined empirically. Friedman's theory requires homogeneity (of degree one) in nominal money balances when there is a change in the price *level*. A doubling of the price level requires a doubling in the demand for money since the flow of services from money depends upon real money balances held. We may represent Friedman's demand for money function as

$$\left(\frac{M}{P}\right)^{d} = f(r, Y^{P}, h, \pi^{e}) \quad f_{Y^{P}}, f_{h} > 0, \ f_{\pi^{e}} < 0 \tag{2.3}$$

where $f_{h} = \partial (M/P)^{d}/\partial h$ etc., r is a vector of interest rates (which may include the return on foreign assets), Y^{P} is a measure of total wealth (usually referred to as permanent income), h is the ratio of human to non-human wealth and π^{e} is the expected rate of inflation.

It is worth noting that Friedman's demand for money function is much more complex than that which is used in IS–LM analysis and its extensions. If borne out by empirical evidence, Friedman's theory would result in a more complex macroeconomic model than we have analysed in chapter 1. For example, using Friedman's demand for money, our macromodel would have to include the determinants of wealth as well as income and the return on a wide range of financial assets. The latter may well involve detailed models of the stock market, the demand and supply of government and private sector long term bonds as well as the determinants of real assets such as fixed investment, stocks and the demand for consumer durables and housing.

2.2.4   *Summary*

In general terms the 'quantity theory' approach indicates that the demand for money should depend upon some measure of transactions some measure of wealth and a vector of assets yields. Apart from positing a positive (and possibly proportionate) relationship between transactions and money, a unit price level elasticity (homogeneity) and a positive 'own yield', the quantity theory leaves 'the signs' on the other variables to be determined by the data.

2.3   KEYNES AND THE DEMAND FOR MONEY

Keynes (1936) analysed the determinants of the transactions and the precautionary demand for money. In general he envisaged these two motives for holding money as depending primarily on income and interest rates on alternative assets. We concentrate here on Keynes's speculative motive. The individual is assumed to choose between a 'capital certain' asset such as money whose nominal value is known with certainty at the end of the fixed holding period. Any capital certain asset, that is one whose market price does *not* vary, may be used in the analysis but we shall use money in what follows. The alternative asset available to the individual is one whose market price varies. This 'risky' asset we will call a bond, although again any risky asset (such as an equity or debenture) would suffice. The main predictions from Keynes's theory are, first, that individuals do *not* hold a diversified portfolio of assets: they hold either all bonds or all money. Second, a downward sloping demand for money function with respect to the interest rate only occurs for the *aggregate* demand for money. Finally the theory predicts that in certain circumstances the elasticity of the demand for money with respect to the interest rate may become infinite: this is the liquidity trap.

2.3.1   *Speculative model*

The expected return on the risky asset R^e over the fixed holding period is made up of the running yield or interest rate r and the expected capital gain or loss g^e

$$R^e = r + g^e \tag{2.4}$$

where $g^e = (P^e_{t+1} - P)/P$, the expected percentage change in the market price of the bond (based on the information available at time t). The market price and the interest rate are inversely related since the price is merely the discounted present value of the future coupon receipts C plus the redemption value of the bond B_T at the maturity date T

$$P = \sum_{i=1}^{T-1} \frac{C_{t+i}}{(1+r)^i} + \frac{B_T}{(1+r)^T} \tag{2.5}$$

It is easy to see that $\partial P/\partial r < 0$. If the bond is a perpetuity, that is yields a fixed coupon and is never redeemed ($B_T = 0$) then the above formula reduces to

$$P = C \sum_{i=1}^{\infty} (1+r)^{-i} = C[(1+r)^{-1} + (1+r)^{-2} + \ldots] = \frac{C}{r} \tag{2.6}$$

where we have used the fact that the sum of an infinite geometric series $1 + x + x^2 + \ldots = 1/(1-x)$ (for $|x| < 1$ and here $x = (1+r)^{-1}$). For a perpetuity the percentage change in the bond price is given by the percentage change in the interest rate (with the sign reversed).

Suppose the individual has a fixed holding period and forms expectations about the price of the bond at the end of the holding period, with perfect certainty; that is, he has 'inelastic' expectations. Clearly, if he expected the return on the bond to exceed the known interest rate on money r_m and he holds this expectation with perfect certainty then he will put *all* his wealth in bonds. The individual does not hold a diversified portfolio, he is a 'plunger'.

To obtain a smooth money demand function in the aggregate we have to assume that different individuals form different expectations about the rate of change in the bond price. Keynes hypothesized that individuals have a subjective view about the 'normal' rate of interest r_N, that is the rate of interest rate to which the current interest rate will eventually return. If the current rate is above the normal rate, people expect the interest rate to fall in the future, and hence they expect to make a capital gain (the running yield or percentage coupon payment is known with certainty). This regressive expectations formulation may be simply expressed

$$g^e = \alpha(r - r_N) \quad \alpha > 0 \tag{2.7}$$

There are now two ways we can generate a smooth demand for money function in the aggregate. First, if α differs between individuals then as r moves above r_N

some people (α large) will expected a large capital gain and move into bonds. Others might hold money because they expect only a small capital gain which (together with the running yield) does not exceed r_m. The larger the gap $(r - r_N)$ the more people we expect to move into bonds in anticipation of a capital gain. Hence we obtain a smooth relationship between r and the demand for money (and bonds). Second, if people hold different views about what constitutes the normal rate of interest then (for any given α) a rise in the current rate of interest will induce some but not all individuals to move into bonds.

In the aggregate the demand for money (and bonds) depends on the current interest rate, the normal rate on bonds and the interest rate on money. The precise functional relationship (as opposed to the qualitative results derived above) between these variables is a little obscure. How can we aggregate over individuals that have different values of α or of the normal rate of interest? In the above analysis we implicitly assumed that the normal rate remained unchanged when the current rate of interest altered. This may not be realistic because individuals are likely to update their views about r_N on the basis of the current rate. None of these problems is insuperable but they are difficult to overcome in practice and are likely to involve rather arbitrary assumptions. Ignoring these difficulties Keynes's speculative demand for aggregate money balances may be written

$$M = f(r, r_N, r_m, W) \quad f_r < 0; f_{r_N}, f_{r_m}, f_W > 0 \tag{2.8}$$

where W is some measure of wealth.

Clearly the Keynesian speculative demand is unrealistic as far as the individual's demand for assets is concerned since people do hold diversified portfolios. In the aggregate the theory points to possible instabilities in the demand for money (and bonds). People may have volatile expectations about capital gains; either because of changing views about the normal rate or the speed of adjustment coefficient α, or because expectations are influenced by other variables, for example the money supply. Keynes' speculative theory is a joint hypothesis about the determinants of the demand for money and a specific method of expectations formation.

Only a brief discussion of the liquidity trap follows as this aspect has not been prominent in the empirical literature. If interest rates are very low and have been so for some time then the normal rate will be low. At the time Keynes wrote the *General Theory* interest rates had been around 2 per cent for some considerable period. At such low stable rates of interest a *small* rise in the current rate above the normal rate might be expected to be reversed very quickly. (in terms of equation (2.7) we are assuming that α becomes larger, the lower is the absolute level of the normal rate.) Under such circumstances it follows that a large number of individuals might expect a large capital gain and would substantially reduce their money holdings even though the rate on bonds had risen only slightly. In other words at low interest rates we expect the interest elasticity of the demand for money and bonds to be large (infinite). This is the liquid trap.

To test the liquidity trap hypothesis one could posit a non-linear relationship for the expected capital gains function (2.7). The more usual method has been to estimate the interest elasticity in a period when interest rates are low and repeat the exercise for high interest rate periods. The relative size of the two elasticities are then compared. However, if the rate of inflation provides a base-line, below which nominal interest rates cannot fall, then the liquidity trap may apply equally well in high *nominal* interest rate periods. This proposition may also be tested.

2.3.2 *Summary*

The predictions from Keynes's transactions and precautionary motives are similar to those for the quantity theory. The speculative motive explicitly introduces uncertainty, albeit uncertainty about one particular variable, the future yield on bonds. Volatile expectations might cause parameter instability. Also expecta-tions formation may be such as to cause a highly elastic response of money holdings to a small change in the interest rate: that is, the 'liquidity trap'. Port-folio diversification for 'speculative funds' only occurs in the aggregate: indi-viduals are 'plungers', hold inelastic expectations and hence do not hold a diversified portfolio of assets.

2.4 THE TRANSACTIONS DEMAND FOR MONEY: INVENTORY MODELS

2.4.1 *A simple inventory model*

There are several ways of modelling the transactions motive for holding money and we start with an exposition of the inventory-theoretic model (Baumol, 1952; Tobin, 1956). The assumptions of the model are (a) the individual receives a *known* lump sum cash payment of T per period (say per annum) and spends it all, evenly over the period; (b) the individual may invest in 'bonds' paying a *known* interest rate r per period, or hold cash (money) paying zero interest; (c) the individual sells bonds to obtain cash in equal amounts K, and incurs a (fixed) brokerage fee b per transaction. The key element in this inventory model is that all relevant information is known with certainty. The model yields a square root relationship between the demand for money and the level of income, the brokerage fee and the bond interest rate.

If the individual holds no bonds he incurs no brokerage fee but also earns no interest. He will therefore choose to withdraw an amount K so as to 'trade off' brokerage costs against interest income. (Note that the variable K as used here has nothing to do with the Cambridge K of section 2.2.) The number of times he sells bonds is $n = T/K$, incurring a total brokerage cost of $nb = b(T/K)$. Since expenditure is a constant flow, a withdrawal of K involves an average cash balance of $M^d = K/2$ and a loss of interest (opportunity cost of money) of $(K/2)r$ per period. Total cost TC is

$$TC = \frac{bT}{K} + r\frac{K}{2} \tag{2.9}$$

minimizing total cost gives[1]

$$\frac{\delta(TC)}{\delta K} = -\frac{bT}{K^2} + \frac{r}{2} = 0 \qquad\qquad (2.10)$$

$$K = \left(\frac{2bT}{r}\right)^{1/2} \qquad\qquad (2.11)$$

$$M^d = \frac{K}{2} = \left(\frac{bT}{2r}\right)^{1/2} \qquad\qquad (2.12)$$

or

$$\ln\left(\frac{M^d}{P}\right) = \frac{1}{2}\ln\left(\frac{b}{2}\right) + \frac{1}{2}\ln T - \frac{1}{2}\ln r \qquad\qquad (2.13)$$

The demand for bonds B^d is

$$\frac{T}{2} - M = \frac{T}{2} - \left(\frac{Tb}{2r}\right)^{1/2} \qquad\qquad (2.14)$$

We have added a unit price elasticity in (2.13) because a doubling of the price level doubles both b and T and therefore doubles M (T and b must now be considered as real variables rather than nominal variables).[2]

The sawtooth profile of money balances is shown in figure 2.1. In figure 2.1(a) the individual holds no bonds, average balances are $T/2$. In figure 2.1(b) he makes one purchase and sale of bonds ($n = 2$) and the average balance is given by $T/2n$ ($= K/2$). If the number of instalments in which *annual* income is received is $p = 2$ and we keep $n = 2$ then the profile of cash balances is shown in figure 2.1(c) with average cash balances given by $T/2pn = T/8$.

Notice that the individual will always switch into bonds immediately and will always hold zero money balances before switching into bonds; since receipts are perfectly foreseen any other strategy would involve a loss of interest.

The brokerage fee consists of 'inconvenience costs' (particularly of time) as well as any direct pecuniary costs (for example stockbrokers or bank charges). The brokerage fee may vary with the real wage rate, if the latter measures the opportunity cost of time lost, or it may decrease due to changes in payments mechanisms that reduce queuing time. Baumol's model predicts economies of scale in holding money: a doubling in the level of transactions leads to only a 50 per cent increase in money holdings. It follows that the *distribution* of transactions/income influences the demand for money. For example if aggregate transactions (income) is split evenly, the aggregate demand for money is

$$M_1 = \gamma\left(\frac{T}{2}\right)^{1/2} + \gamma\left(\frac{T}{2}\right)^{1/2} = 2^{1/2}\left(\gamma(T)^{1/2}\right)$$

where $\gamma = (b/2r)^{1/2}$, but if *all* income is held by a *single* person $M_2 = \gamma(T)^{1/2}$. Thus the greater the disparity in the income distribution, the lower is the aggre-

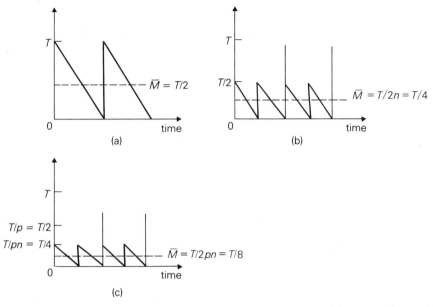

FIGURE 2.1   *Time profile of income: inventory model; (a) no purchase of bonds, income received annually; (b) one purchase and sale of bonds ($n = 2$), income received annually; (c) one purchase and sale of bonds ($n = 2$), income paid twice per annum.*

gate demand for money ($M_2 < M_1$). For the individual the (absolute value) of the income and interest rate elasticities is $\frac{1}{2}$.

The demand for money is independent of the frequency of payments: doubling the period of transactions also implies a doubling in r and hence M^d is unchanged. There is no uncertainty in the model, the demand for money derives primarily from the existence of a brokerage fee. If $b = 0$ then $M^d = 0$ and the individual would then perfectly synchronize bond sales with transactions needs. (If $r = 0$ it appears from (2.12) as if $M \to \infty$ but the latter is impossible since the maximum value of M is T.)

The transactions model views money as an inventory and its demand is determined in the same way as a wholesaler would determine the optimal stock of say refrigerators held in a warehouse. Clearly the model is somewhat unrealistic, particularly for firms who presumably face uncertain receipts and payments. For persons the assumption of a known lump sum payment is more realistic and here the opportunity cost of holding cash is likely to be the interest rate on liquid assets (such as time deposits or building society deposits), rather than bonds. Since a large element of what is usually defined as 'money' is interest bearing, this simple inventory model can only explain the demand for non-interest bearing money such as cash and sight deposits. However, we can easily extend the simple inventory model to include interest payments on money.

2.4.2 *Interest payments on money*

Let the interest payable on money balances be i per cent per period. The average deposit is, as before, $M = K/2$, but this now earns interest payments of $(K/2)i$ per period. Average 'bond' holdings of $[(T/2) - M]$ earn payments of $((T/2) - M)r$. The individual chooses K to maximize total profit Π[3]

$$\Pi = \frac{Ki}{2} + \left[\frac{T}{2} - \frac{K}{2}\right]r - b\frac{T}{K} \tag{2.15}$$

$$\Pi_K = \frac{\delta\Pi}{\delta K} = \frac{i - r}{2} + \frac{bT}{K^2} = 0$$

$$M^d = \frac{K}{2} = \left[\frac{bT}{2(r - i)}\right]^{1/2} \tag{2.16a}$$

$$B^d = \frac{T}{2} - M = \frac{T}{2} - \left[\frac{bT}{2(r - i)}\right]^{1/2} \tag{2.16b}$$

The transactions elasticity is again $\frac{1}{2}$ but the interest elasticity is now no longer $\frac{1}{2}$ as in the simple model, but is $E_r = -\frac{1}{2}r/(r - i)$.

In principle the above model may be easily estimated in log linear form with coefficients of $\frac{1}{2}$ expected on T and $(r - i)$.

Sprenkle (1966) has pointed out that if the *own rate* on money is excluded from the regression equation, a transactions elasticity greater than $\frac{1}{2}$ may ensue; however, this would not necessarily imply that money is a 'luxury' good. Firms may receive a higher return on their 'money' balances the greater the volume of their transactions, that is $\delta i/\delta T > 0$. The transactions elasticity may then be calculated by taking logarithms of (2.16) and differentiating

$$\frac{dM}{M} = \frac{1}{2}\frac{dT}{T} - \frac{1}{2}\frac{1}{(r - i)}\frac{d}{dr}(r - i) \tag{2.17}$$

$$E_r = \frac{dM}{dT}\frac{T}{M} = \frac{1}{2} + \frac{1}{2}\frac{T}{(r - i)}\frac{di}{dT} \tag{2.18}$$

Thus (for $r > i$) the estimated transactions elasticity may exceed $\frac{1}{2}$ because i rises along with T and provides an additional increase in the demand for money.

By a similar argument if banks raise i along with market rates r, then the response of M to a change in r may differ from $-\frac{1}{2}r/(r - i)$ given above. Further, if banks increase i by more than the market increase in r, the response of M to a rise in the market interest rates will be perverse.[4] This is a consequence of M depending upon *relative* interest rates and may account for some of the rapid growth in money demand in the UK in 1972/3 after the introduction of the policy of competition and credit control (CCC) in September 1971 (see section 8.2). Under the CCC policy the interest rate on bank deposits was no longer fixed by a cartel arrangement and i could vary in response to changes in r.

Further extensions of the inventory model are possible[5] but all emphasize the importance of transactions, relative interest rates and the 'brokerage fee'. These are briefly discussed in section 2.7.

2.4.3   Criticisms of the inventory model

Sprenkle (1969) provides a damaging critique of the inventory model when applied to large firms. First, Sprenkle argues that cash holdings of large firms may be explained by the existence of multiple accounts as much as by optimal inventory behaviour. Second, it may not be profitable for firms to undertake optimal cash management if receipts of each branch of the firm are small: the firm can minimize costs by *not* purchasing any securities at all but keeping all their receipts in cash. Third, Sprenkle demonstrates that if firms hold some optimal and some non-optimal balances the proportion of non-optimal receipts in total receipts does not have to be very large for non-optimal balances to dominate money holdings. We demonstrate these points below, assuming for ease of exposition that $i = 0$.

Multiple accounts. Consider the first point concerning multiple accounts. If the jth branch of the firm with its own bank account optimizes its cash inventory then

$$M_j = \left(\frac{x_j Tb}{2r}\right)^{1/2} \tag{2.19}$$

where x_j is the proportion of total receipts T accruing to the jth subsidiary. Total money holdings of all J subsidiaries are then

$$\sum_{j=1}^{J} M_j = \left(\frac{Tb}{2r}\right)^{1/2} \sum_{j=1}^{J} x_j^{1/2} = C^* \sum_{j=1}^{J} x_j^{1/2} \tag{2.20}$$

where C^* is optimum cash holdings of the centralized firm. With complete decentralization $x_j = 1/J$ and

$$M_J = C^* J \left(\frac{1}{J}\right)^{1/2} = C^* J^{1/2} \tag{2.21}$$

Thus a firm with 25 branches will have five times the cash holdings of an equivalent firm with completely centralized accounts.

Is cash management worthwhile? The second point concerning profitability and the timing and frequency of receipts is a little more involved. If the firm *does* find it profitable to engage in optimal cash management then the optimal stock is independent of the timing of payments. For example, if receipts are obtained p evenly spaced times *per year* then receipts per *period* are $T' = T/p$ and the interest rate per period is $T' = r/p$ (where T and r refer to the *annual* time period). Using (2.12) the optimal cash balance for the centralized firm with at least one purchase and sale of bonds per year (i.e. $n \geqslant 2$) is

$$C^* = \left(\frac{T'b}{2r'}\right)^{1/2} = \left[\frac{(T/p)\,b}{(2r/p)}\right]^{1/2} = \left(\frac{Tb}{2r}\right)^{1/2} \tag{2.22}$$

and is therefore independent of the timing of payments p.

If the number of sales and purchases of bonds is n per year, the average cash balance is $T/2n$ and the average holding of bonds is $[(T/2) - (T/2n)]$. However, the average holding of bonds *per period* is $(T/2p - T/2pn^*)$ where $n^* = n/p$ is the number of sales and purchases of bonds *per period*. It is only profitable to buy and sell bonds during the period if

$$\Pi = \frac{r}{p}\left(\frac{T}{2p} - \frac{T}{2pn^*}\right) - n^*b \geqslant 0$$

For minimal switching between cash and 'bonds', $n^* = 2$ and thus

$$\frac{r}{p}\left(\frac{T}{2p} - \frac{T}{4p}\right) - 2b \geqslant 0 \tag{2.23}$$

$$T \geqslant 8p^2\,\frac{b}{r} \tag{2.24}$$

For example for $b = \$20$, $r = 0.05$, then for switching to occur for yearly receipts $(p = 1)\,T > \$3200$ per annum and for weekly receipts $(p = 52)\,T > \$8.6$ million per annum. Thus if there are frequent receipts, T must be large before any gains from cash management will occur.

Are non-optimal cash balances large? Non-optimal cash balances are $T/2p$. If x per cent of T received is by small branches for which optimization is unprofitable, and $(1-x)$ by centralized firms who engage in optimal cash management, total cash balances are

$$M = \left[\frac{(1-x)\,Tb}{2r}\right]^{1/2} + \frac{xT}{2p} = C_1^* + C_1 \tag{2.25}$$

M now depends upon a linear term T as well as the familiar square root relationship. We can now demonstrate the conditions under which non-optimal balances dominate money holdings.

For non-optimal balances to exceed optimal balances $C_1 > C_1^*$. From (2.25) this requires $x^2/(1-x) > 2pb/Tr$. Take $b = \$20$, $r = 0.05$ and $p = 12$ (monthly receipts). For $T = \$960$ million per annum which is approximately the value of transactions for the hundredth largest US firm out of the top 500 (in 1969), then $x > 0.1$ per cent. Thus the proportion of non-optimal receipts in total receipts need only be very small before non-optimal cash balances exceed optimal inventory holdings.[6]

Some evidence. Sprenkle (1969) finds that only about 1–3 per cent of actual cash holdings of firms are explained with the simple inventory formula (that is taking representative values of T, r, b in $C^* = (Tb/2r)^{1/2}$. If actual cash holdings are *assumed* to be held by a completely decentralized optimizing firm (that is actual cash $= M_J$) then we can calculate J from $J = (M_J/C^*)^2$ (equation (2.21)). Using the average value of M_J for the largest 50 US firms, Sprenkle calculates that $J = 10\,000$ branches which implies average yearly receipts *per branch* of about \$200 000. Such a level of receipts seems unlikely to be sufficient to make optimal inventory management profitable, since for monthly receipts ($p = 12$), calculations using equation (2.24) show that T must exceed \$450 000 to make 'minimal switching' profitable. Thus the decentralized inventory model is unlikely to explain actual cash holdings of firms. Sprenkle feels that empirical relationships between cash and firm size (transactions/sales) found in cross-section studies probably reflect the need for additional branches J as sales increase and does not reflect the square root law of optimal inventory management.

If cash holdings of firms cannot be explained by the simple inventory model either with or without decentralized cash holdings then what does? Sprenkle believes that cash holdings of US firms are primarily determined by compensating balances. Rather than pay bank charges directly, US firms hold compensating balances, even though they earn zero interest, in order to provide an *implicit* payment to banks for their banking services (that is payments mechanism, loans, advice etc.). Thus if we wish to determine the size of compensating balances we need greater information on the costs and demand for banking services: the level of transactions and interest rates will not influence such balances. Clearly, the inventory model of the transactions demand for money should not be applied to the demand for (transactions) money balances of large firms.

In the UK, bank charges are incurred by firms in payment for banking services and cash management is more centralized than in the US, therefore compensating balances should be relatively small and the inventory model more applicable. However Sprenkle (1972) suggests that even in this case the inventory model is inappropriate for large firms as they will not hold cash in excess of the minimum amount required to invest in the overnight inter-bank market (\£500 000 in 1972). Thus the demand for money will vary neither with interest rates nor the level of transactions but with any institutional changes in this 'minimum overnight trading amount'. The fact that current (sight) and deposit accounts of companies increased by about 6 per cent between 1959 and 1971 while those of the personal sector increased over the same period by 120 per cent is consistent with Sprenkle's view since (nominal) sales would have also increased substantially over this period.[7]

Sprenkle (1972) also notes that it is end of day cash balances that are important and not the *average* balance derived in the inventory model. Let the average end of day (observed) cash balance be M^e. Let p be the number of times (days) payments are made per year. Then the average (daily) payment is T/p and[8]

$$M^e = C^* - \frac{T}{2p} = \left(\frac{Tb}{2r}\right)^{1/2} - \frac{T}{2p} \tag{2.26}$$

for $C > T/2p$. Since data consists of end of day cash balance then (using equation (2.25)) we see that the transactions and interest elasticities are much more complex than in the simple inventory model and the transactions elasticity may become negative.[9]

2.4.4   *Summary*

The inventory model may be applicable to persons but should not be applied to (large) firms whose money balances are likely to be determined by compensating balances (in the US) or the minimum overnight trading amount (in the UK). Since it is *end of day balances* that are important for both firms and persons the simple inventory model is inappropriate and the relationship between interest rates and the level of transactions is rather more complex than a simple square root relationship. Decentralization of receipts and the frequency with which cash is received imply that firm's demand is probably related to the number of branches used and it is unlikely that either firms or persons have a level of transactions that make it profitable to switch between money and 'bonds' in the manner of the inventory model. Our discussion appears to preclude the possibility of the demand for money by *firms* being 'explained' by interest rates and the level of transactions. For persons, the inventory model may have some relevance but the relationship between money, interest rates and transactions is likely to be more complex than in the simple inventory model.

2.5   THE TRANSACTIONS DEMAND FOR MONEY: TARGET-THRESHOLD MODEL

The inventory theoretic models of Baumol (1952) and others discussed above predict an income elasticity lying between $\frac{1}{2}$ and 1. Empirical studies, as we shall see, typically find short-run income elasticities that are very small (of the order of 0.2 in quarterly data), but long-run elasticities near unity. These empirical results are consistent with the procyclical movements in the velocity of circulation of money and the near constancy of velocity in the longer run.[10]

In this section we discuss another approach to the modelling of the transactions demand for money in which money holdings are only actively adjusted when they hit an upper or lower threshold level. This target-threshold model (Akerlof and Milbourne, 1980) is consistent with the above stylized facts since the short-run income elasticity is around zero and may even take a small negative value.

We discuss two variants of the Akerlof-Milbourne (A-M) model. In the first there is no uncertainty but in the second we assume that the timing of lump sum[11] expenditure plans by agents is uncertain. Broadly speaking, the 'certainty' model is an inventory model while the second is more akin to the 'precautionary demand' model, which we discuss in the next chapter. In the A-M model we relax two rather restrictive assumptions of the inventory models discussed above. First, we do not have to assume that agents continuously adjust their money balances to maintain them at their optimal level: adjustments take place infrequently and only when the threshold points are reached. Second, we include 'uncertainty' in the portfolio choice problem.

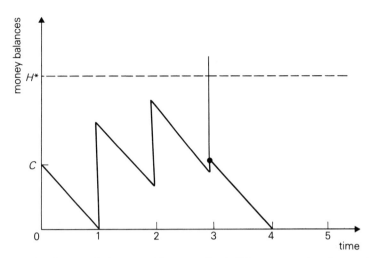

FIGURE 2.2   *Money balances with upper limit H^*, return point C, spending at a constant rate and lump sum inpayments.*
(Source: Akerlof and Milbourne (1980)).

2.5.1   *The model with 'certain' net receipts*

In its simplest form, the model assumes (a) a lump sum receipt of Y per period and (b) spending of C at a constant rate through the period. Money balances accumulate via savings, $S \equiv Y - C$. When the money balance hits the upper threshold H^*, it is returned to C, so that money balances are exhausted by the next receipt date. Figure 2.2 shows the time profile of money balances where the threshold is reached every third period. The threshold H^* is reached after an integral number of periods n such that

$$C + nS \geqslant H^* \geqslant C + (n-1)S \tag{2.27}$$

or

$$n \geqslant \frac{H^* - C}{S} \geqslant n - 1 \tag{2.28}$$

which determines n in terms of H^*, C and S.

K periods after the last induced transfer of money, the beginning of period balance is $C + (K-1)S$. Since C is spent during the period, the end of period balance is $(K-1)S$ and the average balance is $\frac{1}{2}C + (K-1)S$. Over all such periods, the average money balance between transfers is

$$
\begin{aligned}
M^d &= \frac{1}{n}\left[\frac{C}{2} + \left(\frac{C}{2} + S\right) + \left(\frac{C}{2} + 2S\right) + \ldots + \left(\frac{C}{2} + (n-1)S\right)\right] \\
&= \frac{C}{2} + \frac{S(n-1)}{2}
\end{aligned}
\tag{2.29}
$$

and n is the number of periods before the threshold is attained. Substituting from (2.28) for the values of $h_{max} = [(H^* - C)/S] + 1$, and $n_{min} = (H^* - C)/S$ in (2.29) gives

$$M_{max}^d = \frac{H^*}{2} \quad M_{min}^d = \frac{H^* - S}{2} \tag{2.30}$$

and an average balance $\bar{M} = \frac{1}{2}(M_{max}^d + M_{min}^d)$ of

$$\bar{M} = \frac{H^*}{2} - \frac{S}{4} \tag{2.31}$$

and

$$\frac{\partial \bar{M}}{\partial Y} = -\frac{S_Y(Y)}{4} \tag{2.32}$$

where $S_Y = \partial S/\partial Y$ is the marginal propensity to save and is assumed to be positively related to income. Hence, the short run income elasticity is negative and takes a larger negative value the higher the level of income. This result is in sharp contrast to the Baumol result and to the 'classical' Fisher (1911) view. The latter may be represented (following A-M) as $M^d = \lambda Y$ where Y equals the constant inflow of receipts and λ is the average time each dollar is held. Fisher's constant lag monitoring rule (λ is assumed constant in the short run) gives a short-run income elasticity of unity.

An intuitive interpretation of the negative income elasticity is that at higher income levels, but positive saving, the fixed threshold H^* is reached more quickly. Money balances are returned to C more frequently.

2.5.2 *Uncertainty added*

The model is generalized by A-M to incorporate uncertainty about spending plans in the form of small stochastic lump sum purchases of durable goods. When a durable good is purchased, money balances immediately fall (but not below zero since such purchases are 'small') and the time profile of money balances is shown in figure 2.3 where purchases are made in periods $t = 2$ and $t = 4$. After lengthy calculations and assuming the saving ratio $s = S/Y$ is a constant, A-M obtain

$$\bar{M} \approx \frac{H^*}{2} - s(1 + p)\frac{Y}{4} \tag{2.23}$$

$$\frac{\partial \bar{M}}{\partial Y} = -\frac{s}{4}(1 + p + Yp'(Y)) \tag{2.34}$$

where p = probability of a durable purchase (in any time period). Equation (2.34) reduces to the 'constant spending' case (equation (2.32)), when $p = 0$ and $p'(Y) = 0$. If the probability of a durable goods purchase increases with income $p'(Y) > 0$, then the income elasticity of the demand for money is negative. A-M show that the latter result also holds when durables purchases are large.

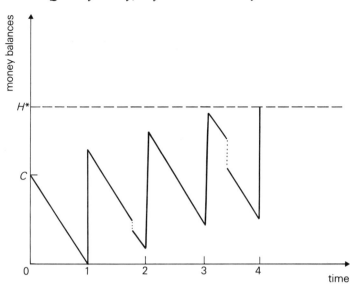

FIGURE 2.3   *Money balances with small lump sum purchases and lump sum inpayments.*

(Source: Akerlof and Milbourne (1980)).

2.6   EXTENSIONS TO THE INVENTORY MODEL

There have been a number of refinements to the simple inventory model and for completeness we briefly discuss some of these below.

The Baumol (1952) model neglects integer constraints on the number of sales of assets. Tobin (1956) rectified this and found that it may be worthwhile for some individuals to hold no earning assets at all (a 'corner solution'); their demand for money is then *proportional* to the lumpy income receipts as in the Fisher model. Barro (1976) aggregated Tobin's 'corner solution' and 'square root' money holders (assuming a gamma distribution for the cross sectional distribution of income) and found, not surprisingly, that the aggregate income elasticity lay between $\frac{1}{2}$ and unity.

Karni (1974) proposed that the brokerage fee depended on the value of time. If the latter rises in proportion to real income, then the Baumol model yields an income elasticity of unity ($\frac{1}{2}$ from transactions and $\frac{1}{2}$ from the brokerage fee).

Feige and Parkin (1971) and Santomero (1974) introduce commodities into the choice set of the inventory framework. There are transactions costs in moving into and out of durable goods, the yield on which is the expected rate of inflation (less storage and depreciation costs). The expected rate of inflation enters the determination of the demand for money (and bonds) but somewhat surprisingly, its sign remains ambiguous (Grossman and Policano, 1975).

Barro (1970) and Santomero (1974) endogenize the period between income receipts in the money–bonds–commodity inventory model. The 'corner solution' now depends upon interest rates and transactions costs and in Barro's model (where earnings assets are excluded) money and expected inflation are negatively related. Clearly, results vary depending on the assumptions used and it is dangerous to generalize.

2.7 SUMMARY OF TRANSACTIONS MODELS

The classical and Cambridge economists concentrated on the determinants of the transactions demand for money. In Friedman's restatement of the quantity theory, the demand for money is placed in the context of the choice between money and a wide range of other financial and real assets. In Friedman's view the demand for money depends on a *set* of interest rates, a transactions variable and some measure of wealth. In the main, the qualitative (and quantitative) relationship between these variables and the demand for money is to be determined by empirical work.

By making more specific and sometimes more restrictive assumptions, inventory models provide rather precise forms of the demand for money function. The essence of the inventory theoretic models of the transactions demand for money (and bonds) is the assumption of certainty: certainty concerning the timing of income receipts of the return on money and bonds and the brokerage fee. Even in this model the demand for money only obeys the square root 'law' in the simplest case. Following Sprenkle we have expressed major reservations concerning the ability of the inventory theoretic models to explain the demand for transactions balances of firms and persons. Extensions of the model to include commodities in the choice set although of interest, particularly as regards the impact of the expected rate of inflation on money holdings, have not proved very tractable.

Akerlof and Milbourne have presented a transactions model of the target-threshold type with lump sum receipts and payments, and this results in the demand for money having a very low (even negative) income elasticity. They extend the model to include an element of uncertainty in the timing of lump sum durables expenditures, and again a low income elasticity is a feature of the model. The model seems particularly applicable to explaining the demand for money by persons. Models of the precautionary demand for money, to be discussed in the next chapter, take up the assumption that receipts may be stochastic, although continuous rather than a 'lumpy' profile of receipts is usually assumed.

NOTES

1 The second-order condition for a minimum $\delta^2 TC/\delta K^2 = 2bT/K^3 > 0$ is met. An equivalent result is obtained if one chooses n to minimize $TC = bn + rT/2n$ and then substitutes for n in $M = T/2n$. Given T, K and n are uniquely related via the identity $n = T/K$. Another equivalent formulation is to note that the average bond holding is $(T - K)/2$, hence net revenue

$\Pi = [r(T-K)/2] - b(T/K)$. Maximizing Π with respect to K yields the demand for money equation (2.12).

2 If $\ln M = \frac{1}{2}\ln T + \frac{1}{2}\ln(b/2)$, then $\ln(M/P) = \frac{1}{2}\ln(T/P) - \frac{1}{2}\ln(b/2P)$; or $\ln M' = \frac{1}{2}\ln T' - \frac{1}{2}\ln(b'/2)$ where the prime indicates a real variable.

3 The second-order condition for a maximum $\Pi_{KK} = -2bT/K^2 < 0$ is met. Note also that positive solutions for M require $r > i$.

4 $\delta(\ln M)/\delta r = -\frac{1}{2}(r-i)^{-1}(1-\delta i/\delta r) > 0$, if $\delta i/\delta r > 1$ (assuming initial values are such that $r - i > 0$).

5 Sprenkle (1966) also considers brokerage costs that vary proportionately with the value of purchases or sales of bonds. Broadly speaking the 'square root law' of the simple model no longer holds and $M = T/2n$, where $n = [Tr(1-2b*/r)^2 - Ti]^{1/2}/2b$, where $b*$ is the cost per 'dollar' of the purchase/ sale and b is the fixed cost per transaction.

6 When optimal balances are held in completely decentralized firms, then using equations (2.21) and (2.25), $M = [(1-x)Tb(J/(2r))]^{1/2} + (xT/2p)$ and decentralized optimal balances are larger than for the centralized firm. Under these circumstances x may have to be larger for the decentralized firm before non-optimal balances exceed optimal holdings.

7 Speculative balances are assumed to be a very small proportion of actual money holdings of firms because of the existence of higher yielding (capital certain) liquid assets other than money, while precautionary balances are also thought to be small because of frequent dealings in the money market and because (in the UK) of the existence of automatic overdraft facilities.

8 The formula for M^e is obtained by noting that for a three day period ($p = 3$), receipts of R yield an average balance of $R/2$ over the three day period. However, observed end of day balances are $\frac{2}{3}R$, $\frac{1}{3}R$, 0 and therefore the average observed end of day balance is $R/3$. But $R/3 = R/2 - \frac{1}{2}(R/3)\ldots(i)$, that is the average balance over the three day period $(R/2)$ minus one half of the daily payments $(R/3)$. In the text, average daily payments are T/p and average balances $C^* = (Tb/2r)^{1/2}$, hence, by analogy with (i), $M^e = C^* - \frac{1}{2}(T/p)$.

9 $dM^e/dT = \frac{1}{2}(b/2rT)^{1/2} - 1/2p$. Hence dM^e/dT falls as T increases and is negative for $T > p^2b/2r$. For completeness the reader may easily verify that the interest elasticity $(r/M^e)(\partial M^e/\partial r) = -\frac{1}{2}C^*/[C^* - (T/2p)]$. When T is small the interest elasticity is $-\frac{1}{2}$ and increases as T increases.

10 To see why the procyclical movement in velocity in the short run, and constancy in the long run, is consistent with a demand for money function with a small short-run nominal income elasticity and a unit long-run elasticity, consider the log linear function $M^d = K_0 Y_t + (1-K_0)Y_{t-1}$. This demand for money function has a 'small' short-run elasticity if $0 < K_0 < 1$ and a unit long run elasticity. Money market equilibrium yields $M = M^d$, where M is the money supply. In the short run $\partial Y_t/\partial M_t = K_0^{-1} > 1$ while in the long run $\partial Y/\partial M = 1$. The logarithm of the velocity of circulation $V \equiv Y - M$, increases as income rises since in the short run $\partial Y_t > \partial M_t$. In the long run $\partial Y = \partial M$, and hence velocity is constant. In general, movements in velocity depend on *all* the determinants of the demand for money.

11 Akerloff (1979) has also developed a constant target-threshold model with a continuous (binominal) distribution of receipts and payments, and this model implies a zero income elasticity of the demand for money. The Miller and Orr (1966) precautionary demand model, to be discussed in the next chapter, is also of the target-threshold type and also assumes a continuous distribution for net cash receipts.

3

Precautionary and Risk-aversion Models of the Demand for Money

3.1 INTRODUCTION

In this chapter we extend our analysis of the possible determinants of the demand for money (and other assets) by introducing 'uncertainty' into our models. Our analysis is limited to a discussion of two sources of uncertainty, namely uncertainty concerning the timing of receipts and payments and uncertainty about the future price of an asset (bond). Nevertheless a detailed analysis of these types of model provides useful practical insights into the behaviour of the demand for assets by persons, firms and financial intermediaries, including banks. The portfolio behaviour of banks is crucial for modelling the money supply process and analysing alternative monetary control techniques and we draw on the material in this chapter when discussing these issues later in the book. The two broad approaches to modelling the demand for money discussed in this chapter are precautionary demand models and 'risk-aversion' models.

Models of the precautionary demand are based on the transactions motive for holding money. However, in contrast to most inventory models we relax the assumption that receipts and payments are known with certainty. The motive for holding money is still to enable one to minimize the cost of undertaking transactions. Costs again consist of brokerage fees and the interest foregone on alternative assets (bond). Although the latter is known with certainty the former is not because of uncertainty about the size of net cash inflows. Hence agents minimize expected transactions costs. In general, the precautionary demand for money depends on the brokerage fee and the interest rate on bonds (as in the inventory models) but in addition some measure of the variability of transactions also influences demand.

Risk-aversion models deal with the problem noted by Keynes, of choice amongst a set of assets some of which have uncertain capital values in nominal terms. As the name suggests these models assume that individuals maximize utility by trading off risk and return subject to a wealth constraint. Holding more of the risky asset (bond) increases the return to be obtained on the whole portfolio but may also increase the riskiness of the portfolio due to the possibility of capital gains and losses on the risky assets. Under such circumstances it may be worthwhile holding a capital safe asset such as money even if the latter does not earn interest. Risk aversion models allow the demand for money and bonds to depend upon the relative expected return on alternative assets, wealth and the variability in the return on bonds. There is a parallel here with the precautionary demand for money. The latter invokes uncertainty about the level of transactions while in risk-aversion models, uncertainty about future bond prices influences the demand for money.

The reader may have noticed that in all of our theories of the demand for money, the individual simultaneously chooses his money balances *and* his non-money balances (for example his bond holdings). Variables that influence the demand for money also affect the demand for alternative assets. This may lead to the coefficients in different asset demand functions being interrelated. Put more technically, some theories imply cross-equation restrictions on the parameters in a set of asset demand functions.

3.2 THE PRECAUTIONARY DEMAND FOR MONEY

We consider two approaches to the precautionary demand for money. In the first, the individual does not have access to any liabilities such as bank advances and must meet his uncertain transactions needs by switching between money and a 'bond' with a known yield. The second model allows access to bank overdrafts (loans).

3.2.1 *Money, bonds and the precautionary demand*

The distinguishing feature of most inventory models of the transactions demand for money is certainty. Receipts, interest rates (yields) and the brokerage fee are all known. We have noted certain criticisms of the model when applied to large firms. Firms and to a lesser extent individuals are subject to variable and uncertain receipts and payments. Precautionary demand models assume net receipts are uncertain but reduce the uncertainty to the one of 'risk', that is the probability distribution of receipts–payments is assumed known. The assumptions of the model are as follows. The firm incurs a brokerage cost b if net payments per period N (that is payments less receipts) are greater than money holdings M. The brokerage fee involves costs of selling interest bearing assets at short notice. These may involve time, inconvenience, possible interest penalties or an unexpected capital loss (on marketable assets). On the other hand, holding a higher level of money balances (which for the moment we assume earn zero interest) to reduce brokerage fees, involves a loss of interest on 'bonds'. (The 'bond' is most likely to be a capital certain short-term asset). The firm will therefore trade off expected brokerage fees against interest foregone, in choosing its optimal money (and bond) holdings, in much the same fashion as in the non-stochastic inventory model.

If the probability distribution of net payments is centred on zero and the probability distribution of net payments exceeding money holdings $(N > M)$ is p then total brokerage costs are bp. Interest payments foregone are rM (r = yield on the alternative asset) and expected total costs TC are

$$TC = Mr + pb \tag{3.1}$$

Precautionary demand models give different results depending upon the assumption made about the probability of illiquidity p, and the results involve reasonably complex derivations. Here we illustrate Whalen's (1966) most simple precautionary demand model (which assumes very risk-averse behaviour). It may be shown that the probability p of $N > M$ takes a maximum value $p = \sigma^2/M^2$ where $\sigma =$ standard deviation of net payments.[1] Substituting for p in equation (3.1) and minimizing TC with respect to M gives

$$\partial(TC)/\partial M = r - \frac{2\sigma^2 b}{M^3} = 0 \tag{3.2}$$

$$M = \left(\frac{2\sigma^2 b}{r}\right)^{1/3} \tag{3.3}$$

and the second derivative $\partial^2(TC)/\delta M^2 = 6\sigma^2 b/M^4 > 0$ indicates a minimum.

As with the transactions models we obtain the result that the individual's demand for money is positively related to the brokerage fee and negatively related to the interest rate on 'bonds' (but with an interest elasticity of one-third). The demand for money also increases with the (cube root) of the *variance* of expected net payments.

One is tempted to enquire whether income, which has featured so prominently in estimated demand for money functions, has any precise role to play in the precautionary demand model. The answer is yes, provided some rather restrictive assumptions are made about the distribution of net receipts which here we take to be normally distributed. If the frequency of receipts and payments increases but the *value* of each receipt stays the same then it may be shown (Whalen, 1966) that $\sigma^2 = K_1 Y$ where $K_1 =$ constant and $Y =$ volume of transactions: if the converse holds then $\sigma^2 = K_2 Y^2$. Substituting these expressions in equation (3.3) we see that the income elasticity of the demand for money will vary between one-third (increased frequency) and two-thirds (increased 'value'). Since an increase in the value of receipts will presumably be accompanied by a proportionate increase in the brokerage fee b (with an elasticity of one-third) the 'price level' elasticity will be unity (that is two-thirds 'transactions value' plus one-third brokerage 'value').

For the individual the relationship between income and the variance of transactions is likely to be more complex than the above. For example, as incomes rise the frequency of transactions may fall as people attempt to economize on 'time', since the opportunity cost of time in terms of income foregone, will be higher. Over time both 'value' and the frequency of transactions are likely to alter in such a manner that the relationship between money holdings and income is impossible to determine. In the aggregate it is difficult to see how adequate measures of the variance could be constructed. Another problem in testing the theory is that actual money balances are likely to simultaneously comprise inventory balances and precautionary balances; however, actual data on money cannot be separated into these two separate 'demands'.

The Miller–Orr precautionary demand model (Miller and Orr, 1966, 1968) is similar to the one described above but the individual only switches between 'bonds' and 'money' when upper or lower bounds for money are reached

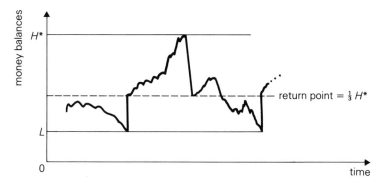

FIGURE 3.1   *Miller-Orr precautionary demand model.*

(figure 3.1). The decision variable is then the amount transferred at these limiting points. This gives rise to a demand for money (assuming a binominal distribution for the net cash drain with a zero mean) of the form:

$$M = \frac{4}{3}\left(\frac{3bm^2t}{4r}\right)^{1/3}$$ (3.4)

where m is the amount the cash balance is expected to alter (with a probability of $\frac{1}{2}$) and t is the frequency of transactions. The variance of transactions is proportional to m^3t and therefore implicitly appears in the above formula. The result is almost identical to Whalen's with a frequency elasticity $E_t^M = \frac{1}{3}$, the 'value' elasticity $E_m^M = \frac{2}{3}$ and the interest elasticity $E_r^M = -\frac{1}{3}$. The Miller-Orr model therefore implies homogeneity (of degree one) for nominal money balances with respect to the price level.

The Miller-Orr model, like the Akerlof-Milbourne (1980) model is also a target-threshold model and therefore has the intuitively appealing idea that money balances are not adjusted continuously but only when money balances reach a ceiling or floor. Temporary or transitory changes in money are voluntarily held. This idea will appear in a slightly different context in the section on buffer-stock money.

3.2.2   *Money, liquid assets and bank advances in a precautionary demand model*

Sprenkle and Miller (1980) have extended the precautionary model to include the possibility of meeting an unexpected cash drain by (automatic) overdrafts at an interest cost r_0 as well as by running down liquid assets (with an interest rate r). The model may therefore be particularly useful in analysing the demand for money (and bank advances) by large firms who have automatic overdraft facilities. We apply some of the results of this model to our analysis of monetary control in chapter 8.

In the model we assume 'money' earns zero interest. There are no brokerage fees and the 'trade-off' involves the probable cost of overdrafts r_0 relative to the return from investing in (alternative) liquid assets r. Let A be the desired cash holding and x the forecast error for the end of day net money balance. If x lies between minus infinity and A (that is $x \in (-\infty, A)$) then there is an excess of money $(A - x)$ at an opportunity cost of r, the return on alternative assets. For $x \in (A, \infty)$ there will be overdrafts $(x - A)$ at an opportunity cost $(r_0 - r)$. Note that the opportunity cost of overdrafts is $(r_0 - r)$ and not r, since an amount equivalent to the overdraft will have been invested in liquid assets at a rate r. It is the *relative* interest rate $(r_0 - r)$ that provides novel results in the model.

Assuming x has a zero mean and probability distribution $f(x)$, the individual chooses A to minimize total cost

$$TC = r \int_{-\infty}^{A} (A - x)f(x)\,dx + (r_0 - r) \int_{A}^{\infty} (x - A)f(x)\,dx \qquad (3.5)$$

$$\frac{\partial TC}{\partial A} = r \int_{-\infty}^{A} f(x)\,dx - (r_0 - r) \int_{A}^{\infty} f(x)\,dx = 0$$

$$= r \int_{-\infty}^{\infty} f(x)\,dx - r_0 \int_{A}^{\infty} f(x)\,dx$$

$$= r - r_0(F(\infty) - F(A))$$

$$= r - r_0(1 - F(A)) = 0 \qquad (3.6)$$

$$F(A^*) = \frac{r_0 - r}{r_0} \qquad (3.7)$$

where we have used

$$\int_{-\infty}^{\infty} f(x)\,dx = 1$$

$F(\infty)$ is the cumulative probability which equals 1 and $F(A)$ is the cumulative probability that cash requirements are equal to optimal cash holdings. For optimal cash holdings to exceed zero (i.e. $A^* > 0$) we require $F(A^*) > \frac{1}{2}$ and from equation (3.7) this implies $r_0 > 2r$. In general, the borrowing rate is less than twice the return on liquid assets and therefore the model predicts that optimal cash holdings are negative, that is firms should usually plan to use their overdrafts. By assuming a normal distribution it is possible to show that optimal cash holding depends upon the variance of the forecast error of cash balances, but *explicit* demand functions are difficult to derive. Sprenkle and Miller are able to show that the demand for 'broad money' depends on relative interest rates and demand will rise *continuously* (in the form of increased overdrafts which appear on the liabilities side of the banks balance sheet as 'money') as r rises relative to the overdraft rate r_0, even when $r < r_0$. This could account in part, for the rapid rise in the broad money supply in the UK in some periods in the 1970s and highlights the need to use relative interest rates in the demand function for broad money.[2]

3.2.3 *Summary*

Precautionary demand models are applicable for agents whose money holdings are subject to a stochastic element. Our first model of precautionary demand predicts that the demand for money depends on the brokerage fee, the opportunity cost of holding money and some measure of uncertainty of net receipts. The latter may often be adequately represented by the variance of net receipts. This version of the precautionary model may therefore capture some elements of the demand for money by persons who usually do not have access to automatic overdraft facilities. Milbourne (1983) provides an elegant synthesis of the various target-threshold models.

The precautionary model of Sprenkle and Miller (1980) explicitly introduces automatic overdraft facilities and hence may be applicable to the demand for money (bank advances and other liquid assets) by large firms. An interesting result is that the demand for 'broad money' and bank loans increases when the relative cost of advances $r_0 - r$ narrows (even though the latter may still be negative). Unfortunately the difficulties in measuring the uncertainty of receipts, particularly when using aggregate data, has severely limited empirical tests of these models.

3.3 RISK-AVERSION MODELS

Risk-aversion models have been widely applied in empirical work on asset demand functions and these models may be applied in many other branches of economics. We therefore examine them in some detail. The distinguishing feature of risk-aversion models is that some assets (for example, bonds, equities) have an uncertain nominal return because capital gains and losses may occur.

Our analysis of risk aversion models proceeds in easy stages. First we present a model in which there are only two assets, a 'risky' asset and a (capital) 'safe' asset and the expected capital gain on the former is assured to be zero. We present this rather simple model geometrically and algebraically. From the analysis of the above simple model it becomes obvious that we need an unambiguous measure of the 'riskiness' of holding bonds. In section 3.3.2 we discuss the conditions under which the variance of uncertain returns provides such a measure. (In appendix 3A we develop some of these points.) In the next section we examine the choice between two risky assets with non-zero expected capital gains. In section 3.3.3(b) we return to our original problem of choice between one safe and one risky asset but this time we allow expected capital gains to be non-zero. Although the above models have been couched in terms of only two assets for pedagogic reasons we show how the model may be extended to many assets in appendix 3B. To anticipate some of our results we find that risk-aversion models indicate that the demand for money and other assets depends on a set of expected yields, wealth and the variability of asset prices (yields).

In section 3.4 we consider a number of general issues that arise from our analysis in this and the previous chapter. First, we briefly discuss 'homogeneity' in asset demand functions. Second, we outline how one might combine various models of the demand for money into a composite model that might include say, inventory and risk-aversion models. Thirdly, under the heading of 'interdependent asset demands' we examine the restrictions on the parameters of asset demand functions implied by the budget constraint. Finally in section 3.5 we discuss some issues in testing and discriminating between our various models.

3.3.1 *A simple mean-variance model:*
one safe, one risky asset, zero expected capital gains

Risk-aversion models are based on the idea that individuals like wealth but dislike risk. Thus in choosing the amount of each asset they wish to hold, individuals trade off risk against expected return. Risk arises from uncertainty concerning the future price of the asset. If the holding period for an asset with a variable interest rate is less than its term to maturity then the total return on the asset will not be known with certainty. For example the running yield or interest rate r on a bond is known at the time of purchase but the price at the end of the holding period is not. The total expected yield R_{t+1}^e on the bond is made up of the running yield r_t and the expected percentage capital gain between t and $t + 1$ (based upon information known at time t), that is g_{t+1}^e

$$R_{t+1}^e = r_t + g_{t+1}^e \tag{3.8}$$

where $g_{t+1}^e = (P_{t+1}^e - P_t)\,100/P_t$ and P is the market price of the bond. Even if the expected capital gain is zero the bond holder is still subject to risk since he knows that his expectation may not be fulfilled *ex post*. The question immediately arises as to how we may measure 'riskiness'. Perhaps the most obvious answer is to use the variance of the probability distribution of possible future prices of the bond: the greater the variance in the price of the bond the greater the risk attached to that individual bond.

Suppose the individual has a well-behaved utility function depending only on the expected return on the *whole* portfolio Π^e and the riskiness of the *whole* portfolio of assets as measured by the variance of the portfolio σ_Π^2

$$U = U(\Pi^e, \sigma_\Pi^2) \qquad U_1 > 0, U_2 < 0, U_{11} < 0, U_{22} < 0 \tag{3.9}$$

The sign of the first-order partial derivatives (U_1, U_2) imply that expected return adds to utility while more 'risk' reduces utility. The second-order partial derivatives indicate *diminishing* marginal utility to additional expected 'returns' and increasing marginal disutility with respect to additional risk. The indifference curves for the above utility function are shown in figure 3.2.

At a point like A on indifference curve I_1 the individual requires a higher expected return as compensation for a higher level of risk, if he is to maintain the level of satisfaction (utility) pertaining at A: the indifference curves have a positive slope in risk-return space. The indifference curves are convex to the 'risk axis' indicating that at higher levels of risk, say at C, the individual requires

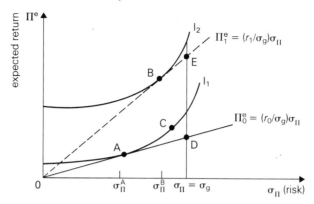

FIGURE 3.2   *A simple mean-variance model.*

a higher expected return for each additional increment to risk he undertakes, than he did at A: the individual is 'risk averse'. Below we demonstrate the special assumptions required to enable 'riskiness' to be expressed solely in terms of the variance of returns but for the moment we merely note that the assumptions in equation (3.9) are consistent with the indifference curves in figure 3.2. The individual, in attempting to maximize utility, will attempt to reach the highest indifference curve but his choices are limited by his budget constraint. If all wealth is held in money, which we assume for the moment earns no interest, then expected return and 'risk' are both zero and graphically we are at the origin. If *all* wealth is held in bonds the individual incurs maximum risk and (for a given expected yield R^e) a maximum expected return on the whole portfolio. He is therefore at a point like D. A combination of money and bond holdings is represented by points on the line OD, the budget constraint. Given the budget constraint OD, the individual attains the highest indifference curve at point A which involves a diversified portfolio of money and bonds. This, in a nutshell, is the basis of mean-variance models of asset choice which we elaborate below.

An algebraic representation. Assume that money earns zero interest ($i = 0$); the expected capital gain on the risky asset (bond) is zero and that wealth is held in either money or bonds

$$M + B = W \tag{3.10}$$

$$M/W + B/W = W/W = m + \beta = 1 \tag{3.11}$$

The *actual* return Π and the *expected* return Π^e on the whole portfolio, as a percentage of initial wealth, are respectively

$$\Pi = \frac{iM + B(r + g)}{W} = \beta(r + g) \tag{3.12}$$

$$\Pi^e = \frac{B(r + g^e) + iM}{W} = \frac{B}{W} r = \beta r \tag{3.13}$$

since $g^e = i = 0$ by assumption. From (3.12) and (3.13) $\Pi - \Pi^e = \beta g$. The variance of the whole portfolio is

$$\mathrm{var}\,(\Pi) = \sigma_\Pi^2 = E(\Pi - \Pi^e)^2 = E(\beta g)^2 = \beta^2 E g^2 = \beta^2 \sigma_g^2$$

Hence

$$\sigma_\Pi^2 = \beta^2 \sigma_g^2 \quad \text{or} \quad \sigma_\Pi = \beta \sigma_g \tag{3.14}$$

where σ_g^2 is the variance of the price of the bonds.[3]

The variance of the whole portfolio therefore depends upon the variance of the returns on the risky asset σ_g^2 and the amount of the risky asset held (as a proportion of wealth) β. For given σ_g^2 the riskiness of the whole portfolio increases linearly with β. When all wealth is held in bonds $\beta = 1$ and $\sigma_\Pi^2 = \sigma_g^2$ (if $\beta < 1$ then $\sigma_\Pi^2 < \sigma_g^2$ and the riskiness of the whole portfolio σ_Π^2 is reduced by holding some of the non-risky asset, money).

Returning now to expected profit we see that this depends linearly on β and r, $\Pi^e = \beta r$. However, substituting for β from (3.14) in (3.13) we obtain

$$\Pi^e = (r/\sigma_g)\sigma_\Pi \tag{3.15}$$

This is the opportunity locus in (Π^e, σ_Π) space and is linear for given r and σ_g. For higher values of r and lower values of σ_g the slope increases, (compare OD and OG in figure 3.1). From the above we know that the maximum value of $\sigma_\Pi = \sigma_g$ and at this point all wealth is held in bonds. Points between 0 and σ_g indicate a diversified portfolio, in which both bonds and money are held simultaneously, by the individual. Maximizing utility subject to the opportunity locus gives a diversified portfolio with equilibrium at A.

A higher interest rate on bonds yields an equilibrium at B which involves a higher value of σ_Π and therefore higher bond holdings and lower money holdings. However, this result depends on the shape of the indifference curves and it is possible for an increase in r to give *lower* bond holdings. This is the familiar case where the 'income effect' (or more precisely the 'wealth effect') is negative and outweighs the 'substitution effect'. A higher interest rate encourages a move into bonds, at unchanged levels of wealth or utility: this is the 'substitution effect'. However, for a given initial holding of money and bonds the increase in r increases expected wealth and this will lead to less bond holdings if the bonds are 'inferior goods'. If we make the reasonably plausible assumption that bonds are 'normal goods' the wealth effect reinforces the substitition effect and $\partial B/\partial r > 0$. Finally, a decrease in the 'risk' on the bond σ_g for a given interest rate also shifts the opportunity locus upwards and again would normally result in an increase in bond holdings.

Our demand for bonds and demand for money function are therefore of the form

$$\frac{B}{W} = B(\sigma_g, r) \quad B_1 < 0, B_2 > 0$$

$$\frac{M}{W} = M(\sigma_g, r) \quad M_1 > 0, M_2 < 0 \tag{3.16}$$

The budget constraint equation (3.11) implies that a change in either σ_g or r cannot alter the portfolio shares (since these must always sum to unity) and therefore the cross equation restrictions $B_1 + M_1 = 0 = B_2 + M_2$ hold. Also, as the budget shares (B/W) and (M/W) must sum to unity then the constant terms in the demand functions for (B/W) and (M/W) must also sum to unity.

These cross equation restrictions are a prediction of the model (more precisely of the 'budget constraint') and if the model is 'true' they may be imposed which considerably reduces the number of parameters to be estimated. (In this simple example, estimation of either the bond or money demand equation enables one to algebraically determine the parameters of the non-estimated function.) Explicit functional forms for $B(.)$ and $M(.)$ require an explicit utility function and we return to this issue below.

3.3.2   Measures of risk

In our previous discussion we measured 'risk' by the *variance* of the probability distribution of the future price of a bond and we asserted that our representative individual was 'risk averse'. We now present a far more formal measure of the individual's degree of risk aversion and derive an explicit utility function which embodies a certain view about the degree of risk aversion. This enables us to see why portfolio diversification may reduce risk and also allow us to derive explicit (and estimable) functional forms for asset demand functions, based on the assumption that individuals maximize the *expected* utility from wealth.

Risk aversion. We restrict ourselves to defining 'risk aversion' in terms of only one variable which we take to be wealth W. Consider a concave utility function $U(W)$ (figure 3.3). An individual offered W_0 (say £100) with certainty will

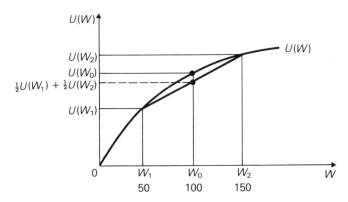

FIGURE 3.3   *Risk aversion and utility.*

obtain a level of utility $U(W_0)$. If the individual is offered a gamble of W_1 (£50) and W_2 (£150) each with a probability of $\frac{1}{2}$, his expected wealth EW, $(= \frac{1}{2}W_1 + \frac{1}{2}W_2) = \frac{1}{2}(50) + \frac{1}{2}(150) = £100 = W_0$, the same as in the certainty case. However the expected utility from wealth, $\mathrm{E}[U(W)]$ is $[\frac{1}{2}U(W_1) + \frac{1}{2}U(W_2)]$ and as indicated in figure 3.3 is less than the utility to be obtained from the certainty case. Thus our individual with a concave utility function gains more utility by taking the certainty case rather than the bet: such an individual is said to be 'risk averse'. It is easy to see that the individual would be indifferent between the certainty case or the gamble if the utility function were a straight line. Such an individual is said to be risk neutral. An individual who expects to achieve more utility from taking the bet has a utility function that is convex (to the horizontal axis). He is described as a 'risk lover'.

For all the cases considered above $U'(W) = \partial U/\partial W$ is positive, that is, the marginal utility from wealth is positive. However for a risk averse individual the slope of the utility function decreases as wealth increases since $U(W)$ is concave to the horizontal axis: that is, $U''(W) < 0$. We can define our three types of risk taker in terms of the second-order derivative of the utility function.

$U''(W) < 0, (= 0), > 0$ implies a risk averse, (neutral), lover

$U''(W)$ is an indicator of the degree of risk aversion: the more negative is $U''(W)$ the more risk averse the individual. However $U''(W)$ is unique only up to a linear transformation (Phlips, 1974) and to avoid the latter problem, we use the Arrow-Pratt measure of *absolute* risk aversion $R_A(W)$, defined as

$$R_A(W) = -\frac{U''(W)}{U'(W)} \tag{3.17}$$

$U''(W)$ is negative for a risk averse individual and $U'(W)$ is always positive hence the greater the degree of risk aversion the greater is R_A. R_A is positive/zero/negative for a risk averse/neutral/lover.

$R_A(W)$ is dependent on the choice of units of W. To obtain a measure of risk aversion that is independent of the units of W we may use the coefficient of *relative* risk aversion $R_R(W)$

$$R_R(W) = WR_A(W) = -\frac{WU''(W)}{U'(W)} \tag{3.18}$$

For $W > 0$, $R_R(W)$ has the same properties as $R_A(W)$ discussed above. In general R_A and R_R are functions of wealth and are therefore *local* measures of risk aversion. As a useful special case we assume that R_A and R_R are constant and equal to c (that is independent of wealth). We may then integrate equations (3.17) and (3.18) to give explicit utility functions. For example, assuming constant absolute risk aversion $R_A(W) = c$ and integrating (3.17) twice we obtain

$$\ln U'(W) = K_1 - cW$$

or

$$U'(W) = \exp(K_1 - cW)$$

hence

$$U(W) = K_2 - (c^{-1}) \exp(K_1 - cW)$$

where K_1 and K_2 are constants of integration. If we define $b = (c^{-1}) \exp(K_1)$ and $a = K_2$ the constant absolute risk aversion utility function is

$$U(W) = a - b \exp(-cW) \qquad (3.19)$$

Similarly, assuming a constant coefficient of relative risk aversion $R_R(W) = d$ and integrating (3.18) twice we obtain the constant relative risk aversion utility function

$$U(W) = a - bW^{-d+1} \qquad b > 0, d \neq 1 \qquad (3.20)$$

The constant absolute risk aversion utility function is used frequently in applied work since it reduces to a particularly tractable form if we assume (a) portfolio choice is governed by a desire to maximize the expected utility of terminal wealth, (b) wealth (which depends upon uncertain outcomes concerning future asset prices) is a normally distributed random variable with mean Π^e and variance σ_Π^2. Under these conditions the expected value of (3.19) becomes

$$E[U(W)] = a - b\left[\exp\left(-c\Pi^e + \frac{c^2}{2}\sigma_\Pi^2\right)\right] \qquad (3.21)$$

Since c is constant by assumption, maximizing $E[U(W)]$ is equivalent to maximizing (for $c > 0$) the simple expression

$$\Pi^e - \frac{c}{2}\sigma_\Pi^2 \qquad (3.22)$$

Thus under our assumptions the expected utility from wealth may be expressed simply in terms of the mean (expected) value of wealth and its variance and as we see below this provides tractable asset demand functions. Not surprisingly this special case of the risk aversion approach is often referred to as the mean-variance model of the demand for assets.

For constant absolute risk aversion $(R_A = c)$ and normally distributed returns, the variance of the distribution of returns turns out to be a useful measure of risk; increasing variance implying increasing risk. However, a priori we might find the proposition that absolute risk aversion *diminishes* as one becomes wealthier rather more plausible than an assumption that it is constant (as used to derive equations (3.19) and (3.22)). The assumption of a normal distribution for wealth implies identical subjective probabilities of an equal capital gain or loss. This is a rather restrictive assumption both for the individual and in the aggregate where market participants may form views based on other peoples views. However, these two 'drawbacks' have not unduly quelled the enthusiasm of economists for the special case of equation (3.22) as it allows the derivation of tractable estimating equations for assets demand functions.

As an alternative to the above, a quadratic utility function with respect to wealth, $U(W) = a + bW + fW^2$, also allows one unambiguously to use variances as a measure of risk. However, the quadratic utility function has the drawback of exhibiting negative marginal utility and increasing absolute risk aversion over some of its range (appendix 3A).

To summarize, except in two special cases where the distribution of asset returns are (a) all normal distributions or (b) a quadratic utility function, it is possible for a risk-averse individual to prefer a distribution with a larger variance than a smaller one. If we are to unambiguously measure 'risk' by the *variance* (of the risky outcome), then we are forced to use either one of our two special cases, even given their other drawbacks.[4]

3.3.3   *Extensions of the simple mean-variance model*

(a) *Two risky assets: non-zero expected capital gains.* We can now demonstrate the derivation of explicit asset demand functions for two risky assets A_1 and A_2 using the special case of the mean variance framework of the risk-aversion model. A_1 may be considered to be gilts and A_2 to be 91 day Treasury bills, with a holding period less than 91 days. The aggregate saving decision has been made and it only remains for wealth to be apportioned between A_1 and A_2 to maximize $E(U(W))$.

Using our above results the problem is to choose A_1 and A_2 to maximize

$$\Pi^e - \frac{c}{2}\,\sigma_\Pi^2 \quad \text{subject to } (A_1 + A_2) = W \tag{3.23}$$

where $W = $ total wealth. Actual profit (*not* as a proportion of wealth) and expected profit are given by

$$\Pi = A_1 R_1 + A_2 R_2$$

$$\Pi^e = A_1 R_1^e + A_2 R_2^e \tag{3.24}$$

where $R_i = r_i + g_i$ and $R_i^e = r_i + g_i^e$ $(i = 1, 2)$ and we do not assume that g_1^e and g_2^e are zero. The variance of total returns $\sigma_\Pi^2 = E(\Pi - \Pi^e)^2$ may be calculated as follows

$$\Pi - \Pi^e = A_1(R_1 - R_1^e) + A_2(R_2 - R_2^e)$$

$$= A_1(g_1 - g_1^e) + A_2(g_2 - g_2^e) \tag{3.25}$$

$$\sigma_\Pi^2 = A_1^2 \sigma_1^2 + A_2^2 \sigma_2^2 + 2A_1 A_2 \sigma_{12} \tag{3.26}$$

where σ_1^2 is the variance of the capital gain on asset '1', around a (possibly) non-zero expected value g^e (σ_i^2 is also equal to the variance of the *price* of the risky asset) (see note 3). σ_{12} is the covariance of capital gains on A_1 and A_2.[5]

From (3.26) we immediately see why portfolio diversification might be attractive. Negative covariances $\sigma_{12} < 0$ between asset returns (for example when gilt prices rise, the price of treasury bills falls) may reduce the overall variance (risk) of the portfolio. For example, choosing A_1 and A_2 to minimise σ_Π^2 subject to $A_2 = 1 - A_1$ yields $A_1 = (\sigma_1^2 + \sigma_2^2 - 2\sigma_1\sigma_2\beta_{12})^{-1}(\sigma_2^2 - \sigma_1\sigma_2\beta_{12})$ where $\beta_{12} = \sigma_{12}/\sigma_1\sigma_2$ is the correlation coefficient of asset returns. For $\beta_{12} = -1$, $A_1 = \sigma_2/(\sigma_1 + \sigma_2)$ and $A_2 = \sigma_1/(\sigma_1 + \sigma_2)$ and substituting for these expressions in (3.26) we obtain $\sigma_\Pi^2 = 0$. Hence with perfect negative correlation we obtain a certain return on a diversified portfolio even though each asset is risky. In the general case, the addition of a single asset to the portfolio of assets adds only one variance term but many covariance terms. If sufficient (weighted) covariance terms are negative this may reduce the total variance of the portfolio.

Using equations (3.23), (3.24) and (3.26) we form the Lagrangean

$$\max_{A_1, A_2} L = A_1 R_1^e + A_2 R_2^e - \frac{c}{2}(A_1^2 \sigma_1^2 + A_2^2 \sigma_2^2 + 2A_1 A_2 \sigma_{12})$$

$$+ \lambda(A_1 + A_2 - W) \tag{3.27}$$

The first-order conditions for a maximum are

$$L_{A_1} = R_1^e - c(A_1 \sigma_1^2 + A_2 \sigma_{12}) + \lambda = 0 \tag{3.28}$$

$$L_{A_2} = R_2^e - c(A_2 \sigma_2^2 + A_1 \sigma_{12}) + \lambda = 0 \tag{3.29}$$

$$L = A_1 + A_2 - W = 0 \tag{3.30}$$

Equating equations (3.28) and (3.29) and substituting for A_2 from the wealth constraint and rearranging we obtain

$$R_1^e - R_2^e + c(\sigma_2^2 - \sigma_{12})W = A_1 c(\sigma_1^2 + \sigma_2^2 - 2\sigma_{12})$$

$$A_1 = \frac{R_1^e - R_2^e}{c(\sigma_1^2 + \sigma_2^2 - 2\sigma_{12})} + \frac{\sigma_2^2 - \sigma_{12}}{\sigma_1^2 + \sigma_2^2 - 2\sigma_{12}} W \tag{3.31}$$

$$A_1 = K_1(R_1^e - R_2^e) + K_2 W \tag{3.32}$$

where K_1 and K_2 are constants, if the variances, covariance and the coefficient of absolute risk aversion c are constant. Using the budget constraint and equation (3.32) we obtain

$$A_2 = (-K_1)(R_1^e - R_2^e) + (1 - K_2)W \tag{3.33}$$

Before commenting on these results we derive the asset demand functions when one asset is a 'safe' asset.

(b) *One risky, one safe asset: non-zero capital gains.* The model discussed above may be applied to the demand for interest bearing money which is subject to a variable interest rate (that is a non-zero variance of return) over the holding period (for example marketable 'certificate of deposit' where the holding period is less than the term to maturity). However, we can easily adapt the model to consider the choice between a risk free asset A_2 (such as cash yielding zero interest or demand deposits yielding a *known* interest rate r_2) and a risky asset such as bonds A_1. For the risk free asset $R_2^e = r_2$ ($g_2^e = 0$), $\sigma_2^2 = \sigma_{12} = 0$, and using equation (3.32) we have[6]

$$A_1 = \frac{R_1^e - r_2}{c \sigma_1^2} \tag{3.34}$$

and

$$A_2 = W - A_1 = W - \frac{1}{c \sigma_1^2}(R_1^e - r_2) \tag{3.35}$$

The demand for 'bonds' and 'money' depend on relative expected yields $(R_1^e - r_2)$. The demand for the risky asset bonds, does *not* depend on wealth and all increments to wealth add to money holdings $(\partial A_2/\partial W = 1)$. We discuss the empirical implementation of the above model when we discuss the demand for bonds, that is gilt-edged stock (Spencer 1981; Cuthbertson, 1983), and the demand for broad money (Grice and Bennett, 1984) in chapter 5.

Summary. Taking the more general model of case 3.3.3 (a) above (as elaborated in appendix 3B) the results of the mean-variance approach are as follows

1 The demand for risky assets depends upon relative expected holding period yields $(R_1^e - R_2^e)$ and wealth W, with the coefficients depending upon variances and covariances and the (constant) coefficient of absolute risk aversion c. With constant values for variances and covariances asset demands are linear in the relative expected yield and wealth. The measurement of expected yields is discussed in sections 4.3 and 4.4.1.

2 The 'own' relative rate has a positive effect $(K_1 > 0)$ provided $\sigma_1^2 + \sigma_2^2 > 2\sigma_{12}$. The latter will always hold for $\sigma_{12} < 0$ and the second-order conditions for a maximum guarantee $K_1 > 0$ even when $\sigma_{12} > 0$.[7]

3 The wealth effect may be positive or negative but is always positive for $\sigma_{12} < 0$. The second-order condition for a maximum $\sigma_1^2 + \sigma_2^2 - 2\sigma_{12} > 0$, does not guarantee a positive wealth effect for asset A_1. If K_2 is negative because A_1 is an inferior good then the coefficient on wealth in the demand function for A_2 must be greater than unity in order that the budget constraint holds.

4 There is a symmetry of cross interest rate effects $\partial A_1/\partial R_2^e = \partial A_2/\partial R_1^e$ and in the two variable case A_1 and A_2 are (gross) substitutes (that is $\partial A_i/\partial R_j^e < 0$) (this is not necessarily the case when more than two assets are considered).

5 The budget constraint imposes cross equation restrictions: the interest rate coefficients sum to zero and the wealth coefficients to unity (equations (3.32) and (3.33)).

6 The parameters K_i on the relative yield and wealth variables depend upon the variances and covariances of asset returns. If agents use rational expectations when predicting the future course of bond prices, the parameters of the demand function will not remain constant under alternative monetary policy rules. For example, if the authorities have a policy of smoothing interest rate movements, agents correctly perceive that the variance of bond prices is small: the risk in holding bonds is low and the interest elasticity (in a simple money bonds model) of the demand for money will be large. (equation (3.35) $\sigma_1^2 \to 0$). Suppose that the authorities switch to a policy of controlling the money supply which will involve larger swings in bond prices (section 8.3). Rational agents correctly recognize that 'bonds' are now more 'risky' and hence the interest elasticity of money demand falls. Hence the estimated coefficients of the demand for money may appear to be unstable even though the mean-variance model is the 'true' model of the demand for money. Put another way, the variance in interest rates after a move to monetary control will be larger than predicted under the assumption that the original (high) interest elasticities hold (Walshe, 1984). This is a form

of the Lucas policy evaluation critique referred to in chapter 1, and is directly applicable to our analysis of the move to monetary base control in the US as described in section 8.3.

Even if one does not accept a (Muth) RE approach, the assumption that the parameters K_i are constant over time is somewhat heroic. An attempt to measure the movement over time in the variance and covariance terms is clearly required. The (weakly) rational expectations hypothesis is of use here and we discuss this aspect in section 5.5.2.

7   The mean-variance model is applicable to a portfolio that includes liabilities (for example bank loans) as well as assets and 'foreign' as well as domestic assets. The expected return on a risky foreign asset includes the expected capital gain (in foreign currency) *and* the expected change in the exchange rate.

3.3.4   *Money and short-term assets*

There has been a lengthy debate in the literature concerning the relevance of the mean-variance model in explaining the demand for money. One side of the argument goes like this. In a world where there exists a wide array of virtually (capital value) risk-free 'short term' assets with low transactions costs, these will dominate the 'low' interest asset 'money', for speculative purposes. The mean-variance model therefore determines the demand for 'short term' assets (and bonds) but not the demand for 'money': the latter is not held at all in a speculative model. It may be demonstrated that with three assets, 'money', a short-term asset and a bond (with normally distributed asset returns and either a quadratic or constant absolute risk aversion utility function) then 'money' will be dominated in the portfolio by the short-term asset, if the return on 'money' is less than the return on 'shorts' and the variance on 'shorts' is small (Sprenkle, 1974; Chang et al., 1983).

Now on logical grounds one cannot fault this argument but it is easy enough to demonstrate that for some definitions of 'money', holdings of the latter are likely to be determined by the mean-variance model. If 'money' includes certificates of deposit and the holding period is short (that is less than the term to maturity), then 'money', in part, consists of a risky asset and the analysis of section 3.3.3(a) applies. Similarly, if deposit accounts are designated as 'money', and earn a known interest rate, we have the model of section 3.3.3(b) with 'money' as the non-risky asset, which has a well-defined demand function. The latter argument also applies to an increasing proportion of 'narrow money' transactions balances which now earn interest. We may summarize the above arguments by noting that the wider the group of assets paying 'competitive' interest rates, that are included in the definition of 'money', the more likely it is that the mean-variance model will be applicable, even in the presence of other virtually risk-free short-term assets.

When trying to equate the mean-variance model with the 'real-world', one must also recall that the model ignores brokerage costs of switching between different assets. A switch between longs and shorts involves two 'brokerage fees', whereas only one is required if the switch is into (narrow) money. Although the cost of switching may be small per transaction, nevertheless if frequent switching takes place, total transactions costs may not be negligible. If 'switching costs' are included in the mean-variance model, which 'realism' dictates they should be, then this biases the decision away from (narrow) money being dominated by short-term assets. Hence in a more 'realistic' mean-variance model there may be additional brokerage cost reasons for holding money (Sprenkle, 1984; Chang et al., 1984).

In section 3.5 we present a simple model which explicitly incorporates brokerage costs into the mean-variance framework (Buiter and Armstrong, 1978). However, in the latter model, money is held to undertake a known expenditure flow (as in the Baumol inventory model) and the brokerage cost is therefore somewhat different from the differential switching costs referred to above where agents move between different assets which act purely as stores of value.

We conclude, by noting that although the mean-variance model may not explain holdings of non-interest bearing money we cannot rule out, on a priori grounds, its possible relevance in explaining holdings of interest bearing 'money', particularly when the pace of 'financial innovation' (section 8.6) means that the latter earn very competitive interest rates (together with low switching costs into checking accounts).

Summary. Risk aversion models assume that the individual in choosing amongst a set of assets with an uncertain return (and with the possibility that one of the assets is a 'safe' asset), seeks to maximize the expected utility from terminal wealth subject to the wealth or 'budget' constraint. To make the model more tractable it is frequency assumed that the problem can be reduced to maximizing a function that depends only upon terms in the expected (mean) return and the variance of the portfolio. Hence the title mean-variance models is often applied. Naturally different utility functions yield different functional forms for the asset demands. The simple mean-variance models that we looked at yield asset demand functions that depend upon expected yields (including capital gains) over the fixed holding period, wealth, a coefficient of risk aversion and the variances and covariances of asset returns. In empirical work the latter two factors are often assumed to be constant. The model is easily generalized to include many risky assets, including real assets where the expected return might be measured by the expected rate of inflation. The risk-averse *individual* holds a diversified portfolio (unlike Keynes' 'plunger') and aggregation over risky assets is possible. (The latter applies for any utility function for which the marginal utility of wealth is isoelastic in a linear function of wealth (Stiglitz, 1972), the quadratic and negative exponential functions used here satisfy this property.)

The possibility of instability in the asset demand functions arises if the variances and covariances of asset returns alter. This seems a definite possibility in time series data particularly if the authorities frequently alter their policy stance in the market for government debt. For example a move from a policy of fixing interest rates to one of controlling the money supply by open market operations could alter the variance of returns on government long-term debt and the covarance between government debt and private sector assets. More volatile rates of inflation that are expected to be reflected in more volatile interest rate movements might also alter the variance of asset returns. This is a form of the Lucas (1976) critique.

The informational requirements in using a mean-variance approach to asset holdings might limit the applicability of the model to sophisticated financial firms such as banks, insurance companies and pension funds, however, this covers the main agents who operate in 'risky' financial markets; persons comprise only a small part of this market. Alternatively one could assume that agents apply the mean-variance analysis to broad aggregates of homogeneous assets (for example gilts, equities, liquid assets).

3.4 SOME GENERALIZATIONS AND LIMITATIONS

3.4.1 *Homogeneity*

Friedman and Roley (1979a) show that maximizing the expected utility from terminal wealth coupled with the assumption of constant *relative* risk aversion and (joint) normally distributed asset returns can yield asset demand functions linear in expected holding period yields R^e and having wealth homogeneity. When all the assets are risky the demand functions are of the form $A_i/W = K_i R^e$, where K_i depends on $R_R = c$, the coefficient of relative risk aversion, and the variance and covariances of asset returns. With one non-risky asset A_0 the demand functions for the risky assets A_i are similar to the above while the non-risky asset is determined as a residual

$$\frac{A_0}{W} = 1 - \sum_1^N \frac{A_i}{W}$$

The demand for the non-risky asset (with interest rate r_0) therefore depends on relative expected yields $(R_i^e - r_0)$ and is homogeneous with respect to wealth. The analysis is similar to that given in section (3.3.3) but with the values of A_i representing asset *shares*. This model will reappear when we discuss Friedman's 'optimal partial adjustment model' (section 4.2.2).

Wealth homogeneity is not implied by *all* mean-variance models but it is sometimes taken to be a desirable property on intuitive grounds. A non-unit wealth elasticity implies that as wealth grows, asset shares either go to zero (if the elasticity < 1) or infinity (if the elasticity > 1). Nevertheless rather than impose a unit wealth elasticity one might view a non-unit elasticity as an approximation valid for the data period in question and for small variations in wealth. Alternatively, in practice other variables might be included in the equation, such as income, which grow in the long run at the same rate as wealth and allow a unit elasticity with respect to both variables.[8]

3.4.2 *Mixed models*

It appears that there is a rather bewildering variety of models of the demand for assets with little common ground between them. Up to a point this is true. More general models that embrace transactions, precautionary and speculative elements are not available because one very quickly runs into difficulties in obtaining tractable results. An exception here is the work of Buiter and Armstrong (1978) who have succeeded in combining the Baumol inventory model of choice between two assets with the assumption of an uncertain return on 'the' bond. This mixed inventory-risk-aversion model can under certain restrictions yield tractable estimating equations and provides one of the few examples of a 'mixed' model. The expected return on the portfolio is similar to that in the simple inventory model

$$\Pi^e = R^e \frac{Y-K}{2} - b \frac{Y}{K} \tag{3.36}$$

where K is the amount withdrawn and $(Y-K)/2$ is the average bond holding. In this mixed model the return on the bond R^e is not known with certainty and includes expected capital gains and losses. If the variance on the bond is σ^2 then the variance of returns on the whole portfolio σ_Π^e is obtained from

$$\sigma_\Pi^e = \frac{Y-K}{2} \sigma \tag{3.37}$$

These expressions are then substituted in an appropriate mean-variance utility function such as the quadratic, which is then maximized with respect to K, in the usual way. We do not pursue the details here but not surprisingly perhaps, the demand for money depends on a mixture of 'transactions' and 'risk aversion' vaiables, the former consisting of income and the brokerage fee and the latter the expected return and the variance of the return on the risky asset. These independent variables have the expected signs (when the satiation level of return in the quadratic utility function has a sufficiently high value) but the income elasticity may be greater than unity in contrast to the Baumol 'pure transactions' model.

Rather than attempting the impossible, that is, developing a 'super-model' covering all three motives for holding money simultaneously, practitioners have used a useful subterfuge. One can obtain what appears to be a super-model by invoking the assumption of 'separability' (or independence). We assume that agents' decisions concerning, say their risk aversion demand for assets, is made independently of their decisions concerning their transactions balances. We cannot discuss the concept of separability in detail but we may note that if the utility from a group of n assets is 'separable' from the utility obtained from another group of m assets then the demand for the first n assets depends only upon the returns (interest rates) on this subgroup of assets and on the wealth placed in this subgroup of assets: it is independent of the rates of return on the other m assets. A simple example will illustrate the methodology employed.

Consider a portfolio consisting of a risky and a safe asset, A_1 and A_2 respectively (as in section 3.3.3(b) on the mean-variance model) and another asset 'money' M that is used solely for transactions needs (and earns no interest). Suppose the utility from transactions exhibits positive and diminishing marginal utility, for example

$$U = xM - \frac{y}{2} M^2$$

$$U' = x - yM \tag{3.38}$$

$$U'' = -y$$

where x and y are positive constants. Marginal utility is positve (for $M < (x/y)$) and diminishing (for positive y) as required. If we assume our mean-variance utility function is (additively) 'separable' from the transactions utility then the Lagrangian for the 'super-model' is

$$L = A_1 R_1^e + A_2 r_2 - \frac{c}{2} A_1^2 \sigma_1^2 + xM - \frac{y}{2} M^2 + q(A_1 + A_2 + M - W) \tag{3.39}$$

where q is the Lagrangean multiplier. The first-order conditions are

$$R_1^e - cA_1 \sigma_1^2 + q = 0 \tag{3.40a}$$

$$r_2 + q = 0 \tag{3.40b}$$

$$x - yM + q = 0 \tag{3.40c}$$

From (3.40a) and (3.40b) we obtain the same asset demand function for A_1 as in our earlier mean-variance model, namely equation (3.34). Using (3.40b) and (3.40c) the demand for transactions balances is given by $M = (x - r_2)/y$. As in section 3.3.3(b), A_2 is the residual from the budget constraint $A_2 = (W - A_1 - M)$ and therefore depends on the variables that influence the determinants of the risky asset and the transactions asset (money).

Although 'separability' enables one to set up a general utility function and yet still obtain tractable equations the crucial factor is whether the economics which lies behind this assumption is realistic for the problem at hand (see Deaton and Muellbauer (1980) and Spencer (1984) for further discussion). But even if we cannot adequately formulate 'a super-model' we may still be able to usefully apply a particular theory of the demand for assets to a particular group of agents in the economy. For example, we shall see that the mean-variance model has been applied to the asset holdings of banks and pension funds.

3.4.3   *Interdependent asset demands*

Brainard and Tobin (1968) popularized the interdependent asset demand approach particularly with respect to adjustment lags. We deal with the latter in section 4.2.2 but concentrate here on the equilibrium (or 'static') theories of asset demands. In all our models of the demand for assets it has been an implicit assumption that an increase in the demand for one asset implies a reduction in holdings of another asset. Consider now, an *explicit* budget constraint where the sum of all asset holdings must equal wealth. This 'adding up' constraint appears explicitly in our risk-aversion model and gave rise to cross equation restrictions on the parameters of the demand function for money and bonds (equations (3.32) and (3.33)). We may generalize this result slightly by considering the following long-run equilibrium demand functions that could arise from a combination of a transactions and risk-aversion model. If we have only two assets, money M and bonds B, with yields RM and RB, *linear* demand functions and a 'budget constraint' then

$$M^* = a_0 + a_1 Y + a_2 RM + a_3 RB + a_4 W \qquad (3.41)$$

$$B^* = b_0 + b_1 Y + b_2 RM + b_3 RB + b_4 W \qquad (3.42)$$

$$M^* + B^* = W \qquad (3.43)$$

where Y is income and W is wealth. When expressed in terms of the *desired* values M^* and B^*, the 'budget constraint' is known as the rational desires hypothesis: individual's total *desired* demand for assets equals current period wealth. We could equate M^* and B^* with actual M and B respectively and apply the wealth constraint $M + B = W$ without affecting our subsequent argument.

The 'constraint' implies the following cross equation restrictions $a_4 + b_4 = 1$ and $a_j + b_j = 0$ $(j \neq 4)$. For example if an increase in income (transactions) raises the demand for money $(a_1 > 0)$ it must lower the demand for bonds by an equal amount $(b_1 = -a_1)$. 'Sensible' coefficients in any one asset demand function may result in 'implausible' coefficients in other asset demand functions if the budget constraint is ignored. Hence there must be a strong presumption in favour of estimating *systems* of asset demand equations. (We discuss the empirical implementation and problems of lagged adjustment in systems of equations in the next chapter.)

3.5 DISCRIMINATING BETWEEN MODELS

Although the theories of the demand for assets outlined in this and the previous chapter appear to provide competing explanations of the demand for 'money' it can equally well be argued that they are complementary in that each theory may be useful for explaining the demand for a particular set of assets by a particular sector or institution. For example, it appears that non-interest bearing (nib) money balances are likely to be dominated by 'liquid assets' (including interest bearing money) for speculative purposes, and hence the mean-variance model is unlikely to be applicable here. Such nib money balances are more likely to be explained by the inventory or precautionary models.

Turning now to the sectoral breakdown of assets, pension funds and insurance companies deal mainly in interest bearing money, short-term liquid assets, bonds and equities and their transactions needs are low. Hence the mean-variance model would seem to be applicable here. Similar arguments apply to the demand for assets by other financial intermediaries such as the discount houses (in the UK) and to a lesser extent banks and (UK) building societies (saving loan associations in the US). Banks are able to use the interbank market to obtain 'cash' but may also hold a small amount of (nib) 'cash' to cover unforeseen net withdrawals. In this case, we might consider their demand for 'cash' and some capital certain short assets as being 'separable' from their demand for other assets (for example long-term debt, advances). The former may be explained using a precautionary model and the latter using the mean-variance model. Similarly, a 'separability' argument could be applied to the asset demands of building societies. We also noted that the inventory model is likely to be applicable to the demand for narrow (transactions) money balances by persons rather than firms, with a precautionary model being applicable to the latter. However, as we see in future chapters, 'financial innovation' may alter the above demarcation lines.

Economists favour theories with 'strong' testable restrictions, for then a model is capable of refutation. Our theories differ in the scope of their a priori restrictions. The quantity theory approach does not impose strong a priori restrictions, whereas the simple Baumol inventory model, the (Whalen and Miller-Orr) precautionary models and the risk-aversion models do. The Baumol model implies income and interest elasticities of a half (in absolute value) and the Whalen precautionary model also has quantitative a priori restrictions. On the other hand, Friedman's restatement of the quantity theory provides a formidable list of potential independent variables but in the main their signs (and size) are 'to be determined by the data' and are not suggested by a priori considerations. Any model that has an explicit budget constraint implies 'adding up' constraints *across equations.* The mean variance model falls into the latter category and here theory also implies symmetry restrictions.

A major problem in testing theories is data availability. For example, precautionary models require a measure of the variability of transactions; the only available data series on 'money' may not separate out nib from interest bearing money or disaggregate into holdings by persons, firms, and so on. Clearly when aggregating across sectors and different types of asset, testing specific theories becomes hazardous: the available monetary aggregate may include components that are held for transactions, precautionary and risk aversion motives. Here there is little the researcher can do other than construct an 'eclectic' model where unfortunately many of the a priori restrictions implied by each individual model cannot be expected to hold.

Thus although in some cases our theories may be viewed as providing competing explanations of the demand for a specific asset (for example inventory and precautionary models of the demand for nib money by firms), often they are complementary: each being applicable to a particular set of assets. In practice, data limitations often imply the construction of an 'eclectic' model. Even here interesting questions remain: 'Is it wealth or income that is important?' 'Are asset demand homogeneous in the scale variable(s)?' 'Should the vector of returns include foreign interest rates, expected or actual yields?' 'Do adding-up restrictions hold?' The answers to such questions can profoundly influence our view of the transmission mechanism of monetary and fiscal policy.

All our theories of asset demands have been of a comparative static nature: different (long-run) equilibrium positions are compared. Before we test these models we need to form a view of how the demand for assets alters through time and how expectations variables are to be measured. We now turn to these issues.

APPENDIX 3A QUADRATIC UTILITY FUNCTION

The quadratic utility function may be written

$$U(W) = a + bW + fW^2 \tag{3A.1}$$

We now demonstrate that the quadratic utility function allows expected utility to depend only upon expected returns (wealth) EW, and the variance of returns (wealth) σ^2. Taking expectations of (3A.1) we see that expected utility from wealth is given by

$$E(U(W)) = a + bE(W) + fE(W^2) \tag{3A.2}$$

To prove our proposition we therefore need to show that $E(W^2)$ depends only upon EW and σ^2. For any random variable such as W

$$\sigma^2 = E(W - EW)^2 = E(W^2) - (EW)^2$$

hence

$$E(W^2) = \sigma^2 + (EW)^2 \tag{3A.3}$$

Substituting (3A.3) in (3A.2)

$$E(U(W)) = a + b(EW) + f(EW)^2 + f\sigma^2 \tag{3A.4}$$

and expected utility depends only upon the mean and variance of wealth.

To show that the quadratic utility function implies increasing absolute risk aversion at 'high' levels of wealth note that differentiating (3A.1) gives

$$U'(W) = b + 2fW \tag{3A.5}$$

$$U''(W) = 2f \tag{3A.6}$$

$$R_a(W) = -\frac{U''(W)}{U'(W)} = -\frac{2|f|}{b - 2|f|w} \tag{3A.7}$$

For diminishing marginal utility from wealth we require $f < 0$ and this implies that marginal utility and the coefficient of absolute risk aversion become *negative* as W approaches infinity ($W > b/2|f|$ is sufficient).

APPENDIX 3B THE MEAN-VARIANCE MODEL IN MATRIX NOTATION

The mean-variance model is frequently presented in matrix notation. This provides a fairly compact method of deriving the asset demand functions, although to obtain any insight into the signs of the coefficients one still needs to look inside the matrix at the individual elements. For completeness, however, we think it worthwhile comparing the matrix approach to the approach used in the text. For ease of exposition we assume there are only two risky assets in the choice set. The generalization to n assets is easily accomplished.

Our expression for Π and Π^e may be expressed in vector notation as

$$\Pi = R'A \tag{3B.1}$$

$$\Pi^e = R^{e'}A \tag{3B.2}$$

where $R' = (R_1, R_2)$, $A' = (A_1, A_2)$ and a prime indicates the transpose of the vector or matrix.

We now incorporate a useful simplification in notation by representing the error in forecasting R^e as a *vector* ϵ. Thus

$$(R - R^e)' = \epsilon'$$

where

$$\epsilon' = (\epsilon_1, \epsilon_2)$$

hence

$$E(\epsilon\epsilon') = E\begin{bmatrix} \epsilon_1^2 & \epsilon_1\epsilon_2 \\ \epsilon_1\epsilon_2 & \epsilon_2^2 \end{bmatrix} = \begin{bmatrix} \sigma_1^2 & \sigma_{12} \\ \sigma_{12} & \sigma_2^2 \end{bmatrix} = S \tag{3B.3}$$

S is therefore the matrix of variances and covariances of 'returns'. The variance of the portfolio is

$$\sigma_\pi^2 = E(\Pi - \Pi^e)^2 = E[(R - R^e)'A]^2 = E[\epsilon'A]^2 \tag{3B.4}$$

Since $\epsilon'A$ is a scalar it is equal to $(\epsilon'A)' = A'\epsilon$ and hence (3B.4) may be written

$$\sigma_\pi^2 = E(\Pi - \Pi^e)^2 = E(\epsilon'A)^2 = E(A'\epsilon\epsilon'A) = A'E(\epsilon\epsilon')A = A'SA \tag{3B.5}$$

Given our definition of S above we see that equation (3B.5) gives the variance of the portfolio as a weighted average of the variances and covariances of asset returns, the weights being determined by A_1 and A_2. This corresponds to equation (3.26) in the text.

The maximization problems is then

$$\max L = R^{e'}A - \frac{c}{2}A'SA + \lambda(A'i - W) \tag{3B.6}$$

where i is a unit column vector and W is wealth.

First-order conditions are

$$L_A = R^e - cSA + \lambda i = 0$$

$$L_\lambda = A'i - W = 0$$

Hence

$$\begin{bmatrix} A \\ \lambda \end{bmatrix} = \begin{bmatrix} cS & -i \\ -i' & 0 \end{bmatrix}^{-1}\begin{bmatrix} R^e \\ -W \end{bmatrix}$$

and

$$A = \begin{bmatrix} A_1 \\ A_2 \end{bmatrix}$$

$$= \frac{1}{c} \left[S^{-1} - \frac{S^{-1}ii'S^{-1}}{i'S^{-1}i} \right] R^e + \left[\frac{S^{-1}i}{i'S^{-1}i} \right] W$$

$$= K^a R^e + K^b W \tag{3B.7}$$

where K^a is a 2×2 matrix and K^b a 2×1 vector of coefficient estimates. The coefficients on expected returns R^e and wealth W are given by the bracketed terms. The reader might like to try the very tedious task of demonstrating that for two assets the above equation (3B.7) yields equations (3.31) and (3.33) given in the text. He might then realize why matrix methods do not *always* provide a short cut. Some clues are in order

$$S^{-1} = \begin{pmatrix} \sigma_2^2 & -\sigma_{12} \\ -\sigma_{12} & \sigma_1^2 \end{pmatrix} \frac{1}{D}$$

where

$$D = \sigma_1^2 \sigma_2^2 - (\sigma_{12})^2$$

$$S^{-1}i = \begin{pmatrix} \sigma_2^2 - \sigma_{12} \\ \sigma_1^2 - \sigma_{12} \end{pmatrix} \frac{1}{D}$$

$$i'S^{-1}i = (\sigma_1^2 + \sigma_2^2 - 2\sigma_{12})D^{-1}$$

However, the matrix approach is useful when investigating the adding-up restriction $\Sigma A_i = W$ and the symmetry restrictions on the yield (R^e) coefficients, particularly when the vectors A and R^e contain many assets and 'returns'.

To show that our asset demand functions in (3B.7) obey the adding-up restriction $i'A = W$, premultiply (3B.7) by $i' = (1, 1)$

$$i'A = \frac{1}{b} \left[i'S^{-1} - \frac{(i'S^{-1}i)i'S^{-1}}{iS^{-1}i} \right] R^e + \frac{i'S^{-1}i}{i'S^{-1}i} W \tag{3B.8}$$

$i'S^{-1}i$ is a scalar and we may cancel this out in the numerator and denominator of (3B.8) yielding $i'A = W$ as required. The *column* sum of the coefficients on R^e is given by $i'K^a$ and they therefore sum to zero across equations. Similarly the coefficients on W across equations sum to unity. Equation (3B.7) is *derived* under the restriction $i'A = W$ so these results should not come as a surprise but merely provide a check on the matrix algebra.

The *symmetry* of the cross interest rate effects $\partial A_i / \partial R_j$ arise because S, the matrix of variances and covariances of returns, is symmetric ($\sigma_{ij} = \sigma_{ji}$). If S is symmetric, S^{-1} is also symmetric. Therefore $(S^{-1})' = S^{-1}$. Taking the transpose of the term in square brackets on the R^e term in (3B.7) and noting that $(i'S^{-1}i)$ is a scalar and $(S^{-1})' = S^{-1}$ we have

$$(K^a)' = \left[(S^{-1})' - \frac{(S^{-1})'ii'(S^{-1})'}{(i'S^{-1}i)} \right] = K^a$$

The coefficients of the R^e terms in any *one* equation also sum to zero. This follows directly given that the column sums are zero and the matrix of coefficients on R^e is symmetric. Alternatively this result may be established by post-multiplying K^a in equation (3B.7) by 'i', the 2×1 column vector. This restriction implies that the demand for all assets in the choice set depend on *relative* yields.

To summarize. The budget constraint implies cross equation restrictions on the asset demand functions. The coefficients on any one asset return R_i^e sum to zero across all equations while the sum of the coefficients on the wealth term is unity. The variance–covariance matrix of asset returns is symmetric and hence cross-interest rate coefficients (in different equations) are equal, $\partial A_i/\partial R_j^e = \partial A_j/\partial R_i^e$. These restrictions are testable and (particularly the last set) allow one to substantially reduce the number of coefficients to be estimated: an issue we take up in chapter 5.

NOTES

1 The result is based on Chebyshev's inequality. This states that the probability p of a variable x (net payments) deviating from its mean by t times its standard deviation σ is equal to or less than $1/t^2$, that is

$$p(-t\sigma > x > t\sigma) \leqslant \frac{1}{t^2}$$

Net payments are assumed to have a zero mean, so the probability of net payments equal to M which is $M/\sigma = t$, standard deviations from zero is

$$p(N > M) \leqslant \frac{1}{t^2} = \frac{\sigma^2}{M^2}$$

where the equality indicates we have taken the highest possible probability.

2 In practice, broad money and overdrafts cannot rise indefinitely because of overdraft limits. In the UK, in the 1970s, rates of interest on broad money (for example certificates of deposit) sometimes exceeded those on overdrafts and this was thought to encourage large firms to 'round trip' from overdrafts to money and earn a risk free positive return. However Sprenkle and Miller's model indicates that 'round tripping' might take place even when this interest differential moves to a lower *negative* value. The differential $r_0 - r$ need not be positive for round tripping to occur.

3 The variance in the price of the bond is defined as $E[(P_{t+1} - P_{t+1}^e)/P]^2$. The variance of the capital gain σ_g^2 is defined as $E(g - g^e)^2$, where $g = (P_{t+1} - P)/P$ and $g^e = (P_{t+1}^e - P)/P$. Two points follow. First if $g^e = 0$ then $\sigma_g^2 = E(g^2)$. Second $g - g^e = (P_{t+1} - P_{t+1}^e)/P$, hence the variance of the capital gain $E(g - g^e)^2$ is equal to the variance in the price of the bond.

4 Alternatively we could use another measure of risk such as the 'risk premium'. We do not invoke the latter in our analysis (see Hey (1979) for further details).

5 Our 'simple model', earlier, has $R_2 = \sigma_2^2 = \sigma_{12} = 0$ and hence $\Pi^e = A_1 r_1$ and $\sigma_\Pi^2 = A_1^2 \sigma_1^2$.

6 The second-order condition becomes $\sigma_1^2 > 0$ (for $c > 0$) and always holds. Our simple graphical exposition of section 3.3.1 involves a further simplifi-

cation, namely $g_1^e = 0$. Then equations (3.24) and (3.26) reduce to $\Pi^e = A_1 r_1$ and $\sigma_\Pi^2 = A_1^2 \sigma_1^2$ and the mathematical equivalent of our graphical solution of figure 3.2 is given by equations (3.34) and (3.35) with $R_1^e = r_1$ and $r_2 = 0$.

7   The second-order conditions for a maximum are that the determinant of the boarded Hessian $|H| > 0$, where

$$H = \begin{vmatrix} 0 & g_1 & g_2 \\ g_1 & Z_{11} & Z_{12} \\ g_2 & Z_{21} & Z_{22} \end{vmatrix} \quad \text{and} \quad L = Z(A_1, A_2) + \lambda g(A_1, A_2) = 0$$

Using (3.27), $g_1 = g_2 = 1$, $Z_{11} = -c\sigma_1^2$, $Z_{22} = -c\sigma_2^2$, $Z_{12} = Z_{21} = -c\sigma_{12}$. For a risk averse individual $c > 0$ and hence $|H| > 0$, then implies $\sigma_1^2 + \sigma_2^2 - 2\sigma_{12} > 0$.

8   Consider $\ln A_i = a_1 \ln W_i + a_2 \ln Y_i$ where $Y_i = $ income. If $\Delta \ln W = \Delta \ln Y$ then $\Delta \ln A_i = (a_1 + a_2) \Delta \ln W$. (A/W) is constant if $a_1 + a_2 = 1$. Hence a_1 may be less than unity and (A/W) remain constant in the long run. However, the use of a *log* linear relationship here is not consistent with the risk-aversion models discussed.

4

Lag Structures and Expectations

4.1 INTRODUCTION

In previous chapters we derived comparative static results for a number of alternative theories of the demand for assets: these demand functions are usually referred to as 'long-run equilibrium' demand functions. In such models the speed of adjustment between two equilibrium positions is instantaneous. The inventory and precautionary models implicitly incorporate costs of adjustment in the form of the brokerage fee. Agents trade off this cost of adjustment against interest foregone, when deciding on their desired level of money balances. But having done so, adjustment to equilibrium is instantaneous. Things are a little different with the risk-aversion model where there are no costs in adjusting the portfolio of assets.

In general, if the above models are fitted to quarterly time series data on money balances they do not perform well statistically. However, the addition of lagged values of money as independent variables, improves their statistical performance considerably. It is probably correct to say that the latter empirical fact led to a search for 'theories' to explain this phenomenon. As we shall see below, there are a number of legitimate ways of including lagged values of money as independent variables: two methods frequently used being the partial adjustment and adaptive expectations hypotheses.

In this chapter we shall be concerned with the theoretical basis for determining the speed of adjustment of money balances to their long-run equilibrium value and how expectations may be adequately incorporated in asset demand functions. Our other major area of interest is to examine whether we can obtain the parameters of the long-run demand for money function and the adjustment or expectations parameters from our estimated demand for money functions – this is usually referred to as 'single equation identification'.

Consider adjustment costs. Ideally one would like a theory of the demand for money (and other assets) in which *all* costs of adjustment are included in the constrained optimization problem facing the individual. However, such 'complete' theories quickly become analytically intractable.[1] (Readers familiar with neo-classical theories of real investment will realize that incorporating costs of adjustment of the capital stock in an optimizing multiperiod framework involves similar difficulties.)[2] As a result we are virtually forced to assume that the individual undertakes a two stage decision process. First he decides on the 'long-run' optimal amount of assets to hold in accordance with the theories set out in the previous chapters. Second, he undertakes a completely separate optimization problem concerning the speed at which he wishes to adjust towards this equilibrium. Thus it is assumed that the adjustment path chosen does not influence the desired (optimal) long-run level of demand for the asset.

In section 4.2 we discuss the partial adjustment and error correction (feedback) models of adjustment. Both result in the (own) lagged asset stocks appearing as independent variables in the demand function. In the (first-order) partial adjustment model the actual change in money balances depends only upon the disequilibrium between 'long-run' balances and previous periods balances. It was recognized that because of the budget constraint, disequilibrium in money balances implies disequilibrium in at least one other asset stock. Put another way, the change in money balances might also depend on the size of the disequilibrium in *other* asset stocks. This is the basis of the interdependent asset adjustment models: we discuss two models of this type in section 4.2.2.

After presenting the theoretical basis for each of these adjustment models we derive the implied 'short-run' demand for money function and consider whether we can obtain the structural parameters of interest (that is the parameters of the long-run demand for money function and the adjustment parameters) from this 'estimation equation'.

After discussing adjustment mechanisms we move on to consider the modelling of expectations in section 4.3. The latter appear in a number of theories of the demand for money discussed earlier. Survey data on expectations may be available for some variables (for example inflation and output). If this is of a qualitative nature (for example the proportion of the sample that believes inflation will go up), methods exist to transform this into quantitative measures (Carlson and Parkin, 1975; Batchelor 1981). Once we have quantitative survey data over time, we can use it directly in the demand for money function as an independent variable. Published forecasts may also provide reasonable proxy variables for expectations. When the above types of data are not available we then need a method (model) to proxy or generate an expectations series. In the empirical literature on asset demands two main approaches are used.

Much early empirical work invoked the adaptive expectations hypothesis, whereby people adjust their expectations of say inflation based on their previous forecast errors; extrapolative and regressive expectations have been used less frequently. The second approach involves the rational expectations hypothesis (REH) whereby expectations are formed using the underlying model that generates the data. In empirical work on asset demands, use of the REH is in its infancy. In section 4.3 we discuss the adaptive, regressive, extrapolative and RE methods of modelling expectations variables.

In the final part of the chapter we attempt to provide some points of comparison in the modelling of lags and expectations. In section 4.4.1 we compare the different expectations models. This is followed by a model in which both adaptive expectations and partial adjustment appear. In section 4.4.3 we consider alternative methods of modelling lagged responses before finally presenting a brief summary.

Although in this chapter our adjustment and expectations models are mainly applied to the demand for money they are nevertheless perfectly general. We also use absolute levels of the variables but most of the analysis follows if log linear functions are used.

4.1.1 *Lag polynomials*

Before proceeding further we wish to derive some results concerning lag polynomials. A distributed lag response of money M to income Y may be written

$$M_t = a_0 Y_t + a_1 Y_{t-1} + a_2 Y_{t-2} + \ldots \tag{4.1}$$

If we let $a(L) = a_0 + a_1 L + a_2 L^2 + \ldots$ where $L^n Y_t = Y_{t-n}$ this may be written more compactly as

$$M_t = a(L) Y_t \tag{4.2}$$

where $a(L)$ is a lag polynomial and L a lag operator. Lag responses may also be incorporated by using lagged dependent variables

$$M_t = aY_t + \gamma M_{t-1} \qquad 0 < \gamma < 1 \tag{4.3}$$

The response of M to a step change in Y through time is given by $a, a + \gamma a$, $a + \gamma a + \gamma(a + \gamma a) \ldots$, that is $a, a(1 + \gamma), a(1 + \gamma)^2, \ldots$ By using the lag polynomial notation this may be expressed as

$$M_t = aY_t + \gamma(LM_t)$$

$$(1 - \gamma L) M_t = aY_t$$

$$M_t = (1 - \gamma L)^{-1} aY_t \tag{4.4}$$

and expanding $(1 - \gamma L)^{-1}$ in a Taylor series (for $|\gamma| < 1$)

$$M_t = (1 + \gamma L + \gamma^2 L^2 + \gamma^3 L^3 + \ldots) aY_t \tag{4.5}$$

The response of M is therefore directly given as $a, a + \gamma a, a(1 + \gamma + \gamma^2)$, etc. The long run effect is $M_t = [a/(1 - \gamma)] Y$ where we have used $1 + \gamma + \gamma^2 + \ldots = 1/(1 - \gamma)$. We shall use the polynomial lag operator frequently in our discussion of lag effects in asset demand functions.

If we have lagged values of the independent as well as the dependent variable this is an autoregressive distributed lag model (ADL)

$$M = a_0 Y_t + a_1 Y_{t-1} + \ldots \gamma_1 M_{t-1} + \gamma_2 M_{t-2} + \ldots$$

$$M = a(L) Y_t + \gamma(L) M_t \tag{4.6}$$

where $\gamma(L) = \gamma_1 L + \gamma_2 L^2 + \gamma_3 L^3 + \ldots$ This is sometimes written

$$c(L) M = a(L) Y_t \tag{4.7}$$

where $c(L) = 1 - \gamma(L)$. The response of M over time to a step change in Y is given by

$$M = [(c(L))^{-1} a(L)] Y_t = d(L) Y_t \tag{4.8}$$

and if $d(L)$ is a high order polynomial then simulation methods may be required to work out the time path of the response of M. The lag response $d(L)$ may be very flexible if $a(L)$ and $c(L)$ are high order polynomials.

4.2 MODELLING LAG RESPONSES

4.2.1 *The partial adjustment and error feedback models*

Partial adjustment and error feedback models are based on minimizing a cost function that depends only upon current and past variables and results in the lagged money stock appearing as an independent variable in the demand for money function. We assume that the desired long-run equilibrium demand for money M^* is given, and depends upon such variables as interest rates, income and wealth.

Partial adjustment. There may be costs, for example, in terms of interest income foregone or inability to make a purchase of goods, if the individual's asset stock is out of (long-run) equilibrium. If costs of being above and below equilibrium are equal, we may represent this by the quadratic term $a(M - M^*)^2$, where a is the cost per unit of disequilibrium. Similarly costs of *changing* the stock of assets (that is inconvenience and time)[3] may be represented by $b(M - M_{t-1})^2$. Given M^* and M_{t-1} the individual chooses M to minimize (one period) total costs C

$$\min C = a(M - M^*)^2 + b(M - M_{t-1})^2 \tag{4.9}$$

$$\frac{\partial C}{\partial M} = 2a(M - M^*) + 2b(M - M_{t-1}) = 0 \tag{4.10}$$

$$M = \frac{a}{a+b} M^* + \frac{b}{a+b} M_{t-1} = \gamma M^* + (1 - \gamma) M_{t-1} \tag{4.11}$$

where $\gamma = a/(a + b)$. Equation (4.11) is the first-order partial adjustment model. If costs of being out of equilibrium are zero, $a = 0$, then $\gamma = 0$ and $M = M_{t-1}$. If costs of adjustment are zero, $b = 0$, $\gamma = 1$ and $M = M^*$.

It is easy to obtain higher order lagged dependent variables using partial adjustment. For example, if there are costs when money is adjusted more *rapidly*, we have an additional term $c(\Delta M - \Delta M_{-1})^2 = c(M - M_{t-2})^2$. Minimizing cost then gives an additional term $c(M - M_{t-2})$ and the (second-order) partial adjustment equation is

$$M = (a + b + c)^{-1}(aM^* + bM_{t-1} + cM_{t-2}) \tag{4.12}$$

$$M = \mu_1 M^* + \mu_2 M_{t-1} + (1 - \mu_1 - \mu_2) M_{t-2} \tag{4.13}$$

where $\mu_1 = a/(a + b + c)$, $\mu_2 = b/(a + b + c)$. The coefficients on M^*, M_{t-1}, M_{t-2} sum to unity, hence the coefficient on M_{t-2} is $(1 - \mu_1 - \mu_2)$.

In general, partial adjustment implies that short-run desired money balances M are a weighted average of desired long-run balances M^* and lagged values of money balances. If we believe that an increase in the demand for money is always met by an increase in supply (as for example under a constant interest rate target by the authorities) then we can equate the short-run *desired* demand derived above with *actual* money balances and estimate the demand function.

As we shall see in the section on the buffer-stock approach to the demand for money this is not always a realistic assumption, even though it has been widely adopted in the empirical literature.

A possible defect of the first-order partial adjustment mechanism is that short-run money balances may *continually* differ from long-run balances. If M^* is rising, say due to a continuous rise in real income, then because short-run balances adjust towards M^* with a lag, they will continually lie below long run balances.[4] There are a number of counter-arguments to this proposition. First, if in the data income does not rise continuously but fluctuates around a roughly constant mean, the first-order partial adjustment mechanism will not involve M continuously diverging from M^*. Further, changes in the other independent variables that influence M^* may offset the effects of rising income, so that M^* does not continuously rise or fall. Of course, an equation estimated using data where M^* is non-trended should not necessarily be used to simulate the effect of a steady growth in income on the desired demand for money, since the parameters of the demand function may change under this alternative regime (the argument has a parallel in the so-called Lucas policy evaluation critique (cf. section 1.2.4 and 4.4.3 below).

The continuous under- or over-prediction of the short-run demand for money in relation to the long-run demand is a consequence of the (first-order) partial adjustment equation being a first-order difference equation. Higher order lagged dependent variables would not necessarily produce such a result. Hence, a higher order partial adjustment process could be invoked for data in which M^* is expected to be trended. A broadly equivalent procedure is to assume that γ in the first-order partial adjustment equation increases as the growth in income increases: that is, adjustment is quicker the faster income grows. (The latter is suggested by Flemming (1976) in the context of modelling inflationary expectations.)

In the partial adjustment mechanisms discussed above, it is recognized that it is costly to alter money balances in the current period but they fail to allow for the fact that, where one ends up in this period, will influence next period's costs of adjustment: they are backward looking in assessing costs of adjustment. In section 6.4.3 we rectify this by looking at cost of adjustment in a multiperiod framework.

The first-order partial adjustment mechanism imposes a similar geometric lag response of M to a change in *any* of the independent variables. Whatever the effect in the current period, the change in M in subsequent periods is $(1 - \gamma)$ per period regardless of the independent variable that caused the initial change. This is a highly restrictive lag response. Casual introspection might suggest that the profile over time in M may be different if the change in M is triggered by a change in income rather than in the interest rate. We discuss this issue further but now merely note that, in principle, different lag structures may always be tested against the data to assess their validity.

Researchers do not usually present a rationalization of the quadratic cost function of equation (4.9) and it must be admitted that it is very *ad hoc*. Costs of being out equilibrium are assumed to be symmetric but it seems likely that the cost of being below equilibrium may be greater than being above equilibrium owing to differential lending and borrowing rates and non-pecuniary costs. For large firms, marginal costs of adjustment in terms of labour time and brokerage fees are unlikely to vary in proportion to the amount of funds transacted and *b* will vary with improvements in payments technology (Section 0). Equation (4.9) is probably more applicable to behaviour of the personal sector. For persons who normally deal in relatively small transactions, costs of adjustment may be more than proportionate because of increasing costs of obtaining information on the terms offered on 'new' savings instruments. For persons, costs of being out of equilibrium, '*a*', may be much less than costs of adjustment, '*b*', especially if only small amounts are normally transacted and an unregulated market keeps the relative yield between money and close substitutes within narrow bands. Although not formally included in equation (4.9) it is likely that estimated lags in the demand for money function are picking up 'recognition lags' by persons. There have been some advances recently in modelling the adjustment process for money balances (Milbourne et al, 1983) but the quadratic cost formulation continues to be widely used mainly because it yields tractible estimating equations.

Estimation equation. How does the addition of the (first-order) partial adjustment mechanism alter our view of the form of the demand for money function? For expositional purposes let us assume our equilibrium theories yield a desired demand for money M^*, depending on current income Y, and the expected yield on alternative assets R^e, for example, bonds. We ignore simultaneous equation and identification problems and assume the demand function is linear with an additive stochastic error u. (The assumption of a log linear relationship would not invalidate the analysis.)

$$M^* = m_y Y - m_r R^e + u \tag{4.14}$$

The observed amount of money may not equal the desired long-run value because people adjust their money holdings only slowly. First-order partial adjustment gives

$$M - M_{t-1} = \gamma(M^* - M_{t-1}) \tag{4.15}$$

or

$$M = \gamma M^* + (1 - \gamma) M_{t-1}$$

or

$$[1 - (1 - \gamma) L] M = \gamma M^* \tag{4.16}$$

Substituting our long-run equilibrium relation in equation (4.16) and assuming the actual money stock always equals the short-run desired demand for money we obtain our estimating equation

$$M = \gamma m_y Y - \gamma m_r R^e + (1 - \gamma) M_{t-1} + \gamma u$$

$$M = b_1 Y + b_2 R^e + b_3 M_{t-1} + V \tag{4.17}$$

where b_1, b_2, b_3 are the estimated coefficients and $V = \gamma u$. Can the structural parameters γ, m_y, m_r, be retrieved from our estimated coefficients? That is, do we have 'single equation identification' (SEI).[5] In this case, the answer is yes, $b_3 = 1 - \gamma$, provides an estimate of $\gamma(= 1 - b_3)$ and the other parameters are then derived very simply (e.g. $m_y = b_1/\gamma$ etc.).[6] We have *exact* identificatio namely just enough estimated coefficients to determine the structural parameters.

Error feedback approach. We can derive the so-called error feedback equation by a simple addition to the cost function (4.9). If we are willing to assume that costs are less when the actual change $(M - M_{t-1})$ is in the same direction in the desired change $\Delta M^* = (M^* - M^*_{t-1})$ then the cost function has an additional term $-d\,\Delta M^*(M - M_{t-1})$. This gives rise to an additional term $\Psi \Delta M^*$, where $\Psi = d/(a + b)$, in the short-run desired demand for money function. This formulation allows the change in all the variables determining the equilibrium level of M^* to be included in the estimating equation (as well as their levels). The adjustment equation for this basic error feedback approach is

$$\Delta M = \mu_1(M^* - M_{t-1}) + \Psi \Delta M^* \tag{4.18}$$

Equation (4.18) may be interpreted as an 'error feedback equation' (EFE) (Davidson et al., 1978). The EFE in the language of control theory (Turnovsky, 1977) involves proportional and derivative control. The actual change in M is a function of the level of disequilibrium $(M^* - M_{t-1})$, that is proportional control, and the *change* in the determinants of M^*, that is derivative control.[7] The equation suffers from the 'underprediction problem' if M^* is continually rising or falling. This may be solved by introducing an 'integral control' term,

$$\Psi_1 \sum_{j=2}^{m} (M^*_{t-j} - M_{t-j})$$

The change in M now depends upon *past* disequilibria (Hendry and von Ungern Sternberg, 1983) and therefore on higher lags in M.[8]

The estimation equation for the EFE is the same as that for the partial adjustment equation with the addition of ΔM^*. The latter gives additional terms in the change in the variables that determine M^*, hence

$$\begin{aligned} M &= \mu_1 m_y Y - \mu_1 m_r R^e + (1 - \mu_1) M_{t-1} + (\Psi m_y)\,\Delta Y - \Psi m_r \Delta R^e \\ &= b_1 Y - b_2 R^e + b_3 M_{t-1} + b_4 \Delta Y - b_5 \Delta R^e \end{aligned} \tag{4.19}$$

It is obvious that the structural parameters μ_1, Ψ, m_y, m_r are over identified. As in the first-order partial adjustment equation the geometrically declining lag response still occurs for all the independent variables but does not begin to operate in the EFE until the second period.

Autoregressive distributed lag ADL approach. In much applied work the EFE has been written in a very general 'autoregressive distributed lag form' (ADL)

$$M = a(L)\,Y + b(L)\,R^e + c(L)\,M_{t-1} \tag{4.20}$$

where a, b and c are lag polynomials, that is $a(L) = a_0 + a_1 L + a_2 L^2 + \ldots$ etc. (where $L^n Y = Y_{t-n}$). Here the lag response of money to a change in an independent variable can be very flexible and, if enough lags are included, the lag response is unrestricted and differs for each independent variable (Hendry et al., 1984). However the ADL approach is not necessarily consistent with an optimizing framework of the kind developed above. (Nevertheless much ingenuity has been displayed in producing one period cost minimizing models of adjustment to justify equations of the ADL type; see for example Hendry and Anderson (1977) and Hendry and von Ungern Sternberg (1983).) The partial adjustment models (of any order) are special cases (nested versions) of the ADL model (as are adaptive *expectations* models). One strategy, recently applied, is to start from a very general ADL model and to *test* the restrictions required to yield, say, the first-order partial adjustment model. (We discuss this 'general to specific' modelling strategy further in appendix A.) For example, if $a(L) = a_0$, $b(L) = b_0$ and $C(L) = c_0$ we have the first-order partial adjustment model of equation (4.17).

4.2.2 *Interdependent asset adjustment*

In the simple partial adjustment model the change in the short-run desired demand for money depends only on the disequilibrium in (long-run) money holdings that is on $(M^* - M_{t-1})$. However, disequilibrium in money holdings must imply that at least one other asset is also in disequilibrium. In principle the speed of adjustment in money holdings might depend on the disequilibrium in other assets stocks such as building society deposits. (We ignore the possibility that disequilibria in *real* assets or expenditure flows might influence the speed of adjustment of individuals money balances: on this see Smith (1978).) These ideas are based on the common-sense notion that if I want to move out of money I must also alter some other asset stock. This is the basis of the inter-dependent asset adjustment model. Before discussing this approach we wish to examine the deficiencies of the simple partial adjustment approach when it is recognized that individuals face (a) a wealth (budget) constraint

$$\sum_i A_i = W$$

where A_i is actual holdings of the ith asset and W is wealth, and (b) the rational desires hypothesis

$$\sum_i A_i^* = W$$

where A^* is the desired long-run stock of the ith asset.

If one starts from equilibrium and adjusts all assets only partially towards the new equilibrium then the rational desires hypothesis cannot hold in the current period (see appendix 4A for the proof of this and the following assertions). In fact, the simple first-order partial adjustment mechanism if applied to *all* assets, implies that all assets are always in equilibrium! Also if simple partial adjustment is applied to a subset of explicit assets in the portfolio and the residual assets are not explicitly modelled, the residual set of assets fully adjust to their own dis-equilibria and passively absorb any funds that are not fully adjusted in the set of 'explicit' assets. So, for example, models that use simple partial adjustment for liquid assets only, implicitly assume that illiquid assets (such as equities or long-term government stocks) adjust completely to equilibrium in the current period. A somewhat implausible result.

Brainard-Tobin approach. To avoid the above problems Brainard and Tobin (1968) propose a system of interdependent asset adjustments. The adjustment of the *i*th asset (A_i) depends upon disequilibria in *other* assets stocks as well as that in the 'own' asset stock

$$\Delta A_i = \gamma_{i1}[A_1^* - A_1(-1)] + \gamma_{i2}[A_2^* - A_2(-1)] + \gamma_{ii}[A_i^* - A_i(-1)] + \dots$$
(4.21)

where we expect $\gamma_{ii} < 0$ but we cannot sign γ_{ij}, a priori.

Christophides (1976) has demonstrated that equations such as (4.21) may be derived from minimizing the (quadratic) costs of being out of equilibrium and of adjustment costs, for *all* assets, that is, by minimizing

$$C = \Sigma \alpha_i (A_i - A_i^*)^2 + \Sigma \beta_i (A_i - A_i(-1))^2$$
(4.22)

subject to the rational desires hypothesis $\Sigma A_i^* = W$.

Equation (4.21) introduces lagged 'other' asset stocks (as well as the lagged own asset stocks) into the equation determining the change in the own asset stock. To satisfy the wealth constraint, the coefficients on any lagged assets stocks across equations must sum to zero. For the two-asset model

$$M^* = a_0 + a_1 Y + a_2 RM + a_3 RB + a_4 W$$
(4.23a)

$$B^* = b_0 + b_1 Y + b_2 RM + b_3 RB + b_4 W$$
(4.23b)

where *RM* and *RB* are the yield on money and bonds respectively, the above adjustment mechanism yields short-run desired asset demands of the form

$$\begin{bmatrix} M \\ B \end{bmatrix} = \gamma \begin{bmatrix} a_0 & a_1 & a_2 & a_3 & a_4 \\ b_0 & b_1 & b_2 & b_3 & b_4 \end{bmatrix} [1, \ Y, \ RM, \ RB, \ W]'$$

$$+ (I - \gamma)[M_{t-1}, B_{t-1}]'$$
(4.24)

which may be written

$$A_t = \gamma dX + (I - \gamma)A_{t-1} = DX + (I - \gamma)A_{t-1}$$
(4.25)

where *I* is the identity matrix, *d* is the matrix of long run parameters (a_i, b_i), γ is the 2×2 matrix of adjustment parameters γ_{ij}, $A = [M, B]'$ and $X = (1, Y, RM, RB, W)'$. The short-run response for the asset stocks is given by $A = \gamma dX$ and therefore depends upon the 'cross lag' coefficients γ_{12}, γ_{21} as well as the own lag coefficients γ_{11}, γ_{22}. It follows that the short-run coefficient on any independent variable does not guarantee that the long-run coefficient will be of the same sign.

The simple partial adjustment model is a special case of (4.24) (that is a 'nested' version) which is easily tested by the joint hypothesis $\gamma_{12} = \gamma_{21} = 0$ (although if accepted would violate the rational desires hypothesis).

The dynamic response of a change in *M* to a change in an exogenous variable (e.g. *RM*) depends upon all the coefficients in γ and allows a more varied dynamic response than simple partial adjustment. (Stability in the lag response requires the eigenvalues of $(I - \gamma)$ to have modulus less than one, or equivalently for $(I - \gamma)^n \to 0$ as $n \to \infty$.)

In most cases the estimation problems involved in the set of equations in (4.25) are no more severe than the usual single equation case. OLS and instrumental variable estimates applied to each equation *separately*, automatically satisfy the adding up constraints if all equations contain the same set of independent variables. (Under the latter assumption, OLS estimates are equivalent to estimates obtained using seemingly unrelated regression estimation (SURE) procedures.) Adjustment for autocorrelation is possible equation by equation, if we are willing to accept equal autocorrelation coefficients for each equation. However, if particular variables are excluded from a subset of equations then 'restricted estimation' of the whole system of equations is required to ensure that cross equation restrictions hold. The interdependent asset demand approach, if it is to *exactly* satisfy the 'adding-up' constraints' requires the equations to be linear in variables. Use of log linear variables is possible if one merely wishes to approximate the adding up constraint (Masson, 1978).

The interdependent asset demand approach appears to provide tractable, fairly general dynamic equations based on cost minimization and has more intuitive appeal than the simple partial adjustment model. This model has been frequently applied to the demand for assets for a wide variety of economic agents, such as banks, insurance companies and persons. There is, however, one drawback to the interdependent asset demand approach. The coefficients of the determinants of the long-run desired demand for money cannot be identified unless *all* the equations are estimated. This arises because the coefficients a_i and b_i appear in the estimating equation (4.25) in the form γd and since the γ_{ij} ($i \neq j$) cannot be identified in a *single equation* context we cannot identify the a_i and b_i from any *one* equation.

Friedman's 'optimal partial adjustment model' retains the interdependent asset adjustment approach but allows identification of the parameters of the long-run demand for money after estimation of the demand for money function only.

Friedman's optimal partial adjustment model. Friedman (1977) provides an interdependent asset demand approach whereby the sign of some important structural coefficients may be determined without having to run equations for *all* the assets in the choice set. In this model it is less costly to allocate new savings flows amongst alternative assets than to rearrange the portfolio within a given level of wealth. Allocation of new savings requires only one transaction (a purchase); rearrangement requires a sale and subsequent purchase. One further refinement is incorporated. New savings are not allocated in arbitrary fixed proportions but are determined by the desired long-run equilibrium proportions $\alpha_i^*(t) = A_i^*(t)/W_t$, where A_i^* is the desired long-run nominal holdings of the ith asset and W is nominal wealth.

Desired portfolio shares α_i^* are given by

$$\alpha_i^*(t) = \frac{A_i^*(t)}{W(t)}$$

$$= \sum_{K=1}^{N} \beta_{ik} r_k^e(t) + \sum_{h=1}^{M} \delta_{ih} X_h(t) + \Pi_i \qquad (4.26)$$

The rational desired hypothesis

$$\sum_i \alpha_i^*(t) = 1$$

implies that the sum of β_{ik} and δ_{ih} across equations is zero and the sum of Π_i is unity. r_k^e are expected holding period yields. X_h are 'other variables' (for example variances and covariances of returns) that might influence α_i^*, and Π is a constant. Equation (4.26) may be derived from a mean-variance model. The unit wealth elasticity and linearity of the function arises from an assumption of constant relative risk aversion and normally distributed asset returns (section 3.5).

The optimal partial adjustment model incorporating interdependent adjustment terms is

$$\Delta A_i = \sum_{k=1}^{N} \gamma_{ik}(\alpha_k^* W_{t-1} - a_k(-1)) + \alpha_i^* \Delta W_t \quad i = 1, \ldots, n \tag{4.27}$$

Since $\alpha_i^* > 0$, an increase in wealth (savings flow) adds to all asset stocks to maintain desired portfolio shares.[9]

Substituting from (4.26) in (4.27) gives

$$\Delta A_i = \Pi_i \Delta W_t + \sum_{h=1}^{M} \delta_{ih}(X_h(t) \Delta W_t) + \sum_{k=1}^{N} \beta_{ik}(r_k^e(t) \Delta W_t) - \gamma_{ii} A_i(-1)$$

$$- \sum_{k=1}^{N} \beta_{ik} A_k(-1) + \sum_{k} \Pi_k \gamma_{ik} W_{t-1} + \sum_{j} \sum_{k} \beta_{jk} \gamma_{ij}(r_i(t) W_{t-1})$$

$$+ \sum_{h} \sum_{k} (\delta_{kh} \Theta_{ik})(X_h(t) W_{t-1}) \tag{4.28}$$

It is possible to sign, a priori some of the structural coefficients and identify them from the single regression equation (4.28). This arises from Friedman's inclusion of the term $\alpha_i^* \Delta W_t$ in the partial adjustment equation (a feature excluded in the Brainard–Tobin (1968) framework).

Assume we can 'sign' the long-run parameters β_{ik} and δ_{ih} a priori. These parameters are identified in the regression equation (4.28) and are given by the coefficients on the 'composite variables' ($r_k^e \Delta W$) and ($X_h(t) \Delta W_t$). Presumably $\beta_{ii} > 0$, while an assumption of gross substitutability implies $\beta_{ik} < 0$ ($i \neq k$). γ_{ii}, the 'own adjustment coefficient', is expected to be negative and is also identified. All the coefficients on the composite variables ($r_i(t) W_{-1}$), ($X_h(t) W_{-1}$) and γ_{ik} ($i \neq k$) cannot be signed. They are weighted averages which include γ_{ik} ($i \neq k$) and the latter cannot be signed a priori. This is the reason we cannot identify the long-run parameters (β_{ik}, δ_{ih}) in the Brainard–Tobin approach by estimation of a single asset demand equation.

Friedman has applied the above model both to the supply and the demand for assets together with a number of variants on the basic model and these are discussed in section 5.5.2.

The useful element in Friedman's model is therefore the ability to identify long-run parameters from a *single* regression equation which also incorporates a form of interdependent asset adjustment. The idea that new savings are allocated in 'optimal' proportions is also intuitively appealing.

4.3   MODELLING EXPECTATIONS

Expectations about the rate of inflation, the level of income and the yield on assets appear in our theories of the demand for assets. Survey data on expectations and publicly available forecasts of economic variables may both be used directly in asset demand functions and we do not discuss these aspects further here. The most popular model used in the empirical literature for modelling expectations has been some variant of the adaptive expectations hypothesis. We discuss this model in some detail and in particular we demonstrate the conditions under which this expectations scheme provides optimal forecasts. We briefly discuss regressive and extrapolative expectations formation although these have not been widely used in empirical work. We demonstrate that all three forecasting schemes mentioned above may be considered as restricted versions of a general autoregressive distributed lag model. As far as estimation is concerned the main feature of the adaptive expectations framework is that it introduces lagged dependent variables into asset demand functions.

When discussing the rational expectations hypothesis we must make a clear distinction between mathematical and subjective expectations. An individual's subjective expectation of a variable is that which influences his behaviour in some way. A conditional mathematical expectation is a relationship obtained by using the 'expectations operator' on an economic 'model'. The subjective expectations of 'Muth–RE' agents (Muth, 1961), are *assumed* to be identical to conditional mathematical expectations. This assumption allows us to make the concept of subjective expectations an operation one, since if we can *estimate* the 'true' model we may obtain a data series for the unobservable subjective expectations.

The basic idea behind Muth–RE is that in forming his expectations, the agent uses all the available information about the economy he finds it worthwhile to collect. Stated thus the hypothesis appears innocuous enough and indeed it is the substantial information requirements and the assumption of zero learning costs that make Muth–RE contentious. It is assumed that the individual has complete information on the true structure of the economy and immediately (and costlessly) learns about any changes in structure that occur. Agents do not persistently over- or under-predict a particular variable over several periods. Because the RE agent is assumed to use the true model, he therefore uses all *relevant* information when making his predictions: no information known at the time the forecast is made can improve the individual's forecast.

In forming RE the individual is concerned with three factors: the time expectations are formed, the horizon over which expectations are formed and the information set available to him. For simplicity we assume only one-period ahead expectations and because it is the dating of the information set available to individuals that is important, we ignore the time at which expectations are formed. Hence expectations about a variable S, formed for period t, on the basis of information available at time $t - 1$ may be written $E_{t-1}S_t$, which we write more simply as ES where no ambiguity is likely to arise.

An RE agent uses all relevant information when forming his expectations and is correct on *average*. Suppose ES represents the individuals *subjective* expectation, I is a set of variables known to the individual at the time the forecast is made and S is the actual (*ex post*) value of the variable. A general relationship between these variables may be expressed

$$S = a_0 + a_1(ES) + a_2 I + u$$

However, if expectations ES are Muth-rational then $a_0 = 0$, $a_1 = 1$ (this ensures *unbiased* forecasts) and $a_2 = 0$. The latter ensures that information available at time $t - 1$ or earlier, provides no additional useful information in predicting S (that is that ES utilizes all relevant information). This is often referred to as the orthogonality property. In addition the error term must be a zero-mean random error (actually an 'innovation').

The use of the REH in empirical work on asset demands is relatively recent. Two broad approaches have been adopted. The first invokes the unbiasedness property of RE whereby the *actual* future value of the variable provides an unbiased predictor of the *expected* value. The second approach uses the fact that the REH predicts that the expected value of a variable is formed by the individual using forecasts from the economic model that is thought to generate the variable in question. A regression of the future values of the variable on the exogenous (predetermined) variables from the whole model provides an equation for generating future expected values. This is known as 'weakly rational' expectations. ('Full Muth-rational' expectations requires the imposition of cross-equation parameter restrictions, Wallis (1980).) Weakly rational predictors are not necessarily inconsistent with the ADL approach used in some early studies. We begin with an account of the adaptive expectations hypothesis and use the concept of expected (or permanent) income as an example.

4.3.1 *Adaptive expectations*

Because of lack of data on wealth, early studies of the demand for money excluded an explicit wealth variable and used a related concept 'permanent income'. Permanent or expected income is a measure of long-run income to be obtained from human and non-human wealth *in the future*. With some simplifying assumptions we may equate permanent income with future expected income. Further (heroic) simplification allows one to invoke first-order adaptive expectations as a measure of permanent or expected income.[10]

First-order adaptive expectations assumes that revisions to expected income $(Y_t^e - Y_{t-1}^e)$ are a *fraction* Θ of the difference between *current* income and expected income $(Y_t - Y_{t-1}^e)$

$$Y_t^e - Y_{t-1}^e = \Theta(Y - Y_{t-1}^e) \quad 0 \leqslant \Theta \leqslant 1 \tag{4.29a}$$

or

$$(1 - (1 - \Theta)L) Y^e = \Theta Y$$

or

$$Y^e = [1 - (1 - \Theta) L]^{-1}(\Theta Y) = \Theta \sum_{j=0}^{\infty} (1 - \Theta)^j Y_{t-j} \qquad (4.29b)$$

where L is the lag operator $L^n Y = Y_{t-n}$. The term $(Y_t - Y_{t-1}^e)$ is the forecast error.

First-order adaptive expectations embodies some intuitively plausible properties. Expected income is a weighted average of past income with a relatively higher weight being given to more recent income. If current income remains constant for a long period of time, expected income will eventually equal this constant level of actual income.[11] Adaptive expectations contain two extreme cases: $\Theta = 1$, that is expected income equals current income, and $\Theta = 0$, expected income is never revised. A major defect of first-order adaptive expectations is that if income is growing, Y^e will always lie below the actual value of current income. This arises because Y^e reacts with a monotonic lag to changes in current income. Such systematic errors, if costly, should encourage learning by agents, who then correct such errors. However, relatively simple methods may alleviate the under-prediction of first-order adaptive expectations. For example, we may make the adjustment parameter Θ a positive function of the growth in Y or we may assume expectations adjust to forecast errors further in the past. This introduces terms in higher lags of Y which allows Y^e to have other than a monotonic response to changes in Y.[12] As we have already remarked first-order partial adjustment suffers similar problems.

The above discussion prompts the question as to whether first-order adaptive expectations provides optimal forecasts of future income under *any* circumstances. It turns out that partial adjustment is 'optimal' when the actual data on income follows a particular stochastic process (Muth, 1960). Suppose the economic system is such that, to a good approximation, income is generated by the following stochastic process known as integrated moving average, IMA $(1,1)$

$$Y_t = Y_{t-1} + u_t - \Theta^* u_{t-1} = Y_{t-1} + (1 - \Theta^* L) u_t \qquad (4.30)$$

where u_t is a white noise error term (see appendix A). With information available at time t this equation may be used to provide an optimal prediction of income in period $t + 1$

$$E_t Y_{t+1} = E_t Y_t + E_t u_{t+1} - \Theta^* E_t u_t = Y_t - \Theta^* u_t \qquad (4.31)$$

where we have used the result $E_t Y_t = Y_t$, $E_t u_t = u_t$ and $E_t u_{t+1} = 0$. Substituting from (4.30) for u_t in (4.31) and multiplying through by $(1 - \Theta L)$

$$E_t Y_{t+1} = Y_t - \Theta^*(1 - \Theta^* L)^{-1}(Y_t - Y_{t-1}) \qquad (4.32a)$$

$$(1 - \Theta^* L) E_t Y_{t+1} = (1 - \Theta^* L) Y_t - \Theta^*(Y_t - Y_{t-1}) \qquad (4.32b)$$

$$E_t Y_{t+1} - E_{t-1} Y_t = (1 - \Theta^*)(Y_t - E_{t-1} Y_t) \qquad (4.32c)$$

The last equation is a type of first-order partial adjustment equation usually written as

$$Y_t^e - Y_{t-1}^e = \Theta(Y_{t-1} - Y_{t-1}^e) \qquad (4.33)$$

where we have lagged equation (4.32c) one period and defined $Y_t^e = E_{t-1}Y_t$ etc. and $\Theta = (1 - \Theta^*)$. (4.33 differs from 4.29a only in the dating of Y.)

For period $t + 2$, it is easily seen from (4.31) that $E_t Y_{t+2} = E_t Y_{t+1}$ as $E_t u_{t+2} = E_t u_{t+1} = 0$. Hence the first-order partial adjustment mechanism provides the optimal forecast for *all* future periods (given information at time t).

If income is *growing* and follows a stochastic process

$$\Delta Y_t = \Delta Y_{t-1} + u_t - \Theta^* u_{t-1} \tag{4.34}$$

then first-order adaptive expectations applied to the *growth* in income (Y is in logarithms) would provide unbiased (optimal) forecasts. (This is Flemming's (1976) change-of-gear idea.)

While it is true that a large number of economic time series may approximate an IMA $(1, 1)$ process (Granger, 1966) this need not necessarily be the case for all variables. Adaptive expectations may provide biased forecasts if the model generating the data does not conform to the IMA $(1, 1)$ process.

It is useful to note that the adaptive expectations hypothesis predicts that expected income is a geometrically weighted average of past income

$$Y_t^e = [1 - (1 - \Theta L)]^{-1} \Theta Y_t = [1 + (1 - \Theta) L + (1 - \Theta) L^2 + \ldots] \Theta Y_t$$

$$Y_t^e = \Theta \sum_{j=0}^{\infty} (1 - \Theta)^j Y_{t-j} \tag{4.35}$$

A second-order partial adjustment equation would yield a similar qualitative result but the coefficients on lagged income would be more complex.

There is a possibility of a logical inconsistency when adaptive expectations is embodied in a 'complete' model. A complete model will yield predictions of Y over time (the reduced form solution for Y) depending on the future course of the exogenous variables in the complete model. A rational agent, *if he knew the complete model* would therefore base his predictions of future income on the predictions from the model, which in turn require his best guess of the future course of the exogenous variables. (By definition, he does not know the structural model for the *exogenous* variables and he may therefore base his predictions on 'time series' equations.) Such 'Muth-rational' predictions are unlikely to coincide with predictions based solely on past observations of income, as in adaptive expectations. Thus, the REH highlights a possible inconsistency when using adaptive expectations since the latter does not take account of *all* relevant information potentially available to the individual. This logical inconsistency is, in part, a consequence of the extreme assumptions taken to get from the theoretical definition of expected income (which depends on future income) to the adaptive expectations formula. However, the informational requirements of full rational expectations (for example that the individual knows and uses the complete model) may be too 'costly' for the individual to implement. Rules of thumb, like adaptive expectations may then prevail. These defects of first-order adaptive expectations have not prevented its widespread and continuing use in applied economics and in particular in demand for money functions.

Estimation equation. Replacing current income with expected income Y^e, assuming $R^e = r$ and $M = M^*$ (no adjustment lags), we have

$$M = m_y Y^e - m_r r + u \qquad (4.36)$$

$$Y^e = \frac{\Theta Y}{1 - (1 - \Theta) L} \qquad (4.37)$$

substituting (4.37) in (4.36) and rearranging we obtain

$$[1 - (1 - \Theta) L] M = m_y \Theta Y + [1 - (1 - \Theta) L] [-m_r r + u]$$

$$M = m_y \Theta Y - m_r r + (1 - \Theta) m_r r_{t-1} + (1 - \Theta) M_{t-1} + u - (1 - \Theta) u_{t-1} \qquad (4.38)$$

$$M = b_1 Y + b_2 r + b_3 r_{t-1} + b_4 M_{t-1} + u - (1 - \Theta) u_{t-1} \qquad (4.39)$$

An estimate of $(1 - \Theta)$ may be obtained directly from b_4 and indirectly as the ratio $-b_3/b_2$. Thus ignoring the error term for the moment, we see that the equation is 'over identified'. The model is distinct from the partial adjustment model discussed above, since it contains an additional term in r_{t-1} and a moving average error.[13]

4.3.2   *Regressive and extrapolative expectations*

Individuals with regressive expectations assume that the variable will move towards its long-run equilibrium value (for example as determined by the 'complete model'). In simple terms

$$E_t Y_{t+1} = Y_t + \alpha(\bar{Y} - Y_t) \qquad \alpha > 0 \qquad (4.40)$$

where α may be considered as a lag polynomial if one wishes to generalize the model a little. If Y_t is below its current long run value $\bar{Y}$, then individuals expect income to rise in the next period. Regressive expectations do not necessarily lead to systematic forecasting errors (e.g. Dornbusch (1976) model) but, like adaptive expectations, are only optimal in certain special circumstances. Keynes's theory of the speculative demand for money assumes regressive expectations. If we are willing to make the rather strong assumption that the normal or long-run value of the variable $\bar{Y}$ is formed by looking at known current and past values of the variable (that is $\bar{Y} = \beta(L) Y_t$) then the regressive expectations equation becomes a general ADL equation

$$E_t Y_{t+1} = Y_t + \alpha(L) [\beta(L) Y_t - Y_t] = d(L) Y_t \qquad (4.41)$$

The extrapolative expectations model assumes that recent *changes* in the variable will persist in the future. This may be represented by the equation

$$E_t Y_{t+1} = Y_t + \delta(L) (Y_t - Y_{t-1}) \qquad (4.42)$$

Again this provides a general ADL model of expectations formation.

4.3.3   *Rational expectations*

If we believe that actual income is generated in a 'complete model' of the economy by a set of predetermined variables X_t, that is *known* exogenous and lagged endogenous variables (excluding income), then a regression of actual income on X and lagged income provides a 'weakly rational' predictor of expected income (we assume X_t is known at time t).

$$Y_t = \hat{b}X_t + \hat{c}(L) Y_{t-1} + u \tag{4.43}$$

where $c(L)$ is a lag polynomial and u is a white noise error term. Predictions $\hat{Y}_t = \hat{b}X_t + \hat{c}(L) Y_{t-1}$ provide an estimate of the one-period ahead *expected* income which can then be directly used in asset demand equations. The predictions are unbiased since the error term (and the residuals) are zero on average. If expected income for several periods ahead is required, that is $E_t(Y_{t+j})$, then we may need future values of the exogenous variables: these may be obtained by a separate time series regression of the exogenous variables on their own lagged values, $X_t = a(L) X_{t-1}$. Thus, for example $E_t Y_{t+1}$ is obtained by calculating $\hat{Y}_{t+1}$ from

$$\hat{Y}_{t+1} = \hat{b}\tilde{X}_{t+1} + \hat{c}_0 \tilde{Y}_t \tag{4.44}$$

where $\tilde{X}_{t+1}$ are the predictions from the time series regression equation $\tilde{X}_{t+1} = \hat{a}_0 X_t + \hat{a}_1 X_{t-1} + \dots$ and $\tilde{Y}$ is the prediction worked out using (4.43) for period t (which only requires *known* values of X_{t-i+1} and $Y_{t-i}, i \geqslant 1$).

The second method employed in the RE approach is to use *actual* income as a proxy variable for expected income since the former is an unbiased predictor of the latter. However, the use of actual income creates an econometric problem known as 'error in variables bias' (appendix A). The solution to the latter is to use an 'instrumental variables' estimator rather than the OLS estimator (McCallum, 1976; Wickens, 1982). We shall not delve into the finer points here, but note that the instrumental variable approach is similar to the weakly rational method described above.

The RE approach therefore replaces an expected variable by a suitable proxy variable and does not explicitly introduce any lagged dependent variables into the demand for money function.

4.4 FURTHER ISSUES

4.4.1 *Expectations models: a comparison*

Do the expectations models that we have outlined give very different estimating equations for the demand for assets? If strictly applied they do give different results. The adaptive expectations hypothesis as usually applied in the empirical literature introduces lagged asset stocks into the demand function, the other approaches do not. However, there are some similarities between the way in which adaptive, regressive and extrapolative expectations are formed. All of these expectations mechanisms indicate that the expected value of the variable depends upon a distributed lag of past (actual) values. In principle therefore one could simply replace Y^e in the demand function by a distributed lag of *actual* values of Y and provided we do not impose any constraints on this lag pattern we would encompass all three hypotheses in our regression equation. This has sometimes been done in the empirical literature.

The rational expectations approach is in some respects not radically different from the above when it is applied in its 'weak' form.[14] It could be argued that the important variables determining Y in the reduced form of the whole model are lagged values of Y. In this case the RE approach reduces to the autoregressive distributed lag ADL model that encompasses the other three non-rational expectations mechanisms mentioned above. Alternatively one might argue that the informational requirements of RE are too severe and individuals are unlikely to use the complete model to forecast Y and merely use a less costly form of expectations generating mechanism such as an autoregressive mechanism. However, if variables other than lagged values of Y influence expectations – as in equation (4.43) – then RE differs from the other approaches. Even if 'weakly rational' expectations depend only on past values of Y the RE approach has encouraged the use of a *separate* equation for generating Y^e: predictions from the autoregressive equation $\hat{Y} = \hat{a}(L) Y_{t-1}$ are used in the demand for money equation in place of the unobservable Y^e. This has the merit of separating the expectations mechanism from the structural demand equation. If lagged values of Y are included in the demand function and the coefficients are unstable (over time) then we cannot say whether the instability is due to the parameters of the demand function or the expectations process. This problem is avoided in the 'weakly rational' expectations approach, but not in the 'non-rational' methods discussed above. The 'weakly rational' approach may therefore be less prone to the Lucas critique (section 1.2.4). We discuss this issue further in section 4.4.3 below.

4.4.2　*Partial adjustment and adaptive expectations*

It is possible to combine the adaptive expectations hypothesis with the partial adjustment model and to separately identify the adjustment and expectations parameters as well as the structural parameters of the long-run desired demand for money function. Using equations (4.16) and (4.37) and assuming a long-run demand for money function of the form

$$M^* = m_y Y^e - m_r r + u$$

we obtain

$$(1 - (1 - \gamma) L) M = \gamma M^* = \gamma \frac{m_y \Theta Y}{1 - (1 - \Theta) L} - \gamma m_r r + \gamma u \qquad (4.45)$$

multiplying through by $(1 - (1 - \Theta) L)$ and rearranging we obtain

$$M = \gamma m_y \Theta Y - \gamma m_r r + \gamma m_r (1 - \Theta) r_{t-1} + (2 - \gamma - \Theta) M_{t-1}$$
$$- (1 - \Theta) (1 - \gamma) M_{t-2} + \gamma (u - (1 - \Theta) u_{t-1}) \qquad (4.46)$$

$$M = b_1 Y + b_2 r + b_3 r_{t-1} + b_4 M_{t-1} + b_5 M_{t-2} + V \qquad (4.47)$$

where

$$V = \gamma (u - (1 - \Theta) u_{t-1})$$

Ignoring the error term, we have five estimated coefficients $(b_1, b_2, \ldots, b_5)$ and four structural parameters γ, Θ, m_y, m_r. It thus appears that we have 'single equation over-identification', that is, we have more than one equation to determine one of the structural parameters. To be consistent with the structural model, (4.46) must be estimated subject to one non-linear restriction between the values of b_i. It turns out that the structural parameters can be identified, so we can investigate whether lags are due to expectations adjustment $(\Theta \neq 1)$ or partial adjustment $(\gamma \neq 1)$ or both.[15] The model embodied in equation (4.46) is more general than either the partial adjustment or adaptive expectations model, taken in isolation. Either model may be retrieved under the restrictions $\gamma = 1$ and $\Theta = 1$ respectively. These models are 'nested' (that is a special case) of the general model. It follows that models that use either instantaneous adjustment or partial adjustment only, or adaptive expectations only, may be deficient and produce biased estimates of the 'true' structural parameters. There are plenty of examples where the 'maintained hypothesis' has been restricted in this manner, which casts doubts on the validity of the results.

Our analysis above highlights an important methodological issue. An empirical research strategy that starts with a very general model and tests for restrictions (leading to more restrictive models) may be preferable to starting with a restrictive model and adding potentially relevant variables at a later stage. This is because including irrelevant variables in the equation does not bias the coefficients of the 'true' variables, whereas omitting relevant variables does ('omitted variables bias'). However, adding irrelevant variables does increase the standard error of the equation and may lead to 'large' standard errors for the 'true' variables, so there is a limit to the generality of model with which we may begin our empirical research. We discuss the issue of the 'general' to 'specific' modelling strategy in appendix A.

Particularly in the context of rational expectations, it is worth noting that the estimated *coefficients* in equation (4.47) consist of long-run equilibrium parameters (m_y, m_r), a short-run adjustment parameter γ and an expectations adjustment parameter Θ. Rational expectations theorists have pointed out that if the form of the expectations generating mechanism changes (for example Θ increases due to a credible government policy to alter the growth in income) then an equation such as (4.47) may exhibit coefficient instability even though the underlying long-run equilibrium relationship (that is m_y and m_r) remains constant. To avoid this source of instability we need direct expectations on variables (which are not usually available) or a mechanism for generating a Y^e series from other data before we include it in the demand for money function. The former solution does not tell us how expectations are formed, but does remove one source of instability (that is unstable Θ) in the demand for money function. Similarly, *prior* estimation of Y^e by a sensible (not necessarily fully rational) method, would enable one to begin to determine the *source* of any instability be it from m_y, m_r or the coefficients generating the expectations variables. A simple example of an equation to determine Y^e is the autoregressive equation

$$Y = a_0 + a_1 Y_{t-1} + a_2 Y_{t-2} + \ldots = a(L) Y \qquad (4.48)$$

where the predictions from this equation (that is $\hat{Y}$) are used as a proxy variable for Y^e. Instability in the expectations mechanism would manifest itself in unstable a_i coefficients (which would then probably produce instability in the b_1 coefficient of Y^e in the demand for money function). However, instability in b_1 but stability in the values of a_i provides evidence that m_y (or γ) rather than the expectations mechanism is at fault.

4.4.3   *Alternative approaches to lag responses*

Adjustment costs and some expectations mechanisms yield a lag response of observed money balances to changes in the independent variables of the demand for money. If one does not wish to constrain the lag response on a priori grounds but would rather let the data determine the lag profile, then several approaches are possible. We have already mentioned the ADL approach. This gives very flexible lag responses and as it includes lagged dependent variables it allows an infinite lag response without having to estimate a large number of parameters, that is it uses up few degrees of freedom.[16]

One can proxy an infinite lag by including a large number of lags of the independent variables only this may quickly become impractical as one has to estimate a large number of parameters on a limited data set. The estimating equation in this case is of the form

$$M = b_0(L)\, Y + b_1(L)\, R \qquad\qquad (4.49)$$

One can proxy a fairly flexible lag response by using the 'Almon lag' technique. This approximates the large number of b_i coefficients by a low order polynomial function. For example, by assuming that all the elements of $b_0(L)$ lie on a quadratic function we need only estimate three parameters. However, this method has become less popular in recent empirical work on the demand for assets and we do not discuss it further.

By using very general but unrestricted lag structures to proxy *both* lagged adjustment and the formation of expectations it becomes impossible to identify the expectations and adjustment parameters. The estimated lags are a convolution of expectations and adjustment lags. If such an equation should exhibit parameter instability this may be due to instability in the adjustment parameters, the expectations parameters or the parameters of the long-run demand for money function, but since we cannot identify these we cannot diagnose the source of the parameter instability.

If the structural model of the demand for money contains expectations variables, then in a general unrestricted lag representation, for example the ADL model

$$M = a(L)\, M + m_y(L)\, Y + m_r(L)\, R \qquad\qquad (4.50)$$

where $a(L)$, $m_y(L)$, $m_r(L)$ are polynomial lag operators, the long-run solution will contain a mixture of adjustment, structural and expectations lags. Care must be taken in interpreting the 'long-run solution' of an ADL model. For example, if we assume that agents use rational expectations we can show that 'long-run' solutions using an ADL model do not yield estimates of the 'true' long-run structural parameters. Put another way, an unrestricted ADL model may give misleading predictions if the mechanism used to generate expectations alters. This is a form of the Lucas critique. It may therefore be more useful to model expectations formation explicitly, as suggested by the RE approach, since this may allow the expectations, adjustment and structural parameters to be correctly identified.

To see why the 'long-run' solution of an ADL model may give 'incorrect' results in the presence of rational expectations, assume a very simple 'true' *structural* model (in logarithms)

$$M_t = m_y Y_t^e \tag{4.51}$$

where Y_t^e is the expectation of Y based on information available at $t-1$ (that is $Y_t^e = E(Y_t | I_{t-1})$). Assume that over the data period of estimation actual Y_t is generated by the following autoregressive model

$$Y_t = \delta_0 + \delta_1 Y_{t-1} + \delta_2 Y_{t-2} + u_t \tag{4.52}$$

where for the moment we assume $\delta_1 + \delta_2 < 1$ (so that Y_t is a stationary stochastic process (Sargent, 1971)), u_t is 'white noise' and $E(u_t | I_{t-1}) = 0$. Rational agents would use predictions from (4.52) in forming expectations and therefore the 'true' model for this data set is

$$M_t = m_y(\delta_0 + \delta_1 Y_{t-1} + \delta_2 Y_{t-2}) \tag{4.53}$$

Equation (4.53) is an ADL model and after estimation may be solved for a 'dynamic equilibrium' $\bar{M}$ in which Y is assumed to grow at a constant rate, that is $Y_{-j} = Y - jg_y$ (see appendix A6), hence:

$$\bar{M} = m_y \delta_0 + m_y \delta_1 (Y - g_y) + m_y \delta_2 (Y - 2g_y) \tag{4.54}$$

$$\bar{M} = m_y \delta_0 + m_y(\delta_1 + \delta_2) Y - m_y(\delta_1 + 2\delta_2) g_y \tag{4.55}$$

Notice that if $\delta_1 + \delta_2 < 1$, then in the static equilibrium solution of the ADL model (i.e. $g_y = 0$), the long run effect of Y is $m_y(\delta_1 + \delta_2)$ which does not equal the 'true' value m_y. For example if $m_y = 1$ we do not expect the *estimated* long run (static) coefficient on Y in the ADL model to be unity. Under RE therefore, it is generally incorrect to constrain the long run static equilibrium of the ADL model to be unity (see appendix A.6 for further details).

The estimated ADL model (4.53) is the 'true' model given that Y_t is generated as in (4.52). However, the question we pose is whether the 'dynamic equilibrium' solution of the ADL model in (4.55) gives the true 'structural' model. If under a constant rate of growth in Y_t the expectations equation (4.52) continued to hold, then the ADL dynamic equilibrium equation for $\bar{M}$ is correct. However, if we assume agents use RE, they correctly forecast Y (except for a random error) and hence under a constant rate of growth

$$Y_t^e = Y_t \equiv Y_{t-1} + g_y$$

Thus, under RE, the 'true' model is simply

$$M_t = m_y Y_t \tag{4.56}$$

Comparing (4.55) and (4.56) we see that when income grows at a constant rate, the dynamic equilibrium of the ADL model yields the true (RE) structural model only if $\delta_0 = 0$, $\delta_1 + \delta_2 = 1$ and $\delta_1 + 2\delta_2 = 0$, that is $\delta_0 = 0$, $\delta_1 = 2$, $\delta_2 = -1$. Thus, in general, the 'dynamic solution' and static long-run solution (that is $g_y = 0$ in (4.55)) of the ADL model does not yield the true structural model $M = m_y Y_t$. This is a consequence of the ADL parameters in (4.53) and (4.55) being convolutions of structural and expectations parameters (we have no adjustment parameters in our simple model $M = m_y Y_t^e$), and under RE the expectations parameters alter as the actual path of Y alters. RE agents use (4.52) in forming their expectations in the period of estimation since this yields unbiased predictions over this period $(E_{t-1} Y_t = \delta_0 + \delta_1 Y_{t-1} + \delta_2 Y_{t-2}$ and $Y - E_{t-1}(Y_t) = u_t)$ but they use $Y^e = Y_{-1} + g_y$ when Y grows at a constant rate.

The ADL 'dynamic equilibrium' solution (4.55) gives the 'true' model if $\delta_0 = 0$, $\delta_1 = 2$, $\delta_2 = -1$. Substituting these values in (4.52) we obtain $Y_t = 2Y_{t-1} - Y_{t-2} = Y_{t-1} + \Delta Y_{t-1} = Y_{t-1} + g$. Not surprisingly, the 'constant growth' ADL solution for M gives the 'true' structural model if the data set underlying the expectations mechanism (4.52) actually embodies a constant growth in Y in *all* periods. Since the latter is unlikely to be the case in general, the static and dynamic equilibrium solutions of the ADL model may give misleading inferences concerning the structural parameters if agents use RE and the process of expectations formation alters. One answer to this problem is to use the *predictions* $\hat{Y}_t$ $(= \hat{\delta}_0 + \hat{\delta} Y_{t-1} + \hat{\delta}_2 Y_{t-2})$ from the expectations equation (4.52) as a separate variable in the structural equation (4.51) to obtain an estimate of the true structural parameter(s) m_y.

The above observations apply in the more general model where M adjusts slowly and is determined by current and past expectations of Y_t^e, that is $a(L) M_t = m_y(L) Y_t^e$ where $a(L)$ and $m_y(L)$ are polynomial lag operators (Cuthbertson, 1985c). Thus in the presence of RE, the dynamic and static equilibrium solutions of an ADL model must be interpreted with care and the best procedure is to include the expectations variables *directly* in the structural equation rather than simply including their lagged actual values. In the next chapter we provide examples of both approaches.

4.5 SUMMARY

It is widely known that many economic time series are highly autoregressive: 'money' when regressed on its own lagged values gives a good fit. It is not surprising therefore that many empirical studies use lagged dependent variables (ldv) when estimating asset demand functions. One of our tasks in this section was to examine the theoretical basis for the inclusion of such variables. We find that adaptive expectations and partial adjustment provide a rationale for the inclusion of ldv.

Although based on cost minimization, the adaptive expectations hypothesis is tagged on to our equilibrium theories of the demand for money. Individuals are assumed to make a two stage decision process, first determining their equilibrium money balances and then, indepndently of this decision deciding on the speed of adjustment to equilibrium; this is somewhat unsatisfactory particularly for the behaviour of companies. Partial adjustment severely constrains the profile of the lag response although higher order partial adjustment mitigates this problem. The error feedback approach is slightly less restrictive in its lag response than the partial adjustment model. The interdependent asset adjustment approach highlights further deficiencies of the simple partial adjustment and error feedback models. The former approach yields a flexible lag response and may also be rationalized on the basis of costs of adjustment (subject to a wealth constraint). Friedman's optimal partial adjustment model utilizes the interdependent adjustment approach but adds the novel idea that new savings flows may be 'optimally' allocated more quickly than existing assets. In principle all these lag structures may be tested against the data to see which one provides the best 'fit'. However, in practice we may be testing more than one hypothesis in a particular equation (for example adjustment and expectations lags) and it may not be possible to provide a direct comparison of different lag structures.

The adaptive expectations hypothesis provides a further rationale for the inclusion of ldv, and higher order adaptive mechanisms may provide optimal forecasts. The 'weak form' of the REH may not be radically different from a general distributed lag approach to expectations. However, 'weak-form' RE allows one to generate a separate expectations series based on a single regression equation. This allows expectations lags to be separated from adjustment lags, even when the latter are rather complex. Such a separation (identification) is possible only when *simple* (first-order) versions of the *adaptive expectations* and partial adjustment models are used.

The basis of our partial adjustment model is optimization over a single period. This applies to the interdependent asset demand approach too. When the partial adjustment model is extended to a multiperiod framework, a very different model emerges in which *future* values of the independent variables of the demand for money appear (section 6.4.3).

The autoregressive distributed lag ADL model which allows the money stock to be regressed on a large number of lagged values of itself and lagged values of the determinants of the demand for money provides a very flexible lag response for all the independent variables. However, these lags may be a convolution of expectations and adjustment lags and it may be difficult to disentangle these separate effects; misleading inferences concerning long-run parameters may ensue if agents use rational expectations.

The expectations and adjustment mechanisms we have discussed have played a major role in empirical work on the demand for assets. We are now able to examine this work with a thorough understanding of the theoretical strengths and weakness of these hypotheses. This is important because if the empirical work proves to be deficient it is as important to examine the adjustment and expectations mechanisms as it is to question the theories of the long-run demand for assets outlined in previous chapters.

APPENDIX 4A   PARTIAL ADJUSTMENT AND THE BUDGET CONSTRAINT

The rational desires hypothesis and the wealth constraint are respectively

$$\sum_i A_i^* = W \quad \text{and} \quad \sum_i A_i = W \tag{4A.1}$$

hence

$$\sum_i [A_i^* - A_i(-1)] = \Delta W = \sum_i \Delta A_i \tag{4A.2}$$

where A_i is the individual's holding of the asset i at time t.

If we assume simple first-order partial adjustment for all assets then the partial adjustment coefficients γ_i for *all* assets must be unity, that is, equilibrium prevails at all times. To demonstrate this, note that summing the simple partial adjustment terms gives

$$\sum \Delta A_i = \sum \gamma_i (A_i^* - A_i(-1)) \tag{4A.3}$$

But $\Sigma \Delta A_i = \Delta W$ by the budget constraint and is also equal to $\Sigma(A_i^* - A_i(-1))$ because of the rational desires hypothesis. Hence from (4A.3) and (4A.2)

$$\sum \gamma_i (A_i^* - A_i(-1)) = \sum_i (A_i^* - A_i(-1)) \tag{4A.4}$$

Equation (4A.4) can only hold for all values of $[A_i^* - A_i(-1)]$ if $\gamma_i = 1$ for all assets. $\gamma_i = 1$ implies $A_i^* = A_i$, that is equilibrium holds in all periods.

Suppose the simple first-order partial adjustment mechanism only applies to a subset q of all n assets. What does this imply for the residual set of assets $q + 1, \ldots, n$? We have

$$\Delta A_i = \gamma_i (A_i^* - A_i(-1)) \quad \text{for } i = 1, \ldots, q, only \tag{4A.5}$$

The residual set of assets, as a group, that is

$$\sum_{q+1}^{n} A_i$$

may then be shown to fully adjust to any disequilibrium within its own group and passively absorb any disequilibrium holdings in the q assets $(1, 2, \ldots, q)$ that are subject to simple partial adjustment

$$\Delta \sum_{q+1}^{n} A_i = \Delta W - \sum_{1}^{q} \Delta A_i$$

Using (4A.2) we may express ΔW as the sum of disequilibrium in the assets 1 to q plus disequilibrium in assets $q + 1$ to n: that is terms in $(A_i^* - A_i(-1))$. In addition we can replace

$$\sum_1^q \Delta A_i$$

by the partial adjustment equation (4A.5) for these assets

$$\Delta \sum_{q+1}^n A_i = \sum_1^q (A_i^* - A_i(-1)) + \sum_{q+1}^n (A_i^* - A_i(-1))$$

$$- \sum_1^q \gamma_i(A_i^* - A_i(-1))$$

$$= \sum_{q+1}^n (A_i^* - A_i(-1)) + \sum_1^q (1 - \gamma_i)(A_i^* - A_i(-1))$$

The first term indicates complete adjustment to disequilibrium in the 'residual assets' and the second indicates that any remaining disequilibrium in the first q 'partial adjustment' assets is absorbed in the set of residual assets.

For these reasons simple partial adjustment applied to a subset of assets may yield 'implausible' adjustment mechanisms for the residual set of assets. This is particularly true if 'liquid assets' are explicitly modelled using simple partial adjustment and illiquid assets are *implicitly* treated as the residual assets.

NOTES

1 Milbourne et al. (1983) provide an explicit model of the process of adjustment in a Miller–Orr (1966) precautionary demand model. They assume that cash balances follow a random walk and, although a partial adjustment model ensues, the partial adjustment coefficient γ depends on the interest rate r, the variance of receipts σ^2 and the brokerage fee b. In the partial adjustment models discussed in this chapter the adjustment coefficient is assumed to be constant. The Milbourne et al. model appears to work reasonably well on Australian data for M1. This is an interesting extension which explicitly incorporates the adjustment process in the precautionary demand model. Space precludes a detailed examination here.

2 Sargent (1979b) provides an integrated analysis of this type for employment decisions in a multiperiod framework. The final reduced form equation is rather complex.

3 One has to admit that the nature of these costs for asset markets is rarely analysed in great depth. For real variables, such as employment, adjustment costs and 'disequilibrium costs' are more plausible.

4 This is most easily demonstrated by assuming partial adjustment in terms of the logarithm of M ($= m$) and noting that $m - m_{t-1} = g$, the rate of growth in m. Substituting for m_{t-1} in the partial adjustment equation we obtain

$m = \gamma m^* + (1 - \gamma)(m - g)$ and $m = m^* - [(1 - \gamma)/\gamma] g$. Thus, if $g > 0$ then $m < m^*$ (unless adjustment is instantaneous, that is $\gamma = 1$).

5   We use the term 'single equation identification' to avoid confusion with 'identification' in the context of simultaneous equations.

6   Even if the values of b are unbiased, the structural parameters will be biased if they involve non-linear transformations of the values of b (for example $m_y = b_1/\gamma$ is biased). However, the estimates of the structural parameters are unbiased in large samples (that is asymptotically unbiased) if an appropriate estimation procedure is used.

7   The change in some, but not all, variables determining M^* also *implicitly* appear in some of the lag equations reported above. Wherever terms in $a_0 X_t$ and $a_1 X_{t-1}$ appear, these may be 'reparameterized' as $a_0 \Delta X_t + (a_1 + a_0) X_{t-1}$ (see appendix A).

8   The definition of proportional, derivative and integral control may vary from author to author (compare Salmon (1982) and Turnovsky (1977)).

9   Adding-up constraints imply that

$$\sum_i \gamma_{ik} = \bar{\gamma}$$

is a constant. To avoid perfect collinearity whilst retaining W requires one to drop one term in $(\alpha_k^* W_{t-1} - \alpha_k(-1))$ (Smith, 1975).

10 End period wealth W_t is existing non-human wealth NW_t plus the discounted present value of expected future income ${}_t Y_{t+i}^e$ (where the first subscript indicates the information available when expectations are formed). Thus

$$W_t = NW_t + \sum_{i=0}^{N} \frac{{}_t Y_{t+i}^e}{(1 + r)^i}$$

where N is the life of the individual and r is the discount (real interest) rate. Given W_t there is an annuity equivalent $\bar{Y}$ (that is a constant amount payable each year until death at N) which could be obtained in exchange for W_t today (assuming away uncertainty and legal restraints on slavery!). $\bar{Y}$ is given by

$$W_t \bigg/ \sum_{i=0}^{N} \frac{1}{(1 + r)^i}$$

and therefore depends on NW_t, future income and r (assumed constant). $\bar{Y}$ is permanent income. Neglecting NW_t, we assume somewhat implausibly that ${}_t Y_{t+i}^e$ is a constant for all future periods $\bar{Y}$. Letting $N \to \infty$, we have $W_t = \bar{Y}(1 + (1 + r)^{-1} + (1 + r)^{-2} + \ldots) = \bar{Y}/r$, where we have used the formula for the sum of an infinite geometric series $S = 1 + a + a^2 + \ldots = 1/(1 - a)$ for $|a| < 1$. Hence for a constant real interest rate, wealth may be expressed in terms of expected long run income $\bar{Y}$. The latter and permanent income are closely related concepts and both require a view about the path of future income.

11 By expanding $(1 - (1 - \Theta) L)^{-1}$ in a Taylor series, we obtain

$$Y^e = (1 + (1 - \Theta) L + (1 - \Theta)^2 L^2 + \ldots) \Theta Y$$
$$= \Theta Y + (1 - \Theta) \Theta Y_{t-1} + (1 - \Theta)^2 \Theta Y_{t-2} + \ldots; \quad 0 < \Theta < 1$$

which gives Y^e as weighted average of current past income levels with declining weights $\Theta > \Theta(1-\Theta) > \Theta(1-\Theta)^2 > \ldots$ This result may also be obtained by back substitution for Y_{t-1}^e. Using

$$Y_t^e = \Theta Y_t + (1-\Theta) \, Y_{t-1}^e \tag{1}$$

lagging one period and substituting back into (1) we obtain

$$Y_t^e = \Theta Y + (1-\Theta) \, (\Theta Y_{t-1} + (1-\Theta) \, Y_{t-2}^e)$$

Repeated back substitution yields the required expression. If $Y_{t-1} = \bar{Y}$ for all past time periods then

$$Y^e = \Theta \bar{Y}(1 + (1-\Theta) + (1-\Theta)^2 + \ldots) = \Theta \bar{Y}(1-(1-\Theta))^{-1} = \bar{Y}$$

12 Higher order terms have been used in explaining price expectations (Carlson and Parkin, 1975; Foster and Gregory, 1977; Figlewski and Wachtel, 1981). The differential equation explaining Y^e is then of order greater than one, allowing a wide variety of response of Y^e to Y, including overshooting.

13 The moving average error provides an additional overidentifying restriction for $(1-\Theta)$. Ideally the equation should be estimated subject to the restriction that the coefficient on M_{t-1} equals that on u_{t-1}, but this is rarely done. (The restriction $b_4 = (b_3/b_2)$ as noted in the text, should also be imposed.)

14 When applied in its 'strong form' RE gives very different results from the other expectations mechanisms. The strong form gives *cross equation* restrictions on the parameters of the whole structural model (Wallis, 1980). However, the 'strong form' has not been widely used in the asset demand literature.

15 We have

$$b_2 = -\gamma m_r \tag{1}$$

and

$$b_3 = (1-\Theta) \, \gamma m_r \tag{2}$$

hence

$$(1-\Theta) = -\frac{b_3}{b_2} \tag{3}$$

Using $b_5 = -(1-\Theta)(1-\gamma)$ we obtain

$$1-\gamma = -\frac{b_5}{1-\Theta} = \frac{b_2 b_5}{b_3} \tag{4}$$

But we also have $b_4 = (2 - \Theta \quad \gamma)$ and substituting for γ and Θ from (3) and (4) we obtain our non-linear restriction between the values of b. Note that once γ and Θ are known, m_y is calculated from $m_y = b_1/\Theta\gamma$ and $m_r = -b_2/\gamma = b_3/(1-\Theta)\gamma$ using (1) and (2). The reader may easily verify that the latter two expressions give identical estimates for m_r in terms of b_i. Notice that the moving average error term provides an additional (overidentifying) restriction.

16 Rational lags are very similar to the ADL approach plus an assumption of serial correlation in the error terms. A rational lag model is

$$Y = \frac{a(L)}{b(L)} X + \frac{c(L)}{d(L)} u_t$$

where u_t is a white noise error term. This gives rise to an estimating equation

$$b(L)\, d(L)\, Y = a(L)\, d(L)\, X + b(L)\, c(L)\, u_t$$

where the error term is now a moving average error. We could append an error model to the ADL model which would then closely resemble the rational lag model. In practice the ADL is usually investigated using only autoregressive errors (common factors) since these are computationally less burdensome than moving average errors and provide a reasonable approximation to the latter (Hendry, 1977). We do not discuss the rational lag approach further.

5

Empirical Approaches to the Demand
for Assets

5.1 INTRODUCTION

In previous chapters we discussed the role of the demand for assets (particularly money) in the transmission process, the theoretical derivation of static equilibrium asset demand functions and the role of lagged adjustment and expectations in the determination of asset demands. For example in chapter 1 we found that the size of the interest and wealth elasticities of the demand for money play a crucial role in the transmission mechanism of both fiscal and monetary policy. The existence of lags and expectations effects in asset demands influence the time profile of the response of output and prices, for example.

The empirical literature on the demand for assets is vast. We do not attempt to give an exhaustive account of the empirical evidence even for the demand for money function. Nor do we present a detailed econometric evaluation of specific equations. Rather, our main aim in this chapter is to provide illustrative examples of recent empirical work that highlight the themes outlined in the previous three 'theoretical' chapters dealing with asset demands. In the main we shall concentrate on the demand for money function since this has been the chief area of study for obvious reasons. In subsequent chapters it becomes clear that demand functions for assets other than money are of importance for control of the money supply. We therefore present some results on 'other' asset demand functions, in particular the demand for long-term government debt and bank advances.

In the next chapter we discuss 'buffer-stock money' where some further recent empirical work on the demand for money is presented, albeit from a somewhat different theoretical standpoint from that discussed below. In discussing empirical work one cannot avoid econometric terminology even though we recognize that non-specialists are frequently bemused by it. We have therefore tried to clearly delineate the purely econometric points in the text or relegate them to notes. In addition we have provided an appendix at the end of the book which deals with a few important selected topics in applied econometrics that have recently appeared in the literature. The reader who is familiar with this material will glean more from the analysis presented in this chapter. However, we concentrate on the economic interpretation of the empirical results and therefore the non-specialist should be able to follow the main points in the argument.

We begin this chapter with a discussion of some definitional problems and a brief overview of some early studies of the demand for money using data prior to the 1960s. We have chosen to be brief for a number of reasons. First studies of the demand for money for the period 1880–1950 can be no more than indicative of what might pertain in the 1980s, particularly given the recent pace of innovation in financial markets. Second, over the data period considered, the money supply may well have been endogenous and therefore these results may not be of relevance for periods when the authorities choose to target monetary aggregates (that is the Lucas critique applies: see section 6.4 on buffer-stock money for further elaboration). Third, later studies are likely to incorporate better statistical techniques. Finally, a survey, even a detailed one, can only provide a summary of a set of fairly disparate results, for example over different data sets using different definitions etc. What is needed is a systematic econometric comparison but thse are few and far between (see, for example, Hendry and Ericsson (1983)). However, in each section of the chapter we give key references so that the reader may undertake further analysis of the issues raised.

The topics covered in the rest of the chapter are organized to mirror those in the previous chapter. A broad division between single equation studies and a systems approach is made. Under the former we begin in section 5.3 with studies of the demand for money that use the partial adjustment and adaptive expectations hypotheses.

We move on in section 5.4 to analyse the autoregressive distributed lag–error feedback (ADL–EFE) approach. We spend a disproportionate amount of time on this approach, partly because it tends to be rather complex and hence less well understood than earlier approaches, and partly because it is widely used in the recent empirical literature. (Appendix A provides useful additional material on this model.) We present examples for the demand for narrow and broad money: the former is a key policy variable in the US and the later in the UK. Still within the single equation ADL–EFE framework, we present some results on the demand for long-term government debt and the demand for bank advances. Both variables play a key role in the 'flow of funds' method of monetary control adopted in a number of industrialized nations. Hence these studies complement our analysis of the determination of the UK money supply in chapter 8. In addition, our analysis of the demand for government debt provides an example of the use of rational expectations in measuring the impact of expected yields on asset demands.

In section 5.5 we consider systems of asset demand equations. Here we are particularly interested in the implications of imposing cross equation restrictions and analysing the resulting lag responses. First we present 'eclectic' models of the interdependent asset adjustment variety before considering Friedman's approach, namely the 'optimal partial adjustment' model. The mean-variance model is a systems approach and we consider the wide range of tests of this model in its static and dynamic form. The mean-variance model has been applied to the demand for assets by banks, pension funds and insurance companies all of whom play an important role in the determination of the money supply and the transmission of monetary policy through financial markets.

In section 5.6 we briefly discuss a number of issues that are not crucial in understanding other themes in the book, but nevertheless provide interesting approaches to the estimation of asset demand functions. These include non-market clearing models, different functional forms, stochastic parameters and the use of 'foreign' interest rates. A brief summary is given at the end of the chapter.

In assessing the equations presented below the criteria discussed in appendix A should be borne in mind, although for any particular study we shall often not mention all of these criteria.

A final caveat. Our analysis in this chapter covers aspects of both economic theory and theoretical and applied econometrics. Space considerations imply that we do not cover some issues in a fully rigorous fashion although we hope the analysis is not misleading. Therefore the reader should not consider our conclusions as definitive, but merely illustrative of particular approaches. There is no substitute for reading the articles fully or better still trying a few regressions oneself! The latter provides a very salutary experience concerning our empirical knowledge in this area.

5.2 EARLY EMPIRICAL WORK

5.2.1 *Data and definitional problems*

Our theories of the demand for money do not give an unambiguous indication of what constitutes 'money'. The transactions and precautionary models perhaps give the clearest indication suggesting the use of 'cash plus demand deposits' as the appropriate definition since these are universally recognized as the means of exchange in most industrialized nations. However, even here recent innovations in financial markets have rendered this distinction less clear cut than previously (section 8.6). The risk-aversion model gives no clear indication of the appropriate definition of money since a wide variety of assets (both real and financial) may act as a store of value.

Empirical work, in the main, has treated money as consisting of various elements of the liabilities of the banking system. M1, the 'narrow' definition, usually consists of 'cash' and current (checking) accounts held by the non-bank private sector (NBPS). M2 consists of M1 and usually also includes certain interest bearing bank deposits of small denomination that are not marketable (for example seven-day time deposits) – although in the UK it also includes most building society deposits. For the US, M2 is often referred to as 'broad money' but in the UK (and some other European countries) the latter usually refers to a wider set of assets held by the NBPS. In the UK, £M3 is the most widely discussed of the 'broad' monetary aggregates and consists of M1 plus sterling 'time deposits' plus certain large denomination fixed term deposits (wholesale deposits) some of which are marketable (for example certificates of deposit). Early empirical studies found such definitions useful. First it was generally the case that all three definitions gave similar conclusions concerning the appropriate form for the demand for money function, including the stability of such relationships. Second, the authorities could attempt to control such aggregates, a prerequisite for their use as intermediate targets. As we shall see below, in the post 1970 period both of the above facets became problematic and the view that the appropriate definition of money was 'an empirical matter' became even more prevalent than hitherto. That is 'money' was to be defined as that financial asset which had a stable demand function and which could be controlled by the authorities.

The empirical work summarized in this section deals mainly with the data period prior to about 1960 and beginning around 1900. Most of these empirical studies use annual data and therefore the issue of *adjustment* lags tends to play a minor role. Laidler (1977) provides a useful summary of this work particularly for the US and the UK. The basic equation used is the 'static' demand for money function

$$m = a + bx + cr + dp \qquad (5.1)$$

where m is nominal money balances, x is the scale variable, usually taken to be current income, financial wealth or permanent income, r is the opportunity cost of holding money (either a rate on short term assets or a rate of interest on long term bonds), later studies included the own rate on money, p is the price level. The variables are in logarithms (except on occasions for r which might appear as its absolute value).

Some early studies impose untested unit income and price elasticities which render their results somewhat suspect. One of the first studies to avoid these pitfalls is that of Meltzer (1963) using US data 1900-58 for various definitions of money and of the scale variable. Brunner and Meltzer (1964) and Laidler (1966) refined this work for the US and Laidler (1971) and Barratt and Walters (1966) repeated this kind of analysis for the UK with broadly similar results. In these studies it is generally found that the results obtained are fairly invariant to the definition of 'money' chosen. The demand for money appears to be related to a representative interest rate (and again the *fit* of the equation is fairly invariant to the choice of a short or long rate) and to permanent (expected) income which was usually proxied using the adaptive expectations mechanism. Permanent income performed better than current income but only marginally better than financial wealth (of which there was a paucity of accurate data). The evidence favoured a unit price level elasticity and hence d could be be constrained to be unity in annual data. Some outside sample forecast tests and Chow tests for parameter stability (note 1) were conducted by a minority of investigators and in general indicated stability in the relationships over sub-periods. For example Laidler (1966) finds that the interest elasticity of the short rate with respect to M2 over the period 1892-1960 in the US varies roughly between -0.12 and -0.15 and with respect to the long rate between -0.2 and -0.6. Artis and Lewis (1981, p. 14) report studies on UK data on 'old' M2 (excluding building society deposits) over the period 1880-1960 as giving an income elasticity of about unity and an interest elasticity with respect to the long rate between -0.3 and -0.8. Extending the data period Artis and Lewis (1984) find that a demand function for ('old') M2 using annual UK data over the period 1920-57 accurately predicts demand over the period 1958-81 except for the years 1973-6. This result is all the more remarkable as the only independent variable is the long bond rate with an elasticity of about -0.6. (Note however that the income elasticity is constrained to unity and no tests of this restriction are given.) As we see in subsequent chapters, explanations of the breakdown of the demand for money function in the UK in the 1973-6 period include the view that large independent changes in the money supply led to either, 'disequilibrium' or buffer-stock holdings of money.

Some early studies include a wide variety of interest rates in the demand for money. For example, for broad money in the US, Lee (1967, 1969) and Hamberger (1966) find evidence in favour of the inclusion of the return on saving and loan association deposits and the return on equity, as well as the 'time deposit' rate. Klein (1974a, 1974b) and Barro and Santomero (1972) find evidence that the 'implicit service return on money' (that is a form of own rate on demand deposits) is a significant determinant of narrow money holdings.

Evidence supporting the liquidity trap is mixed. Studies that test for a higher interest elasticity in periods of low interest rates (and vice versa) do not generally find any change in the elasticity (Bronfenbrenner and Mayer 1960 and Laidler 1966). Direct tests of the liquidity trap replace r in equation (5.1) above by $(r - r_m)$ where r_m is the 'minimum' level of interest rates (to be chosen by the data in some way, for example, by assuming adaptive expectations or a 'grid search' over alternative values for r_m). Laidler (1977) takes the view that 'on the whole the evidence goes against the hypothesis'. (For a contrary view using US data see Spitzer 1976, 1977.)

In hyperinflations (for example in Germany in the 1920s and South American countries in the post-1945 period) the expected rate of inflation (usually proxied by an adaptive expectations mechanism) is found to be significant.

Studies that explicitly consider the supply and demand for money and hence the identification and simultaneous equations problems (for example Brunner and Meltzer (1964) and Teigen (1964)) find that the results are little different from the single equation studies when annual data for the US is used. (Note that some single equation studies use simultaneous equations *estimators* even though they do not explicitly consider the form of the supply function for money.)

In summary, we note that studies for this early data period using annual data, suggest a well-determined, fairly stable demand for money function. Broadly speaking stability applies under different definitions of money, for different interest rates and over different data periods. As we shall see in subsequent sections it appears to be the case that in recent years economists have become more circumspect concerning our knowledge of the demand for money.

5.3 PARTIAL ADJUSTMENT AND ADAPTIVE EXPECTATIONS

Prior to Feige's (1967) study of the demand for narrow money in the US, researchers had assumed that either partial adjustment *or* the adaptive expectations hypothesis (usually on income) were responsible for the lags in the demand for money. Feige considered both hypotheses *simultaneously*, with different expectations parameters on income and interest rates. However, as the adaptive coefficient on interest rates is found to be unity we present this simplified model below (see equation (4.46)).

$$M_t = (\gamma m_y \theta) Y_t - \gamma m_r r_t + \gamma m_r (1-\theta) r_{t-1} + (2-\gamma-\theta) M_{t-1}$$
$$- (1-\theta)(1-\gamma) M_{t-2} + \gamma[u_t + (1-\theta) u_{t-1}] \tag{5.2}$$

$$= b_1Y + b_2r + b_3r_{t-1} + b_4M_{t-1} + b_5M_{t-2} + v_t \tag{5.3}$$

The equation is estimated on annual data over the period 1915–63 and the overidentifying restrictions are imposed using a non-linear instrumental variable procedure. Feige found the results satisfactory (for M1 and M2) on a priori grounds and, in particular, $\gamma = 1$ and $\theta = 0.4$. Hence *instantaneous* adjustment (on annual data) and adaptive expectations on income are indicated. On quarterly US data Goldfeld (1973) finds less than instantaneous adjustment.

Laidler and Parkin (1970) apply Feige's model with $r_t^e = r_t$ to UK quarterly per capita data on M2, 1956(2)–1967(4) and obtain ambiguous results concerning adjustment and expectations lags. Laidler and Parkin do not in general find the interest rate significant and in this case the adjustment and expectations parameters γ and θ cannot be separately identified in the unrestricted equation 5.3. (To see this, put $m_r = 0$ in equation 5.2; γ and θ then enter symmetrically in the estimating equation.)

To impose the overidentifying restrictions, Laidler and Parkin search over values of γ and θ in the range (0, 1) to maximize the $\bar{R}^2$ of the regression. However, two local maxima are found, one with a large value of θ and small value of γ, and the other where these values are reversed. On a priori grounds, Laidler and Parkin favour the permanent income interpretation with short adjustment lags. It is argued that the failure of the interest rate in the equation is due to the failure of the Treasury bill rate to provide a satisfactory proxy variable for the *relative* return on money: the omitted variable being the own rate on money.

Meyer and Neri (1975) add a little twist to the Feige-type equation. They assert that individuals distinguish between current, permanent and short-run expected income $_tY_{t+1}^e$. People expect their actual current income eventually to converge on their permanent (or long-run) income, but if convergence is slow they may base their demand for money on short-run expected income. The latter is therefore a weighted average of current income Y_t and permanent income Y_t^P

$$_tY_{t+1}^e = \delta Y_t^P + (1 - \delta)Y_t$$

If $\delta = 1$, then $_tY_{t+1}^e = Y_t^P$ and if $\delta = 0$, $_tY_{t+1}^e = Y_t$. Using annual data for the US, Meyer and Neri find that $0 < \delta < 1$ for both narrow and broad money, supporting the use of $_tY_{t+1}^e$. This result is interesting in that, in principle, $_tY_{t+1}^e$ is a forward looking expectations variable and it seems plausible that today's money balances should be influenced by the level of expected future transactions. We follow up this line of enquiry when discussing 'buffer-stock money'.

Thus, early attempts to separately identify adjustment and expectations lags were more successful with US than UK data, particularly with annual data. (For evidence on other OECD countries see OECD (1979) and Blundell-Wignall et al. (1984)). Later studies apply the own rate on money as an additional variable and as an example, we now turn to the Artis–Lewis (1976) study of the UK demand for money function.

5.3.1 *Partial adjustment only*

(a) *Post-war UK results.* For the UK, for various definitions of money, Artis and Lewis (1976) look at the stability of coefficient estimates, as the sample period which begins in 1963(2) is extended from 1970(4) to 1973(1). For *broad* money, they include the interest *differential* between the 'own rate' on money and the rate on long-term government debt. In *all* equations, the variance of bond prices (measured as a moving average) is included to measure 'riskiness'. Equations are presented with nominal and real balances as the dependent variable and first-order partial adjustment is invoked. In all cases, the equations fail the Chow test for parameter stability over the period 1971(1)–1973(1) and, for broad money, the equation is dynamically unstable over the 'long data period' (as the lagged dependent variable exceeds unity). Obviously, parameter instability is not due to the erroneous exclusion of the own rate and the riskiness of bonds and Artis and Lewis reject the view that it is caused by a large change in the non-interest service flow on current accounts (sight deposits). They favour the view that the apparent instability in the demand for *broad* money is due to disequilibrium in the money market and we discuss this evidence in the section on buffer-stock money.

As we shall see below, it appears that for the UK the conventional demand function for M1 exhibits parameter stability when a more flexible (EFE) lag response is allowed (Hendry, 1979). Also a conventional demand function for *broad* money in the UK, has relatively stable parameters when a dummy variable (for the policy of competition and credit control) and a wealth variable are added to the equation and a more flexible lag structure is allowed (Grice and Bennett, 1984). We comment further on these results below.

A further investigation into the instability in the demand for broad money in the UK considers disaggregated functions for companies and the personal sector where nominal partial adjustment is assumed. Goodhart (1984) finds that the nominal demand for M3 is reasonably stable over the period 1963(4)–1973(4). Nominal M3 is regressed on itself lagged, a real current income variable, the current price level, an 'alternative' interest rate (local authority rate), the 'own rate' (that is certificate of deposit (CD) rate) together with the differential between the CD rate and the rate on bank lending. The latter picks up the effects of 'round tripping' out of bank advances into certificates of deposit, the latter being a component of broad money (see section 8.2). Somewhat surprisingly, it is the demand for broad money *by persons* (where the rate on long term government debt is the only interest rate) which appears to be unstable.

(b) *Post-war US results.* It is probably fair to say that most work in the US using quarterly data on the demand for money has used and continues to use a conventional long-run function of the form (5.1) with the addition of a lagged dependent variable. The latter is taken to represent either (first-order) partial adjustment in real or nominal terms or, perhaps less frequently, the result of the adaptive expectations hypothesis. There are few new analytic points to emerge from this work and as recent empirical studies are well documented elsewhere (Laidler, 1980; Judd and Scadding, 1982) we content ourselves here with an overview of the main conclusions.

Over the period 1952(2)–1973(4), Goldfeld (1976) found a stable demand function for narrow money (M1) which was positively related to real GNP, negatively related to a representative market short rate (for example commercial bill rate) and the rate on time deposits, and incorporating first-order partial adjustment in nominal terms. However, this function seriously overpredicted money balances (in a *dynamic* simulation) over the period 1974–6 ('the case of the missing money') and is also found to be unstable over the 1979–81 period.

Attempts to account for the temporal instability by permutations of different interest rate and 'transactions' variables has not proved wholly successful. Admittedly the use of bank debits as an additional transactions variable along-side GNP (which excludes intermediate transactions and transactions in financial assets but includes some inputed items for which no transactions take place) does improve matters somewhat (Judd and Scadding, 1982). Also the use of the dividend price ratio (Hamberger, 1977) improves the performance of the M1 equation – but other criticisms of this equation have been raised (Hafer and Hein, 1979; Laidler, 1980).

The most likely causes of the observed instability in the demand for money in the US, post-1973, appear to be financial innovation and the role of money as a 'buffer-stock'. We discuss the latter in the next chapter and the former in chapter 8. However, it is worth briefly outlining the methods used to measure the impact of 'financial innovation' on the demand for money. Financial inno-vation took the form of the banks offering interest bearing accounts that were easily transferable to 'checking accounts' and in allowing the centralization of accounts (of different branches of the firm – 'cash concentration accounts'). Ideally one would like direct measures of the change in brokerage fees and of the reduction in the variance of net cash flows facilitated by these innovations. These variables could then be used directly in the inventory and precautionary models of the demand for money. Unfortunately such direct measures are not available and the most 'successful' variables include the number of 'wire transfers' and previous peak interest rates. The former reflects the increased use of cash management techniques by firms and the latter represents the increased incentive *to begin* using these services more frequently. When either of these variables is added to the demand for M1 they are statistically significant and the (outside sample) forecast errors of the equation, post-1973, are reduced (Judd and Scadding, 1982). In contrast to the above, the demand for narrow money in other industrialized countries does not appear to have been affected by financial innovation variables even though they also experienced high interest rates in the 1970s (Boughton, 1981; Arango and Nadiri, 1981). The pace of financial innova-tion (chapter 8) appears to be accelerating in other industrialized nations and we may see similar problems with instability in the demand for M1 in these countries in the near future. (There is already some evidence for this in the demand for M1 in the UK in 1983/4.)

Although there have been acute problems in finding a stable demand function for M1 in the US, post-1973, the difficulties with M2 (which consists of M1 plus small savings accounts at commercial banks) have been far less severe.

Laidler (1980) reports that the 'conventional' demand function for M2 exhibits much greater outside sample temporal stability than does M1 and is less sensitive to alternative specifications of the arguments in the function (for a counter-argument, see Hamberger (1980)). Interest however tends to centre on M1 as this is the targeted aggregate in the US.

There has been an interesting attempt in the US to correctly measure 'money' and the return on money using Divisia aggregates and to use these measures to test the stability of the partial adjustment model (Barnett et al., 1984). The approach recognizes that the components of the money supply (for example currency, demand and time deposits) may not be perfect substitutes for each other and should not be given equal weight as in official statistics on monetary aggregates. In the Divisia approach the separate components are *weighted* together, according to their contribution to 'money services' to form a 'consistent' series for money. 'User costs' measure the marginal 'money services' yielded by each component and are proportional to the difference between the yield on a 'benchmark' asset and the component's own yield. The share of each component's user cost in total user cost is used to weight each component in forming the Divisia aggregate.

In the demand for money function, conventional aggregates are replaced by their Divisia counterparts and interest rates are replaced by the user cost indexes. On US data, for narrow money there is no improvement in the performance of the 'Divisia equation' over the conventional function; however, for broad aggregates, where we expect conventional measures to incorrectly measure 'money services', the Divisia measures do produce a more stable demand function. The approach is probably most useful where interest rates (which make up the user cost variables) are market determined rather than subject to regulation and hence may prove useful in an increasingly competitive financial environment.

We noted in the previous chapter that the partial adjustment and adaptive expectations hypotheses *impose* rather rigid lag responses and this may account for some of the apparent observed instability. The ADL model does not impose a restrictive lag structure and the partial adjustment models are special cases (that is nested versions) of the ADL model. Hence the ADL approach may improve the statistical performance of money demand functions and it is to this we now turn.

5.4   THE ADL–EFE APPROACH

In this section we illustrate the ADL-EFE approach with respect to the demand for narrow and broad money, the demand for long term goverment debt and bank advances. The key elements in this approach are that an unrestricted ('general') ADL equation is initially chosen so that the lag structure is not unduly constrained at the outset. The equation is then simplified ('reparameterized') into 'plausible' decision variables that are data acceptable. The simplified (parsimonious) equation usually involves some form of error-feedback term as well as differenced variables. The former (levels and ratio) terms determine the long-run 'static' equilibrium parameters of the asset demand function (as discussed in chapters 2 and 3). The 'differenced variables' model the short-run dynamics around this 'static' equilibrium position. This modelling strategy is frequently referred to as moving from 'the general to the specific'. Broadly speaking the aim in this approach is to obtain a well-fitting (data coherent) equation that has 'good' statistical properties, forecasts well outside of its sample period of estimation, and conforms to the a priori notions given by the static equilibrium model (these issues are elaborated by Hendry (1983)).

Frequently, adjustment and expectations lags are not separately identified in the ADL–EFE approach but an exception here is provided by our discussion of the demand for long-term government debt. In general terms the results from some of the equations presented below are referred to in later chapters on the money supply.

The ADL–EFE approach has been widely adopted in recent UK empirical work but appears to be catching on elsewhere (Gordon, 1984). Our examples are therefore drawn from UK studies but also provide a basis for investigating this approach in the literature generally.

5.4.1   The demand for narrow money

Hendry (1979) provides a recent econometric study of the demand for transactions balances M1 in the UK, by the NBPS. Hendry assumes the demand curve for M1 is identified and since M1 is assumed to be demand determined, actual balances equal (short-term) *desired* balances given by 'theory'. Both seem plausible assumptions. In long-run equilibrium, the real demand for M1 is assumed to depend upon real income Y, and expected yield on alternative assets r, and the expected rate of inflation π^e. A long-run unit income elasticity is proposed. In obvious notation, the static long run equilibrium is

$$\frac{M}{PY} = Kr^\alpha(\pi^e)^\beta \quad \alpha, \beta < 0 \tag{5.4}$$

A general unrestricted ADL equation in the logarithms of the levels of Y_{t-j}, r_{t-j}, P_{t-j} and M_{t-j-1} ($j = 0, \ldots, 4$) and with $\ln M$ as the dependent variable, is reparameterized and simplified to produce the following data-coherent dynamic error feedback equation (EFE)[1]

$$\Delta \ln (M_t/P_{t-1}) = \underset{(0.28)}{0.86} \, \Delta \ln Y_t^* - \underset{(0.023)}{0.119} \, \Delta \ln r_t^* - \underset{(0.23)}{0.90} \, \Delta \ln P_{t-2}$$

$$+ \underset{(0.26)}{0.54} \, \Delta \ln P_{t-3} - \underset{(0.036)}{0.096} \, \ln (M/PY)_{t-1}$$

$$- \underset{(0.011)}{0.035} \, \ln r_{t-2} - \underset{(0.017)}{0.026} \tag{5.5}$$

$$\text{OLS } 6301\text{–}7603, \text{ SE } (\%) = 1.3 \quad \text{RC}(11) = 15, \text{ LM}(6) = 6.5,$$

$$\text{HF}(7) = 8.1, \text{ CH}(7, 42) = 0.75$$

where figures in parentheses indicate standard errors, the $\Delta \ln P$ terms proxy the expected rate of inflation or lagged price level adjustment and

$$\Delta \ln Y^* = \frac{1}{3} \sum_{i=0}^{2} \Delta \ln Y_{t-i}$$

is the average growth rate in income; similarly

$$\Delta \ln r_t^* = \frac{1}{3} \sum_{i=0}^{2} \Delta \ln r_{t-i}$$

Statistically the equation, as it was designed to do, performs well. There is no evidence of autocorrelation in the residuals (RC, LM), the equation forecasts well outside the estimation period (HF), and has 'stable' parameters (CH).[1] The within-sample standard error of the equation SE is 1.3 per cent of M1. The equilibrium, or error feedback term, $\ln (M/PY)_{t-1}$ is statistically significant; a unit income elasticity is accepted by the data and the long-run interest rate and (annual) inflation rate elasticities are (minus 0.36) and (minus) 0.9 respectively.[2]

Although the lag response is eventually geometric because of the single lagged dependent variable, nevertheless the lag profiles are relatively flexible in the 'first year' because of the presence of lags in the independent variables themselves. The median lags for Y and r are 0.6 and 4 quarters respectively. If we are willing to assume that there is little simultaneous feedback from Y_t or r_t to u_t, then given the absence of autocorrelation, OLS provides consistent estimates of the structural parameters (including σ^2, the variance of the errors).

As far as the terms in Y and r are concerned, the reparameterized variables provide plausible decision variables: the growth in real money balances depends upon the average growth in real income and the interest rate and upon disequilibrium (error) in the level of $\ln (M/PY)_{t-1}$. The inflation terms are a little difficult to rationalize either in terms of a proxy for the expected rate of inflation or as a lagged adjustment to the price level. Also, the long-run inflation effect seems rather large if it is measuring the switch from transactions balances to real goods due to expected inflation.

Notice that in this model, as is typical in the ADL–EFE approach in general, the lag response could be a mixture of expectations and adjustment lags and there is no attempt to separate out the two. (Our analysis in appendix A indicates that errors in variables may cause statistically significant lag effects when in the 'true' model there are none.)

It is worth mentioning that Hendry and Ericsson (1983) fit an EFE to narrow money on UK annual data from about 1870 and find some temporal instability in the relationship, contrary to the earlier assertions of Friedman and Schwartz (1982). Also Gordon (1984) finds only weak support for the EFE when applied to US data on M1 including the 1970s (although alternative models do not fare particularly well either).

The above results for the UK indicate that the ADL–EFEs for M1 are an improvement on the partial adjustment–adaptive expectations models. For the US the results are less clear cut.

5.4.2   *The demand for broad money*

Hendry and Mizon (1978) criticize the earlier work of Haache (1974) on the demand for M3 (that is sight and interest bearing deposits) by the UK *personal* sector. Hendry and Mizon's criticism is that Haache began his study with an unduly restrictive model, namely one that had only first differences in the variables. A model that contains only first differences may be tested in two equivalent ways starting from an unrestricted ADL equation in the levels of the variables. First we can test the common factor restriction (autocorrelation) and then test to see if the common factor has a root of unity (that is $\rho = 1$) (appendix A). Second we can reparameterize the equation into difference and levels terms and test the statistical significance of the latter. Mizon and Hendry demonstrate that the implicit common factor restrictions in the Haache model are statistically invalid, however, we shall concentrate on the second approach. The data acceptable reparameterized equation is

$$\Delta \ln (M/P)_t = \; 1.6 + \; 0.21 \, \Delta \ln Y_t + \; 0.81 \, \Delta \ln (1 + r_t)$$
$$\quad\quad (0.6) \quad (0.1) \quad\quad\quad\quad (0.3)$$

$$+ \; 0.26 \, \Delta \ln (M/P)_{t-1} - \; 0.40 \, \Delta \ln P_t$$
$$\quad (0.1) \quad\quad\quad\quad\quad\quad (0.1)$$

$$- \; 0.23 \ln (M/PY)_{t-1} - \; 0.61 \ln (1 + r_{t-4})$$
$$\quad (0.05) \quad\quad\quad\quad\quad (0.2)$$

$$+ \; 0.14 \ln Y_{t-4} \tag{5.6}$$
$$\quad (0.04)$$

$$\text{OLS } 6301\text{–}7503, \text{SE } (\%) = 0.9, \quad R^2 = 0.69, \text{RC}(12) = 6.4$$

where figures in parentheses indicate standard error, Y is real personal disposable income, r_t is the yield on long-term government debt and P is the consumer price index (and the data is seasonally adjusted). The statistically significant 'levels terms' $\ln (M/PY)_{t-1}$, $\ln (1 + r_{t-4})$ and $\ln Y_{t-4}$ reject the hypothesis that the equation should only contain first differences in the variables. The unit income elasticity implicit in the error feedback term $\ln (M/PY)_{t-1}$ is 'broken' by the inclusion of $\ln Y_{t-4}$. The long-run *dynamic* equilibrium solution, using $\ln X_{t-j} = \ln X_t - jg$, where g is the constant growth rate in an independent variable X, is[3]

$$\ln \frac{M}{P} = K(1 + r)^{-2.6}(1 + g_p)^{-1.7}Y^{1.6} \tag{5.7}$$

where $K = \exp (7 - 4.2g_y)$.

The 'static' elasticities are all of the expected sign and of a plausible magnitude. Economic theory does not indicate any a priori relationship between the level of real balances and the rate of growth in real income g_y. The equation indicates that the higher is g_y the lower the equilibrium level of real money balances (at any given level of income) which may appear a little strange on intuitive grounds. As argued in appendix A, this 'growth effect' although large may not be statistically different from zero and ideally one should test this proposition. The within-sample statistical properties of the equation are good and if we assume simultaneity problems are negligible, OLS provides consistent estimates.

Wealth and capital gains. Grice and Bennett (1984), in a study of the demand for £M3 by the UK NBPS over the data of the 1960s and 1970s, introduce a dummy variable to proxy the large shift in demand after the introduction of CCC. Gross financial wealth, as well as a transactions variable (that is total final expenditure), is included and the *relative* return on money is used in preference to using only the return on alternative assets. The relative return is measured by the own rate on money less the return to holding gilts which includes the one-period ahead expected capital gain. This relative expected return is proxied by a 'weakly rational' predictor.

A general ADL equation is reparameterized and the resulting long-run effects are acceptable on a priori grounds, and the step response functions are relatively smooth. However, the reparameterized variables are not readily interpreted as behavioural, since the lag coefficients on a particular variable frequently change sign. The ADL model in this case becomes a convenient parsimonious method of approximating lag responses rather than being interpreted as an error feedback equation. Wealth plays a more important role than income/transactions, the former having a long-run elasticity of 1.4 and the latter 0.3. The semi-elasticity of £M3 with respect to the relative yield on money and long-term government debt is 0.3. However, because expected capital gains can be substantial, the impact of the latter on the demand for money may be large. CCC has a substantial long-run effect of about 13 per cent on the demand for £M3. The within sample statistical properties of the equation are good, as one might expect from the ADL approach. The outside sample, one-step ahead (static) forecasting performance of the equation is tolerable.

Grice and Bennett provide an interesting Monte-Carlo study of the effect of errors in variables on estimated lagged responses (Grether and Maddala, 1973). The wealth variable causes potential estimation problems because it may be measured with error (see appendix A). The experiments indicate that there is considerable elongation of the 'true' lag structure and bias in the OLS estimate of the long-run wealth elasticity of the demand for money.

There are some further problems with the equation. First the lagged responses might be thought to be implausibly long, and terms in the lagged dependent variable (of up to $t-5$) provide much of the statistical explanation. The lag response to changes in the expected capital gain on long-term debt imply that in the short run, it is possible for the demand for money to *increase* when the expected return to long-term debt increases (section 4.2). However the study is one of the first systematic attempts to model both wealth effects and expected capital gain in the UK demand for money function.[4]

5.4.3   *The demand for long-term government debt*

Spencer (1981) and Cuthbertson (1983) estimate 'single equations' to explain the UK–NBPS demand for gilt-edged stock G, which incorporate expected capital gains. Both reach similar conclusions. Both estimate the *relative* return to gilts R^e (the running yield plus the capital gain on gilts less the yield on alternative capital safe short assets RS), using a McCallum (1976) weakly rational predictor. The equation for R estimated by Cuthbertson is

$$R^e = -58 + 10.3R_{t-1} + 2RS_{t-1} - 4R^f + 7.5R^f_{t-2}$$
$$\quad (2.3)\,(3.7) \qquad (0.9) \qquad (1.6)\,(1.6)$$
$$\quad - 6.6R^f_{t-3} + 2\dot{E}_{t-1} + 0.8\dot{E}_{t-2} \tag{5.8}$$
$$\quad (2.4) \qquad (2.2) \quad (1.2)$$

OLS 7201-8102, $\quad R^2 = 0.42$, $\quad dw = 2.4$

where figures in parentheses indicate the t-statistic, R_{t-1} is the running yield (interest rate) on gilts, R^f is the three-month Eurodollar rate and $\dot{E}$ is the annual percentage change in the effective exchange rate. The positive coefficient on R_{t-1} probably reflects the authorities' behaviour in engineering expectations of a capital gain. By raising long rates abruptly by a large amount, the NBPS are led to believe that interest rates will fall in the future, yielding a capital gain. (In the UK this is referred to as the Grand Old Duke of York strategy.) The negative effect of the Eurodollar rate may reflect the authorities' desire to raise domestic rates to stabilize the exchange rate or is the result of short-term capital flows to preserve uncovered arbitrage. The latter argument also applies to the sign of the exchange rate variable.

Predictions from the above equation yield a series for the expected return $\hat{R}^e$. The demand for gilts equation is a reparameterized version of an unrestricted ADL model, and yields an error feedback equation

$$\Delta \ln (G/P)_t = 0.015 + 1.24\,\Delta \ln (W/P)_t + 0.00043\hat{R}^e_t$$
$$\qquad\quad (3.4) \qquad (3.1) \qquad\qquad\qquad (1.6)$$
$$\qquad\quad - 0.158 \ln (G/Y)_{t-1} \tag{5.9}$$
$$\qquad\quad (1.5)$$

7203-8102, IV, $SE = 0.021$, $\quad dw = 2.4$, $\quad LM(8) = 9.8$,

$$HF(10) = 1.2, \quad CH(10,18) = 0.1,$$

$$IE(5) = 5.8$$

where IV indicates an instrumental variables regression, IE is a chi-squared statistic to test the independence of instruments and errors (Sargan, 1958), Y is real income and W is a measure of gross wealth of the NBPS. A short-run influence only was found for gross wealth $\Delta \ln (W/P)$, and in the long run the (real) demand for gilts is determined by income (as a proxy for human and non-human wealth) and the expected relative yield on gilts.[5] Although the standard error of the equation is only 2.1 per cent this figure can be misleading since it assumes $\ln G_{t-1}$ is known. In dynamic single equation simulations $\ln G_{t-1}$ is the *predicted* value from the previous period and dynamic prediction errors can often be substantial.[6]

5.4.4   *The demand for bank loans by UK industrial and commercial companies (ICC)*

In the UK, attempts to control the money supply have centred on the interest elasticity of bank advances. Open market operations by the authorities influence market yields which then spread to interest rates on bank deposits and bank advances. The higher the own interest elasticity of the demand for bank advances, the larger the fall in advances and hence the money supply, for any given change in the own rate of interest. These issues are discussed in detail in section 8.2 on control of the money supply in the UK. Here we provide background material for this later discussion by presenting illustrative statistical results of the demand for sterling advances by ICC from UK banks.

For ICC, bank advances are a very close substitute for 'money' transactions balances and the latter are likely to be held only as minimum overnight trading balances (Sprenkle, 1966). We might therefore expect a higher demand for bank advances (and liquid assets), the higher the expected level of turnover (output) of the firm, *ceteris paribus*.

In a precautionary demand model the choice between an increase in bank advances or running down liquid assets depends in part on the *relative* interest cost, *RS–RBL* (Sprenkle and Miller, 1980).

ICC may also obtain finance from the sale of foreign assets or by borrowing in foreign markets, for example from offshore banks. If the borrowing is in foreign currencies these may be switched into sterling in the spot market. The forward market can be used to eliminate exchange risk (for maturities of up to about one year) or the UK firm might take an open position. For a UK based multinational firm the exchange risk could be eliminated by using the retained profits of a foreign based subsidiary or by future sales in export markets. We therefore expect sterling bank lending to ICC to be *positively* related to the return to foreign borrowing (or the return on foreign assets held by ICC).

Having discussed the role of relative interest rates we now turn to the influence of real interest rates and inflation. Taking a portfolio view, firms may consider real assets, such as stocks, as substitutes for financial assets. If so, we expect the *real* cost of loans to have a negative relationship with bank lending and therefore for inflation to have a positive impact, *ceteris paribus*. On the other hand, claims have been made for an independent influence of the nominal cost of bank borrowing and the rate of inflation on bank lending. The nominal cost of borrowing may provide a proxy variable for a high gearing ratio which would tend to reduce the demand for bank finance. Short-run *changes* in the nominal rate on bank lending together with 'sticky' price expectations may lead to changes in bank lending because of a *temporary* postponement or advancement of investment projects. If high inflation is associated with highly variable rates of inflation, particularly of relative prices (see Parks (1978) and Hesselman (1983) for example), this may increase the risk associated with the returns to investment. Hence we might expect a negative inflation effect from this source. A negative inflation effect might also ensue if nominal bank lending reacts with a lag to changes in the price level (but is homogeneous in the long run).

On a priori grounds the sign of the inflation effect on bank lending is indeterminate. If we include the nominal cost of borrowing and the rate of inflation as separate variables in our bank lending equation, we implicitly include a real interest rate and a separate inflation effect.

The precautionary model of Miller and Orr (1966) suggests that the variability of net receipts influences the demand for bank advances (and other 'liquid assets') but measurement and aggregation problems have prevented the use of such a variable in applied work. Clearly in such 'target-threshold' models actual (as opposed to average) balances act as a buffer stock absorbing shocks which do not push asset balances beyond the 'return points'. Hence, some measure of the unanticipated financing requirement of companies is required in the demand function for bank advances. The (net) borrowing requirement of ICC appears to provide a useful proxy variable here. We assume that the firm attempts to cover its expected current costs (including expected costs of physical stocks) from revenues and its long-term investment plans (including investment overseas) from retained profits. Any *unanticipated* changes in 'working capital' or net receipts (for example trade credit) will therefore be reflected in the borrowing requirement. The trended income variable may therefore be viewed as measuring the expected change in transactions needs that are met by bank advances while the borrowing requirement measures unanticipated financing requirements.

Cuthbertson (1985a) starts with an unrestricted ADL model and 'tests down' to produce a (complex) error feedback equation

$$\Delta_4 \ln (BL/P)_t = 0.59 \, \Delta_2 \ln (BL/P)_{t-1} + 0.98 \, \Delta \ln (BL/P)_{t-3}$$
$$\quad\quad\quad (10.7) \quad\quad\quad\quad\quad\quad (14.1)$$

$$+ 0.22 \, \Delta_4 \ln Y_t - 0.16 \ln (BL/PY)_{t-4}$$
$$\quad (2.2) \quad\quad\quad\quad (3.8)$$

$$- 0.005 \, \Delta RBL_{t-1} - 1.29 \, \Delta \ln P_{t-1}$$
$$\quad (2.5) \quad\quad\quad\quad (4.0)$$

$$- 0.76 \, \Delta \ln P_{t-2} + 0.006 \, \Delta(RS - RBL)_t$$
$$\quad (2.4) \quad\quad\quad\quad (2.1)$$

$$+ 0.015 \, (RS - RBL)_{t-2} + 0.029 \, RB_t$$
$$\quad (4.1) \quad\quad\quad\quad\quad (5.8)$$

$$+ 0.002 \, (REU^* - RBL^*) + 0.038 \, (CCC_t + CCC_{t-1})$$
$$\quad (4.1) \quad\quad\quad\quad\quad (10.3) \quad\quad\quad\quad\quad (5.10)$$

6501–8003 OLS, SE(%) = 1.5,   dw = 1.8,   RC(16) = 18,   LM(8) = 10

where parentheses indicate the t-statistic, BL is sterling bank lending to ICC, P is the price index, Y is total final expenditure, RBL is the interest rate on bank lending, RS is the representative 'short rate' on liquid assets held by ICC, REU is the Eurodollar rate, REU^* and RBL^* contain lagged terms in REU and RBL, RB is the real net borrowing requirement of ICC, CCC is a (0, 1) dummy variable to capture the 'non-price' effects on lending after the introduction of the policy of competition and credit control CCC (see section 8.2). The long-run static equilibrium solution for equation (5.10) is

$$\ln \frac{BL}{P} = \ln Y + 0.025 \, (REU - RBL) + 0.094 \, (RS - RBL)$$

$$- 3.2 \, \Delta_4 \ln P + 0.46CCC \tag{5.11}$$

These results conform to a priori views.[7] In particular there is a unit transactions elasticity, a *relative* yield elasticity with respect to *REU* and *RS* of 2.5 and 9.4 respectively. Collinearity between the *CCC* variable and inflation in the early 1970s may mask their individual contributions but both are large. Although the EFE looks rather complex the (step) response of lending to changes in any of the independent variables (excluding the price level) are fairly smooth.

5.4.5 *Summary: ADL-EFE approach*

The ADL-EFE approach appears to be a useful method of estimating lag structures and avoids the problem of constraining the lag structure at the outset of the investigation. Partial adjustment and adaptive expectations may be obtained as 'special cases' if they are data admissible. In principle the ADL-EFE allows expectations variables to be explicitly included in the equation (although this is not always done, in which case the parameters may be a convolution of expectations and adjustment parameters). In the examples discussed above the ADL-EFE approach performed well on a number of statistical criteria.

However, in the examples considered so far, disequilibria in 'other' asset stocks do not influence the speed of adjustment in money balances. We now turn to discuss how such interdependent asset adjustment equations perform empirically.

5.5 A SYSTEMS APPROACH: INTERDEPENDENT ASSET DEMANDS

In this section we consider a number of applications of the interdependent asset adjustment models discussed in the previous chapter. We begin by looking at studies that use a fairly eclectic model of the long-run demand function to which they then apply the interdependent adjustment model. This is followed by various models that apply Friedman's optimal partial adjustment approach.

Asset demand functions that contain long and short rates can be 'solved' to yield a term structure equation. We discuss the latter in detail in chapter 9, but our asset demand results provide a useful introduction to this area. In the final part of this section we review various models that apply the mean-variance model of the long-run demand for assets, some of which also model short-run dynamics using the interdependent asset adjustment model.

5.5.1　*Eclectic approach*

Christofides (1980) has applied the Brainard–Tobin (1968) interdependent asset demand model to explain Canadian NBPS holdings of money M, short-term bonds S and long-term bonds B. Each asset is assumed to have an (eclectic) long-run demand function depending upon a short rate RS, a long rate RL, the level of transactions (income) Y, and wealth W (that is the sum of the three assets). The interest rate on money is assumed to be zero. The equations are estimated in real terms thus imposing an instantaneous unit price level elasticity for all assets. Unitary expectations (that is expected capital gains are assumed to be zero) and endogenous asset supplies are assumed.

The empirical results (table 5.1) indicate gross substitutability and both income and wealth are statistically significant. The statistically significant lagged dependent variables in 'other' asset stocks support the interdependent asset adjustment model, in preference to the simple partial adjustment approach. It may be shown that the long-run coefficients all have the correct sign and the system is dynamically stable. Most of any increase in wealth in the *current* period is held in money and short-term bonds but in the long run the bond equation has the largest wealth effect. In the short run an increase in income (transactions) leads to an increase in money and short assets and a reduction in holdings of bonds. In the long run these qualitative relationships continue to hold except in the case of short assets where the long-run transactions effect is also negative. These are plausible and interesting conclusions that might not emerge from simple partial adjustment applied to each equation in turn.[8]

In view of our discussion of theories of the term structure of interest rates in chapter 9, it is worth noting that these asset demand equations imply a particular term structure (which Freidman (1977) has called a 'restrictive' term structure equation). Assuming that asset supplies are exogenous and the market clears, the system of equations may be used to solve for the long and short bond rate.[9] Long and short rates both depend upon Y, M, S and B in the long run and also on lagged values of M, S and B in the short run. The yield curve, that is the relationship between RB and RS, may be altered by changes in Y, W and the outstanding stock of assets. For example, it is found that changes in Y, M and S impinge more powerfully on RS than on RL, thus 'shifting the yield curve'.

Some Extensions. Smith and Brainard (1976) and Smith (1981) use the interdependent asset adjustment model to explain the behaviour of the set of assets held by US saving and loan associations. Noting that earlier studies found that expected yield variables were poorly determined because of multicollinearity, they suggest using a Bayesian approach. Prior values (guesses) are presented for the means of *all* the parameters of the model, together with their prior variances and covariances. The latter are difficult to determine a priori, and because there are a large number of covariances:[10] they 'put a great strain on our intuition' (Smith and Brainard, 1976, p. 1310).[11] The results of this 'mixed' or Bayesian estimation were not widely encouraging overall, but were no worse than non-Bayesian methods. A number of 'wrong' signs persisted in the 'mixed estimators'

TABLE 5.1 Canadian interdependent asset adjustment equations

Dependent variables	Constant	RS	RL	Y	W	M_{t-1}	S_{t-1}	B_{t-1}	R^2	dw
M_t	−3.1 (0.9)	−1.2 (5.3)	0.4 (1.3)	0.076 (3.8)	0.35 (6.8)	−0.5 (10.1)	−0.25 (6.0)	−0.3 (6.5)	0.99	2.1
S_t	8.4 (0.6)	3.7 4.1	−4.3 (3.0)	0.037 (0.5)	0.5 (2.4)	0.5 (2.5)	0.25 (1.4)	−0.5 (2.4)	0.78	2.0
B_t	5.3 (0.4)	−2.5 (3.1)	3.8 (3.0)	−0.1 (1.6)	0.12 (0.6)	0.0 (0.0)	0.0 (0.0)	0.8 (4.4)	0.93	2.1
Coefficient sums	0	0	0	0	1	0	0	0		

OLS, 5502–7404, t-statistics given in parentheses.

Source: Christofides (1980)

and the latter did not produce forecasts that were markedly better than the coefficients estimated from sample data only. A Bayesian approach applied to UK insurance company holdings of assets is given by Honohan (1980) but the results are rather disappointing. Thus although the formal Bayesian approach is novel, it does not appear markedly superior to the *ad hoc* Bayesian approach whereby the researcher chooses the final equation as his own personal weighted average of his priors and the various regression results obtained.

5.5.2 *Friedman's optimal partial adjustment model*

As noted in section 4.2.2 Friedman's (1977) model incorporates the inter-dependent asset adjustment approach but enables the long-run structural parameters for a particular asset to be identified by running a single equation, rather than the complete set of equations as required in the Tobin–Brainard approach discussed above. Cross equation adding-up restrictions are therefore not incorporated in Friedman's model. The terms in $(r_t \ \Delta W_t)$ can be signed a priori as can the coefficient in the 'own' lagged dependent variables. From these two coefficients we can then obtain the long-run structural parameters for the yield variables.

Friedman assumes that a particular version of the comparative static one-period mean variance model determines desired 'long-run' asset demands. The particular version used assumes a unit wealth elasticity and desired asset *shares* $\alpha_i^* = A_i/W$ are determined by relative yields.

For illustrative purposes, consider Friedman's demand equations for corporate bonds (CB) held by pension funds in the US. The *expected* yields are proxied by the actual (running) yield (or 'interest rate'). Asset demands are assumed to be homogeneous (of degree one) in nominal wealth W and to depend on the own yield, the equity yield r_{EQ}, the corporate bond yield r_{CB}, the expected rate of inflation Π^e, lagged assets stocks of corporate bonds CB_{t-1}, government stock GS_{t-1} equities EQ_{t-1} and liquid assets LA_{t-1}. Not all these variables are included in the 'final equation' for pension fund holdings of corporate bonds

$$\Delta CB_t^P = 0.24 W_{-1}^P + 0.15(r_{CB}(t)\Delta W_t^P)^* - 0.71(\Pi_t^e \Delta W_t^P)$$
$$\quad (3.3) \qquad (6.5) \qquad\qquad (4.6)$$

$$\quad - 0.37 CB_{-1}^P + 0.21 GS_{-1}^P - 0.25 EQ_{-1}^P \qquad\qquad (5.12)$$
$$\quad (3.5) \qquad (3.6) \qquad (3.4)$$

$$6000\text{-}7000, \text{IV}, \quad R^2 = 0.67, \quad R^2 = 0.79, \quad dw = 2.3$$

where the parentheses indicate the *t*-statistic. The own rate coefficients on the $(r_{CB}(t)\Delta W_t)$ variables are positive and the own partial adjustment coefficient (on CB_{-1}) is negative in both equations, as expected from a priori considerations.[12] Lagged 'other' asset stocks are also significant, supporting the interdependent asset adjustment approach. The expected rate of inflation (proxied by actual inflation over the previous two years) has a negative effect on equilibrium holdings of bonds by pension funds ($\Pi_t^e \Delta W_t$ term).

There are some minor problems with the equations. The pension fund equation contains no term in $(r_{CB}(t)\,W_{t-1})$ and therefore the equilibrium level of CB^P is independent of r_{CB} (when $\Delta W = 0$). A counter-argument is that the assumption $\Delta W = 0$ is unrealistic and does not occur in the data. When $\Delta W \neq 0$, CB is influenced by r_{CB} via the $r_{CB}\Delta W$ term[13] (see also Cummins and Outreville (1984)).

Simulations and the term structure in Friedman's model. Having estimated demand functions for all holders of corporate bonds and assuming an exogenous supply of bonds, one can solve the system for the predicted bond yield $\hat{r}_{CB}(t)$ that clears the market in period t. By substituting $\hat{r}_{CB}(t)$ in the bond equations, one obtains the equilibrium (total) stock of bonds $CB(t)$. The latter can then be used to generate predicted values for $CB(t+j)$ and hence for the equilibrium values $r_{CB}(t+j)$. The dynamic (single equation) simulation errors for CB and r_{CB} are found to be satisfactory (Friedman, 1977)[14] and provide a reasonably strong test of the model. However, outside sample static or dynamic prediction errors are not presented.

In the complete set of demand equations (for all holders of corporate bonds) the equilibrium long-term bond rate r_{CB} depends upon a wide variety of other interest rates, savings flows and outstanding *past* stocks of bonds and other assets held. The model solves for a term structure type of equation, that is the long rate depends upon short rates, in which asset stocks and flows also play a role. Friedman (1977) considers this to be a 'restricted' term structure equation as opposed to the more usual *unrestricted* equations, for example from the 'expectations hypothesis' which we meet in chapter 9. The latter often assume risk neutral asset holders with zero transactions costs, so that the long rate depends only upon current and future short rates.[15] These unrestricted models sometimes incorporate *ad hoc* asset terms as independent variables whereas Friedman's approach emphasizes that asset stocks appear in the equilibrium solution for r_{CB} because of the restrictions imposed and variables included in the demand functions. Friedman's algebraic solution for r_{CB} produces a *restricted* reduced-form term-structure equation, *consistent* with acceptable asset demand functions. Solving estimated demand functions for the implicit term structure therefore provides an alternative set of models to those usually discussed under the heading of the term structure of interest rates. We compare these approaches further in chapter 9.

Some extensions. Friedman and his associates have extended the optimal partial adjustment model in a number of interesting ways. Friedman and Roley (1979b) extend the basic model by considering alternative expectations generating mechanisms for the 'yield' variables r_k^e that determine the long run portfolio shares of the US corporate bond holders. The 'yield' on any asset consists of the 'running yield' and the *expected* capital gain (or loss) over the (one-period) holding period $(E_t g_{t+1})$. Friedman and Roley consider (a) unitary expectations $E_t g_{t+1} = 0$, where all information about future changes in interest rates is embodied in the current rate: a typical (but not necessary) implication of the 'efficient markets' literature; (b) rational expectations $g_{t+1} = E_t g_{t+1} + $

u_{t+1}, where u_{t+1} is 'white noise' and independent of any information available at time t or earlier; (c) autoregressive expectations

$$E_t g_{t+1} = \beta_0 + \sum_{i=0}^{\infty} \delta_i g_{t-i}$$

This formulation encompasses the adaptive–regressive hypotheses and may also be considered a 'weak form' rational expectations approach, if agents use only past capital gains in forming their expectations.

An instrumental variable (IV) procedure has to be used for the unitary expectations and rational expectations variants. The instruments chosen being (principal components of the) predetermined variables of the demand (and supply) curve. In the case of unitary expectations the IV procedure is required because of simultaneity; an additional reason in the case of rational expectations is the possibility of errors in variables bias when the actual capital gain is used to measure the expected capital gain (McCallum, 1976) (appendix A). Broadly speaking Friedman and Roleys' demand functions for US corporate bonds are similar to those reported above. However, the 'best' equations (in terms of within-sample fit, plausibility of coefficients, etc.) are those using the auto-regressive formulation for expected capital gains rather than the current interest rate alone or the 'weakly rational' variant.

In a further extension of the optimal partial adjustment model Friedman (1980a) 'linearizes' the risk-aversion model so that the desired asset proportions $\alpha_i^*(t)$ depend upon the variance $V_k(t)$ and covariance $C_k(t)$ of returns as well as the mean expected return r_k^e. The variance and covariances of returns are therefore assumed to vary over time. However, Friedman attempts to model only r_k and $V_k(t)$, the latter by means of a moving average of the variance of actual returns

$$V_k = \frac{1}{4} \sum_{t=0}^{4} (r_k(t) - \overline{r_k(t)})^2$$

where

$$\overline{r_k(t)} = \frac{1}{4} \sum_{t=0}^{4} r(t)$$

The expected rate of inflation and its variance are included (in rather an *ad hoc* manner) in the *set* of yields r_k. The expected yields are proxied by autoregressive schemes and McCallum-type 'weakly rational' expectations predictors. Generally, the former performed best in explaining the demand for various US financial assets by persons and the variance terms were not particularly successful. Using this model of asset demands together with a supply function (Friedman, 1979) (or an assumption of exogenous supply), we can solve for the equilibrium level of the long-term bond yield. As before this will depend on the short rates that influence the demand for long-term debt and lagged asset stocks. However, the variance of returns influences the equilibrium long rate in addition to these other variables. The implicit 'restricted' term structure equation therefore has the long depending upon short rates, expected inflation, lagged asset stocks and the variance of 'returns'. A simplified model of this kind, where the term structure is derived from asset demand functions which depend on variances an covariances of returns, is that of Buse (1975) and is discussed in chapter 9.

5.5.3 Examples of the mean-variance approach

Adding-up constraints are a consequence of the budget constraint that holdings of current period assets must sum to current period wealth. The mean-variance model adds an additional constraint, that of symmetry of cross yield effects, which is a consequence of the symmetry of the variance–covariance (matrix) of returns.

As we have seen, in practical applications of Friedman's optimal partial adjustment model, 'adding-up' or symmetry restrictions are not imposed since the demand for only *one* asset is considered. On the other hand, the Christofides (1980) approach imposes the adding-up constraints but the long-run equilibrium model is 'eclectic', and does not require symmetry. Economists enjoy testing models with strong a priori restrictions since these result from very specific theoretical models: the mean-variance model falls into this class. The model has been applied both in static form and assuming interdependent asset adjustment. Interest has centred on the sign of the 'own yield', the empirical validity of the symmetry effects and to a lesser extent perhaps, homogeneity of degree one in the scale variable.

Parkin (1970) applied the *static* mean-variance model to the behaviour of the UK discount houses and sought to explain their holdings of call money, Treasury bills, commercial bills and other short term assets using quarterly data over the period 1955–67. A number of interest rates are statistically significant and not all assets are found to be gross substitutes. However, symmetry is *imposed* on the regression estimates and this restriction is not tested.

Courakis (1975) re-estimated Parkin's (1970) equations for the discount houses using an efficient maximum likelihood technique and tested for symmetry and homogeneity. The latter restrictions do not hold and Courakis's unbiased estimates of the standard errors render far more coefficients as statistically insignificant than in Parkin's original study.

Parkin et al. (1970) apply the static mean variance model to the asset choices of UK commercial banks. White (1975) extended the model to incorporate endogenous advances and interdependent asset adjustment. The choice set of assets in these models included a number of short-term assets (for example Treasury bills, commercial bills, call money to the discount houses) with deposits and special deposits (a tax on banks) being exogenous. White and Parkin et al. impose symmetry, homogeneity and adding-up restrictions. The Parkin et al. static model performs reasonably well, statistically, over the 1950s and 1960s data, giving sensible interest rate effects. White's results which also include data for the early 1970s are rather mixed with some poorly determined interest rate coefficients and rather implausible lagged responses.

Berndt et al. (1980) re-examine the Parkin et al. study of UK commercial banks over the period 1954(1)–1967(1) using two different estimation methods.

The first method yields efficient (that is minimum variance) maximum likelihood estimators, assuming no serial correlation in the error terms. The second is an appropriate estimator in the presence of first-order *vector* autocorrelation (that is the error in one equation is related to its *own* past value and errors at time $t-1$ in the *other* asset demand equations). They test the sensitivity of the parameter estimates and the validity of the symmetry and homogeneity restrictions under these more sophisticated estimation procedures. The symmetry and homogeneity restrictions do not hold under the first estimation technique but do under the second. However, parameter estimates are very different from those of Parkin et al. Serial correlation is found in the residuals (although the common factor test is not undertaken) but not *vector* autocorrelation. (This result indicates that the use of a dynamic rather than static model might be more appropriate, see Anderson and Blundell (1982)).

Bewley (1981) repeats the exercise done by White (1975) on UK banks but allows advances to be endogenous only when severe lending controls were *not* in operation. Using monthly data (1966–71), Bewley finds statistically significant interest rate effects, evidence in favour of interdependent asset disequilibrium and very short lag responses (the mean lag for bank advances for a change in the 'own rate' is, somewhat implausibly, found to be only one month). Liquid assets tend to be substitutes with each other while there is some complementarity between liquid assets and illiquid assets such as long-term bonds. For example, a rise in the Treasury bill rate induces a switch from call loans and commercial bills into Treasury bills but an increase in holdings of government bonds. There are some perverse 'own rate' effects, namely for government bonds and advances.

Tests of symmetry restrictions using the error feedback type of adjustment model (Anderson and Blundell, 1982) are in their infancy and have not yet been applied to systems of asset demand equations.

5.5.4   *Summary*

The interdependent asset demand approach has proved particularly successful when applied to the asset demand functions of financial intermediaries such as banks, insurance companies and pension funds. The latter purchase substantial amounts of government debt and hence their behaviour influences the equilibrium money stock: an issue we take up in chapters 7 and 8.

It does appear that for some assets, disequilibria in 'other' asset stocks influence their speed of adjustment. These 'other' asset stocks that appear in the equation are lagged only one period but taken together as a system they allow a flexible lag response. The latter is obtained in 'single equation' studies discussed in section 5.4 only by higher order lags on a *single* dependent variable. However, the latter are not well grounded in theory and the independent adjustment equation would seem preferable on these grounds.

Evidence on the validity of the symmetry restrictions on asset returns in the mean-variance model is mixed but empirical evidence does seem to favour the inclusion of *expected* returns in asset demand functions.

5.6 FURTHER ISSUES IN THE ESTIMATION OF ASSET
DEMAND FUNCTIONS

There are some interesting empirical approaches that we have not yet touched upon but are nevertheless worthy of mention. Since our exposition will be brief the reader may like to follow up some of the issues raised.

One response to the apparent instability in the demand for money in the 1970s was to assume that an incorrect functional form had been used, another was to assume that the parameters of the demand function might vary *systematically* over time. The former led to the application of the Box–Cox transformation to asset demand functions which allows the linear and log linear functional forms to emerge as special cases.

In all the empirical work cited above we have (implicitly) assumed that asset markets are continuously in equilibrium. The 'non-clearing markets' approach eschews this assumption and we briefly discuss these models below. We take up the issue of 'disequilibrium markets' again in the next chapter.

The final area we look at in this section is the role of foreign interest rates in the demand for money. The degree of asset substitutability plays an important role in exchange rate overshooting models (Dornbusch, 1976). We are only able to examine currency substitution. As capital markets become more open, with the abolition of exchange controls, intercountry asset flows may become increasingly important. The monetary implications of integrated capital markets are taken up in chapter 8 on the Euromarkets.

5.6.1 *Different functional forms*

Asset demand functions are frequently estimated assuming a linear or log linear relationship between the variables. Generally, economic theory gives little indication of the correct functional form. But we may be worried that 'problems' with our equation, for example serial correlation in the errors or coefficient instability in different samples, are caused by an inappropriate functional form.

Rather than running a multitude of regressions, one for each functional form, we may apply the Box–Cox power transformation which allows some 'common' functional forms to emerge as special cases. The Box–Cox transformation of a variable, say X_t, is

$$X_t^\lambda = \frac{X_t^\lambda - 1}{\lambda} \quad \lambda \neq 0, X_t > 0 \tag{5.13}$$

The generalized Box–Cox regression equation for a three-variable model (with a different 'power transformation' on the interest rate) is

$$M_t^\lambda = \beta_0 + \beta_1 Y_t^\lambda + \beta_2 r^\phi \tag{5.14}$$

Coefficient estimates of β_0, β_1, β_2, λ and ϕ are obtained by an appropriate maximum likelihood procedure and the special cases are:

$\lambda = 1, \phi = 1$ linear function

$\lambda = 0, \phi = 0$ log linear function[16]

$\lambda = 0, \phi = 1$ log linear in Y, semi-log in r

$\lambda \neq 0, \phi \neq 1$ a hybrid power function ('general functional form')

If the estimate of λ and ϕ are close to unity or zero then a linear or log linear function is acceptable. If $\lambda \neq 0 \neq 1$, the economic interpretation of the short-run coefficients is problematic. However, the long-run elasticity can still be calculated using, for example, $\beta_1 (X_t/Y_t)^\lambda$ where (X/Y) is usually evaluated at the sample mean of the variables.

Mills (1978) and Oxley (1983) provide estimates of the UK demand for broad and narrow money. A conventional partial adjustment model is used with income and the interest rate, as well as the lagged dependent variable, being subject to the Box–Cox transformation. For M1 over the period 1963 to 1974(4) Mills finds that $\lambda = 0$ and $\phi = 1$ and hence the often used functional form

$$\ln\left(\frac{M}{P}\right) = b_0 + b_1 \ln Y + b_2 r + b_3 \ln\left(\frac{M}{P}\right)_{t-1} \tag{5.15}$$

is appropriate. Oxley finds that the 'general functional form' ($\lambda = -0.8$) fits best for broad money (1963–1979(4)) and is more stable than any of the simpler functions.

The results on US data are adequately summarized by Spitzer (1976, 1977). The double logarithmic functional form is found to be acceptable in single equation studies but the general functional form is superior in a simultaneous system.

For the UK, it appears that one way of obtaining more stable long-run income and interest rate elasticities for broad money is to use a general functional form of the Box–Cox type rather than impose a linear or log linear function. However, the models considered for the test of alternative functional forms are rather restrictive in their lag structure (that is a first-order lagged dependent variable only) and in the choice of independent variables (for example no wealth, or expected capital gains variables), and it may be that a log linear or linear functional form may be appropriate with a more elaborate underlying demand for money function.

5.6.2   *Stochastic parameters*

A rather sophisticated estimation approach to the problem of parameter instability is to assume that the parameters are stochastic rather than constant. This avoids assuming one has a priori knowledge of the point in time when parameter shifts occur. Under this approach the econometric relationship is assumed to be stable if the parameters are not subject to *permanent* changes over time. For example in the Cooley-Prescot (Cooley and Prescott, 1973) variable parameter model

$$Y_t = \beta_t X_t \tag{5.16}$$

β_t is assumed to be adaptive over time, and subject to permanent and transitory changes

$$\beta_t = \beta_t^P + u_t \tag{5.17}$$

$$\beta_t^P = \beta_{t-1}^P + v_t \tag{5.18}$$

The error u_t is a measure of the transitory component of β_t and the permanent component β_t^P follows a random walk. A more general model of this type is the Kalman filter (Chow, 1984). These models produce an estimate of β_t (which varies over time) and one may test to see if β_t is generated by a stable stochastic process (that is β_t does not tend to move towards plus or minus infinity). Lack of the appropriate computer software has probably prevented widespread use of these variable parameters approaches but they are certainly appealing if one believes that people learn from experience and *slowly* change their behaviour accordingly.

Laumas (1978) applies the above method to the demand for broad and narrow money in the UK over two separate data periods – a pre- and post-competition and control (CCC) period – using a conventional partial adjustment demand for money function. *Within* both periods the stochastic behaviour of the parameters is stable but there is a substantial difference in the elasticities in the two sub-periods for both narrow and broad money. The shift in parameter values in 1971(3) when CCC was introduced is therefore left unexplained.

5.6.3 *Non clearing markets*

The non-clearing markets approach has not been widely applied to the demand (and supply) for assets, partly, no doubt, because of technical difficulties in the proposed estimation techniques (Bowden, 1978). The model is most frequently applied to the bank credit (advances) market and the (house) mortgage market where rationing is thought at times to be pervasive. Initially, the method used split the data set into points that should lie on the demand curve and those that should lie on the supply curve using the 'min-condition'.

For example, if the bank lending rate is increasing, the market is assumed to be in excess demand and one would assume that the data points for bank advances over this period lie on the supply curve (that is the minimum of desired or 'notional' supply or demand). Separate supply and demand curves may then be estimated (Fair and Jaffee, 1972). In a variant on this approach, Spencer and Mowl (1978) for UK bank lending assume that observed data points on advances are a weighted average of the notional (desired) demand and supply functions with the weights depending on the degree of excess demand in the market. This pioneering work for the UK was not wholly successful. The supply curve assumed was rather simple (it did not include any relative interest rates) and for industrial and commercial companies they find that the 'weights' are independent of the degree of excess demand. (For US evidence on bank lending see Laffont and Garcia (1977).)

Smith and Brainard (1982) apply a disequilibrium model to US savings and loan association asset holdings, and split the data according to the min-side condition. However, the disequilibrium results are little different from those that assume demand and supply are always in equilibrium.

Technical econometric difficulties apart, the results from disequilibrium studies of the demand for (and supply) of assets tentatively support the view that asset markets clear (within the data period of observation). Precisely how such markets clear remains an open question. The usual assumption is that interest rates adjust instantaneously to clear the market. For credit markets non-price or quality factors (for example collateral, pay back period) might clear the market and micro-theoretic models have recently been developed in this area (Fried and Howitt (1980). An alternative approach assumes that short-term assets and flexible lines of credit act as a buffer stock against unexpected shocks. Such assets are willing held, at least initially, at unchanged interest rates, thus obviating the need for short-run changes in the 'price' of such assets. We investigate this promising line of enquiry in section 6.4.

5.6.4   *Foreign assets*

In the empirical literature to date, there are no major new estimation or theoretical problems that arise when foreign assets are considered as part of the choice set. The equilibrium demand for domestic money by domestic residents is assumed to fall if the return to foreign assets increases. Movements out of domestic money could be into foreign bonds and foreign currency (where the latter is usually assumed to have a zero return in its *own* currency). The return to foreign bonds in terms of domestic currency is the foreign yield r^* plus the expected (percentage) appreciation in the foreign currency $\dot{s}^e$ over the holding period. The response of domestic money to a change in $r^* + \dot{s}^e$ is therefore a measure of the degree of capital mobility. The rate of return to holding foreign currency is the expected appreciation of the foreign currency $\dot{s}^e$ (as the 'foreign' money is assumed to earn zero interest). The responsiveness of domestic currency to changes in s^e measures the degree of currency substitution.

$\dot{s}^e$ is equal to $(s_{t+1}^e - s_t)/s_t$ where s_t is the spot exchange rate at time t in units of domestic per unit of foreign currency and s_{t+1}^e is the spot rate expected to prevail at time $t + 1$ based on information available at time t. Under the efficient markets hypothesis the expected spot rate may be measured by the one-period forward exchange rate, and $\dot{s}_t^e$ then equals the forward premium/discount. Alternatively, assuming weakly rational expectations (McCallum, 1976) the expected spot rate is determined by certain predetermined variables in the economy (for example lagged own value, lagged money supply etc.); an 'instrument' for s_{t+1}^e may then be obtained as predictions from such an equation (see section 4.3.3 for a resumé of this approach). Under the assumption of unitary expectations, this is $\dot{s}_{t+1}^e = 0$, only the foreign interest rate enters the demand function for the domestic asset.

The demand for domestic money incorporating foreign interest rate variables may therefore be written as equation 5.19.

In equation 5.19 r is the yield on domestic assets other than money, and we have assumed a first-order partial adjustment mechanism.

$$\ln\left(\frac{M}{P}\right) = \beta_0 + \beta_1 \ln Y - \beta_2 r - \beta_3(r^* + \mathring{s}^e_{t+1})$$

$$- \beta_4 \mathring{s}^e_{t+1} + \beta_5 \ln\left(\frac{M}{P}\right)_{t-1} \tag{5.19}$$

There has not been a great deal of work incorporating foreign variables in domestic demand for money functions. Hamberger (1977) assumes $\mathring{s}^e_{t+1} = 0$ and adds only a representative foreign interest rate to the demand for (narrow) money functions for Germany and the UK. The results over the period 1963–72 are rather mixed but do support some substitutability between domestic money and foreign assets for both countries in the 1970s.

Cuddington (1983) summarizes much of the recent work in this area and applies the model of equation (5.19) using 1960s and 1970s data for the UK, Canada, US and Germany, both for narrow and broad money aggregates. s^e_{t+1} is measured by the three-month forward rate and in principle one can estimate capital mobility effects β_3 and currency substitution effects β_4. The results even at face value are a little disappointing as a statistically significant value for $\beta_3 (<0)$ is only obtained for the US whilst only Germany shows some evidence of currency substitution $\beta_4 < 0$. The high multicollinearity between $(r^* + \mathring{s}^e_{t+1})$ and $\mathring{s}^e_{t+1}$ masks the separate effect of these two variables when both are included in the regression. The estimated equations suffer from imposing an instantaneous unit price level elasticity, and a common factor (autocorrelation) restriction, neither of which is tested against the data: no attempt to correct for possible simultaneous equations bias is undertaken.

One can also look at the substitutability between foreign and domestic assets by focusing on *domestic* holdings of *foreign* currency bank deposits. For the UK, McKenzie and Thomas (1984) assume that holdings of foreign currency deposits (in UK banks) by UK residents M^F depends positively on the covered (Eurodollar) interest rate r^{cf} negatively on the opportunity cost as measured by the UK commercial bill r^c and the interest rate on sterling deposits r^d, and positively on the level of GDP, Y. They test down from a general ADL model and obtain a data acceptable parsimonious equation 1964(3)–1979(4) whose long-run static equilibrium solution is

$$m^F_t = -10.1r^c - 9.2r^d + 14r^{cf} + 6.9y \tag{5.20}$$
$$\quad\;\; (0.8) \quad (1.1) \quad\;\; (3.5)\;\;(15.9)$$

where m and y are in logarithms. Their ADL representation has desirable diagnostics (R^2, LM, CH, HF) but the long-run effect of the domestic interest rate terms are rather poorly determined. The long-run covered 'own rate' and GDP provide most of the statistical explanation. By using the covered Eurodollar rate and the level of domestic output, we implicitly assume that foreign currency deposits will ultimately finance domestic transactions, but with multinational companies this seems unlikely to be the case. The results are an interesting first step in modelling foreign currency holdings.

Overall it is probably reasonable to conclude that 'foreign variables' do not appear to have had a statistically well-determined effect on the demand for 'domestic money' to date.

5.7 SUMMARY

In this chapter we have provided empirical illustrations of the various asset demand models discussed in previous chapters. Our survey is far from exhaustive, and therefore we only draw broad general conclusions.

A transactions variable influences the demand for narrow and broad money: this is *broadly* consistent with the inventory model (but the square root law of the simple inventory model does not hold). The impact of wealth on the demand for money is less well established because of data and measurement problems. It does appear as if *relative* interest rates influence asset demands and there is some evidence that *expected* yields (including capital gains) influence asset choice when 'risky' assets form part of the portfolio. Expected yields seem to be best approximated by 'weakly rational' predictors rather than by adaptive expectations. Time varying variances and covariances of expected returns do not appear to have a major impact on asset demands.

Foreign interest rates do not appear to have a well-determined influence on domestic asset demands but with the relaxation of exchange controls and the free mobility of capital these may become of greater importance in the future.

Single equation studies using quarterly data favour the use of a more flexible lag structure than first-order partial adjustment (except perhaps for narrow money). The ADL–EFE approach has proved successful in modelling lag structures since it allows a very flexible lag response.

Instability in the demand for broad money in the UK in the 1970s is evident and a (CCC) dummy variable appears to be one (very *ad hoc*) method of coping with this problem: use of alternative functional forms and variable parameter models have only been moderately successful.

In testing our models of the demand for assets we have frequently undertaken a joint hypothesis consisting of the long-run equilibrium theory, an adjustment hypothesis and a hypothesis about the formation of expectations. A poor empirical performance of an equation could be due to the failure of one or all of these hypotheses (Cross, 1982). There is a further difficulty in testing some of our theories of the demand for money: *aggregate* money demand is likely to comprise transactions, precautionary and risk-aversion motives and it is therefore difficult to test any one of these theories in isolation. We have concentrated on tests of highly aggregative relationships although disaggregated studies of the demand for money by firms and persons have if anything proved to be even less successful than aggregate relationships (see Price (1972) for the UK and Goldfeld (1973) for the US).

There have been few explicit tests of the precautionary demand model because of problems in measuring the variance of net receipts. The mean-variance model emphasizes the importance of *expected* returns and this variable has proved reasonably successful in some studies of the demand for money (Grice and Bennett, 1984), long-term government debt (Spencer, 1981; Cuthbertson, 1983) and for corporate bonds (Friedman, 1980b) using 'weakly rational' predictors. The mean-variance model is a systems model and ideally should be tested within a *set* of asset demand equations, one of the strongest ('system') predictions being the symmetry of cross interest rate effects. Formal tests of the mean-variance model (for the UK discount houses and commercial banks, and for US savings and loan associations) are reported but the statistical validity of the symmetry property is a contentious one.

'Eclectic models' using interdependent asset demands have proved reasonably successful in determining the demand for money and other assets. These models have the advantage of allowing a flexible lag response (by including lagged 'other' asset stocks as independent variables) and force one to consider the interaction between different assets in the portfolio. If money is deemed to be an interest bearing risky asset (that is the holding period differs from the term to maturity of 'money' – 'broad' money could be so considered) then the demand for 'money' is equivalent to the demand for any other risky asset. On the other hand if money is a 'safe' asset (for example sight deposit) then it is the residual asset in the 'mean-variance' portfolio and depends on all the variables that appear in all the other demand functions for risky assets. We have not explicitly considered this role for money but do so in section 6.4 on buffer-stock money and in section 10.2 on 'complete' financial models.

Testing asset demand functions has become more sophisticated and our knowledge of the behaviour of the demand for money and other assets is vastly improved. We hope that this chapter has made the reader aware of difficulties and possible pitfalls involved in testing theories. One should always cast a critical eye over published empirical results since 'data mining' is a recurrent disease amongst some economists. It is not hard to see why – there is as yet no journal entitled 'Fruitful Failures in Applied Economics'.

There are two crucial assumptions in the above empirical models (except the disequilibrium approach). First, we have usually implicitly assumed that the actual money supply is always equal to the short-run desired demand for money. Second it is often assumed that expected income may be adequately modelled by the 'backward looking' first-order adaptive expectations hypothesis. In the next chapter we take up these two issues from a theoretical and empirical standpoint. The first issue concerns the role of money as a 'buffer stock' and the second invites the use of forward looking variables in the demand for money function.

NOTES

1   The Box–Pierce portmanteau test (Box and Pierce, 1970) for autocorrelation RC(p), is distributed asymptotically as central chi-squared with p degrees of freedom (where p is the order of autocorrelation) under the null of no serial correlation in the error terms (Harvey, 1981). The Lagrange multiplier LM(p) statistic is also distributed asymptotically as a chi-squared distribution under the null (Godfrey, 1978a, 1978b). In small samples and where the equation contains a lagged dependent variable the LM statistic appears to be the most useful test of serial correlation. If RC or LM exceed the critical value from the chi-squared distribution then we reject the null of no serial correlation in the errors. The Durbin–Watson (dw) statistic for first-order serial correlation is inconsistent in the presence of a lagged dependent variable.

CH(n_1, n_2) is the Chow test for parameter stability (constancy) where n_2 is the degrees of freedom in the 'first' sample period and n_1 is the number of additional data points used to test the stability of the equation. CH has an F-distribution with (n_1, n_2) degrees of freedom under the null of constant parameters in the two sample periods. The Hendry forecast test HF compares the within-sample errors SE with the outside-sample forecast errors f_t

$$HF(n_2) = \left[\frac{1}{(SE)^2} \sum_{n_2} f_t^2 \right]$$

where n_2 is the number of outside-sample data points and $f_t = (y - \hat{y})_t$, $\hat{y}$ are the one-step ahead predictions (forecasts) over the 'outside sample' data points using the coefficient estimates from the regression equation run only on the within-sample data points n^*. The 'within-sample' equation has a standard error SE and y is the actual value of the dependent variable in the outside-sample data. For large n^*, HF is distributed as a χ^2 distribution with n_2 degrees of freedom under the assumption of constant parameters (and constant error variances in the two-data periods). HF $> X_c^2$ (5%) – the critical value – therefore indicates a poor forecasting equation, which may be due to instability in the parameter estimates. Kiviet (1981) has shown that the HF test rejects too often even if the parameters are constant across the two samples. It therefore cannot be used as a test of parameter constancy but remains a useful pormanteau statistic for assessing outside sample forecast accuracy.

2 The dynamic equilibrium solution for a constant growth rate of $\Delta \ln Y = g$ is $\ln(M/PY) = -1.4g - 3.7 \, \Delta \ln P - 0.36r - 0.3$. This strong dependence of M1 on the growth of Y is a common feature of lag models. Currie (1981) indicates that one ought to test to see if the growth effect may be constrained to zero, if it is not acceptable on a priori grounds. *Steady* growth is not a feature of the data and therefore we cannot, perhaps, expect such growth effects to be plausible. See appendix A and section 4.4.3 for further details.

3 See appendix A for the calculation of dynamic equilibrium solutions. The dynamic solution given by Hendry and Mizon (1978) contains 'g terms' in ($g_p - g_m$) but substitution of $g_m = g_p + 1.6 g_y$ yields the solution given in the text.

4 In a complementary study, Grice and Bennett (1984) also consider estimates of UK transactions balances M1 and wider aggregates than £M3, for example PSL2 which includes building society deposits. Although wealth effects are statistically significant in these equations the results are somewhat unsatisfactory for other economic and statistical reasons.

5 On the whole the statistical properties of the equation are good. There is no sign of serial correlation in the residuals according to the LM test, the equation passes the Hendry forecast test (HF) and the Chow test (CH) for parameter stability. The potentially endogenous 'change in wealth' term is estimated using instrumental variables and the IE statistic indicates that the errors are independent of the instruments used.

6 Although an important financial variable in the control of the money supply, examples of single equation studies of the demand for government debt are relatively scarce. Masson (1978) provides an interesting study of the demand for long- and short-term government debt using Canadian data. He finds statistically significant and relatively large substitution effects between shorts and longs.

7 The equation passes the usual diagnostic tests, gives similar results when estimated by instrumental variables and forecasts reasonably well outside its sample period of estimation (Cuthbertson, 1985a).

8 One can point to possible deficiencies in these results. The dw statistic is biased in the presence of lagged dependent variables and any serial correlation implies inconsistent parameter estimates. Simultaneity bias may be a problem in which case OLS again gives inconsistent parameter estimates. The econometric cognoscenti might like to note that there would be no efficiency gain from using Zellner's (1962) SURE or the 3SLS estimator since all the equations contain the same set of independent variables.

9 Although, note that it may be inadvisable to assume that demand equations estimated under conditions of perfectly elastic supply (at the going interest rate) remain unchanged/stable when asset supplies become exogenous. This is a form of the Lucas (1976) critique again.

10 Adding one additional yield variable r_k to a set of n assets adds an additional n covariances (as well as one variance).

11 Smith and Brainard (1976) reduce the number of 'covariance priors' by assuming that they are the same for each equation ('exchangeability'). Smith (1980) provides an alternative method.

12 Friedman finds that the own adjustment coefficient is larger for pension funds than for households indicating a speedier short-run adjustment response of the former. This is to be expected since pension funds are very active in the market.

13 The starred variable in equation (5.12) is estimated using instrumental variables. Also the dw statistic is biased and is an inadequate test for autocorrelation.

14 This procedure was repeated with two *endogenous* supply equations and the 'tracking' of equilibrium values of CB and r_{CB} improved.

15 Friedman's asset demand equations assume risk *aversion* (in determining the desired portfolio shares) and incorporate adjustment cost parameters.

16 For any variable $z(> 0)$ we have

$$z^\lambda = \exp(\log z^\lambda) = \exp(\lambda \log z)$$

$$= 1 + \lambda \log z + \frac{1}{2!}(\lambda \log z)^2 + \frac{1}{3!}(\lambda \log z)^3 + \ldots$$

Hence

$$\frac{(Y_i^\lambda - 1)}{\lambda} = \frac{1}{\lambda}\left[1 + \lambda \log Y_i + \frac{1}{2!}(\lambda \log Y_i)^2 + \ldots - 1\right]$$

$$= \log Y_i + \frac{\lambda}{2!}(\log Y_i)^2 + \ldots$$

For $\lambda = 0$ (and $Y_i > 0$) it follows that $(Y^\lambda - 1)/\lambda = \log Y_i$.

6

Outstanding Problems and Recent Developments on the Demand for Assets

6.1 INTRODUCTION

A number of problems have emerged in our discussion of empirical work on the demand for assets, particularly the demand for money. The demand for broad money appears to have been unstable in the 1970s in a number of countries, and the lag response of money demand to changes in income and interest rates sometimes appears to be implausibly long. As we shall see below, the converse of the latter problem is that these demand for money functions predict acute overshooting of, say, the interest rate in response to exogenous changes in the money supply. We have analysed a number of attempts to solve these problems including more sophisticated estimation techniques, more flexible lag structures, alternative functional forms, stochastic parameter models, addition of variables such as the own rate on money, the riskiness of bonds, the expected rate of inflation and (non-human) wealth into the demand function. Some of these efforts have proved moderately successful but there certainly appears room for improvement.

In the recent literature, there have been three broad attempts to improve our understanding of the demand for assets. Two of the methods recognize that in the *aggregate,* examination of the demand for assets cannot avoid detailed consideration of the supply of assets. The first method considers the possibility of disequilibria in assets markets. We have alluded to this possibility already with respect to credit markets (section 5.6) and here we shall discuss some disequilibrium methods that have been applied to the demand for money. The second method, which we refer to as buffer-stock money (BSM), recognizes that individuals' desired money holdings may comprise an expected (or planned) component and an unexpected or transitory component. The former is governed by planned or expected levels of transactions and rates of return (as discussed in chapters 2, 3 and 4), while the latter are temporary holdings caused by unexpected 'shocks' such as unexpected receipts or disbursements. There is a clear analogy with the treatment of transitory and permanent consumption in Friedman's permanent income hypothesis of the consumption function, but the reader should note that the analogy is by no means exact.

BSM is often referred to as 'disequilibrium money' but we shall clearly differentiate between the two concepts. Both approaches embody the view that it may be incorrect to equate the desired short-run demand for money M_t^d, discussed in chapter 4, with the actual money supply in circulation M_t. Put at its simplest, the disequilibrium model explicitly denies that $M_t = M_t^d$, while the buffer-stock model assumes that $M_t = M_t^d + M_t^T$, where M_t^T are transitory or 'buffer-stock' holdings of money. If the money supply is endogenous and passively responds to changes in demand, then it may be correct to equate desired money holdings in the aggregate to the actual money supply as in the conventional approach. (Of course, it is always the case that the *individual* can achieve his desired money balances.) However, when there is an unexpected shift in the money supply, independent of changes in the demand for money, then, in the aggregate, either the money market may not clear in the current period and disequilibrium prevails, or individuals may experience an unexpected change in their incomes and 'buffer-stock' holdings of money ensue. It is when independent changes in the money supply take place that the disequilibrium model or the BSM approach yield conclusions that differ from the conventional demand for money models of previous chapters. Hence, these two approaches may explain some of the instability in conventional demand for money functions which tended to appear in the 1970s when shocks to the supply of money are thought to have increased.

The third area of recent research we discuss centres on the role of expectations. We have already analysed the role of expected returns in the demand for assets and we now broaden this to include expectations about future transactions. The adaptive expectations hypothesis of the determination of expected income (transactions) results in lags in the demand for money function. It seems intuitively plausible that desired money balances today depend upon expectations formed today about *future* transactions. If so, earlier empirical models of the demand for money may appear unstable because they omit such forward looking variables. In the conventional model, a change in current income has a fixed impact on money demand. If current income influences expectations of future income and the latter affects the demand for money, then the response of the demand for money is allowed to be much more flexible. It turns out that if we generalize the one period quadratic cost model of partial adjustment (section 4.2) to encompass a *multiperiod* optimization, then future values of the determinants of the demand for money enter the estimating equation. With the advent of rational expectations, these forward looking models are being used in many areas of macroeconomic modelling and our analysis of the multiperiod quadratic cost model applied to the demand for money, provides a useful introduction to this class of models.

In the multiperiod quadratic cost model the desired short-run demand for money depends on expected future values of the independent variables. We can add *current* period *unanticipated* changes in the independent variables to this model in a somewhat *ad hoc* fashion. However, with a rather simple modification to the multiperiod quadratic cost model, we can interpret it as a buffer-stock approach, with *forward* looking behaviour as regards expected shocks to money balances. This provides an optimizing microeconomic justification for the more intuitive buffer-stock models used in the empirical literature to date.

This chapter is organized as follows. First, we consider some of the criticisms directed at conventional demand for money functions when the money supply changes independently from the demand for money. We discuss in section 6.2, *inter alia*, the asymmetric response of agents to changes in the *determinants* of the demand for money on the one hand, and to changes in the supply of money on the other. This involves considering the overshooting problem and the possible volatility in the response of interest rates to an exogenous money supply policy: a theme taken up again in the chapter on the supply of money. Next, in section 6.3, we clarify the meaning of disequilibrium and briefly look at attempts to 'solve' the apparent instability in the demand for money using this approach. In the main part of this chapter we present an intuitive approach to buffer-stock money and discuss some empirical results. Finally, we discuss the microeconomic basis for the inclusion of forward looking variables in asset demand functions and a development of this type of model to encompass the buffer stock approach.

6.2   DEFICIENCIES IN CONVENTIONAL DEMAND FOR MONEY FUNCTIONS

In conventional demand for money functions, lags appear either because of adjustment costs (partial adjustment, EFE) or adaptive expectations, or both. If the money supply responds passively to changes in demand, then these models make reasonable sense, but if the money supply changes independently of demand, the implications are rather alarming. Severe overshooting in income, interest rates and real output are possible and the equations involve a peculiar asymmetry in the speed of response of certain variables.

Consider, for example, a long-run (static) desired demand for money function in real terms $\tilde{m}^*$ of the form

$$\tilde{m}^* = (m^* - p_t) = a_0 + a_1 y_t^p - a_2 r_t \tag{6.1}$$

where m_t^*, p_t, y_t^p are (the logarithm of) the desired nominal money stock, the price level and (permanent) income respectively and r_t is 'the' rate of interest. The short-run equilibrium demand may then be determined either by assuming costs of adjustment or by introducing adaptive expectations. Consider first, partial adjustment.

Real partial adjustment. Partial adjustment, in *real* terms, assumes the short-run desired demand for money in real terms $\tilde{m}^d$ adjusts by a fraction of the discrepancy between the desired long-run real demand $\tilde{m}^*$ and last period's short run demand $\tilde{m}_{t-1}^d$

$$\tilde{m}_t^d - \tilde{m}_{t-1}^d = \gamma(\tilde{m}_t^* - \tilde{m}_{t-1}^d) \quad 0 < \gamma < 1 \tag{6.2}$$

For an *individual*, the desired short-run demand can always be achieved but we may commit a fallacy of composition if we apply the partial adjustment model to aggregate data. In empirical work, a crucial but often unstated assumption is invoked, namely that the short-run desired demand for money $\tilde{m}_t^d$, equals the actual real money stock $\tilde{m}_t$ (the 'money supply' in official statistics) in all time periods. When applied to *aggregate* data, the partial adjustment model assumes that the money supply always passively responds to any changes in the (short-run) desired demand for money. Now this assumption may be true for some definitions of money (for example sight deposits) but not necessarily for broad money, in all time periods. A policy of fixing interest rates or the exchange rate (as frequently occurred in the 1960s) may imply that the supply of broad money adjusts to demand. However, a switch from government bonds to other *non-money* assets would imply an increase in the money supply (via the PSBR identity), independently of the demand for money even under a pegged interest rate policy. Further, we do not require the money supply to be exogenous and controlled by the authorities in order that supply moves *independently* of demand. As we see in the chapter on the money supply, commercial banks can institute independent changes in the money supply (see also Brunner and Meltzer (1976)) and changes in the government's borrowing requirement may also provide shocks to the money supply. Thus, particularly under floating exchange rates, it would appear that the conditions required to validly apply the partial adjustment model to actual *aggregate* money balances are unlikely to be met in all time periods.

In defence of the partial adjustment model it could be argued that the *real* money stock is always demand determined even if the *nominal* money stock is exogenous. This would be the case if the current period price level is sufficiently flexible: any change in the determinants of the real demand for money (that is y^p and r) lead to an equilibrating change in the current price level and hence the *real* money supply. This appears to be an unrealistic defence of the partial adjustment model since many prices that make up the aggregate price level are 'sticky' in the short run.

The partial adjustment model yields *partial* adjustment only when the money supply is endogenous. Combining (6.1) and (6.2) (with $y^p = y_t$ for convenience) we have

$$\tilde{m}_t^d = \gamma a_0 + \gamma a_1 y_t - \gamma a_2 r_t + (1 - \gamma) \tilde{m}_{t-1}^d \qquad (6.3)$$

The short-run response of $\tilde{m}^d$ to, say, y_t is γa_1 and the long-run response is greater, being a_1. However, there is a curious asymmetry of response, even when the money supply is considered endogenous. We can write $\tilde{m}_t^d = m_t^d - p_t$ where m_t^d is short-run desired *nominal* money balances (which are equal to the money supply by assumption). Hence, although m_t^d responds with a *lag* to changes in y and r, it responds immediately to, and fully to, a change in the price level.

The implications of the partial adjustment approach when used in a model where the money supply is taken to be exogenous are even more startling.[1] It becomes an overshooting model rather than a partial adjustment model! To see this, note that putting $m_t^s = m_t^d$ for market clearing in the partial adjustment equation (6.2) (holding the price level and income constant) and differentiating, yields $\partial m^*/\partial m^s = \gamma^{-1}$ which is greater than one for $0 < \gamma < 1$. (The long run response is unity.) Equivalently, equation (6.3) gives $\partial r_t/\partial \tilde{m}_t^s = -1/\gamma a_2$. If current period real output and the price level are 'sticky' and we take $\gamma = 0.1$ as a representative empirical result, then the interest rate overshoots its long-run response by a factor of 10! It is not the overshooting *per se* that is the problem but the improbable size of the overshooting. (Note that overshooting occurs in y, if r and p are assumed to be sticky.) Relaxation of the assumption that p and y are fixed, allows a more moderate overshoot in r. In a more complete model that also includes an IS curve containing the current period interest rate and a Phillips curve relating p_t to y_t, overshooting or undershooting in the endogenous variables y, p and r is possible depending upon the size of the coefficients in the whole model. However, the smaller the interest elasticity of aggregate demand and the price response to output, the more likely it is that overshooting will occur. Thus, although overshooting is likely to be substantial when an exogenous money supply is applied to the partial adjustment model, this need not necessarily be the case.[2]

With an exogenous money supply, the *real* partial adjustment model still retains its asymmetrical response with respect to p_t as compared with y_t and r_t. A 1 per cent increase in the nominal money supply m_t^s leads to a 1 per cent increase in p_t, *ceteris paribus*, but an overshoot in r_t and y_t, *ceteris paribus*. The former result might be accepted by rational expectations monetarists if the increase in the money supply were anticipated but not if the increase were unanticipated.

6.2.1 *Nominal partial adjustment*

The nominal partial adjustment model

$$m^d = \gamma m^* + (1 - \gamma) m_{-1}$$

$$= \gamma(a_0 + a_1 y - a_2 r + p) + (1 - \gamma) m_{-1} \tag{6.4}$$

avoids the asymmetry in the response of the desired short-run demand for money to changes in y, r and p. However, it is easily seen from (6.4) that overshooting occurs for all three variables, *ceteris paribus*, when the money supply is exogenous.

Laidler (1982) criticizes the *logical* validity of this overshooting result when the lagged dependent variable is interpreted as representing individual adjustment costs (whether 'real' or 'nominal'). For illustration consider the nominal partial adjustment model with y and r held constant. Adjustment costs imply that the individual changes his demand for goods by less than he would in the absence of such costs, when he receives additions to his money holdings. 'Yet we are asked to believe that the aggregate effect of this *smaller* increase in demand, this *weaker* real balance effect, is to cause the price level to change by a *greater* amount than it otherwise would' (Laidler, 1982, p. 50). According to Laidler this is 'obvious nonsense' and one has to agree. The mathematics may be made consistent with the above by noting that with an *exogenous* money supply the individual's balances at the beginning of his decision period equal the actual *current* money supply m and not m_{-1}. Replacing the latter by the former in (6.4) yields $dp/dm = 1$: the 'overshoot effect' is non-existent and the individual is always on the long-run demand function even in the presence of adjustment costs.

6.2.2 *Adaptive expectations*

Adaptive expectations allows lagged money balances to appear as an independent variable in the demand for money function (section 4.3.1). Mathematically this also produces 'overshooting' in say *current* real income, *ceteris paribus*. However, unlike the partial adjustment case discussed above, there is no logical inconsistency here. An exogenous change in the money supply *must* increase permanent income sufficiently to yield an equal increase the desired long-run demand for money. However, because permanent income changes by only a fraction of *current* income, the latter must 'overshoot' its long-run value.

It must be remarked, however, that the adaptive expectations model does not always provide a good statistical 'fit' and as we have seen it provides a 'rational' forecasting method only in rather restrictive circumstances.

6.2.3 'Sticky prices'

If we cannot logically accept the partial adjustment explanation of the presence of a lagged dependent variable in the demand for money function, when the money supply is autonomous, then what does this variable (which works very well statistically) represent? It could, as argued above, represent adaptive expectations. Another interpretation (Laidler, 1982) is that it represents slow adjustment of the price level. With this interpretation, estimated coefficients of the demand for money function are a mixture of 'price adjustment' and 'demand for money' parameters.

To see how we may obtain a 'plausible' demand for money function from a 'sticky' price assumption suppose that the long-run equilibrium price level p^* is determined by the long-run demand for money function with arguments $f(X)$

$$p^* = m^s - f(X) \tag{6.5}$$

'Sticky prices' may be represented by

$$p - p_{-1} = b(p^* - p_{-1}) \tag{6.6}$$

Substituting (6.5) in (6.6), adding m^s to both sides of the equation and rearranging we obtain

$$m^s - p = bf(X) + (1 - b)(m^s - p_{-1}) + v \tag{6.7}$$

where we have also added an error term v. Comparing (6.7) with the real partial adjustment model of the demand for money

$$m^s - p = bf(X) + (1 - b)(m^s_{-1} - p_{-1}) + u \tag{6.8}$$

we see that the two are equivalent if $u = v + (1 - b)\Delta m^s$. Similarly the *nominal* partial adjustment model is equivalent to (6.7) if $u = v + (1 - b)\Delta(m^s + p)$. Hence if the 'sticky price' model is the 'true' model, the nominal and real partial adjustment models of the demand for money will fit the data reasonably well. The long adjustment lags (that is $1 - \gamma$ close to unity) in estimated demand for money functions may therefore be reinterpreted as long lags in the adjustment of the aggregate price level, that is $(1 - b)$ close to unity (see Gordon (1984) for further elaborations on this theme).

This whole debate has yet to be resolved satisfactorily. Laidler's conjecture about 'sticky' prices requires a complete model of the money-prices interaction and we examine this aspect in the final chapter. As we shall see below there are other ways of rationalizing the lagged dependent variable and avoiding the 'over-shooting' phenomenon. For example, if the demand for money equation is inverted and the interest rate is taken as the dependent variable, then the *estimated* impact of the money supply does not produce overshooting. Also the 'buffer-stock' approach allows the (unanticipated) money supply to be 'absorbed' into the demand for money without any changes in interest rates (or other independent variables of the demand function). It is to these issues that we now turn.

6.3 MARKET DISEQUILIBRIUM MODELS

Market disequilibrum models can, in principle, deal with independent demand and supply régimes. We have discussed the min-side condition and the weighted supply and demand curve approach to estimating the supply and demand for credit (section 5.6). Such models have not been applied to the supply and demand for *money*. Also where supply and demand curves have been simul-taneously estimated, assuming market clearing in all periods (Teigen, 1964; Brunner and Meltzer, 1964), results have been similar to those obtained from the simple partial adjustment approach. (These studies include only 1950s and 1960s data where the assumption that supply is largely demand determined may have a reasonable one.)

'Market disequilibrium', as used here, refers to *market* models and to the 'gap' between the *desired* supply and demand curves at a particular interest rate (AB in figure 6.1). This should not be confused with 'disequilibrium' between the long-run desired demand for money and the short-run desired demand which involves only one side of the money market: examples here include the inter-dependent asset demand system and the simple partial adjustment model.

Artis and Lewis (1976) apply a rather *ad hoc* disequilibrium model to the demand for broad and narrow money in the UK over the period 1963(2)–1973(1). Artis and Lewis's adjustment mechanism appears to be an attempt at a market disequilibrium model with the interest rate adjusting slowly to clear the money market. If the money supply is exogenous and prices and real output are sticky in the short run, the interest rate adjusts to achieve equilibrium and should appear as the *dependent* variable. They assume partial adjustment for the interest rate (that is non-market clearing)

$$\Delta r_t = \alpha(r_t^* - r_{t-1}) \quad 0 < \alpha < 1 \tag{6.9}$$

where r_t^* is the equilibrium interest rate that satisfies the long run (logarithmic) demand for money function, in *nominal* terms;[3] hence

$$m_t^s = m^* = b_0 + b_1(y + p)_t - b_2 r_t \tag{6.10}$$

$$r^* = \frac{1}{b_2}(b_0 + b_1(y + p)_t - m_t^s) \tag{6.11}$$

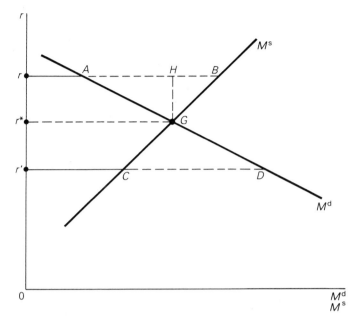

FIGURE 6.1   Disequilibrium in the money market.

The estimating equation is therefore

$$r_t = \frac{\alpha b_0}{b_2} + \frac{\alpha b_1}{b_2}(y+p)_t - \frac{\alpha}{b_2}m_t^s + (1-\alpha)r_{t-1} \qquad (6.12)$$

Notice that there is no overshooting in this model, the short-run response of r_t to m_t^s is (α/b_2) and the long-run response is greater, being $(1/b_2)$.[4] For both broad and narrow money, equation (6.12) is dynamically stable $(0 < \alpha < 1)$ but, more remarkably, the implicit estimates of the income and interest rate elasticities are much more stable over different time periods than in the 'normal' partial adjustment approach. A representative result for broad money is

$$r_t = -1.0 + 1.2(y+p)_t - 1.0m_t + 0.65r_{t-1} \qquad (6.13)$$

$$\quad (1.9)\ (3.9) \qquad\qquad (3.7) \qquad (6.0)$$

$$1963(2)\text{--}1973(1),\ \text{OLS},\ R^2 = 0.90,\ \text{dw} = 1.9$$

which yields long-run income and interest rate elasticities of 1.2 and -0.34 respectively (where r is the yield to maturity on government debt less the own rate on money).

We have some reservations concerning these results. The price level elasticity in the long-run demand function (equation 6.10) is not constrained to be unity and in fact turns out to be 1.2 in the estimated equation (6.13). This violates one's *a priori* views. In the adjustment mechanism for r (equation 6.9) it is assumed that the change in r depends on the degree of excess demand/supply ($CD = AB$, figure 6.1). However, as AB is proportional to GH ($= r - r^*$) we obtain $dr/dt = \gamma(r^* - r)$: the discrete equivalent of the latter is then given by equation (6.9). As market determined interest rates are very flexible 'prices' with rates quoted continuously, it is perhaps a little difficult to accept that they do not *immediately* adjust to equilibrate supply and demand.

Artis and Lewis only present the dw statistic as a test for autocorrelation and this is biased in the presence of a lagged dependent variable and there is no systematic correction for simultaneous equation bias.[5]

Thus, although there may be some doubt as to whether Artis and Lewis have estimated a genuine *market* disequilibrium effect, the results indicate that the response of the interest rate to a change in the money supply appears to be very different to that obtained in the conventional 'overshooting' partial adjustment model. The buffer stock approach provides an account that can reconcile these apparently contradictory results.

6.4   BUFFER-STOCK MONEY (BSM)

We begin with a brief account of some general considerations underlying the idea of money as a buffer stock drawing heavily from Goodhart (1984). Essentially the buffer-stock role arises because the cost of transitory money holdings are less than costs of adjustment for other financial assets and certainly less than costs of adjustment in real assets (for example stocks of goods) or real flows such as consumption (for households) and output and employment (for firms). Thus, transitory money holdings will be willingly held at unchanged levels of income and interest rates. This has three important implications in assessing our earlier models of the demand for money. First (unexpected) changes in the money supply will be willingly held at unchanged interest rates and 'overshooting' need not necessarily occur. Second, if transitory money holdings are a substantial and volatile part of total money holdings, we would expect our conventional theories which ignore such transitory balances to exhibit parameter instability over time. Third, long lags in the response of, say, prices to the money supply may be, in part, due to money initially being held as a buffer stock and gradually being dissipated in increased expenditure.

Below, after a brief introduction to the ideas underlying buffer-stock money, we discuss some applied work in this area.

6.4.1   *Money as a buffer stock*

The buffer-stock approach recognizes that unforeseen as well as expected events lead to changes in money balances and the reaction of economic agents is likely to be different in the two cases. Actual money balances consist of an expected (or permanent) and an unexpected (or transitory) component,[6] and both elements need to be adequately modelled.

Unexpected money balances are likely to occur because (sight) deposits are willingly held as a means of payment. If portfolio decisions are taken somewhat infrequently, or if changes appear to be transitory, it is possible for money balances to vary within an appreciable 'band', regardless of movements in income, interest rates, etc. This is the basic idea behind money as a buffer stock. A more familiar analogy might be the use of inventories (of, say, finished goods) to cushion the firm from unexpected changes in sales or production. As long as goods inventories remain within 'tolerable limits', the entrepreneur does not undertake the costly process of altering his pricing, production and employment policies in an attempt to alter inventories. At any point in time, actual goods inventories will consist of planned (desired) and 'buffer-stock' inventories, and there may be no response to changes in the latter if changes are thought to be due to unexpected events that may soon be reversed. Buffer-stock monetarists argue that much effort (theoretical and empirical) has been expended in modelling desired (short-run) money balances but little attention has been paid to the effect of unexpected or unanticipated money holdings. We shall take the view that unexpected or buffer-stock holdings of money are always willingly held in the short-run and this differentiates the model from disequilibrium models. Clearly, it is logically possible for the desired supply of money (by commercial banks) not to equal the sum of expected (or planned) *and* 'buffer' holdings of money (that is *total* desired holdings of money) but we ignore this 'disequilibrium' buffer-stock approach in this chapter (this 'disequilibrium' money approach is discussed in the final chapter).

Buffer-stock monetarists tend to focus on the different ways in which money enters the system. For example, the response of agents may be different if an increase in the money supply is due to an expected increase in income from employment by the government sector than if it is due to unexpected receipts by a part of the private sector as firms spend additional bank loans. The buffer-stock approach, therefore, explicitly considers the interaction between the supply and demand for money.

By way of an example, consider the probable behaviour of firms in an uncertain environment. The costs of marginal adjustments to prices, wages, production and real stock levels may be very substantial relative to the 'interest foregone' by holding excess money balances. 'Shocks' to the firm's production and employment plans are likely to result in a change in cash balances which will be willingly held in the short run until the shocks are perceived as permanent or temporary. Similarly, shocks to the money supply, for example, caused by an increase in the supply of advances may lead to unexpected changes in money holdings by other agents, when the advances are spent. In the buffer-stock approach, disequilibria originating in either demand or supply are explicitly considered. The speed with which firms adjust their 'excess' holdings of money may depend upon (a) their initial holdings, (b) the width of the 'band' within which money balances are allowed to fluctuate, (c) the review period for decisions, (d) the transactions costs of moving into other assets, goods, or in altering the production process, etc., (e) the source of the change in money balances and a view as to whether they are permanent or transitory (Goodhart, 1984). Taking up the last point, if the source of the change in 'buffer money' is concentrated rather narrowly, then even though each individual agent may adjust fairly quickly, the system as a whole may take considerable time to adjust as 'buffer money' is passed on to different agents.

The buffer-stock approach may be broadly represented by the target-threshold models of the precautionary demand for money (section 3.2). Money holdings drift between the upper and lower limits and the agent's 'preferred return point' is his desired short-run demand for money. Only the 'limits' and the return point are influenced by economic variables and hence it is possible for actual money holdings of the *individual* to differ from his short-run desired ('return point') holdings.

If the money transactions technology is highly efficient and it is relatively costless to transfer between 'money' and 'near money', then buffer assets are likely to consist of a wider set of assets than transaction balances. For large firms in the UK, the automatic overdraft system may also be used as a buffer stock. Excess money may be used to reduce overdrafts.[7] Cash shortages may also lead to increased overdrafts as the spread between money rates and the cost of overdrafts is relatively small for large firms. Thus, it may be *net* liquidity that acts as the 'buffer stock' for large firms rather than simply 'money'.

For persons, the relevant interest spread between liquid assets and credit in the UK is rather large and automatic overdrafts are somewhat uncommon. Therefore, buffer assets are likely to consist of gross liquid assets, particularly money and building society deposits. However, in countries where short term credit is widely and easily available – for example in the US and increasingly so in the UK (bank credit cards) – liabilities may also perform a buffer role.

Buffer-stock monetarism recognizes that the supply of money is not always demand determined. But unlike the disequilibrium approach, it sees supply shocks as resulting in buffer assets that are willingly held (desired) in the short run. Conversely, a *desired* change in money holdings by a group of individuals, say by an increase in expenditures, may lead to an increase in holdings of buffer money by other agents. Even with an unchanged money supply, aggregate money balances are still willingly held in the short run. An autonomous change in the desired short-run demand for money need not require a change in the money supply, or prices, incomes and interest rates, for the aggregate money market to remain in equilibrium in the short run. Of course, as 'buffer money' is perceived as a permanent addition to money balances, individuals attempt to run down these balances producing conventional 'real balance' effects on prices, output and interest rates.

BSM rather neatly copes with shocks to both the demand and supply of money and hence is more general than the partial adjustment model which requires an endogenous money supply and the 'inversion' of the demand function when we assume an exogenous supply of money. Supply side shocks are more likely to arise for broad money and, in the UK, surges in bank advances and the PSBR in the 1970s provide ample evidence that such 'shocks' may well be substantial and frequent.[8]

6.4.2 *Applied research on buffer stock money*

Research in this area is in its infancy, although an article by Darby appeared in 1972 (Darby, 1972). Darby considered that transitory (unexpected) real money balances M_t^T would increase if unexpected (transitory) real savings are positive S_t^T while accumulated transitory balances would be depleted slowly

$$\Delta M_t^T = \beta_1 S_t^T + \beta_2 M_{t-1}^T \quad 1 > \beta_1 > 0, \ \beta_2 < 0 \tag{6.14}$$

If actual consumption always equals planned consumption, transitory savings S^T equal transitory income Y_t^T. Permanent (or expected) real money balances M_t^P depend on permanent income Y_t^P (in Friedman's sense of the term) and interest rates r_t, while *actual* balances M_t are the sum of permanent and transitory balances

$$M_t = M_t^P + M_t^T \tag{6.15}$$

$$M_t^P = \beta_3 + \beta_4 Y_t^P + \beta_5 r_t \tag{6.16}$$

Substituting (6.14) and (6.16) in (6.15) and rearranging, we obtain Darby's estimating equation (in real terms)

$$M_t = \beta_3(1 - \beta_8) + \beta_1 Y_t^T + \beta_8 M_{t-1} + \beta_4 Y_t^{P*} + \beta_5 r_t^* \tag{6.17}$$

where $\beta_8 = (1 + \beta_2)$, $Y_t^{P*} = Y_t^P - \beta_8 Y_{t-1}^P$, etc. Y_t^P is generated from an adaptive expectations equation where current income has a weight of 0.1 (as in Friedman's consumption function estimate) and $Y_t^T = Y_t - Y_t^P$ where Y_t is actual income. For US data on M1 over the period 1947(1)–1966(4), Darby finds the equation fits well with the correct a priori signs. Transitory income has a powerful effect, increasing the demand for money by about 40 per cent of the increase in income ($\beta_1 \approx 0.4$), while transitory money balances are depleted at a rate of 20 per cent per quarter.

Johnston's (1983b) buffer model for broad money, £M3 in the UK, is almost identical to Darby's. A representative equation (in logarithms) for real money balances, $\tilde{m}$ is

$$\tilde{m} = 1.8 + 0.54 y_t^{P*} - 0.009 r_t^* + 2.8 y_t^T + 0.54 \tilde{m}_{t-1} \tag{6.18}$$

$$(2.2) \ (5.2) \qquad (1.6) \qquad (3.1) \qquad (3.9)$$

$$1955(1)–1980(4), \text{ OLS}, \ \bar{R}^2 = 0.99, \text{ SEE} = 0.046, \text{ dw} = 1.6$$

Again transitory income has a powerful effect on (broad) money holdings and the equation is dynamically stable over the 1970s data without having to employ a dummy variable for the effects of competition and credit control.

It is perhaps worth noting that the above buffer stock models are observationally very close to a normal partial adjustment model with new savings flows allocated to money in a different proportion to disequilibrium holdings. To see this, note that $\Delta \tilde{m}_t = \gamma(\tilde{m}_t^* - \tilde{m}_{t-1}) + \gamma_1 S_t$ and $S_t = Y_t - C_t = Y_t - k Y_t^P \simeq Y_t^T$ if k is close to unity. Hence $\tilde{m}_t = \gamma \tilde{m}^* + (1 - \gamma) \tilde{m}_{t-1} + \gamma_1 Y_t^T$.

Carr and Darby (1981) recognize that the *real* partial adjustment model under the RE market clearing assumption is consistent with exogenous but *anticipated* changes in the money supply since the current price level, then adjusts fully and instantaneously and there is no overshooting. However, if the change in the money supply is unanticipated, or if prices are very 'sticky', a change in the money supply may produce substantial overshooting in the conventional model as argued above. Carr and Darby, therefore, seek to amend the conventional partial adjustment model in three ways. First, they assume that a proportion of unanticipated changes in income y_t^T are willingly absorbed in buffer-stock money holdings and second, that *unanticipated* changes in the money *supply* m_t^u also lead to a 'temporary desire to hold more or less money' as the 'synchronization of purchases and sales of assets' is altered. Third, *anticipated* changes in the money supply are immediately reflected in price level expectations. If prices are flexible then *real* money balances are unaffected by anticipated changes in the money supply.

Carr and Darby test for the influence of unanticipated money on money demand using the following equations[9]

$$m^d - p = m - p = bX + a(m - m^a) + u \tag{6.19}$$

$$m = gZ + v \tag{6.20}$$

where we expect $0 < a < 1$ and we assume the money supply m equals the demand for money m^d. The first equation is a 'conventional' demand for money function with the addition of the unanticipated money supply. m is the logarithm of the nominal money stock, p is the logarithm of the price level, X is a set of variables that determine the 'conventional' short-run demand for money function and b is a suitably dimensioned vector of coefficients. m^a is the anticipated value of the money supply and is determined as the predictions from equation (6.20), where Z is a set of variables that agents assume have a systematic influence on the money supply. Unanticipated changes in the money supply $m^u = (m - m^a)$ are the residuals from equation (6.20). u and v are white noise error terms.

Carr and Darby (1981) estimate the above two-equation system over the period 1957(1)–1976(4) for narrow money (M1) for eight industrial countries. They use an autoregressive predictor for the anticipated money supply (that is Z contains only lagged values of M) and obtain encouraging results for a number ' of countries. In particular the coefficient on unanticipated money m^u is positive, less than unity and usually statistically significant.

Carr and Darby recognize that because u determines m in equation (6.19) then u is correlated with $(m - m^a)$ and OLS estimation yields inconsistent (incorrect) estimates of the parameters: hence they use an instrumental variables procedure, namely 2SLS. However, MacKinnon and Milbourne (1984) (MM) argue that their use of a large number of principal components as instruments is unlikely to remove all of the small sample bias (Klein, 1969). Instead they propose an alternative maximum likelihood (ML) procedure which is computationally simple and allows an economic interpretation of the parameters. Rearranging equation (6.19) we have

$$m - p = d^*(m^a - p) + b^*X + u^* \tag{6.21}$$

where $d^* = -a/(1-a)$, $b^* = b/(1-a)$ and $u^* = u/(1-a)$. The problem of correlation between $(m - m^a)$ and the error term has been removed (and it may be shown that OLS estimation of (6.21) is equivalent to the appropriate ML estimation of equation (6.19)). If the Carr–Darby hypothesis holds, then d^* will be non-zero and yields an estimate of a.[10] The additional term introduced by MM into the conventional demand for money function is the anticipated quantity of nominal money deflated by the current price level.

MM point out that the second part of the Carr–Darby hypothesis, namely that anticipated money does not influence real balances may be tested by adding a term sm^a to equation (6.19) which after transformation yields the analogue to the shock-absorber equation (6.21)

$$m - p = d^*(m^a - p) + b^* X + s^* m^a + u^* \tag{6.22}$$

If the Carr–Darby hypothesis is correct we expect $s^* = s/(1 - a)$ to be zero and the estimate of $d^* = -a/(1 - a)$ to be negative (given $0 < a < 1$). MM, using data on M1 for Australia, and Cuthbertson (1985b) using similar data for the UK, find that the above restrictions do not hold.[11] In particular d^* is usually statistically insignificant and s^* is negative. These results cast some doubt on the validity of the Carr–Darby hypothesis. However, when Cuthbertson and Taylor (1985a) generate a series for m^a using the Kalman filter (Chow, 1984) the Carr–Darby hypothesis is accepted on UK data for M1. Thus the jury is still out on this one.

The Carr–Darby model is a very specific shock-absorber hypothesis and the above results do not preclude other models of buffer-stock money being empirically valid. Indeed Laidler (1983) argues that the buffer-stock approach is unlikely to be adequately captured in a single equation framework while Gordon (1984) argues that single equation 'demand' for money functions are likely to contain both supply and demand factors.

Santomero and Seater (1981) present a complex but interesting model where individuals trade off costs of being out of long-run equilibrium and the cost of *searching* for new investment opportunities when a 'shock' causes changes in buffer-stock money. Long-run equilibrium balances are given by the precautionary demand model of Whalen (section 3.2) and depend upon illiquidity cost, relative interest rates and the variance of transactions. Because of incomplete information on alternative assets available, 'buffer stock' holdings are run down only slowly. Search intensity in looking for alternative assets increases with the size of the buffer holdings and the speed of adjustment of the latter therefore depends upon a distributed lag of past shocks. The source of such shocks, for example whether they are interest rate shocks or shocks to income, also influences the speed of adjustment to long-run desired money balances. Although the theoretical model is rather novel, it is vastly simplified in the empirical implementation. Essentially long-run desired real money balances are assumed to depend on two interest rates on alternative assets and permanent income, while shocks are represented by a distributed lag on transitory income plus the change in the money supply (to proxy unanticipated money), all as a proportion of permanent income, that is

$$\log\left[1 + \sum_{j=0}^{1} (0.6)^j (Y_{t-j}^T + M_{t-j}) \Big/ Y_{t-j}^P \right]$$

On US data for M1 and M2 over the period 1952(2)–1972(4), the parameters are all statistically significant and of the correct sign, and the 'shock term' has a positive impact on buffer-stock money holdings, as expected. However, the equation suffers from acute serial correlation of a fairly complex nature and, coupled with the presence of lagged dependent variables, implies biased and inconsistent coefficient estimates.

Judd and Scadding (1981) on US data use the change in bank loans as proxy for unanticipated shocks to the money supply and find the variable significant in the demand for money function, as do Artis and Lewis (1976) for the UK.

Clearly the above empirical results on BSM are far from satisfactory on a number of counts but these pioneering attempts indicate that the idea is by no means devoid of empirical content. We might expect to see an improvement in empirical results as the ideas of buffer money are applied in a more sophisticated manner in the near future. The expected–unexpected distinction appears to be a useful construct to apply to money as a buffer stock. However, if the estimated equations are to be interpreted as structural demand functions, it is probably better to proxy unanticipated money supply shocks by variables that we feel individuals respond to, such as unanticipated changes in income, interest rates and wealth. We discuss this in the next section.

6.4.3 *Microfoundation of the buffer-stock approach*

In the previous section we discussed some empirical approaches to modelling buffer-stock money and briefly discussed a formal model, that of Santomero and Seater (1981). We now round off our analysis of buffer-stock money by presenting a microtheoretic model based on multiperiod quadratic costs. This is a generalization of the one-period quadratic cost model used to derive the simple partial adjustment model (section 4.2). The approach has some interesting features that are of a more general nature than the purely buffer-stock model. The multiperiod model allows expectations about *future* values of variables to determine the demand for money (or assets in general). Implementation of such models requires a theory of how agents form expectations. Rational expectations is often invoked, although it is not the only method one might adopt. Expectations about future values are formed not only for the level of transactions and interest rates but also about future 'shocks' to holdings of buffer-stock money.

Incorporation of expected future values into the demand for money allows a greater diversity in the dynamic response of money to changes in independent variables. For example, a change in interest rates that is *expected* to occur in the future may result in changes in money holdings *today*. On the other hand an *un*anticipated change in interest rates is likely to influence the demand for money in the current period. It should be obvious that a 'conventional' demand for money equation, containing current and lagged interest rate variables, may exhibit parameter instability if the forward looking model is the correct one.

An interesting side issue is that the forward looking model discussed may under certain circumstances be adequately modelled using a backward looking error feedback equation (EFE). The empirical performance of the latter model may, therefore, be consistent with forward looking behaviour. The difficulty in discriminating empirically between forward and backward looking models is familiar in the rational expectations literature and is known as 'observational equivalence'.

This section is arranged as follows. First, we derive the multiperiod quadratic cost model and show how this might be interpreted as an EFE. Next, we extent the multiperiod quadratic cost model to embrace the buffer-stock approach and finally, we briefly comment on some implications of these models when interpreting and assessing the demand for money and monetary policy. It should be noted at the outset that, as yet, there has been little or no empirical application of these models to the demand for money.

Multiperiod quadratic costs.[12] In the one-period quadratic cost model, the agent is aware that last period's stock influences the choice of this period's stock but fails to realize that this period's choice will influence next period's costs of adjustment. To avoid such myopia, we assume that the individual has a known long-run desired money stock M_{t+j}^* ($j = 0, \ldots, T$) in all future periods and, at time t, has to choose M_t to minimize current and *future* quadratic costs of being out of equilibrium and the costs of change[13]

$$C = \sum_{t=1}^{T} a(M_t - M_t^*)^2 + b(M_t - M_{t-1})^2 \tag{6.23}$$

The first-order condition for the 'last' period T is the same as in the 'one-period' partial adjustment model

$$\frac{\partial C}{\partial M_T} = 2a(M_T - M_T^*) + 2b(M_T - M_{T-1}) = 0$$

$$M_T = \frac{a}{a+b} M_T^* + \frac{b}{a+b} M_{T-1}$$

$$M_T = A_1 M_T^* + B_1 M_{T-1} \tag{6.24}$$

where $A_1 = a/(a + b)$ and $A_1 + B_1 = 1$. For $t < T$ we have

$$\frac{\partial C}{\partial M_t} = 2a(M_t - M_t^*) + 2b(M_t - M_{t-1}) - 2b(M_{t+1} - M_t) = 0$$

$$M_t = \frac{a}{a+2b} M_t^* + \frac{b}{a+2b} M_{t-1} + \frac{b}{a+2b} M_{t+1} \tag{6.25}$$

$$= A_2 M_t^* + B_2 M_{t-1} + B_2 M_{t+1} \tag{6.26}$$

where $A_2 + 2B_2 = 1$ and the coefficients on M_{t-1} and M_{t+1} are equal. From (6.26), as expected, *future* values of M influence current period short-run desired holdings of money M_t.

The solution (for $T = \infty$) to the forward looking (Euler) equation (6.25) is most easily obtained using the Sargent (1979b) 'forward operator' (readers who are only interested in the economics of the result may disregard the following details). Multiplying (6.25) through by $(a + 2b)$ and rearranging

$$(a + 2b - bL - bL^{-1}) M = aM^* \tag{6.27a}$$

Hence

$$B(L) M = \left[-L\left(\frac{a + 2b}{b}\right) + L^2 + 1 \right] M = -\frac{a}{b} M^*_{-1} \tag{6.27b}$$

where L^{-1} is the forward operator (i.e. $L^{-n}M = M_{t+n}$). Factorizing $B(L)$ and equating coefficients in powers of L gives

$$\left[-L\left(\frac{a + 2b}{b}\right) + L^2 + 1 \right] = (1 - q_1 L)(1 - q_2 L)$$

$$= 1 - (q_1 + q_2) L + q_1 q_2 L^2 \tag{6.28}$$

Hence, $q_1 + q_2 = (a/b) + 2$, $q_1 q_2 = 1$, and without loss of generality we assume $q_2 > 1$ and hence $q_1 < 1$, $q_1^{-1} > 1$. Equation (6.27b) after multiplying through by $(1 - q_2 L)^{-1}$ may now be written

$$(1 - q_1 L) M = -\frac{a}{b} (1 - q_2 L)^{-1} M^*_{-1} = -\frac{a}{b} (1 - q_1^{-1} L)^{-1} M^*_{-1}$$

$$M = q_1 M_{-1} + \frac{a}{b} q_1 \sum_0^\infty q_1^i M^*_{t+i} \tag{6.29}$$

where we have used the Taylor expansion

$$(1 - \lambda L)^{-1} = -\frac{(\lambda L)^{-1}}{1 - (\lambda L)^{-1}}$$

$$= \frac{-1}{\lambda L} [1 + (\lambda L)^{-1} + (\lambda L)^{-2} + \ldots]$$

$$= -(\lambda L)^{-1} - (\lambda L)^{-2} - (\lambda L)^{-3} \ldots$$

and

$$|\lambda| = |q_1^{-1}| > 1 \qquad (a/b) q_1 = (1 - q_1)^2$$

(Sargent, 1979b). If we assume that agents minimize *expected* multiperiod costs, based on information available at time $t - 1$ then we replace M^*_{t+i} by its expected value $E_{t-1}(M^*_{t+i})$, where E is the expectations operator conditional on information available at time $t - 1$ or earlier. The optimal short-run demand for money M then depends on the lagged actual stock[14] and future *expected* values of the variables that determine M^*. For simplicity assume $M^*_t = kY_t$ then

$$M = q_1 M_{-1} + \frac{a}{b} q_1 k \sum_0^\infty (q_1)^i Y^e_{t+i} \tag{6.30}$$

The model implies a testable restriction between the forward and backward looking variables. The weights on future income variables Y^e should decline geometrically and these 'weights' q_1 should equal the coefficient on the lagged dependent variable. (Note that the latter does not hold if a discount factor is included in (6.23); see Artis and Cuthbertson, 1985).[14]

To estimate equation (6.29) we require expected future values of the determinants of M^*. These may in some cases be directly obtained from survey data on expectations or published forecasts. Lack of data from these sources has led to the use of regression techniques to provide proxy variables for future values. Taking income, for example as the transactions variable, we could use the adaptive expectations model with the weight on current income θ chosen either on a priori grounds or from extraneous sources (for example Friedman's consumption function estimate). Alternatively, we could use a 'weakly rational' method. The adaptive expectations model provides an unbiased predictor of future income only if the data generation process for income is of a special form (that is IMA(1, 1)). The adaptive expectations hypothesis *imposes* a geometric lag structure and does not allow variables other than lagged income to influence expectations. A weakly rational predictor for expected income does not impose these restrictions. A purely autoregressive (weakly rational) model for income is[15]

$$Y_t = a_1 Y_{t-1} + a_2 Y_{t-2} + \ldots + u_t = a(L) Y_t + u_t \tag{6.31}$$

where $a(L)$ is a polynomial lag operator and u_t is a white noise error. Estimation of (6.31) allows us to generate future values of Y_t by the chain rule of forecasting. For example, with $a_i = 0$ $(i > 2)$ and knowing Y_1 and Y_0, then

$$Y_2 = a_1 Y_1 + a_2 Y_0$$
$$Y_3 = a_1(a_1 Y_1 + a_2 Y_0) + a_2 Y_1 = (a_1^2 + a_2) Y_1 + a_1 a_2 Y_0 \text{ etc.} \tag{6.32}$$

and all future values of Y depend only upon the known starting values Y_1 and Y_0. We can, therefore, use (6.31) to generate a series of one-step ahead predictions, that is Y_{t+1} (given Y_t and Y_{t-1}), two-step ahead predictions, that is Y_{t+2} (again given Y_t and Y_{t-1}), etc. Since $Eu_t = 0$, the predictions using the chain rule conform to the unbiasedness property of rational expectations predictors.

In general a 'weakly rational' predictor is the reduced form of the model under consideration and hence predetermined variables other than lagged own values may be used in (6.31). If so, expectations of these additional variables (for example world trade) influence expectations of income. To apply the chain rule, these predetermined variables have themselves to be generated using autoregressive models, if more than one-step ahead predictions are required. (In a full Muth rational expectations model, any cross equation restrictions in the reduced form would also be incorporated in the equation to predict Y.)

Having obtained the one step, two step, etc., *predictions* from (6.31), these variables can then be directly included in the short-run demand for money functions (6.30). This is an instrumental variables approach to estimating the influence of expected variables and yields consistent estimates of the parameters (McCallum, 1976).

Artis and Cuthbertson (1985) have tested the above model on narrow money (M1) for the UK. They also include current period income 'surprises' ($Y - Y^e$) in the equation to proxy the buffer-stock role of money. The expected series for income is generated using an autoregressive model as described above. (The interest rate R is assumed to be a random walk and hence only appears as R_{-1}). The results are moderately encouraging: the equation performs as well statistically as a 'backward looking' error feedback equation (but see below) and the 'backward-forward' restrictions on q_1 appear to hold in the data (see also Cuthbertson and Taylor (1985) who use the Kalman filter to generate the expectations series). However, the reader should treat these results as provisional as there are potentially some acute problems in using a two-step estimation procedure. Pagan (1984) has demonstrated that the two-step estimator produces inconsistent estimates of the *variance* of the expectations parameters (the parameters themselves are estimated consistently if we have white noise errors). In addition, because of the use of future expectations, we might expect moving average errors which with a lagged dependent variable yield inconsistent parameter estimates (see Hansen and Sargent (1982), Hayashi and Sims (1983) and Kennan (1979) for a discussion of this problem). Resolution of these rather acute econometric problems will no doubt lead to more empirical work along these lines (see also Gordon (1984) who adds 'shocks' in the real sector to US demand for money functions and Hall et al. (1984) for applications of this forward looking model to the real sector). Use of the errors in variables RE approach would lead to future expectations being replaced by their ex-post values; $Y_{t+j} = {}_tY_{t+j}^e + v_{t+j}$ and obviate the need for auxiliary expectations equations. However, additional problems include the introduction of moving average errors (Hayashi and Sims, 1983) and the surprise terms subsumed in the error term (Wickens, 1982).

Forward looking behaviour and the EFE. The EFE is backward looking, containing only current and past values. We can reduce our forward looking model to an equation containing only current and lagged variables by making all future values of desired money balances M_{t+J}^* depend only upon current and past variables by using the chain rule of forecasting.

Suppose the actual path of *desired* money balances can be adequately represented by a second-order autoregressive scheme

$$M_{t+1}^* = \beta_0 M_t^* + \beta_1 M_{t-1}^* + \epsilon_{t+1} \qquad (6.33)$$

where ϵ_{t+1} is a white noise error. Using the chain rule of forecasting, *all* future values of M^* depend only upon current and lagged desired money holdings[16] and we can replace $M_{t+J}^* (J \geq 1)$ in our forward looking equation (6.29) by a linear function of M_t^* and M_{t-1}^* only. Ignoring the parameter restrictions on (6.29) and replacing the M_{t+j}^* ($j \geq 1$) by a convolution of M_t^* and M_{t-1}^* (using (6.33)), we have

$$M_t = q_1 M_{t-1} + \delta_0 M_t^* + \delta_1 M_{t-1}^* \qquad (6.34)$$

where δ_i are convolutions of the autoregressive expectations parameters β_0, β_1 and the 'quadratic cost' parameters a, b of equation (6.27a). Reparameterizing (6.34) we obtain

$$\Delta M_t = (q_1 - 1) M_{t-1} - \delta_1 \Delta M_t^* + (\delta_0 + \delta_1) M_t^* \qquad (6.35)$$

Equation (6.35) differs slightly from the error feedback equation (4.18) presented in chapter 4 because the coefficients on M_t^* and M_{t-1} are not equal and opposite. However, when EFE are estimated, the determinants of the desired level of money balances usually appear in place of the M^* terms. Thus, for example, if M^* depends only on income Y_t, equation (6.35) has M_{t-1}, Y_t and ΔY_t as independent variables. This is exactly what one would estimate using our EFE of section 4.2.

Thus, with the rather special assumption that M_t^* is adequately represented by a second-order autoregressive equation, our forward looking model may be represented as an error feedback equation. This is another example of observational equivalence between the rational expectations approach and the more conventional approach.[17] Notice that if the forward looking model is the true model, then the parameters of the EFE regression equation are a mixture of expectational parameters (β_0, β_1) and 'adjustment cost' parameters (a, b). A change in the former because of a change in government policy, for example, will cause apparent instability in the coefficients of the EFE (Lucas (1976) critique). This may account for some of the instability in ADL models of the demand for assets and, to avoid this problem, the expectations equation for Y should be separately estimated (see sections 5.4, 5.5).

Buffer-stock money and shocks. The buffer-stock approach may be incorporated into the multiperiod quadratic cost model but, before doing so, it is worth noting what happens when we make a small change to the simple one-period partial adjustment model. Because money is always accepted as a means of payment, changes in money holdings can occur without any action on the part of the agent: these changes in money holdings involve no costs in terms of time and inconvenience. If X_t is the autonomous *increase* in money holdings, then quadratic costs of adjustment depend upon $b(M_t - M_{t-1} - X_t)^2$ rather than $b(M_t - M_{t-1})$ of our simple partial adjustment model (section 4.2). Costs of being in disequilibrium are $a(M_t^* - M_t)^2$ and minimizing total costs gives

$$M_t = \gamma M_t^* + (1 - \gamma) M_{t-1} + (1 - \gamma) X_t \tag{6.36}$$

where $\gamma = a/(a + b)$. Hence the 'shock' variable X_t enters the short-run demand for money function with the same coefficient as the lagged dependent variable. Carr and Darby's results quoted earlier (section 6.4.2) are consistent with the above one-period partial adjustment model where X_t is a money supply 'shock'. We find that when the above simple model is extended to a multiperiod framework, the above restriction still holds, although forward looking behaviour is also a feature of the model.

In the multiperiod framework, we merely have to replace M_{t-1} by $(M_{t-1} - X_t)$ and proceed as before.[18] M_{t-1} and X_t have equal coefficients λ_1 which are a function of the cost of adjustment parameters b and a. The weights on the *expected future* shocks $E_t X_{t+J}$ decline geometrically as we move further into the future and neglecting the terms $E_t M_{t+J}^*$ to concentrate on the shock variables,[19] we have (see Kanniainen and Tarkka (1983) for further details)

$$M_t = \lambda_1 M_{t-1} + \lambda_1 X_t + \beta M_t^* - (1 - \lambda_1) \sum_{J=1}^{T} \lambda_1^J (E_{t-1} X_{t+J}) \tag{6.37}$$

The form of the solution should now be familiar. M_t depends upon all *expected* future shocks $(E_{t-1} X_{t+J})$ with declining weights, the desired current demand M_t^*, the lagged stock of money M_{t-1} and the known current shock X_t, whether anticipated or unanticipated. The latter result enables us to discriminate between this model and the Carr and Darby (1981) model where only unanticipated current shocks affect M_t. In the multiperiod model, all *past* anticipated shocks are reflected in M_{t-1}. However, the *dynamic* effects of unanticipated shocks X_t differ from those that are anticipated $E_t X_{t+J}$, as reflected in the coefficients on the $(E_t X_{t+J})$ terms. This model has not yet been empirically implemented.

It is worth noting that the expected income terms in these forward looking models are conceptually different from Friedman's permanent income concept. The latter is an annuity equivalent of wealth; the amount one could consume without diminishing one's stock of wealth. But 'expected income' Y_{t+J}^e is the level of transactions expected to prevail in period $t + J$ based on information available at time $t - 1$.

6.5 SUMMARY

The multiperiod quadratic cost model implies that expected future values of variables such as income, as well as current values, influence current money holdings. The omission of such forward looking variables may be one reason why some demand for money functions exhibit parameter instability. Although purely backward looking models are consistent with forward looking behaviour under certain circumstances, nevertheless such models will exhibit parameter instability if the way people form their expectations alters due to changes in government policy or other agents' behaviour (for example OPEC price rises might influence expectations of future real income).

The multiperiod quadratic cost model is derived independently of the way people form their expectations and therefore both rational and non-rational models of expectations behaviour can be appended to it. The buffer-stock or shock absorber approach may also be incorporated in the multiperiod model providing another set of possible omitted variables, namely current actual 'shocks' and expected future 'shocks'.

The impact of a current independent variable on the current period demand for money can be much more varied than in the (fixed coefficient) one-period partial adjustment model. An increase in current income, for example, may have a small effect on the demand for money working via M_t^* in equation (6.29). However, if a change in current income influences expectations about *future* income, the impact on current money balances could be substantial. Conventional empirical studies that use only current (and lagged) income, may find the current period income elasticity unstable.

An anticipated change in the money supply (an expected shock $E_t X_{t+J}$) will lead to a change in money demand today and hence a change in interest rate prior to the change in the money supply. The argument applies to an expected change in income, interest rates or the price level, and renders changes in such current period variables difficult to interpret for policy analysis. An exogenous increase in the money supply to the extent that it leads to revisions concerning the future (expected) path of the arguments of the demand for money function need not result in large changes in *current* independent variables in order to equilibrate the money market. Severe 'overshooting' thus becomes less likely.

Although empirical results todate on buffer stock money have been somewhat mixed, theoretical forward looking models with 'shocks' added, do appear to provide an interesting and possibly fruitful line of future enquiry.

NOTES

1 The Lucas critique suggests that the coefficients of the partial adjustment model estimated on the assumption that the money supply is endogenous may well alter when the latter becomes exogenous. Hence Lucasians might not consider the overshooting results as a valid criticism of conventional demand functions, but only as a criticism of their use in a different policy régime.

2 Starleaf (1970) suggests a model that is valid when the (real) money supply is exogenous. Essentially, Starleaf reverses the usual partial adjustment model so that the short-run *desired* (real) demand $\tilde{m}^*$ responds to disequilibrium in *supply*

$$\Delta \tilde{m}_t^* = \delta (\tilde{m}_t^s - \tilde{m}_{t-1}^*) \quad 0 < \delta < 1 \tag{6.5}$$

hence

$$\tilde{m}_t^s = \frac{1}{\delta} \tilde{m}_t^* + \left(1 - \frac{1}{\delta}\right) \tilde{m}_{t-1}^* \tag{6.6}$$

Substituting for $\tilde{m}^* = a_0 + a_1 y_t - a_2 r_t$, gives $\tilde{m}_t^s$ depending upon y_t, y_{t-1}, r_t, r_{t-1} and no lagged dependent variable. The response of, say, y_t to a change in $\tilde{m}_t^s$ is $\partial y_t / \partial \tilde{m}_t^s = \delta / a_1$ which is less than the long-run response $1/a_1$ for $0 < \delta < 1$; hence partial adjustment of y_t and no overshooting occurs. Unfortunately, Starleaf's empirical estimates yield the unacceptable value of $\delta > 1$ for M2 in the US on quarterly data over the period 1952–66. Of course, the model is not valid in a régime where the money supply is endogenous.

3 The real income and price level elasticities are constrained to be equal.

4 Artis and Lewis also consider the case where m^* depends upon the expected interest rate r^e which is assumed to be determined by first-order adaptive expectations. This model is capable of producing overshooting although empirical results indicate no overshooting.

5 Autocorrelation in the Artis–Lewis disequilibrium model may be consistent with measurement error in an equilibrium model (appendix A). Let the 'true' market clearing model be

$$r_t^e = \beta m_t + u_t \tag{1}$$

where r_t^e is the expected yield, u_t is white noise and we have ignored other terms that influence the demand for money. If r^e is measured with error v_t and the latter is autocorrelated, then

$$r_t = r_t^e + v_t \quad \text{where } v_t = \frac{\epsilon_t}{1 - \rho L} \tag{2}$$

where ϵ_t is white noise and independent of u_t. Substituting for r_t^e and v_t in (1) and rearranging

$$r_t = \rho r_{t-1} + \beta(m_t - \rho m_{t-1}) + (u_t - \rho u_{t-1} + \epsilon_t) \tag{3}$$

Thus (autocorrelated) errors in variables in measuring r_t^e are likely to yield a serially correlated error in a static regression of r_t on m_t (and y_t) as reported by Artis and Lewis. (The error term is in fact a moving average error MA(1)). Further, if the static equilibrium model is correct, we expect r_{t-1} and terms of the form $(m_t - \rho m_{t-1})$ to be significant. The coefficient on r_{t-1} in the Artis–Lewis model may, therefore, be measuring the autocorrelation coefficient of the errors in variables v_t rather than an adjustment/disequilibrium parameter.

Further, when Artis–Lewis invoke the disequilibrium interest rate adjustment mechanism together with an expected interest rate generated by adaptive expectations in the long-run demand for money, we have

$$m^* = \lambda r^e + w_t \quad \text{and} \quad r^e = \frac{\theta r}{1 - \theta' L} \quad \text{where } \theta' = (1 - \theta) \tag{4}$$

Hence equilibrium in the desired long-run demand for money gives

$$r^* = (\lambda\theta)^{-1}[(1 - \theta'L) m_t + (1 - \theta'L) w_t] \tag{5}$$

Substituting this in the disequilibrium equation $\Delta r_t = \alpha(r_t^* - r_{t-1})$ gives

$$r_t = \alpha(\lambda\theta)^{-1}[(m_t - \theta'm_{t-1}) + (w_t - \theta'w_{t-1})] + (1-\alpha) r_{t-1} \tag{6}$$

However, the Artis–Lewis 'disequilibrium model' in (6) and the autoregressive errors in variables (*equilibrium* model (3)) yield identical (unrestricted) estimating equations. Again an errors in variables plus a market clearing interpretation of the Artis -Lewis model is possible.

6   The terms used here need not be synonymous. For example, an *expected* component of money could well be viewed as permanent or transitory. Similarly, for unexpected balances. The terms 'permanent' and 'transitory' have a longer lineage in the literature and are often used somewhat loosely. We use the term 'permanent' as in general usage, rather than the precise definition proposed in Friedman's theory of the consumption function, where the term is the annuity equivalent of the discounted present value of total wealth. Similarly, 'transitory' refers to events that are not expected to persist, rather than Friedman's more precise definition. To simplify the terminology, except where explicitly stated otherwise, we have decided to consider expected events as always perceived as 'permanent' and unexpected events as always perceived as being 'transitory'. We do not believe this unduly distorts the subtleties involved in discussing buffer-stock money. Finally, at a risk of sounding pernickety on this matter, expected and 'anticipated', and unexpected and unanticipated should be considered synonymous.

7   In the Civil Service strike in the UK in 1982, a large proportion of unpaid taxes were used by ICC to reduce bank advances (Bank of England, 1981a).

8   Indirect empirical evidence for supply side shocks is that £M3 is more strongly correlated with *future* income levels than is M1 (Mills, 1983).

9   Strong a priori restrictions are required to identify rational expectations (RE) models consisting of equations (6.19) and (6.20). For identification we must assume that the Z variables do not enter equation (6.19) separately, but only as determinants of m^a. In Darby's empirical work, Z consists of

lagged values of money only. Under these circumstances a sufficient condition for identification is that the order of lags in the time series model for m^a exceeds the order of lags in the 'surprise' terms $(m - m^a)$. The latter only appears contemporaneously and hence the estimated model is identified. For a pessimistic view of the possibility of identification in RE models see Pesaran (1981). Mishkin (1983) and Pagan (1984) provide a lucid account of estimation problems in this type of equation system.

10 The estimate of a is biased (but consistent) since it is a non-linear transformation of the estimated parameter. This does not affect subsequent tests.

11 The income variable used by MM and Cuthbertson differs from that of Carr and Darby (who use a proxy variable for permanent income) but the results are unlikely to be sensitive to the scale variable used since all measures are highly trended. Note also that although the two-step estimator used yields consistent estimates of s^* and d^*, nevertheless the estimates of the *variances* are inconsistent (Pagan, 1984). However this does not affect the *result* of the 'null' H_0: $d^* = s^* = 0$, using the two-step estimator.

12 This section is largely based on the work of Hall et al. (1984) and Nickell (1980) for the error correction interpretation, and Sargent (1979b) who provides a model in which the optimal stock and the speed of adjustment are jointly determined.

13 We ignore a discount factor $\alpha^t = (1 + d)^{-t}$, where d is the subjective discount rate, for simplicity of exposition. If $\alpha \neq 0$, it enters the equilibrium solution for M. Nickell (1985) also includes an additional cross-term $-c(M_t^* - M_{t-1}^*)(M_t - M_{t-1}))$ into the cost function, but this does not alter the general flavour of the results obtained. We are also implicitly assuming a two part decision process: M_{t+j}^* is determined, then costs of adjustment C determine the optimal path of M over time. M^* is, therefore, assumed to be independent of the dynamic path: a rather strong assumption.

14 Again, by analogy with the one-period costs of adjustment case, it is obvious that longer lags in M_t will occur if there are higher order costs of change (Hall et al., 1984) for example costs of changing the rate of growth in money $(\Delta M - \Delta M_{t-1})$. Nickell (1985) demonstrates that higher order lagged dependent variables also ensue when two components (x_1, x_2) of a particular target variable $x = x_1 + x_2$ have different adjustment costs. With discount factor α^t in the cost function (6.23), the solution is

$$M_t = q_1 M_{t-1} + (1 - q_1)(1 - q_1\alpha) \sum_i (q_1\alpha)^i M_{t+i}^*$$

15 A difference form on *all* variables imposes the restriction that the predicted value of the *level* of Y equals the actual value when income is constant, regardless of the values of a_i, and this is often used in weakly rational models. Sargent (1971) arges that we should not necessarily expect, nor impose the restriction that $\Sigma a_i = 1$.

16 A linear equation for M_t^* with its determinants (Y, R, P), each following a second-order autoregressive scheme, would produce such an outcome. Economic time series can frequently be represented by such low order autoregressive equations.

17 Restrictions between the parameters of the forward variables and the lagged dependent variables in (6.29) allow us, in principle at least, to discriminate between the forward and backward looking models.

18 Kanniainen and Tarkka (1983) provide a solution via the Euler equations. The transversality condition, namely that $M_{t+J}^* - E_t M_{t+J} \to 0$ as $J \to \infty$ is imposed.

19 We can eliminate M_{t+J}^* by assuming the time path of M^* is $M_{t+J}^* = (1+g)^J M_t^*$ where g is the growth rate of M_t^* (if M is in logarithms). Otherwise *expected* future values of the determinants of M^*, for example real output, prices and interest rates also appear in the equation.

7

The Supply of Assets

7.1 INTRODUCTION

The financial system in the industrialized nations consists of a highly complex set of interdependent institutions, for example the central bank (CB), commercial banks (who deal in retail and wholesale deposits), merchant banks, overseas banks, savings and loan associations (building societies in the UK) and life assurance and pension funds. The interplay of these institutions together with the personal sector and non-financial company sector, determine a wide variety of asset yields and stocks of assets held. The different institutions specialize in various types of financial assets and liabilities. For example commercial banks in the main operate money transmission services as well as supplying credit mainly in the form of bank loans to persons and companies. Savings and loan associations (building societies) accept short-term deposit liabilities and issue long-term credit (mortgages) for house purchase. Life assurance and pension funds use contractual savings flows to purchase assets with long maturities which finance future retirement pensions and life assurance provisions. It is usual to analyse bank and non-bank financial intermediaries, separately. We shall spend a great deal of time in analysing the money supply process because of its prominence in contemporary policy debates. Hence we shall concentrate on the behaviour of banks rather than financial intermediaries in general. However, we hope to show that banks and non-bank financial intermediaries have many features in common and broadly speaking both may be handled within the general framework provided by theories of the financial firm, which forms the first section of this chapter. Although in this chapter we are mainly concerned with the determinants of the desired supply of assets by financial intermediaries we shall find ourselves discussing the interplay of supply and demand factors when trying to model the determination of the equilibrium stock of assets, particularly 'money'. Since money is traded in a market (along with other assets) the need to simultaneously consider both supply and demand factors should be obvious. Our discussion of the determination of the money supply will focus on two broad approaches; money base control and the flow of funds (or credit market) approach. However, at the outset it is worthwhile briefly considering these approaches within the wider context of models of the *whole* financial system which are discussed more fully in the final chapter.

Recalling our study of the demand for money in previous chapters, it is worth noting that early views of the determination of the equilibrium money stock merely inverted the demand function. If the demand for money depends only on its opportunity cost (for example the rate on long-term government debt) then the authorities may influence the latter (say, by open market operations) and 'slide up and down the demand for money function' (Parkin, 1978) to achieve the desired equilibrium money stock.[1] The monetary base view of the determination of the money supply fits neatly into this model. In its simple mechanical form the authorities merely alter the monetary base (high powered money) to achieve a given money supply. The supply curve is vertical (in the r, M^s plane) and *the* interest rate adjusts to equate the supply and demand for money. However, as soon as we recognize that the demand for money and the money supply may depend on a vector of (relative) interest rates, the apparent simplicity of this model disappears. If the demand for money depends on the 'own rate' r_m which may vary relative to its opportunity cost r_b then to determine the equilibrium stock of money we require a model of the interaction between r_m and r_b. Since banks bid for large deposits (known as wholesale deposits) by altering r_m, a model of the behaviour of the banking firm is required to determine the money stock. The monetary base model can accommodate a simple relationship between r_m and r_b (for example r_m fixed by government regulation) but further complications ensue if other interest rates enter the asset demand and supply functions for money. The possibility of substitution among a wide range of assets led to the so-called 'new view' of the financial system.

In the 'new view' (Tobin, 1963; Gurley and Shaw, 1960), the banks do not react mechanically to changes in base money but weigh up the marginal costs and marginal revenue to be obtained before expanding their deposits (and earnings assets such as advances). The model is a general equilibrium approach whereby many interest rates adjust to equate the supply and demand of a wide variety of assets in the financial system; including money. The monetary base model suitably amended and the flow of funds approach may be considered to be special cases of the competitive equilibrium model of the 'new view'.

Complementary to the 'new view', the disequilibrium approach considers the possibility that *some* asset markets may be in disequilibrium. We have already mentioned this aspect when discussing disequilibrium in credit markets and the min-side condition (section 5.6).

Market disequilibrium in one financial market may 'spill over' and affect other asset demands and supplies. Disequilibrium markets are difficult to model empirically and their interaction with other markets is not easily analysed (Muellbauer and Portes 1978). This has limited the applicability of such models, although some relatively simple disequilibrium approaches have been tried for the financial sector (section 5.6) and for the real sector (section 10.3). To summarize, we have noted that financial models may be *partial* and consider only a subset of assets or just one side of a particular market (for example the simple monetary base model considers only the supply function for money). They may conform to a general equilibrium 'new view' approach, or incorporate disequilibrium in some markets. These general themes are discussed in more detail in chapter 10.

In this chapter we analyse some basic behavioural relationships which are used to construct complete models of the financial *system*. We begin with a discussion of theories of the financial *firm*, which are (in the main) applicable to both bank and non-bank financial intermediaries. There are a wide variety of these models and as yet no all-embracing model of financial intermediaries is available. Rather, each model may be more applicable to a particular type of financial intermediary than to others. Some are partial models and others are simple equilibrium models. The theory of the financial firm yields insights into the possible limitations of empirical models that are currently used to analyse financial markets.

The monetary base (MB) and so-called 'flow of funds' (FOF) approaches to the determination of the stock of money are specific models of the 'banking firms' and these are discussed at some length in sections 7.3 and 7.4 respectively. In section 7.5 we compare these two approaches and conclude that the two models are not as radically different as textbooks and some writers claim. Both approaches are deficient and point to the need to consider the determination of the money supply in a general equilibrium framework, which includes the determination of asset stocks other than money and hence a wider set of interest rates. These issues are taken up, in part, in the next chapter where we analyse methods of monetary control based on the MB and FOF approaches.

7.2 THEORIES OF THE FINANCIAL FIRM

Introduction. The 'standard' microeconomic theories of the firm deal at a minimum with the determination of equilibrium price and output. They are based on the assumption of maximizing some objective function such as profits, sales, managerial utility, etc. We wish to examine whether some of these theories can be successfully applied to financial firms such as banks and non-bank financial intermediaries. This prompts one to ask how the functions of financial intermediaries differ from those of the firm in the standard microeconomic literature.

Broadly speaking, part of the 'output' decision of banks concerns the appropriate level and rate of growth in deposits and loans. Decisions about the optimum size of the 'banking firm' may therefore have considerable bearing on the growth in the money supply and the design of policies for monetary control. The size of the 'banking firm' will be determined by managerial objectives in the light of labour and capital costs (that is real resource costs) and perceptions of risk and return on financial assets and liabilities. For example, the decision to expand loans involves substantial labour costs in processing information, assessing risks and weighing these against alternative investment opportunities such as investment in equities or bonds. The lowest cost method of obtaining 'finance' for the loan, for example through the wholesale money markets also needs to be calculated. This may require a forecast of future money market rates if the 'life' of the loan exceeds that for the initial wholesale deposit. The financial firm faces a complex decision problem. The reader may be aware that the standard theories of the firm such as perfect competition, monopoly, oligopoly and managerial models have not been entirely successful in explaining the pricing, output, investment, employment and growth decisions of firms. Similarly the literature on models of financial intermediaries is rather unsettled, heterogeneous and has not, as yet, yielded a generally accepted theory. Our purpose here is to review a number of theories and draw what conclusions we can concerning monetary control and the transmission mechanism of monetary policy;[2] we will frequently refer to banks rather than financial intermediaries but except where explicitly stated our remarks refer to both.

It is generally accepted (Niehans, 1978) that the two main functions of financial firms are, first, to act as brokers, *reducing the transactions costs* of channelling funds from ultimate lenders to ultimate borrowers and, second, to 'diversify' or transform risks. Like non-financial firms they perform such functions by combining physical capital (that is premises, computers, etc) and human capital (that is 'skilled' employees). Financial intermediaries accept 'money' (savings) from surplus units and in return issue their own secondary market assets (for example deposit with a saving and loan association, life insurance policy). The financial intermediary then lends the funds (money) acquired to primary borrowers (or 'deficit units'). There may be a number of financial intermediaries in the 'chain' from surplus to deficit unit as one financial intermediary on-lends funds to another; such 'pyramiding' is substantial in some secondary banks (for example non-clearing banks and the Eurobanks). Generally speaking, deficit units are the government and industrial and commercial firms. The first frequently has budget deficits that need to be financed and the latter require finance for physical investment and stockbuilding. The personal sector as a whole is frequently a 'surplus unit' while the overseas sector is a deficit unit if the domestic economy is in surplus on current account (and vice versa). Since individual lenders could seek out individual borrowers, the 'brokerage function' requires the financial firm to reduce information and transactions costs.

The financial firm also faces default risk on its loans and a 'withdrawal' or 'liquidity' risk on its liabilities. The secondary banks in the UK, for example, in the early 1970s gave substantial loans to property companies some of whom subsequently went bankrupt. Although the Bank of England, on this occasion, supported the secondary banks (known as 'the lifeboat') the latter suffered substantial losses. Building societies in the UK and savings and loan associations in the US have a considerable proportion of their deposits which may be withdrawn at short notice and changes in the level of deposits can be substantial in periods as short as one month. Transactions balances at banks may be withdrawn on demand.

Although some matching of the maturity of assets and liabilities of financial intermediaries takes place they frequently engage in some element of maturity transformation. Some financial intermediaries borrow short and lend 'long'; for example commercial banks who accept short-term deposits and lend out long-term loans and advances. This is known as positive maturity transformation. Savings and loan associations (building societies) also engage in positive maturity transformation. On the other hand pension funds and contractual life assurance companies could be viewed as borrowing long (through constractual saving) and lending 'short' (for example in short-term government debt). Unless there is perfect matching of assets and liabilities the financial intermediary may be forced to sell off some assets at a penalty cost in order to meet unexpected outflows of 'deposits'. For example a bank may have to sell long-term government debt prior to its maturity date and may incur a capital loss. However, financial intermediaries may be able to reduce ('transform') such risks below those obtainable by individual lenders and borrowers.

A financial firm with a large number of small depositors may find that the variance of its deposits is small. Similarly the variance of the *return* on loans (or other assets held) may fall, the larger the number of loans granted (or assets held).[3] The law of large numbers may therefore reduce (transform) overall risk, making it desirable that lending and borrowing should be centralized in a financial firm rather than undertaken bilaterally.

A satisfactory theory of the financial firm should therefore recognize the existence of risk and uncertainty and the cost of producing brokerage services. Monopoly, discriminating monopoly, risk-aversion models and liquidity management models seek to explain financial (or portfolio) decisions.[4] the latter two models assume some uncertainty, but usually the monopoly models do not. On the other hand, 'real resource models' emphasize the production costs of financial services. Models that combine the portfolio and real resource decisions are relatively rare.

A distinction can also be drawn between 'partial' models that treat the total size of the financial firm as given (exogenously) and discuss only the optimal allocation of the portfolio between various assets in the choice set and 'complete' models which attempt to explain the total size of the portfolio as well as its structure. Three broad types of complete model have been attempted: monopoly models, risk-aversion and real resource cost models. Liquidity management models are partial models that deal only with uncertainty surrounding deposit flows and their implications for holdings of reserve assets. The monetary base view of the determination of the money supply is usually based on this model, which we now discuss.

7.2.1 *Liquidity management models*

This set of models encompasses the target-threshold model of Miller and Orr (1966) discussed in connection with the demand for money. Before discussing this model, however, we outline a basic model which consists of optimization under stochastic deposit flows and is especially applicable to retail banks. Not surprisingly, perhaps, this model results in the optimal level of reserve assets depending upon the relevant opportunity cost of reserve assets and the probability distribution of the net cash drain. Thus this is a 'partial model', the only choice variables are the level of reserve and non-reserve assets. It is an asset allocation model and ignores decisions about the appropriate level of (deposit) liabilities.

We assume (a) a level of deposits D which is given exogenously (we are therefore dealing with a partial model), (b) a distribution of net cash outflows X given by $f(X)$, (c) the net yield on loans r, that is the interest cost less administrative costs, is exogenously given (perfect competition in the loan market), (d) p is the adjustment cost per £ (per time period) due to reserve deficiency (this includes the cost of obtaining alternative finance through emergency selling of assets or borrowing). Given these assumptions the bank chooses the optimal combination of reserve assets R and loans E to minimize total cost N.

The opportunity cost of holding reserves is rR. The *expected* liquidity cost L is the product of the cost of the reserve deficiency $p(X-R)$, and the probability of a reserve deficiency occurring

$$\int_R^\infty f(X)\,\mathrm{d}X$$

Hence

$$N = rR - L = rR + \int_R^\infty p(X-R)f(X)\,\mathrm{d}X$$

and $\partial N/\partial R = 0$ implies

$$r = L_R = p\int_R^\infty f(X)\,\mathrm{d}X \tag{7.1}$$

where $L_R = \partial L/\partial R$. Hence the marginal opportunity cost of holding an extra £ of reserves r is equated to the marginal reduction in liquidity costs L_R.

If $f(X)$ can be approximated by a normal distribution with zero mean, which is reasonable if there are a large number of independent depositors, then (7.1) reduces to

$$R^* = b\sigma_x^2 \tag{7.2}$$

where σ_x^2 is the variance of the net cash drain and b is determined by the ratio p/r. Desired reserves R^* are lower, the lower the variance of cash drain and the adjustment costs of illiquidity, and the higher is the loan rate.

The model assumes zero costs in adjusting to R^* so that equilibrium is maintained continuously. A target threshold model of the Miller and Orr (1966) type would allow reserves to fluctuate between an upper and lower bound before being returned to the optimum. Clearly the existence of transaction costs in adjusting R implies that R will only be adjusted towards R^*, if *adjustment* costs are less than the net gain to be obtained from a reduction of 'other costs' $N = (rR + L)$. Strictly speaking, we should formally incorporate such adjustment costs in the net cost function N, but in practice the partial adjustment model is usually applied to R^*.

Baltensperger (1972, 1980) suggests that σ_x should depend on the volume and structure of bank deposits; a plausible extension of the model. First he argues that σ_x (and therefore R) is a positive function of D; the relationship is less than proportional if D increases because of an increase in the number of independent accounts. Second, he states that σ_x and therefore R should increase if there is a redistribution of deposits in favour of more volatile deposits. For example from interest bearing to sight deposits.

Advocates of monetary base control tend to use the stochastic demand model to explain the behaviour of the reserve to deposit ratio but usually ignore the above qualifications. However, it is not clear that 'wholesale banks' who make up part of the monetary sector (and are included in the money supply statistics) conform to this stochastic demand model. Wholesale banks obtain some of their deposit funds for fixed periods, by bidding in the open market and 'match' the term of their liabilities to that of their assets, thus obviating the need for cash reserves. In contrast retail banks tend to fix interest rates and accept all deposits at this going rate. Thus, although for retail banks deposits are exogenous, for wholesale banks this is not the case and the applicability of the stochastic reserve model where all stochastic cash drain is met by reducing non-reserve assets (for example bank loans and long term government debt), does not seem to be applicable to wholesale banking.

The next model of the financial firm we consider is a 'complete' model based on the ideas of risk aversion already discussed in chapter 3 on the demand for assets.

7.2.2 Risk-aversion model of the supply of assets

The financial firm in a perfectly competitive environment considers the return on its assets and liabilities as exogenous and hence outside its control. (They are determined by the *market* supply and demand curves.) If these returns are subject to uncertainty over the holding period we have the risk aversion model, a special case of which is the mean-variance model of section 3.3. The demand for assets *and* the supply of liabilities (deposits) therefore depends on expected holding period yields, the variance–covariance structure of asset returns and any exogenous items in the balance sheet (such as mandatory or required reserves). In practice the model has often been applied only to the demand for *assets* by financial intermediaries with deposits being assumed exogenous. We discussed empirical results from such models as applied to banks and discount houses in section 5.5.3. The model ignores the possibility of a stochastic cash drain and therefore omits a key element in the behaviour of retail banks and saving and loan associations.[5] It would appear to be more relevant in explaining the composition of assets for life assurance and pension funds under the assumption of an exogenous inflow of funds. These institutions are less prone to stochastic cash drain and the net inflow of funds is largely predictable. As usually applied, the mean variance model assumes one-period maximization (of the expected utility of wealth) and although this is a useful time horizon when considering asset switching within a given amount of total assets, it is not applicable when we wish to consider the *growth* of the financial firm and its balance sheet. Real resource cost models then become important. However, these are rather primitive as we shall see when discussing the real perfect competition and monopoly models.

7.2.3 Perfect competition

If we consider one-period profit maximization under perfect competition utilizing only financial considerations, we do not obtain a deterministic solution for the 'output' of the financial firm. Let E, R and D represent loans, reserves and deposits respectively and r^E, r^R and r^D are their respective interest yields which are given exogenously under perfect competition. If the 'financial firm' maximizes profit Π subject to the balance sheet constraint $R + E = D$ we have

$$\max_{(E,R,D)} \quad Q = r^E E + r^R R - r^D D + \lambda(R + E - D)$$

$$Q_E = r^E + \lambda = Q_R = r^R + \lambda = Q_D = -r^D - r^D - \lambda = 0 \qquad (7.3)$$

and $r^E = r^R = r^D$ is the first order condition. Since the values of r are exogenous they are unlikely to be equal but even if they are equal, the solutions for the 'optimal' values of E, R and D are indeterminate – *any* values of E, R and D produce zero profit.[6]

Real resource costs. By analogy with the standard theory of the firm we can rescue the perfect competition model for the 'financial' firm by invoking real resource costs that depend upon the level of loans $C(E)$. We assume positive and increasing marginal cost $C_E(E)$, $C_{EE}(E) > 0$; the real resource costs depend particularly upon the labour costs of organizing and processing loan applications. Aggregate E will consist of a continuous change in *individual* loan applications, both new and 'roll-over' credits and thus require a continuous labour input (with a fixed wage and diminishing marginal productivity). Assuming, for simplicity that $R = 0$ and therefore $E = D$ we have[7]

$$\max \Pi = (r^E - r^D) E - C(E) \qquad (7.4)$$

$$\Pi_E = r^E - r^D - C_E(E) = 0 \qquad (7.5)$$

The first-order condition implies loans should be expanded until the fixed marginal loan receipts r^E equal the marginal cost of funds $r^D + C_E$. The latter comprise the exogenous deposit rate r^D and the rising marginal real resource costs of providing loans $C_E(E)$. We can solve equation (7.5) for E as a function of $r^E - r^D$ (see figure 7.1 for the usual diagrammatic exposition). Output E (or $D = E$) responds positively to $r^E - r^D$ and negatively to exogenous costs such as the wage rate and capital costs.[8] Thus in this simple model, firm size is determinate and depends on financial and real resource costs. For example an exogenous rise wage rate shifts the marginal cost curve to the left resulting in a fall in the equilibrium level of loans and deposits (figure 7.1). However, the model's main use is of a pedagogic nature in showing the possible interaction between real resource costs and the level of loans. Its defects are in part those of the normal (simple) model of perfect competition. There is no optimization over time and therefore no investment decisions, the size of the firm is indeterminate if there are no long-run decreasing returns to scale (that is 'U' shaped long-run average cost curve) and there is no uncertainty. In addition, the interest rate gap $(r^E - r^D)$ is not explained by the model but is clearly a pre-requisite for 'output' E to depend upon interest rates. For a positive equilibrium level of E we also require a positive interest spread $(r_E - r_D) > 0$.

It is easy to see how a profit maximizing framework under perfect competition may be used to determine the optimal level of different types of 'deposit output' D_1, D_2 with *different* production costs $C = C(D_1, D_2)$ and interest rates (prices) r_1^D, r_2^D.

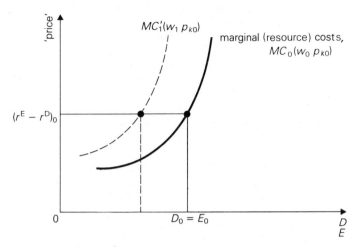

FIGURE 7.1 *Perfect competition: increase in costs.*

The analogous problem in the standard theory of the firm is to choose the optimal combination of output in two plants (q_1, q_2) with different cost structures. Here the solutions for q_1 and q_2 are functions of exogenous wages, the user cost of capital and the price of output. Similarly the problem for the cost minimizing banking firm is to choose D_1 and D_2 such that

$$\max_{(D_1, D_2)} \Pi = r_1^D D_1 + r_2^D D_2 - C(D_1 D_2) \tag{7.6}$$

The marginal cost of additional output of D_1 is given by $C_1 = \partial C / \partial D_1$ and depends upon D_1 and D_2 as well as exogenous input prices such as the wage rate. First-order conditions yield $r_1^D - C_1 = 0 = r_2^D - C_2$.

Since C_1 and C_2 are functions of the level of deposits we can solve the first-order conditions to give $D_i = f_i(r_1^D, r_2^D)$, $i = 1, 2$. Time deposits, where withdrawals are less frequent, probably have a lower marginal cost of production than 'sight deposits' which are used as part of the payments mechanism, so the model has some relevance. However, it is far too simplistic. Perfect competition models are equilibrium models but only equilibrium 'quantities' are chosen by the firm, while 'prices' are exogenous. Monopoly models consider both price and quantity decisions.

7.2.4 Monopoly models

Monti (1971) and Klein (1971) have each proposed a monopoly model for the financial firm but without invoking production costs (which as we saw above are required in the perfect competition model). The model yields a determinate firm size, an optimal allocation of deposits and loans and an optimal setting for interest rates. In this limited sense it is a 'complete model', but it neglects adjustment costs, real resource costs and risk.

The model deals simultaneously with the supply and demand for assets of the financial firm and hence is an equilibrium model. Banks can alter their supply of deposits by altering their deposit rates and similarly alter their demand for loans by changing loan rates (both, relative to the exogenous bond rate). When there are no constraints on banking behaviour these monopoly models yield a loan rate setting equation that is independent of conditions in deposit markets. This dichotomy between loan and deposit markets implies that banks do not alter loan rates when deposit rates rise or when there is a shift in the deposit function (due to changes in income) or changes in reserve requirements. The loan rate is altered only when the exogenous bond rate changes or when there is a shift in the loan demand function. These somewhat counter-intuitive results imply that the authorities cannot influence the loan rate by changes in reserve requirements but only by changes in the bond rate via open market operations.

It turns out that this dichotomy is broken when the financial firm meets a binding liquidity constraint, namely that reserve asset holdings are at the minimum mandatory level. The loan rate is then influenced by the deposit rate and the arguments of the demand for deposits function. The relationship between loan and deposit rates will be seen to be an important one for monetary control under both the monetary base and flow of funds model.

Assumptions. The financial firm is assumed to have (a) downward sloping demand for loans function, (b) upward sloping demand for deposits function, (c) the bond market is perfectly competitive with an exogenous rate on bonds r^b, (d) the bank chooses between three assets, reserves R, bonds B and loans E, and also chooses the level of deposits D;[9] reserves are assumed proportional to deposits $R = kD$, (e) we assume that the objective of the firm is to maximize *current* period profit Π. The budget constraint is $R + B + E = D$ and the Lagrangian Q is

$$\max Q = r^b B + r^E E - r^D D + \lambda(kD + B + E - D) \tag{7.7}$$

where

$$E = E(r^E, r^b) = e_0 - e_1 r^E + e_2 r^b \tag{7.8}$$

and

$$D = D(r^D r^b) = d_0 + d_1 r^D - d_2 r^b \tag{7.9}$$

are the demand funcitions for loans and deposits by the NBPS (here assumed linear). Bonds are assumed to be (gross) substitutes with loans since loans are an alternative form of borrowing. Bonds and deposits are also assumed to be gross substitutes. If the demand functions are linear, $\partial E/\partial r^E$, etc. are constants (given by the e_i and d_i coefficients). Differentiating with respect to B, E and D the first-order conditions are[10]

$$r^b + \lambda = 0 \tag{7.10}$$

$$r^E + E\frac{\partial r^E}{\partial E} + \lambda = 0 \tag{7.11}$$

$$-r^D - D\frac{\partial r^D}{\partial D} + \lambda(k - 1) = 0 \qquad (7.12)$$

The firm equates the marginal revenue from loans $(r^E + E\,\partial r^E/\partial E)$ with the exogenously given bond rate $(-\lambda = r^b)$. The bank meets the loan demand consistent with this solution and any residual funds are invested in bonds. A change in liabilities (deposits) is offset by changes in holdings of bonds and does not influence the loan rate and the equilibrium level of loans.

The size or scale of the firm's operation is determined by the solution for D. The marginal cost (MC) of additional deposits with zero reserves $(k = 0)$ is $MC = (r^D + D\,\partial r^D/\partial D)$. With required reserves, this rises to $MC' = MC/1 - k \cong MC(1 + k)$ for $|k| < 1$. The adjusted marginal cost MC' is equated to the exogenous bond rate (using equations (7.12) and (7.10)) to determine the firm's size. Having determined D and E, reserves follow from $R = kD$ and the optimal level of bonds as the 'residual' item in the balance sheet constraint $(B = D - R - E)$. The solutions for the asset stocks and the interest rates r^D and r^E are given in appendix 7A. The level of loans and the loan rate depend on the bond rate and the parameters of the loan demand function only. The deposit rate and the equilibrium level of deposits also depends on the bond rate and the relevant deposit elasticities together with the required reserve ratio k.

An increase in the bond rate raises both the deposit and loan rate but the effect of this on the level of loans and deposits is ambiguous. This is most easily seen in the case of loan supply by the bank. An increase in r^b leads to an increase in the demand for lending from the financial firm by the non-bank private sector but the increase in r^b leads the financial firm to raise the rate on loans r^E, which tends to reduce loan demand.

Klein's model also has reserves depending upon the variance of deposit flows as in the stochastic inventory model, but reserves are independent of deposit composition and proportional to the aggregate level of deposits. Klein introduces two types of deposit with different demand functions; this merely adds an additional equation whereby the marginal revenue from each type of loan is equalized (as in the normal discriminating monopoly case). The Monti model also includes an exogenous interest rate paid on reserve assets r^R. The reduced form equations for r_D, D, R and therefore B (as the 'residual' asset from the balance sheet) depend upon r^R. An increase in r^R increases r_D, D, R and B but leaves r^E and E unchanged. The latter occurs because of the loan-deposit dichotomy, since the first-order conditions for r^E and E depend only on r^b and the parameters of the loan demand function.

The above monopoly models highlight the fact that banks may set deposit and loan rates as well as determine the optimal level of liabilities and assets. The differential between the loan rate and deposit rate depends upon the elasticities and cross elasticities of demand for deposits and loans. The larger is e_2/e_1 relative to d_2/d_1, the larger is the loan-deposit differential. (See equations (7A.4) and (7A.5) in appendix 7A.) For example the more inelastic is the demand for loans (the smaller is e_1) the higher the loan-deposit differential, an intuitively acceptable result.

The authorities may seek to control the money supply by open market operations, altering the rate of interest on bonds r^b. This leads to a switch out of deposits and into bonds, the partial effect on D being given by d_2. However, our monopoly model reminds us that this will not be the end of the story. Optimizing banks increase the deposit rate which tends to increase the demand for deposits (money). The net effect of an open market operation on the money supply is therefore ambiguous; it depends on the subsequent rise in deposit rates and the size of the 'own' elasticity of demand d_1.

Extensions of the monopoly model. Slovin and Sushka (1983) extend the monopoly model by considering the case where the financial firm faces a binding liquidity constraint, namely that (government) bonds B are at the minimum mandatory level $B = hD$ (where h is the minimum liquidity ratio). The mathematics of the model is a straightforward application of the Kuhn–Tucker conditions using the above Lagrangian. The loan rate setting function is

$$r^E\left(1 + \frac{1}{e^E}\right)(1 - h) + hr^B = r^D\left(1 + \frac{1}{e^D}\right) \tag{7.13}$$

where e^E and e^D are the elasticities of demand for loans and deposits respectively. Thus the marginal cost of additional (wholesale) deposits is bid up to equality with marginal revenue. The latter consists of the return from investing in bonds, at the minimum proportion h, and providing loans with the remaining proportion of funds $1 - h$. The loan rate is now affected by shifts in the deposit market and is a *mark-up* on the deposit rate.

For US banks 1952(3)–1980(4), Slovin and Sushka run various regression equations with the loan rate as the dependent variable. Independent variables are rates on other bank assets (for example commercial paper rate), foreign interest rates, the deposit rate, measures of risk (for example ratio of loans to deposits) and disequilibrium terms (for example growth in loans relative to deposits). They find that loan rates respond to the commercial paper and foreign interest rates very quickly but are uninfluenced by the other rates. It thus appears that for the US the loan rate is independent of the deposit rate and disequilibrium in the loan market, but reacts quickly to other market interest rates. The evidence for the UK (Goodhart, 1984; Spencer and Mowl, 1978) suggests that there were significant lags in the response of the loan rate to the exogenous market rate (as measured by bank rate or MLR) up until the middle of the 1970s. After that period bank loan rates responded quickly to MLR. There is some weak econometric evidence that the loan rate responds to the *deposit* rate but much stronger anecdotal evidence to support this view from pronouncements by bankers to the Wilson Committee (Wilson, 1980, paras. 211–16) at least for the latter half of the 1970s. Spencer and Mowl (1978) and Savage (1978) find little evidence that the loan rate responds to excess demand in the loan market (although the tests are rather indirect like those of Slovin and Sushka above). Thus it *may* be that the loan market could experience periods of disequilibrium although the evidence from these interest rate equations is by no means definitive.

Sales and profits. Monti considers alternative objectives to profit maximization: maximizing deposits (sales) subject to a profit constraint and maximizing a utility function consisting of profits and deposits. The latter is somewhat of a compromise model lying between profit maximization and deposit maximization and we therefore briefly discuss this model. As in the Klein model the loan rate r^E depends only upon the exogenous bond rate and the parameters of the loan demand function (equation (7A.4) in the appendix 7A) and is therefore invariant to this change in the objective function. However, the deposit rate and therefore the level of deposits (reserves and bonds) is greater than in the profit maximization case. The loan deposit differential is smaller the higher the weight given to 'sales' considerations in the utility function.

Real resource costs. Our above monopoly models of the banking firm take no account of the probability of 'redeposits' and therefore the firm must be considered as a monopolist in a local market. Second, in contrast to the usual monopoly models in the theory of the firm, the supply of 'output', that is deposits and loans, differs only with regard to the *demand* characteristics; there are no production costs in supplying loans or deposits. We now correct this defect and examine a monopoly model of the banking firm where there exists cost of producing loans (or deposits) $C(E)$. We also assume reserves are endogenous and earn an exogenous interest rate r^R. We assume all earning assets are loans (that is $B = 0$) to simplify the algebra (Sinclair, 1983). Profit Π is

$$\Pi = Er^E - Dr^D + r^R R - C(E) \tag{7.14}$$

and is maximized with respect to E, D and R subject to the balance sheet constraint $R + E - D = 0$. The bank chooses r^E and r^D in addition to the asset demands and it is shown in appendix 7B that, in general, the equilibrium loan-deposit interest differential and the reserve to deposits ratio depend in a complex way upon the elasticities of demand for deposits and loans as well as the marginal production costs of supplying loans C_E. Given our earlier discussion of the Klein-Monti type models (which exclude real resource costs) these results should not cause surprise. The reader may recall that equilibrium price P and output in the standard monopoly model is determinate but depends upon the position of the demand curve (as expressed in the elasticity of demand with respect to output e_d) as well as the marginal cost curve MC. The equilibrium price–output relationship may be represented by $P = (1 - |e^d|^{-1})$MC, or equivalently marginal revenue equals marginal cost. A shift in the demand curve (unless the latter has a constant price elasticity) alters the value of the elasticity with the result that the equilibrium change in price and output cannot be signed a priori. Our monopoly model of the banking firm suffers similar problems. An *explicit* solution for the level of D, E, R, r^E and r^D as a function of exogenous variables cannot be obtained and unambiguous comparative static results are not obtainable a priori. The model does, however, guard one against wholesale acceptance of simple functions purporting to explain the reserve-deposit ratio of the banking firm. Whilst it may be necessary in practice to postulate (estimate) simple functions, strong conclusions based upon them must be interpreted with extreme caution.

7.2.5 *Other models*

Oligopoly models and models of cartel arrangements can of course also be applied to the financial firm. The commercial banks in the UK, prior to the policy of competition and credit control in 1971, and the building societies, until quite recently, could be usefully slotted into models involving cartel arrangements. Similarly the UK commercial banks after 1971 and the larger building societies after 1983 may exhibit behaviour associated with oligopolies. The latter manifests itself in price leadership, non-price competition, barriers to entry and high advertising expenditure. However, formal oligopoly models yield qualitative results at best and therefore we do not pursue these models here. However, the reader could undoubtedly apply his knowledge of oligopolies and cartels to gain insights into the behaviour of some financial intermediaries. Models that deal with managerial objectives and the growth objectives of the firm are obviously of relevance for the behaviour of the financial firm but space constraints preclude discussion of these (Koutsoyiannis (1982) provides an excellent account of these issues).

7.2.6 *Summary*

Although our theories of the financial form are unlikely to *precisely* monitor the behaviour of financial intermediaries, nevertheless they provide useful insights that would lead one to question the relevance of highly simplified models. The stochastic reserve loss model has some relevance to retail banks where the authorities do not automatically provide reserve assets on demand at zero penalty cost. Thus the model may be more applicable to say US 'clearing banks' in the post-1979 reserve base targeting regime than prior to 1979 when the authorities targeted interest rates Where banks raise funds by bidding for whole-sale deposits, the monopoly model or the mean-variance model are of some relevance. If one believes that the wholesale deposit rate is set in the *market*, the mean variance model yields a desired supply function for deposits depending on a vector of interest rates. On the other hand, if banks have some degree of monopoly power the 'supply function' for deposits and loans are 'interest rate setting functions'. The latter may depend on exogenous market interest rates, real resource costs and perceived elasticities of demand (and in the real world on default risk factors). As we shall see in the sections dealing with the money base and flow of funds approach, the speed with which loan rates respond to deposit rates is a crucial element for successful monetary control.

The real resource cost approach leads one to consider that managerial objectives, which might include staff emoluments, training, technological advancement, etc., are probably important factors in understanding the dynamics of the banking firm. Product diversification (for example UK banks entering the home loan market in 1980–2) requires a complex managerial input involving investment in human and physical capital which may act as a constraint on the growth of the *financial* balance sheet (that is the level of deposits and loans).

The problem in applying the numerous models available to any one type of financial intermediary is that the latter engage in a number of different activities and therefore no single model of the financial firm is applicable. For example most clearing banks take retail deposits at fixed interest rates but also deal extensively in the wholesale money markets. They hold precautionary reserves to avoid the 'liquidity costs' of a cash drain but also decide on the distribution of their assets between default free liquid assets, capital uncertain government bonds and high risk loans. Allocation amongst the default free assets may be determined by mean-variance considerations whereas loans may be determined by the banks setting loan rates and allowing loans to be demand determined, as in the monopoly model. An eclectic model is therefore called for.

A mathematical 'trick' is to invoke 'separability' or independence between the various decisions.[11] (We discussed this in chapter 3 with respect to theories of the demands for assets.) For example the bank may set retail deposit and loan rates leaving these quantities to be demand determined.[12] The 'gap' between these two items may be met by changing the wholesale deposit rate to attract additional funds. Precautionary balances may be determined by the model of stochastic reserve losses and liquid assets may form the residual of the bank's balance sheet. The allocation *within* this residual could be determined by mean-variance considerations. This kind of decision tree (or separability or independence conditions) assumes that factors that influence each type of decision do not influence the others, for example that the loan rate does not influence the choice *amongst* the different liquid assets. (Although the *block* of assets as a whole, that make up the 'residual' in the balance sheet, is dependent on *all* the factors that influence the 'other' asset demands.)

Dynamic considerations concerning the *growth* of the balance sheet may be determined by broad managerial goals and objectives, and are therefore likely to be multidimensional and to vary over time. The Monti model which has 'size' and profits in the objective function is a useful example of a simple static model utilizing a multi-dimensional approach. Over time, changing mangerial goals or changing the weighting given to a fixed set of goals may cause supply parameters to appear unstable. Such regime changes are notoriously difficult to model empirically. Thus, although no formal and tractible 'super-model' of the financial firm is available, our piecemeal models do provide insights into the complexities of the system. With this in mind we now turn to more practical considerations and consider two simplified but tractable approaches to modelling the determination of the money supply.

7.3 THE MONETARY BASE APPROACH

We begin our analysis of the monetary base (MB) approach to the determination of the money supply by examining a simple model of the multiple expansion of deposits. This model although 'unrealistic' is nevertheless a useful pedagogic device. Using this model we examine the sources of changes in 'the base' (or high powered money) and its impact on the level of deposits under the assumption that the reserve ratio of the banks and cash to deposits ratio of the NBPS are constant. In section 7.3.1 we present the above model algebraically but then allow some element of portfolio choice by the banks and NBPS in determining their desired asset ratios. We are able to relate (a simplified version of) this portfolio MBC model to the LM curve of chapter 1. We end the section with some illustrative examples of empirical work on the relevant asset ratios. In secion 7.4 we discuss similar issues with respect to the 'flow of funds' approach. It is not until section 7.5 that we present a critical appraisal of the two approaches. Here the major feature to emerge is that both theories fail to address the problems in modelling the behaviour of wholesale banks who engage in liability as well as asset management.

7.3.1 *Simple bank multiplier*

We establish the conditions under which a multiple expansion of bank deposits may take place and hence explain why banks may 'create' money even though they only 'lend what they receive'. We consider the UK as the domestic economy and sterling as the domestic currency. The initial unrealistic assumptions of the model are later relaxed.

Assume (a) there is only one commercial (retail) bank, with deposits D, (b) reserve assets of the bank R_b are 'till money' and bankers' balances at the CB; the bank's desired reserve ratio $\beta = R_b/D$ is 10 per cent, (c) the NBPS does not wish to hold any additional cash but will hold additional bank deposits or debt instruments of the CB at unchanged interest rates, (d) the balance of payments is always in equilibrium and hence there are no net flows of sterling into the banking system from this source, (e) the money supply is defined to include sterling bank deposits of the UK NBPS only, (f) banks also hold non-reserve assets consisting of long-term government debt and advances to the NBPS. The banks' reserves of 'till money' and bankers' balances *plus* the 'cash' held by the NBPS is referred to as the 'monetary base' or 'high powered money'.

Starting from equilibrium, the reserves of the bank may change only if it has direct or indirect dealing with the CB. The CB may purchase government long-term debt directly from the banks thus increasing reserves (bankers balances at the CB) and reducing non-reserve assets by equal amounts leaving the deposits of the NBPS unchanged. Such 'asset switching' by the banks into reserve assets increases the reserve *ratio* β. The CB 'finances' a government budget deficit (initially) by issuing cheques to the NBPS; deposits and reserves rise by equal (absolute) amounts and the reserve ratio increases. Similarly, when the CB purchases assets (usually government debt) from the NBPS or exchanges foreign currency earned by the NBPS for sterling, commercial bank reserve assets and deposits rise by equal amounts. The foreign currency arises from a *net* sale of goods or financial and real assets to the overseas sector, that is running a balance of payments, current plus capital account, surplus. A freely floating exchange rate or a policy of complete sterilization under fixed exchange rates would ensure that the net effect of such transaction is zero.[13] Any net sales of foreign currency due to intervention in the spot foreign exchange market by the CB results in a change in commercial bank reserves assets, deposits and the reserve ratio.

Faced with an additional £10m of reserve assets and deposits due to the 'financing' of a government budget deficit (for example employing a Civil Servant Mr X), the bank may extend its deposits to £1100m and still maintain a 10 per cent reserve ratio R_b/D (table 7.1, balance sheets (i)–(iii)). The bank may do this either by increasing advances (to the NBPS) or purchasing existing gilts from the NBPS. In each case the assets of the bank increase by £90m and

TABLE 7.1 Simple bank multiplier

1 Multiple expansion of deposits/loans by 'A-bank'

(i)

Assets		Liabilities
R	100	1000 D
B	450	
L	450	
	1000	1000

$R/D = 100/1000 = 10\%$

(ii)

Assets		Liabilities
R	110	1000 D
		+ 10 Mr X
B	450	
L	450	
	1010	1010

$R/D = 110/1010 > 10\%$

(iii)

Assets		Liabilities
R	110	1010
		+ 90 Mr A
		− 90 Mr A
		+ 90 Mr Z
B	450	
L	450 + 90 Mr A	
	1100	1100

$R/D = 110/1100 = 10\%$

Aggregate Reserve Ratio

$$\frac{20 + 190}{2000} \approx 10\%$$

2 Interbank market

(iv) A-bank

Assets		Liabilities
R	(110 − 90) = 20	1100
		− 90 Mr A
B	450	
L	450 + 90	
	1010	1010

$(R/D)_A = 20/1010 < 10\%$

(v) B-bank

Assets		Liabilities
R	100 + 90	1000
		+ 90 Mr B
B	450	
L	450	
	1090	1090

$(R/D)_B = 190/1090 > 10\%$

(vi) A-bank

Assets		Liabilities
R	20 + 90	1010
		+ 90 Mr B
B	450	
L	450 + 90	
	1100	1100

$(R/D)_A = 110/1100 = 10\%$

(vii) B-bank

Assets		Liabilities
R	190 − 90	1090
		− 90 Mr B
B	450	
L	450	
	1000	1000

$(R/D)_B = 100/1000 = 10\%$

members of the NBPS receive an equivalent increase in their deposits. In the case of a purchase of gilts the NBPS current accounts (sight deposits) are credited by £90m. Initially the recipient of the advance has his current account credited. If the recipient (Mr A) spends his advances on goods and services produced in the UK, or on assets held by other members of the UK NBPS (Mr Z) then Mr A's deposit falls by £90m and Mr Z's rises by an equal amount (table 7.1, balance sheet (iii)). The ownership of the deposit alters but not the total outstanding. The latter also occurs if non-bank financial intermediaries hold their reserve assets in the form of bank deposits.

For an injection of base or high powered money of £10m there has been a multiple expansion of deposits of £100m: the deposit multiplier is '10' and is given by $\Delta D = \Delta X_b / \beta$. This process is dubbed the 'widows cruse' by Tobin (1963).

Let us now consider several equal-sized banks all of whom behave identically. If Mr B banks at bank B then when Mr A spends the advance, Mr A's bank will receive a claim on its reserves for £90m from Mr B's bank. Deposits and reserves of A-bank will fall by £90m to £20m and £1010m respectively while those of B-bank will rise by an equal amount (table 7.1, balance sheets (iv) and (v)). But the crucial factor is that the total increase in deposits (in A- and B-banks) is £(10 + 90) as in the single-bank case, and the injection of new 'base' or high powered money does not 'leak out' from the banking system as a whole. We now relax some of the restrictive assumptions of our mechanical bank multiplier and introduce some elementary portfolio considerations into the analysis.

If bank A finds its reserve ratio is low (table 7.1, balance sheet (iv)) it may bid for additional reserve assets from other banks who have surplus reserve assets; this is the function of the interbank market. Alternatively A-bank may attempt to regain its lost deposit and reserves by inducing Mr B to transfer his deposit to A-bank (table 7.1, balance sheets (vi) and (vii)). A-bank does this by bidding for wholesale deposits (of firms) and offering a higher return.

The extent to which either A-bank or B-bank expands relatively faster depends upon: (a) The proportion of deposits that return automatically to each bank because of the payments mechanism. The 'bigger' the bank in the retail deposit market the less the drain on cash reserves after expanding non-reserve assets. (b) The willingness of either bank to offer higher interest rates to attract wholesale deposits (and therefore reserves from other banks). This in turn depends upon the effect of this higher marginal cost of funds on the interest cost of advances and the response of the latter in volume terms. The more efficient in terms of manpower and other real resource costs in administering advances and assessing their riskiness, the smaller the deposit-advance spread can be and the larger the level of advances and deposits for any particular bank.

If we relax assumption (c) (p. 162) and allow the NBPS to hold reserve assets (for example notes and coin) then in principle the banking system *as a whole* can obtain additional reserves assets by 'bidding them away' from the NBPS. Credit card facilities and electronic banking may allow the NBPS to substitute bank deposits for cash. Interest rates paid on current accounts[14] or higher interest rates on seven-day deposit accounts may encourage a switch by the personal sector out of cash into deposits and therefore increase the total amount of reserve assets held by banks. If reserve assets are more widely defined to include short-term assets such as Treasury and commercial bills, the banks can bid for these in the market. (The NBPS then holds less 'bills' and more deposits; a higher price offered for 'bills' would facilitate this.)

Relaxing assumption (d) (p. 162) provides an additional leakage of the monetary base under fixed exchange rates (or government intervention in the foreign exchange market). Expenditure on foreign 'goods' requires a sale of deposits (sterling) to the CB in exchange for foreign currency (for example dollars). Bankers' balances at the CB (that is reserves) fall as do sterling deposits of the NBPS. The reserve to deposit ratio (which applies to sterling funds) falls. Foreign currency deposits of the UK NBPS held in UK banks rise. Payment for goods leads to a fall in foreign currency deposits held in UK banks by residents and an equal rise in foreign currency holdings of foreign residents. These foreign currency deposits need not concern us further here since we have assumed that the money supply consists of £ deposits of *domestic* residents.

To summarize: sources of high powered money (the 'monetary base') arise from CB transactions with the NBPS and the banks. They include a budget deficit, a balance of payments surplus (deficit) and open market operations. If the NBPS is allowed to hold reserve assets, banks may obtain reserves from this source. If banks bid directly for reserve assets from other banks through the interbank market this does not *directly* affect the *total* amount of reserve assets in existence since these transactions do not involve the CB. Similarly, if banks bid away reserve assets from other banks by selling wholesale deposits to the NBPS, the total amount of reserve assets is unchanged. However, if bidding for wholesale deposits leads to a (relative) rise in the 'own' interest rate on money (deposits) the NBPS might (a) switch out of cash into deposits, or (more likely) (b) sell government debt. The former directly increases bank reserves. The latter will also increase bank reserves if the CB (rather than *other* members of the NBPS) purchase the debt sold by some members of the NBPS. If the CB wishes to keep interest rates constant then it has to accept any debt offered at the going market interest rate. Otherwise, an excess supply of bonds (for example sales by NBPS) implies 'bond' prices would fall and interest rates rise. This is the origin of the view that if the CB sets interest rates it cannot control the monetary base and hence the level of deposits (money supply). Note that the CB can *predict* what will happen to the money supply but cannot prevent this happening, given its interest rate target. The amount of any lost reserves recouped by 'competitive bidding' thus depends crucially on the amount by which banks are willing to push up interest rates on deposits and hence advances, the asset preferences of the NBPS and the reaction of the CB to higher interest rates. With this in mind we now turn to a more formal analysis of MBC.

7.3.2 *Monetary base model*

Advocates of MBC argue that control of the money supply relies on the authorities being able to precisely control the base and to predict a small number of behavioural relations of the banks and the NBPS. High powered money or the monetary base B is a subset of the liabilities of the central bank, usually 'till money' and bankers' balances at the central bank (interbank claims net out to zero). The base may be held either by the non-bank private sector R_p or the banks R_b. The money supply M^s is defined as cash held by the non-bank private sector C_p and deposits D of the banking system

$$M^s = C_p + D \tag{7.15}$$

$$B^s = R_p + R_b \tag{7.16}$$

We can rearrange these two identities to give a third identity

$$M^s \equiv \frac{1 + C_p/D}{(R_p/D) + (R_b/D)} B = \left[\frac{1 + \alpha}{\beta_p + \beta_b}\right] B = mB \tag{7.17}$$

where $\alpha = C_p/D$, etc. The money supply may be described by the cash to deposits ratio and reserve asset to deposit ratio of the non-bank private sector (NBPS) (α_p and β_p respectively) and the reserve assets ratio of the commercial banks β_b.[15] There is as yet no behavioural content to equation (7.17) it is an identity, true by definition.

The term in square brackets is often referred to as the money multiplier m, so that changes in the money supply are the product of changes in the base B and in the value of the multiplier

$$\Delta M = m\Delta B + B\Delta m \tag{7.18}$$

or

$$\dot{M} = \dot{m} + \dot{B} \tag{7.19}$$

where a dot over the variable indicates a percentage change.

Since equation (7.19) is an identity it can be used to decompose changes in the money supply into its constituent parts (in the same way as the flow of funds identity). In conventional input–output analysis, changes in the level of output of an industry depends upon changes in the level of material inputs ('the base') and the input–output coefficients. By analogy, B constitutes the level of input and α, β_p and β_b the input–output coefficients.

Advocates of base control assert that since B may be controlled by the authorities and as the asset ratios of the money multiplier are *predictable* (not necessarily constant) then we can predict/control the money supply. Further, we need only concern ourselves with, at most, the behaviour of three asset ratios, a considerable saving in complexity of presentation. Control of the base requires the authorities to accept whatever interest rates are required to remove excess 'cash' from the banks by open market sales of debt to the banks and NBPS.[16] Control over interest rates is therefore relinquished and interest rates are 'market determined'. A floating exchange rate is also required to prevent the 'base' being altered by volatile short-term capital flows that cannot be sterilized in a near perfect capital market.[17]

Some advocates of MBC argue that reserve assets should be narrowly defined so there exists few close substitutes held by the NBPS. This they argue, would help to ensure stability in the relevant asset–deposit ratios. Hence reserve assets of banks are usually defined to exclude 'non-cash' items such as commercial and

Treasury bills. Some go further and advocate a system of 'negotiable entitlements' issued by the authorities independently of funding operations (that is negotiable entitlements do not finance the PSBR) and held only by the banks (Duck and Sheppard, 1978). Thus $X_p/D = 0$; we have one less ratio to worry about in our MBC identity and the base becomes independent of the government borrowing requirement.

Portfolio considerations. Advocates of MBC introduce portfolio considerations into the analysis and they argue that MBC does *not* assume a mechanical response by the banks but is based on rational neo-classical models of behaviour. It is not always clear which neo-classical model of bank behaviour advocates of MBC have in mind. The model presented below as being representative of MBC advocates is that of inventory optimization under stochastic reserve losses. Griffiths (1979, p. 39), in advocating MBC, appears to have this model in mind. However, the reader should recall that different 'maximizing' models (for example monopoly, risk aversion and real resource cost models) will yield different asset demand and supply functions.

In the precautionary demand models, the cash ratio of the public is determined by a set of interest rates such as the banks seven-day deposit rate r_m and other variables Z such as technical change in the provision of money transmission services.

The reserve ratio of the banks is determined by a set of interest rates, the variability of cash flow σ, any imposed minimum reserve requirement RR and the rediscount rate of the authorities r_p,[18]

$$\frac{C_p}{D} = g(\overset{(-)}{r'_m}, Z) \tag{7.20}$$

$$\frac{R_b}{D} = f(\overset{(+)}{r_x}, \overset{(-)}{r_0}, \overset{(+)}{r_p}, \overset{(+)}{RR}, \overset{(+)}{\sigma}) \tag{7.21}$$

where r_x is the rate paid on reserve assets (which could be zero), r_0 is the rate on alternative earning assets including government debt r and advances r_A. Lender of last resort facilities by the central bank are permitted, but at a 'penal' rediscount rate r_p, to encourage the banks to readjust their portfolio of assets (and thus the money supply).

The demand for interest bearing ('liquid') reserve assets (for example commercial bills) by the NBPS, depends on the own yield r_L and that on alternative assets including money r_m

$$\frac{R_p}{D} = f(\overset{(+)}{r_L}, \overset{(-)}{r_m}) \tag{7.22}$$

A simple portfolio MBC model. The usual textbook representation of the money supply process under a monetary base regime is not as complex as the set of equations given above. Indeed policy discussion is often conducted with a rather simple portfolio model in mind. To derive this 'simple model' we need to reduce the set of relationships above to a simple function where the money supply depends only upon variables which could be said to be directly or indirectly determined by the authorities, namely the monetary base B, the interest rate on reserve assets r_x, the (penal) rediscount rate r_p, the required reserve ratio RR and the return on government bonds r. The authorities influence the latter when they engage in open market operations. An upward sloping money supply function with respect to the interest rate on bonds r results, which 'shifts' when the other exogenous monetary policy instruments are altered

$$\overset{(-)\ (-)\ (-)\ (+)\ (+)}{M^s = f(r_x, r_p, RR,\ r\ \ B)} \tag{7.23}$$

If we now add a simple demand for money function $M^d = f(P, Y, r)$ where P is the price level and Y real output, we have a model of the determination of the equilibrium money supply (figure 7.2). A change in the monetary base (or r_x, r_p or RR) by the authorities shifts the money supply function and a new equilibrium is established at r_1 and money supply M_1^s.

The above money supply–money demand model may be incorporated into the derivation of the LM curve with an endogenously determined money supply. The slope of the LM curve is reduced as compared with the exogenous money supply case and the curve shifts when the monetary policy instruments r_x, r_p, RR and B are altered by the authorities. Equating the linear money supply function $M^s = \bar{M} + hr$ where $\bar{M} = f\{r_x, r_p, RR, B\}$ with the money demand function $M^d = m_y Y - m_r r$ gives the LM curve $r = (-\bar{M} + m_y Y)/(h + m_r)$ and the above results follow.

In section 7.5 we argue that the assumptions required to produce this 'simple' model are so unrealistic, in a world where banks bid for wholesale deposits, as to render such an analysis misleading. At best the model is applicable to retail banks who enage only in asset management, that is they do *not* raise their deposit interest rates when faced with a shortage of base money.

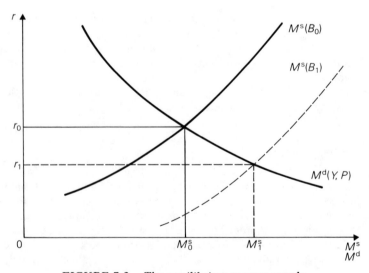

FIGURE 7.2   *The equilibrium money supply.*

To derive the above 'simple' monetary base model (equation (7.23)) for retail banks from our 'general' equations (7.20)–(7.22) we merely have to set σ to zero, assume a fixed rate on money r_m and have the advances and liquid asset interest rates *rigidly linked* to the government bond rate (for example $r_A = (1+a)r$ where a is the mark-up set by the bank on the market rate. The above reserve ratios then depend only on the policy instruments of the authorities and the bond rate. The chain of causation from a change in the monetary base would then be as follows.

Under MBC and 'asset management' by banks, a contraction in the money supply[19] could be accomplished by either a cut in the PSBR (unlikely in the short run) or a sale of debt by the authorities to the NBPS. Bankers' balances at the CB (that is reserves) and deposits fall by an equal amount and the reserve to deposit ratio falls. Although borrowing and lending in the interbank market will reallocate reserves from surplus to decifit banks the authorities must pursue their open market operations until the banking system as a whole has a net shortage of cash.[20] Under a *mandatory* cash base system, if reserves are below the legal minimum the central bank acts as a lender of last resort but does so at a penal rate of interest (that is greater than that which the banks can obtain on earning assets such as advances). Profit maximizing banks simultaneously reduce their earnings assets by selling bonds and the recall and non-renewal of advances. Assets and deposits fall until the level of deposits is consistent with the lower level of reserve assets in the system. Deposits react passively to a decision to alter advances.

Under a mandatory cash base system banks will hold reserves above the legal minimum (so-called free reserves) as a buffer against normal stochastic cash shortages. An open market operation (OMO) may not involve reserves below the legal minimum. At unchanged interest rates the money supply falls by a multiple of the fall in the base. However, the rise in market interest rates due to an OMO, leads to a fall in the free reserve ratio and a movement along the money supply function. However, the net effect of an open market sale of bonds is a fall in the money supply (figure 7.2).

Although textbook descriptions tend to emphasize open market operations at the long end of the market most CBs operate vigorously at the short end of the market. Flows to and from the authorities are large (for example payments of taxes, government expenditures). The CB may offset these flows by the purchase and sale of short-term *non-reserve* assets either to the banks or to the NBPS. In the UK, the CB may create a 'cash' shortage by an over-issue of Treasury bills to the discount houses.[21] The bank can relieve the cash shortage at current market rates and therefore at no penalty cost to the discount houses, or penalize them either by purchasing bills at a lower price (higher interest rate) or instead lend to them at the discount window at a high penal interest rate. Other short-term market rates rise which spreads to the long end of the market via the term structure (see chapter 10).

According to its advocates, the usefulness of MBC therefore depends on the authorities willingness to control the base (rather than interest rates) and on the stability of the cash ratio of the NBPS and the (free) reserve ratio of the banks.

Asset ratios: illustrative empirical results. The demand for currency by the NBPS is usually assumed to depend on some variable to proxy the level of transactions

Y and the opportunity cost of cash, namely a short-term interest rate r^s. In general, results for the UK (Cuthbertson, 1983; Johnston, 1984) indicate that such a relationship is reasonably stable when using quarterly data although quarter to quarter movements are often not accurately predicted. For the US a strong but not particularly well-determined interest rate effect is frequently found (Bryant, 1983; Cooley and LeRoy, 1981). The main problem is in deciding whether these relationships, that have by and large been estimated over data when cash was demand determined, would remain stable if banks started bidding for cash by offering higher interest rates on sight deposits in an MBC regime.

Total bank reserves consist of 'borrowed' and 'non-borrowed' reserves. Borrowed reserves BR are obtained from the central bank who charge an interest rate, the rediscount rate r_d. (We deal with these aspects in more detail in section 8.3 on monetary control.) Non-borrowed reserves are obtained from the private sector. Reserve demand may not be homogeneous with respect to deposits ('size').

Wessels (1982) provides a fairly typical empirical analysis of a commercial bank's demand for borrowed reserves BR from the central bank. The estimated demand function on monthly data for Dutch banks is (variables are all in logarithms)

$$BR = 2.16 - 2.8r_d - 1.2r_p + 1.5r_{cl} + 1.1r_F + 0.98 BQ \qquad (7.24)$$
$$ (0.60) \ (0.32) \ \ (0.28) \ \ (0.09) \ \ (0.18) \ \ (0.14)$$

1973-9, 'quota' periods, $n = 309$, $\hat{\sigma}^2 = 0.81$, $\hat{\sigma}_A^2 = 2.7$ ($\hat{\sigma}^2/\hat{\sigma}_A^2 = 30\%$)

where parentheses indicate standard error, r_p = additional penalty/rediscount rate applied when banks exceed their 'borrowing quota' set by the central bank, r_{cl} and r_F are the rate on call loans and Euroguilder deposits, these being the 'cost' of alternative sources of liquid assets for the banks. BQ is the borrowing quota set by the central bank. The 'basic' rediscount rate r_d applies to 'borrowing' from the central bank if the commercial banks quota is *not* exceeded. In practice r_d is set by the central bank with reference to the Euroguilder rate since Holland is part of the European Monetary System (EMS) and has to maintain its exchange rate within preannounced 'bands'. Domestic and 'foreign' sources of 'reserves' appear to be close substitutes, as the near-equal signs on r_{cl} and r_F indicate.

The coefficients are correctly signed and well determined, overall the equation explains 70 per cent of the variation in borrowing from the CB. (However, there are no test statistics given for autocorrelation, it is not clear whether a simultaneous estimation technique has bee used and no outside sample prediction errors are presented.)

Note that the question is only a first step in empirically validating monetary base control. Faced with a rise in r_d or r_p by the central bank, the commercial banks would 'bid' for call loans (and probably wholesale deposits) raising r_{cl}. The net effect on BR is indeterminate a priori since the model is not designed to tell us the size of the induced change in r_{cl}. Wessel also finds that the quota BQ is determined by bank size (that is deposits) but the elasticity of borrowed reserves BR to deposits is less than unity. Hence reserves *may* not be homogeneous as assumed in the MBC literature. However, R does not include *all* bank reserves; inclusion of other reserve assets might raise the elasticity of reserves with respect to deposits. (See also Langohr (1981) for examples of borrowed reserves functions for Belgium and Richter and Teigen (1982) for 'free reserves' functions for W. Germany.)

Bryant (1983) tests the outside sample performance of an excess or free reserves function for US banks. The equation is similar to that above with the opportunity cost of holding free reserves given by the (short-term) federal funds rate. Although the equation fits well in the period up to 1979 when the Federal Reserve Board used the interest rate to influence the money supply, it underpredicts markedly for the three years since the introduction of reserve asset targets. We discuss these issues further in section 8.3 on the US experience with reserve assets targets.

7.4 THE FLOW OF FUNDS (FOF) APPROACH

The FOF or 'credit aggregates' approach to the determination of the money supply is applicable to a broad monetary aggregate such as £M3 as used in the UK, although the general apporach has been adopted in other countries (for example Australia, France, Italy). It is usually contrasted with money base control and we compare the two in the next section. Here we use the UK system as an example of the FOF approach. We interpret FOF analysis as involving a 'package deal' approach to control of the money supply although the transmission mechanism in all cases is primarily via interest rates.

The FOF approach is based on three identities: one dealing with the balance sheet of the commercial banks, another with the financing of the budget deficit (public sector borrowing requirement, PSBR) and finally, the definition of the money supply as cash plus bank deposits. For expositional purposes we neglect some minor items in the balance sheets.

A banks balance sheet has sterling deposit liabilities D matched by assets in the form of (a) sterling bank lending to the UK NBPS (either as advances, overdrafts or by the banks' purchasing commercial bills) ΔBL_p and (b) sterling bank lending to the government (public sector) ΔBL_g in the form of short term government assets such as Treasury bills, bankers balances, till money, as well as long-term government bonds (gilt-edged stock) held by the banks[22]

$$\Delta D \equiv \Delta BL_p + \Delta BL_g \tag{7.25}$$

Δ£M3 is defined as $(\Delta D + \Delta C_p)$, therefore the *change* in £M3 expressed in terms of its *credit* counterparts is

$$\Delta\text{£M3} \equiv \Delta BL_p + \Delta BL_g + \Delta C_p \tag{7.26}$$

The PSBR must be financed by issuing notes and coin to the NBPS, ΔC_p, by selling government debt (Treasury bills, government bonds, national savings) to the NBPS, ΔG_p, by sales of foreign currency which provides external sterling 'finance' for the PSBR, ΔExt. The banking system is the residual source of the government's financing requirements. Net spending by the government initially results in an increase in bankers balances or 'till money' which are then usually switched by the banks into higher earning government assets such as Treasury bills and gilt-edged stock; these are all forms of bank lending to the government ΔBL_g, hence

$$\text{PSBR} \equiv \Delta G_p + \Delta C_p - \Delta Ext + \Delta BL_g \qquad (7.27)$$

Combining (7.26) and (7.27) we obtain the key FOF identity

$$\Delta \pounds M3 \equiv \text{PSBR} - \Delta G_p + \Delta Ext + \Delta BL_p \qquad (7.28)$$

This identity emphasizes the 'package deal' approach to control of £M3. £M3 may be influenced by fiscal changes, debt sales to the NBPS, dealings in the foreign exchange market and by the CB influencing bank lending to the private sector via changes in interest rates.

Until recently UK governments have not used PSBR as an instrument of monetary policy: fiscal policy was determined independently of monetary policy. In principle, debt sales to the NBPS can be used to influence the money supply but the authorities must be willing to allow interest rates on long-term government debt to fluctuate. This they are not always willing to do because of possible adverse effects on expectations about gilts prices and hence a possible reduction in demand for government debt in the future (that is the 'cashiers view' of the demand for government debt). Although intervention in the foreign exchange market by the authorities does influence the money supply this policy is usually not actively pursued for monetary policy ends, under a floating exchange rate regime. (Intervention may of course be used to influence the exchange rate and have an impact on the money supply but this is not the same as using intervention to *control* the money supply.) Having eschewed the above methods, the authorities are left with the possibility of controlling the money supply primarily by operations at the short end of the market. Short-term interest rates then influence bank lending rates and the *demand* for advances and hence lead to a change in deposits and the money supply. We can demonstrate the mechanisms involved in general terms assuming that banks, when faced with a shortage of reserve assets, adjust their non-reserve *assets* (rather than 'bidding' for reserves by raising wholesale deposit rates).

If the authorities wish to reduce the money supply they sell short-term assets (for example commercial bills, Treasury bills) to the NBPS thus reducing deosits and bankers balances at the CB and raising interest rates. To try and obtain 'cash' the banks sell short-term assets to the NBPS, lowering the price of these assets and pushing up short-term interest rates further. If the banks cannot initially obtain the additional cash, they are forced to borrow from the CB at a penal interest rate. The latter and the loss on sales of short-term assets, may lead the banks to raise their interest rates on advances, which applies *a fortiori* if the banks have to raise their seven-day deposit rate and thus incur higher costs. The rise in the interest rate on advances reduces the demand for advances and the money stock. The FOF approach embodies a portfolio analysis and is broadly consistent with the 'new view'. The mechanism ultimately works via a change in advances. Hence the term 'credit market approach' is often used. The above analysis applies regardless of the *source* of the change in bankers balances (for example from PSBR, sales of long-term government debt).

In the UK the mechanism is slightly different because of the special position of the discount houses acting as 'brokers' between the Bank of England and the banks. Prior to August 1981 a cash shortage was instigated by an 'over-issue' of Treasury bills to the discount houses who then requested additional call money from the banks, pushing up interest rates on the latter. Alternatively, the discount houses borrowed from the CB at a rate chosen by the CB. This could be at a penal level thus signalling a rise in interest rates to the market, which was usually reinforced by an announced rise in the administratively determined 'bank rate' (later minimum lending rate MLR).

As described above the banks engage in *asset* management. When applied in the UK, post-1971 the FOF approach ran into difficulties because there was a failure to consider the importance of the wholesale deposit market and the complex determinants of the demand for advances. We discuss this in the next chapter.

One final point, the reader may be wondering what has happened to the demand for money function in this analysis. There is an implicit demand for money in the model but only *in equilibrium*. The money stock is equal to notes and coin held by the NBPS (C_p) plus the stock of bank lending held by the private sector (BL_p) plus the deposits counterpart of bank lending to the government sector BL_g (equation (7.26)). In the FOF analysis C_p and bank lending are often assumed to be demand determined, at the going interest rates, set either in the market or by the banks. Essentially BL_g is the difference between the PSBR and the demand for government debt. The former is assumed to be given by the real sector of the economy and the latter is usually assumed to be demand determined. Hence the determinants of the demand for money in equilibrium consist of the determinants of the equilibrium demand for government debt, notes and coin and bank advances. In the FOF model the equilibrium demand for money is a complex relationship depending on all the variables that influence the demand for its counterparts. It therefore depends on the bank lending rate, the expected return in government debt, income, etc.

It is possible, for the level of bank advances to be willingly held (that is purely demand determined) and the deposits which ensue when the advances are spent to be accepted by other members of the NBPS since money is the means of payment. But it could be argued that such money balances are willingly held for a short period only. This is the idea of money as a buffer stock which we examined in section 6.4. For the moment we shall accept that the FOF model delivers an implicit equilibrium demand for money function.

7.4.1 *Domestic credit expansion: a digression*

The FOF approach is useful in analysing the concept of domestic credit expansion. This is frequently used by the IMF in assessing the monetary stance in open economies and it forms part of the monetary theory of the balance of payments. Domestic credit is an attempt to isolate those elements in the broad money supply due to transactions in domestic currency between domestic residents; primarily the authorities, the banks and the NBPS, and those which originate from transactions with the overseas sector.

The PSBR, net of sales of government debt $(\text{PSBR} - \Delta G_p)$, gives rise to an injection of 'credit' to the banks ΔBL_g and to the NBPS in the form of cash ΔC_p. The banks and the NBPS extend 'credit' to the CB. 'Credit' is also provided by the banks when extending bank loans in the domestic currency ΔBL_p. Hence the *total* increase in bank credit or 'domestic credit' DC is defined as

$$\Delta DC = (\text{PSBR} - \Delta G_p) + \Delta BL_p \qquad (7.29)$$

Hence using the £M3 identity equation (7.28) we have

$$\Delta \text{£M3} = \Delta DC + \Delta Ext \qquad (7.30)$$

$$\frac{\Delta \text{£M3}}{\text{£M3}} = \frac{DC}{\text{£M3}} \frac{\Delta DC}{DC} + \frac{Ext}{\text{£M3}} \frac{\Delta Ext}{Ext} \qquad (7.31)$$

If $\delta = DC/\text{£M3}$ is approximately constant, which will be the case for small changes in £M3, etc., then $Ext/\text{£M3} = (1 - \delta)$ and

$$\dot{\text{£M3}} = \delta \dot{DC} + (1 - \delta) \dot{Ext} \qquad (7.32)$$

where a dot indicates a percentage change in the variable. This is the origin of the money supply equation used in international monetary models where Ext is equated with the change in foreign exchange reserves (measured in units of the domestic currency).

In fact external flows Ext consist of items other than reserve changes, which may often be substantial. To see this, note that the full PSBR identity is

$$\text{PSBR} - \Delta G_p - OB + FER = \Delta BL_g + \Delta C_p \qquad (7.33)$$

The PSBR may be financed by borrowing overseas in foreign currency OB and selling these funds (to the exchange equalization account) for sterling, as well as by a decline in the foreign exchange reserves FER which also provide sterling finance: these two items constitute external finance of the public sector. The UK banks' balance sheet is as follows:

Assets	*Liabilities*
£ Lending to UK public sector ΔBL_g	UK residents £ deposits ΔD
£ Lending to UK private sector ΔBL_p	Non-resident £ deposits ΔD_o
£ Lending to overseas sector ΔBL_o	Non-deposit liabilities NDL
	Switched position S

NDL consist of bank capital and the 'switched position' is the excess of foreign currency deposits over foreign currency loans. Given our definition of the increase in £M3 $(= \Delta C_p + \Delta D)$ we can rearrange these identities to give

$$\Delta \text{£M3} = \text{PSBR} - \Delta G_p + \Delta BL_p + (FER - OB - \Delta D_o - S + \Delta BL_o) - NDL \qquad (7.34a)$$

$$\Delta \text{£M3} = \Delta DC + FER - (OB + \Delta D_o + S - \Delta BL_o) - NDL \qquad (7.34b)$$

Thus non-intervention by the authorities ($FER = 0$) does not imply that net external flows have no effect on £M3. It is not the cessation of intervention *per se* that insulates £M3 from external flows but continuous equilibrium in the foreign exchange market. The composite item in brackets in equation (7.34a) is referred to as 'external and foreign currency finance' in official statistics (Bank of England, 1984, table 11.3).

7.5 MB AND FOF: AN INITIAL COMPARISON

To the general reader there must appear a number of paradoxical elements in the debate on monetary base versus the FOF methods of control. It appears that alternative rearrangements of a set of identities with no behavioural content yield very divergent views. The demand for money, so prominent in discussions about monetary policy in the early 1970s, appears to have been forgotten or at least relegated to a very minor role. MB control is frequently presented as an alternative to fiscal and interest rate policy that were once advocated as methods of influencing the demand for (and therefore the equilibrium supply of) money. Friedman (1980a, para 11, p. 57), for example, states: 'Direct control of the monetary base is an alternative to fiscal policy and interest rates as a means of controlling monetary growth.' Friedman offers an analogy to control of the money supply by influencing the determinants of demand: 'A precise analogy is like trying to control the output of motor cars by altering the incomes of potential purchasers and manipulating rail and air fares. Far easier to control the output of motor cars by controlling the availability of ... say steel to the manu-factures – a precise analogy to controlling the money supply by controlling the availability of base money to banks and others.'

In contrast to the flow of funds approach there is a presumption in MB control that the output of the banking industry (that is deposits) can be easily controlled and predicted by controlling the inputs (that is cash base) to the industry and analysing a small number of behavioural functions. Friedman's quotation above suggests that similar simple methods may be used to control the output of other industries such as the car industry. Such revelations may come as a surprise to students of the theory of the firm where complex models have not achieved unequivocal success in predicting the subtle interactions of the behaviour of firms. In particular, MB control appears to eschew interest in the behaviour of non-reserve items of the banks balance sheet (for example non-reserve liquid assets and advances). Griffiths (1979, p. 39) expresses this view succinctly when he states: 'If cash within the banking system is limited, then regardless of the private sectors' demand for advances its ability to expand its lending and in turn the volume of deposits is limited.'

Control of the base by the authorities is assumed to be a relatively easy matter: 'it is something over which the authorities, if they so desire *have com-plete control*. As the authorities know their balance sheets daily and are in a position to adjust them by selling or purchasing bills and gilt-edged securities' (Griffiths, 1980, p. 36).

By the end of the next chapter we hope to have resolved some of these para-doxical elements. Our general view is that the MB model, as generally discussed in the textbooks and policy debates, is incomplete. There is a failure to consider the complex decisions faced by banks in determining the optimal level of not only reserve assets but also non-reserve assets such as bank advances. In addition the MB model requires a theory of how banks determine their interest rates on, say, advances and wholesale deposits. These decisions then interact with those concerning the desired level of reserves. In short the determination of the money supply is the outcome of an equilibrium between a number of asset demand functions of the banks and the NBPS such as reserve assets, government debt and advances (as well as the operating policy of the monetary authority).

The MB model requires just as much information as the FOF approach. The banks' demand for reserve assets depends upon the interest rate on alternative assets, namely non-reserve liquid assets, long-term government debt and bank loans to the NBPS. Thus, for example the decision to increase the *supply* of advances may well be made simultaneously with decisions concerning desired reserves. Both decisions may be influenced by similar variables. To 'complete' the MB model we require knowledge of how *all* the interest rates that influence the banks' asset demand and supply functions are determined. This requires either interest rate setting functions for the banks or alternatively desired supply and demand functions for assets which may then be solved for the equilibrium interest rate (if two assets are perfect substitutes then of course their rates will be equal).

Suppose for example under MB control the target for the base was achieved but the money supply target was not, because the money multiplier behaved 'abnormally'. One is virtually forced to look to other elements in the bank's balance sheet to discover the source of this abnormality since all available infor-mation about the influences on the reserve ratio are already in the equation. For example, knowledge of the financial state of companies, and its influence on bank lending might provide additional information to explain why the reserve ratio is 'abnormally low'. The argument against MB control does not necessarily rely on the equations explaining the asset-ratios of the money multiplier being unstable, but that the 'model' is incomplete, since it fails to explain how the banks or the 'market' will react in determining the interest rates that influence the asset ratios (particularly the reserve ratio of the banks). This applies *a fortiori* when the banks considered are rather heterogeneous, consisting of retail banks, wholesale or consortium banks and foreign banks.

It is easy enough to artificially present the FOF model as requiring knowledge of the base and two behavioural relations, as is often done for the MB model. The £M3 identity is

$$\Delta\pounds M3 \equiv PSBR - \Delta G_p + \Delta Ext + \Delta BL_p \tag{7.35}$$

The definition of the monetary base is cash held by the NBPS plus bank lending to the government in the form of reserve assets. The latter is given by ΔBL_g *less* bank holdings of non-reserve assets (for example long-term government debt) ΔG_b; hence

$$\Delta B \equiv \Delta C_p + (\Delta BL_g - \Delta G_b) \tag{7.36}$$

$$\equiv \Delta C_p - \Delta G_b + (PSBR - \Delta G_p + \Delta Ext - \Delta C_p) \tag{7.37}$$

where we have used the definition of ΔBL_g from equation (7.27). From (7.35) and (7.37) we obtain

$$\Delta £M3 \equiv \Delta B + \Delta G_p + \Delta BL_p \tag{7.38}$$

Thus control of £M3 in the FOF model requires control of the base together with two behavioural relations, one for long-term government debt held by the banks ΔG_p and the other for bank lending to the NBPS. The analogy merely shows that one gains no economic insights by the rearrangement of identities.

Miller (1981) has forcefully made the point that MB control is not qualitatively different from control via interest rates in a world where banks undertake liability management (that is bid for wholesale deposits when faced with a shortage of reserves). MB control works via changes in interest rates that ultimately must equate the *supply* and *demand* for money. Using Friedman's 'supply of steel' versus 'adjusting incomes and prices' (see above), Miller notes that it is only in a rigid centrally planned economy at the micro-level that the supply of steel to particular firms may be controlled and this may influence the output of say UK produced cars. Inefficiencies would probably abound and as long as there existed close substitutes for UK cars (for example Japanese imports) this would not lead to control of the *total* sales of cars to UK residents. This is an example of disintermediation into 'offshore markets' (for example Euro-sterling market in the case of the UK). UK manufactures might then switch to fibreglass cars, that is, disintermediation in the domestic market (for example bank acceptances when the 'corset' was imposed in the UK, see section 8.6.1).

In a market economy the authorities can only restrict the *total* supply of steel (the 'base') to *all* firms. Car firms would then bid for steel (or a 'negotiable entitlement' for y tons of steel from the authorities stockpile), the price of steel would rise, the supply curve of cars shift to the left, the price of cars would rise and the latter would reduce *demand*, in line with the lower supply. The rise in the price of *steel* depends upon the elasticity of demand for steel (the supply curve is vertical). The amount by which the price of *cars* would rise depends upon the objectives of UK car firms. Cost mark-up pricing with a constant profit margin would yield a rise in price of $\Delta p_c = (x) \Delta p_s$ where p_c and p_s are the price of steel and cars respectively and x is the proportion of 'steel costs' in total costs of production. The reduction in demand for *cars* will be larger the larger is $\Delta p_s x$ and the price elasticity of demand for cars. The latter is determined by the existence of close substitutes. We are also neglecting any second-round effects of reduced car production on incomes and thus the demand for cars.

Since the mechanism is triggered by a rise in the price of steel it may be more efficient to accomplish this by taxing steel production or (better still) a tax on UK car production. For the latter the chain of causation is shorter and may therefore be more predictable.

Miller applies the above 'model' to MB control and argues that to control the money supply under MB control either requires acceptance of substantial disintermediation (into offshore banking) or requires large changes in the absolute level of interest rates. The latter may have serious repercussions for the exchange rate and the level of traded goods output.

A large *mandatory* reserve ratio x leads to a substantial wedge between wholesale deposit rates r_m and the advances rate r_a (that is $\Delta r_a = (1 + x) \Delta r_m$) and hence advances and the money supply may fall substantially. However, the mandatory reserve ratio is a 'tax' on banking activity and will lead to disintermediation, particularly into offshore banks On the other hand if x is small, the *absolute* level of interest rates has to rise by a *large* amount to drive a wedge between advances and deposit rates, although disintermediation is less in this case. However, a sudden increase in the *absolute* level of interest rates may have adverse consequences on output. Exchange rate 'overshooting' may result in a loss in competitiveness and a fall in real output (Dornbusch, 1976).

Miller's argument applies equally to control via interest rates or the base (since the two are equivalent under certainty). It implies that the authorities should probably consider the exchange rate as an additional intermediate target. Under any monetary control system the authorities should trade off deviations of the money supply from its target range against exchange rate deviations. This might minimize the deviation of the 'ultimate targets', inflation and real output, from their desired values (Artis and Currie, 1981).

In the next chapter we highlight the difficulties of operating either a FOF approach or a MB approach by focusing on the behaviour of the UK and US monetary systems. Our brief historical account suggests that an analysis in terms of stochastic shocks is required to decide (at least in principle) whether an interest rate target or a target for the monetary base is most appropriate in controlling the money supply.

7.6   SUMMARY: THE SUPPLY OF MONEY

We have presented our theories of the supply of money within the wider context of the behaviour of the financial firm. Perhaps the most obvious but nevertheless important conclusion from our analysis is that the behaviour of the balance sheet of the financial firm will vary depending on the objectives and constraints we believe operate on it. For example an assumption of monopoly power in the market for loans and deposits implies that a profit maximizing 'banking firm' will determine its loan and deposit interest rates in the light of other market rates such as the government bond rate and its perception of the size of the elasticity of demand for loans and deposits The authorities can therefore only influence the money stock indirectly by altering the government bond rate. However, as the firm gives greater weight to 'sales' (or size) relative to profits the loan–deposit interest spread narrows and the bank expands its balance sheet. If the banking firm alters its objectives (or the weight it gives to different objectives) over time, then this may manifest itself in apparent instability in the money supply function. Although the theories of the financial firm we have discussed are relatively complex, they are basically static models and in the main, ignore the general problems of risk. They therefore do not deal adequately with the *growth* of the firm and its balance sheet over time, in a risky environment. No single model of the financial firm emerges as superior overall, but each provides an insight into the complex mechanisms that underlie portfolio decisions of financial intermediaries and guards against over-enthusiastic acceptance of simple models.

Control of the money supply by MB control requires one to control the 'base' and for the 'cash' to deposits ratio of the bank and the NBPS to be predictable. Except possibly for retail banks, the monetary base approach requires one to model the behaviour of a *set* of interest rates and possibly other elements in the bank's balance sheet besides 'reserve' assets'; as usually presented in textbooks and by some commentators, it provides only a partial account of the money supply process.

The flow of funds (FOF) model emphasizes the 'package deal' approach to controlling the money supply, although short-term market interest rates, which are thought to influence the rate charged on bank loans, are a key element in the transmisson process. In its simplest version banks are assumed to engage in *asset* management.

In the final section we briefly discussed similarities between the FOF and MB models and came to the conclusion that both approaches require a more complete model when banks engage in liability management. In the next chapter we examine the practical aspects of the two approaches in the context of attempts to control the money supply in the UK and the US.

APPENDIX 7A   SOLUTIONS TO THE MONOPOLY MODEL

The first-order conditions are

$$r^E + E\frac{\partial r^E}{\partial E} = r^b = \frac{r^D + D\,\partial r^D/\partial D}{1-k} \tag{7A.1}$$

and the demand functions are

$$E = e_0 - e_1 r^E + e_2 r^b \tag{7A.2}$$

$$D = d_0 + d_1 r^D - d_2 r^b \tag{7A.3}$$

Substituting for E and D from (7A.2) and (7A.3) in (7A.1) and rearranging

$$r^E = \frac{(e_1 + e_2)\,r^b + e_0}{2e_1} \tag{7A.4}$$

$$r^D = \frac{-d_0 + r^b(d_1(1-k) + d_2)}{2d_1} \tag{7A.5}$$

Using (7A.4) and (7A.5) for r^E and r^D in (7A.2) and (7A.3) gives the equilibrium levels of E and D

$$E = \frac{e_0 + (e_2 - e_1)\,r^b}{2}$$

$$D = \frac{d_0 + (d_1(1-k) - d_2)\,r^b}{2}$$

Thus $\partial r^E/\partial r^b$, $\partial r^D/\partial r^b > 0$ but the sign of $\partial E/\partial r^b$ and $\partial D/\partial r^b$ is ambiguous depending on the sign of $(e_2 - e_1)$ and $(d_1(1 - k) - d_2)$ respectively.

APPENDIX 7B   MONOPOLY MODEL WITH REAL RESOURCES COSTS

$$\max Q = Er^E - Dr^D + r^R R - C(E) + \lambda(R + E - D) \tag{7B.1}$$

$$Q_E = E\frac{\partial r^E}{\partial E} + r^E - C_E + \lambda = 0 \tag{7B.2}$$

$$Q_D = -D\frac{\partial r^D}{\partial D} - r^D - \lambda = 0 \tag{7B.3}$$

$$Q_R = r^R + \lambda = 0 \tag{7B.4}$$

$$r^E(1 + |\epsilon|^{-1}) = r^E E_1 = C_E + r^R \tag{7B.5}$$

$$r^D(1 + |\delta|^{-1}) = r^D d_1 = r^R \tag{7B.6}$$

where ϵ and δ are the loan and deposit elasticities of demand respectively and $E_1 = 1 - |\epsilon|^{-1}, d_1 = 1 - |\delta|^{-1}$. From (7B.5) and (7B.6)

$$r^E E_1 - r^D d_1 = C_E$$

and

$$\frac{r^E}{r^D} = \frac{(C_E/r_D) + d_1}{E_1} \tag{7B.7}$$

Using (7B.2) and (7B.3) and $\lambda = -r^R$ we obtain

$$E = \frac{r^R + C_E - r^E}{\partial r^E/\partial E} \tag{7B.8}$$

$$D = \frac{r^R - r^D}{\partial r^D/\partial D} \tag{7B.9}$$

$$\frac{R}{D} = 1 - \frac{E}{D} = 1 - \frac{(r^R + C_E - r^E)(\partial r^D/\partial D)}{(r^R - r^D)(\partial r^E/\partial E)} \tag{7B.10}$$

The reserve ratio therefore depends in a complex way on the yield on reserve assets, earning assets the marginal cost of expanding loans and the marginal response coefficients of the deposit and loan demand functions. Note that equation (7B.10) is *not* the reduced form of the model but merely shows the interrelationship between several endogenous variables.

The expression for r_E/r_D in equation (7B.7) reduces to the perfect competition model of the text when ϵ and δ approach infinity, that is E_1 and d_1 equal unity. Under these conditions $r_E = C_E + r_D$ as one would expect.

NOTES

1 For simplicity of exposition assume that income Y is determined outside the financial sector so that we know the *position* of the demand for money function in the (r, Y) plane.

2 We do not discuss microeconomic questions of efficiency, welfare considerations, prudential controls and the desirability of regulation, all of which require a satisfactory theory of the behaviour of the (unregulated) financial intermediary.

3 Here we are relying on negative covariances of returns reducing the overall risk (variance) of the portfolio (as in the mean-variance model of section 3.3.3). Bilateral lenders and borrowers can reduce 'risk' by hiring specialist risk assessors but cannot diversify risk unless sufficient funds are available to issue a large number of loans. Banks usually assess loan risks themselves, other financial firms such as insurance companies and some building societies might hire specialist risk assessors (for example surveyors for property).

4 We do not discuss theories of the liability *structure*. Assuming portfolio size is given, the latter models explain the distribution between deposits and equity; considerations that are determined by the probability and costs of insolvency (Niehans, 1978, chapter 9).

5 We discuss the issue of 'separability' of decisions at the end of the section. This allows the stochastic cash drain model to be applied to 'cash' and the mean-variance model to be applied to other assets.

6 Needless to say the second-order conditions for a maximum are not met.

7 We have imposed the constraint $E = D$ in the maximand and therefore do not require the Lagrange multiplier λ. The second-order condition $Q_{EE} = -C_{EE} < 0$ indicates a maximum.

8 If w is the wage rate and P_k is the user cost of capital, both of which are exogenous, then total labour and capital costs are wL and $P_k K$ respectively where L and K are the labour and capital input. If we have a well-behaved production function $E = f(L, K)$ with the usual properties then the model solves (for exogenous w, P_K and $r^E - r^D$) to give 'output' E $(=D)$ labour demand L and capital stock K as functions of input costs w, P_K and the 'output price' $r^E - r^D$.

9 Klein's model includes two types of deposits which have different demand elasticities and also includes 'liquidity costs' proportional to the level of deposits. We ignore these aspects but this doesn't affect our general conclusions.

10 The second-order conditions for a maximum are satisfied. Note that the first-order conditions are equivalent if Q (and therefore Π) is maximized with respect to r^E, and r^D. The firm simultaneously chooses both r^E and E and r^D and D.

11 See Deaton and Muellbauer (1980) for a formal discussion of separability, and Spencer (1984) for a realistic application of this concept to the asset-liability decisions of UK banks.

12 There are problems in meeting the balance sheet constraints in models of this type when the demand curve (for say loans) is stochastic (Melton and Roley 1981).

13 Most but not all influences of the foreign sector on the domestic money supply are nullified under flexible exchange rates (Lomax and Mowl, 1978).

14 Interest is implicitly paid on most sight deposits by the real resource costs of administering such accounts. Interest is sometimes explicitly paid.

15 If the base consisted solely of cash and bankers' balances and the latter were *not* held by the NBPS then R_p/D and C_p/D would be equivalent and $M^s = [(1 + \alpha)/(\alpha + \beta_b)] B$. However, if the base includes 'non-cash' assets held in part by the NBPS (for example commercial bills) R_p/D would consist of C_p/D and the 'non-cash' assets to deposits ratio of the NBPS.

16 The 'debt' can be either private sector assets held by the authorities (for example commercial bills) or government debt, but the debt must not be part of reserve assets.

17 A payments surplus leads to an increase in bank reserves (and deposits) as the NBPS exchanges foreign currency for domestic currency at the CB. The CB can attempt to sterilize the increase in bank reserves by selling government debt to the (domestic) NBPS. To do so it must offer higher interest rates. But if the demand for domestic debt by foreigners is infinitely elastic, foreigners purchase all the government debt offered for sale. Domestic residents holdings of money and their banks' holdings of 'reserve assets' remain unchanged. Sterilization then becomes impossible. It is the view of many advocates of MBC that the base cannot be insulated from capital flows, under fixed exchange rates.

18 We have subsumed any *mandatory* minimum reserve requirement into *total* reserves. The latter therefore consist of 'free reserves' chosen by the banks and required reserves. Some textbooks separate out these and write $R_b = RR + R_F$ where R_F is the free reserve ratio. In the US system there are also 'excess reserves' and 'borrowed reserves' where the latter refer to banks that have borrowed from the central bank (that is the Federal Reserve Bank). We discuss the US system in section 8.3.

19 In the discussion that follows we assume 'cash' is the reserve asset.

20 It is usually assumed that the demand for cash by the NBPS is fairly interest inelastic. Advocates of MB control favour a narrow range of reserve assets so that R_p/D is either notes or coins or negotiable entitlements. In the former case R_p/D is determined by factors that influence the NBPS's cash ratio and in the latter case $R_p/D = 0$.

21 For analytic purposes we may consider the discount houses acting as a broker between the commercial and the central bank (Bank of England). The discount houses obtain funds (call loans) from the banks and use these funds to purchase Treasury bills. Analytically we take this to be equivalent to the banks directly purchasing Treasury bills and subsume the discount houses into our definition of the banking system.

22 Here the presentation of the FOF is deliberately simplified. In equation (7.25), the banks' balance sheet, we have omitted 'net non-deposit liabilities' of the banks, and certain *net* transactions of the banks in foreign currency (and for the overseas sector in sterling too). These items are then subsumed in *Ext* in equation (7.28). In addition bank lending in sterling to the private sector ΔBL_p, includes the issue department's purchase of commercial bills. These points are elaborated in the later section on domestic credit expansion, and further details may be found in the Bank of England Quarterly Bulletin (Bank of England, 1984, table 11.3 and 'supplementary details').

8

Control of the Money Supply

8.1 INTRODUCTION

In the previous chapter we mainly discussed the theoretical aspects of the behaviour of the banking firm and analysed two models of the money supply process, namely the flow of funds FOF and money base control MBC. This chapter concentrates on the practical aspects of monetary control. We begin in section 8.2 with a description of the UK system since 1960 but concentrate mainly on the era of competition and credit control CCC in the 1970s. Since the mid 1970s the UK has had some form of intermediate monetary target and the authorities method of control has been based on the FOF model with the emphasis on control via changes in interest rates. In contrast we then move on in section 8.3 to give an account of the US system, post-1979, where a form of monetary base control has been operating. Both methods of control were subject to acute difficulties. In section 8.4 we therefore present a formal analysis of the issues involved in choosing between interest rates and a quantitative operating target when seeking to control a monetary aggregate. The informational requirements needed to determine the optimal operating target are substantial, even in our simple stylized model and this makes it difficult to choose between them in practice.

In the second half of the chapter we discuss the implications of structural changes in domestic and overseas markets for the control and interpretation of domestic monetary aggregates. Our analysis highlights the importance of the dynamic behaviour of the banking firm operating in an uncertain environment, where managerial goals may be multidimensional (and possibly changing over time). Theories of the financial firm discussed in the previous chapter again provide useful insights.

Innovations in domestic markets discussed in section 8.6.1, include liability management, variable rate lending and improvements in payment technology. We find that such changes make the impact of any method of monetary control more uncertain and they may also distort the informational content of particular monetary aggregates. Our discussion of offshore markets in section 8.7 centres on the Euromarkets. We analyse the ability of the Eurobanks to undertake credit and liquidity creation and to facilitate disintermediation. We find that the Eurobanks provide an efficient method of *distributing* credit and liquidity rather than creating excess liquidity or a multiple expansion of deposits. In small open economies without exchange control, the Eurobanks, rather than thwarting monetary control, impose a severe constraint on the authorities ability to reduce domestic monetary aggregates without a high absolute level of domestic interest rates.

In the final section of this chapter we summarize the main implications for monetary control of the increase in financial innovation in domestic and offshore markets.

8.2 MONETARY CONTROL IN THE UK, 1960–84

Broadly speaking the conduct of monetary policy in the UK may be analysed using the FOF model. Different elements in this 'package deal' approach have been prominent at different times as the authorities have switched the emphasis of policy when faced with new difficulties. We split the historical analysis into four sub-periods: 1960–71, the pre-competition and credit control (CCC) period; 1971–4, the mark I CCC period; 1974–81, the mark II CCC period; and 1981 to the present we dub the 'new measures'. When discussing these historical events we use them in the main to provide a further analysis of the FOF model and to draw analogies with the theory of the financial firm presented earlier: we do not attempt a definitive blow by blow account of events (for the latter see Zawadzki (1981) and Llewellyn et al. (1982)).

8.2.1   *Pre-CCC, 1960–71*

In the 1960s it was 'credit' rather than 'money' which dominated policy. Credit ceilings on lending by the clearing banks were frequently introduced in an attempt to curb spending, in non-priority areas such as consumer goods and investment by property companies.

The clearing banks were subject to a mandatory 8 per cent cash ratio and a liquid assets ratio of around 30 per cent. A large proportion of liquid assets were held in the form of short-term government debt, namely Treasury bills. The clearing banks did not deal directly with the CB (the Bank of England) but lent short-term funds to the discount houses (that is call money) who then purchased Treasury bills from the central bank (CB). For the purpose of analysis we can treat the discount houses as pure brokers acting on behalf of the clearers in their dealings with the CB.[1] These relatively high mandatory reserve ratios were a form of tax on the clearing banks since the latter could not freely choose the portfolio of assets which maximized profit. The clearing banks operated a cartel arrangement in setting rates of interest on deposits and advances; they fixed interest rates and accepted loans and deposits at these rates. An increased demand for loans with an unchanged deposit inflow would be met by a sale of 'other assets' such as long-term government debt held by the banks (that is asset switching).

In the 1960s the 'cashiers view' on debt sales prevailed. It was believed that holders of gilt-edged stock (long-term government debt) were extremely averse to the risk of a capital loss. The government broker therefore tried to avoid sharp changes in long-term interest rates by 'leaning into the wind', that is selling gilts when prices were rising and vice versa. Any changes in the demand for money by the NBPS which resulted in a change in the demand for government debt, were met at the going interest rate by the authorities. An interest rate target (at least for the short run) meant that under free market conditions the money supply was endogenous. Also, fiscal policy was set largely independently of monetary policy and the PSBR was not used as an instrument of monetary control.

The authorities therefore chose to influence bank credit not through interest rates or the PSBR but through moral suasion and direct controls.[2] This policy was reinforced by calls for 'special deposits', a forced loan from the banks to the CB which raised the banks' mandatory reserve requirement. To the extent that special deposits increased bank costs (that is foregone interest on other eaning assets), the authorities expected the banks to either increase the rate on advances or directly reduce advances that were now no longer profitable at the margin.[3]

The policy of direct controls on advances appears to have been successful (Artis, 1978; Spencer and Mowl, 1978) but at the cost of penalizing the clearing banks relative to banks not subject to mandatory reserve requirements and direct controls on advances.

These 'unregulated' secondary banks (broadly speaking foreign and overseas banks, merchant banks and accepting houses) expanded rapidly over this period. They operate in wholesale deposits in both the domestic and Euromarkets. They undertake substantial 'matching' in the term to maturity of their assets and liabilities. Any deficiency between loan demand and deposits is met by bidding for large fixed-term deposits. Similarly any deposit funds that cannot be profitably lent on advances is on-lent to other secondary banks. Because they did not pay the 'reserve tax' they could operate on finer margins between deposit and loan rates and expand at the expense of the clearing banks. The clearing banks set up secondary banks as subsidiaries in order to share in the expanding secondary banking market. While the commercial banks undertook substantial positive maturity transformation, by borrowing short and lending long, the secondary banks issued fixed-term loans whose maturity broadly matched that of their liabilities. They therefore had little need to voluntarily hold low yielding liquid reserve assets for precautionary reasons and this also enabled them to operate on finer margins.

8.2.2 *Mark I CCC, 1971–4*

By the end of the 1960s the authorities were aware that control over advances by the clearing banks did not prevent expansion by the secondary banks and, perhaps, that the clearers were being unfairly treated. The policy of CCC introduced in September 1971 aimed to put all banks on an equal footing with greater competition between banks and greater reliance on interest rates to control bank lending. But the emphasis was still on credit rather than money.

The tax on the clearing banks was reduced and the secondary banks included in the new ('eligible') reserve assets ratio which was $12\frac{1}{2}$ per cent of deposits (or 'eligible liabilities'). Reserve assets consisted of balances with the CB, Treasury bills, gilts with less than one year to maturity, eligible local authority bills and call money to the discount houses[4] ('till money' was excluded from the definition). Calls for special deposits were to be used to 'mop up' excess liquidity and put upward pressure on short-term interest rates as the banks sold reserve assets to obtain funds for the special deposits call (that is asset switching). The gilts market was not to be actively used to reduce liquidity. However, support for the gilt-edged market was to be limited, so that banks could not obtain reserve assets by selling gilts to the *authorities* at unchanged interest rates (that is prices). The banks agreed to abandon the interest rate cartel and it was thought that the upward pressure on short-term rates brought about by the authorities would spread to the advances rate and the *demand* for advances would fall (and hence the money supply). In October 1972 the CB linked its so-called minimum lending rate (MLR) to the Treasury bill rate; changes in MLR are a signal to the banks to alter their rate on advances.

The new policy of monetary control quickly ran into difficulties. First, there was the pent-up demand for advances caused by direct controls on lending to persons and property companies which led to an immediate rapid rise in these two categories of advances. Second, the banks (including the clearers) began to raise funds in the wholesale money markets. Certificates of deposit are wholesale bank deposits held by the NBPS for a fixed term (usually 3–6 months) but they may be bought and sold in the open market. Wholesale deposits also comprise large fixed-term deposits placed with banks by the NBPS but these are not marketable. Both forms of wholesale deposits pay market determined interest rates. In addition the so-called 'parallel money' market in local authority bills had grown rapidly prior to 1971 and these assets were widely held and traded by the banks and the NBPS. The banks could therefore bid directly for reserve assets in the 'established' markets' for Treasury and commercial bills and also for parallel money market assets and wholesale deposits. The implications of *liability* management and its interaction with the determinants of bank advances (particularly to industrial and commercial companies) may be analysed by considering the actual events that ensued over the 1972–4 period. Over this period the authorities made calls for special deposits in an attempt to control bank advances by market means. The banks bid for wholesale deposits increasing the own rate on money. This encouraged the NBPS to switch out of government debt into deposits. To the extent that the CB purchased this debt, the reserve position of the banks was eased.

Consider next the impact of the CCC policy on advances to companies, Assume that the banks set the loan rate and advances are then demand determined (the overdraft system in the UK suggests that this is a reasonable assumption). In section 5.4.4 we saw that the demand for sterling bank advances by companies depends upon (a) the interest rate on liquid assets RS (such as certificates of deposit) relative to the interest cost of advances RBL; (b) the level of the 'own rate' of interest RBL relative to a representative foreign rate R^f (which picks up the cost of borrowing in the Eurosterling market or the Eurodollar market); (c) the net borrowing requirement B of companies, representing their short-run need for bank financing as a buffer stock; (d) the level of transactions PY; (e) the rate of inflation Δp

$$BL = f(\overset{(+)}{PY}, \overset{(+)}{B}, \overset{(+)}{RS-RBL}, \overset{(+)}{R^f\text{-}RBL}, \overset{(-)}{\Delta p}) \qquad (8.1)$$

Arithmetically most of the fluctuations in £M3 are due to changes in bank lending, particularly to companies.

A rise in the interest rate on wholesale deposits encourages companies to finance their borrowing requirement by increasing bank advances rather than running down their 'profitable' liquid assets. Thus the impact on advances of a rise in the *absolute* level of interest rates (brought about by the authorities) depends in part on the response of the banks, whose actions influence the wholesale deposit rate *RS*. Advances are strongly influenced by *relative* interest rates and a narrowing of the *RS–RBL* differential leads to an increase in bank lending and the money supply (section 5.4.4).

The monopoly model of section 7.2.4 seeks to explain the determinants of this differential albeit under the assumption of zero risk. The differential is narrower the greater the elasticity of demand for advances as perceived by the bank. In the new competitive environment post-1971, the banks may well have believed this elasticity to be high and therefore kept the differential low. In fact, the banks' lending rates were so sticky over much of this period that money market rates exceeded the lending rate to prime borrowers on a number of occasions. 'Round tripping' ensued, that is, companies borrowed on overdrafts to reinvest in wholesale deposits, thus swelling the bank lending and money supply figures.

When the general level of interest rates rises, a proportion of the 'high' interest rates received on advances is financed by zero interest current accounts (sight deposits). Nominal bank profits may rise (the 'endowment effect') and create a positive 'supply side' response, leading to an increase in advances on risky loans, but at the going interest rate. This type of supply side response would be predicted by Monti's (1971) model of sales maximization subject to a profit constraint, or the similar model whereby the banks maximize a utility function depending upon 'size' and profits. Anecdotal evidence supporting this model in the CCC period when banks entered a new era of competing for market share can be found in the Wilson committee report (Wilson, 1980).

The rise in the general level of interest rates has further perverse effects on bank lending figures. First, the interest cost of the outstanding level of advances increases and this interest debiting is automatically added to the outstanding stock. Second, if a tight monetary policy leads to a fall in real output or prices whilst employment and the wage bill are 'sticky', then an increase in the borrowing requirement of companies will in part be financed by increased bank loans.

An additional complication is provided by offshore banks. If foreign rates on Eurosterling and Eurodollar deposits happen to rise when there is a tight monetary stance in the UK, then there will be a switch out of Euro-loans into UK bank loans. Although UK interest rates if anything may tend to follow foreign rates because of arbitrage or government policy in supporting the exchange rate, nevertheless independent changes in foreign rates over short periods may exacerbate the control of credit and money in the UK. We discuss these issues further in section 8.7 on the Euromarkets.

In the second half of 1973, strong loan demand increased the banks *demand* for reserve assets and the rate on Treasury bills fell. Under the 'formula' this led to a fall in MLR and a widening of the wholesale deposits – bank lending margin – thus encouraging further 'round tripping'. Partly for this reason, the formula was abandoned in November 1973 and MLR fixed by administrative decision.

Given these problems in controlling loans by market means, the authorities introduced the supplementary special deposit (SSD) scheme in December 1973, to limit the growth in wholesale deposits. The SSD was popularly known as the corset (Bank of England, 1982b).

8.2.3 *Mark II CCC, 1974–81*

The authorities saw that aggressive bidding for wholesale deposits was a major cause of its inability to control credit. The SSD scheme is an incremental tax on interest bearing deposits designed to drive a wedge between the marginal cost of funds to the banks (that is wholesale deposit rate) and the marginal revenue from loans (that is the rate on advances). If wholesale deposits ('interest bearing eligible liabilities', IBELS) exceeded a pre-announced figure the banks had to place x per cent of the wholesale deposits in a *zero* yield account at the CB: 'x' increased steeply with the degree of overshoot.[5] This tax on wholesale deposits can be viewed either as increasing the 'after tax' marginal cost of funds, or as reducing the marginal revenue to be earned on earning assets. The downward pressure on the wholesale deposit rates as banks bid less aggressively and the upward pressure on bank lending rates because of the higher marginal cost of funds would lead either to a fall in the *demand* for bank lending (as $RBL–RLA$ and $RBL–R^F$ increased) or a rationing of advances by non-price factors.

It is easier to analyse the problem by noting that the SSD scheme raised the marginal cost of funds (Wills, 1982). Suppose the reserve *ratio* (that is mandatory reserves plus special deposits plus desired free reserves) is β. To obtain one pounds worth of funds to on-lend in the form of advances, the banks have to obtain $1/(1-\beta) \approx (1+\beta)$ pounds of wholesale deposits at an interest rate r'_m (inclusive of administrative costs). However, a fraction β of these wholesale deposits are held as interest bearing reserve assets at a rate r_R and hence the *net* marginal cost (MC) of obtaining one pounds worth of funds for advances is

$$\text{MC} = (1+\beta)r'_m - \beta[(1+\beta)r_R] = r'_m + \beta(r'_m - r_R) \tag{8.2}$$

$$= r'_m + t_1 \tag{8.3}$$

where we have assumed $\beta^2 r_R$ is negligible. With a fractional reserve system the tax on acquiring funds is $t_1 = \beta(r'_m - r_R)$ and therefore rises with β and the interest gap $(r'_m - r_R)$.

After the introduction of the SSD scheme, to raise one pound for on-lending as advances requires a deposit of wholesale funds of $(1 + \beta + x)$, where x is the proportion placed in SSD. The marginal cost of funds is then

$$\text{MC} = (1+\beta+x)r'_m - \beta[(1+\beta+x)r_R]$$

$$= r'_m + \beta(r'_m - r_R) + x(r'_m - \beta r_R) \tag{8.4}$$

$$= r'_m + t_1 + t_2 \tag{8.5}$$

and we have again assumed that $\beta^2 r_R$ is negligible. The SSD scheme therefore introduces an additional tax t_2 which may be substantial as x can rise to 50 per cent under the scheme. A short-run profit maximizing bank would equate the marginal revenue from loans r'_A (net of administrative costs and a default risk premium) to the marginal cost of funds.[6] r'_A therefore could be expected to rise as x and hence t_2 increase. The banks could only avoid the SSD tax by refraining from bidding for wholesale deposits thus lowering r'_m (relative to r_A). This increases the relative cost for companies of borrowing on overdrafts rather than by running down liquid assets and would result in a fall in the demand for bank advances according to our bank lending equation (8.1) (where $RS \equiv r'_m$, $RBL \equiv r'_A$).

How much of the increase in the marginal cost of funds is passed on in a higher rate on advances depends upon the *incidence* of the bank tax. With high substitutability between wholesale deposits and parallel money market assets, for the NBPS, the 'tax' is unlikely to be 'passed back' in the form of a lower r'_m. The banks could absorb some of the tax in lower profits and this might reduce the 'endowment effect' on the supply of advances. Some of the tax is likely to result in higher loan rates and these were certainly altered more quickly under the SSD, so that few profitable arbitrage opportunities between wholesale deposits and advances occurred.

Thus the authorities at this time had not given up the possibility of control of monetary aggregates by market measures since the SSD was an attempt to supplement interest rate control. Although the corset was a constraint on the liabilities side of the banks balance sheet, and may be interpreted as a shift towards control of monetary as opposed to credit aggregates, it is widely thought that the latter was the prime target.

Over this period the authorities also used OMO at the long end more vigorously, to aid monetary control. The authorities probably still adhered to the view that the gilts market was volatile because of the volatility in expectations about future capital gains. They therefore contrived to give speculators a near certain short-term capital gain by the 'Grand Old Duke of York' strategy. Interest rates on long-term government debt were increased sharply and without warning so that the NBPS would predominantly take a view that interest rates could only fall, thus giving an expected capital gain. Large sales then ensued. There was also increased product diversification in the supply of government debt. New types of long-term debt were introduced (index linked gilts, conversion stock and variable rate stock) to increase demand at existing interest rates. National savings became more competitively 'priced' and again product diversification took place. Broadly speaking the PSBR was largely funded outside of the banking system over this period.

Although the corset did aid monetary control, it was bedevilled by two major problems. First, the banks' tended to build up their 'deposits' (that is interest bearing eligible liabilities, IBELS) prior to the announcement of a growth ceiling. Second, the scheme encouraged disintermediation on a large scale as banks arranged loans (in the form of bank acceptances held outside the banking system) directly between companies, thus 'distorting' the monetary figures it was attempting to control. Disintermediation into offshore markets after the abolition of exchange controls in 1979 was also a factor in the demise of the SSD scheme in June 1980 (section 8.7).

Formal target bands for the growth in the money supply were introduced after the visit of the IMF in 1976, and these received new force in the medium term financial strategy (MTFS) in the 1980 budget. In the MTFS the interdependence of monetary and fiscal policy was stressed and the PSBR advocated as an arm of monetary control; fiscal policy was to become subordinate to monetary policy. The emphasis switched from concern over credit aggregates to monetary aggregates. The targeted aggregate was a broad definition of money £M3, although after 1982 target bands were also announced for narrow money (M1) and a liquidity aggregate PSL2 which includes building society deposits.

The method chosen to control £M3 was still the 'package deal' approach utilizing the FOF framework. Debt sales were pursued more vigorously than in the past, there was an attempt to reduce the PSBR, and cash shortages at the short end of the market were used to influence the general level of interest rates. There was considerable overshoot in the £M3 target in the first two years of the policy caused partly by reintermediation, partly by the impact of the recession on company borrowing and partly by the entry of the banks into the home loan market. When the demise of the corset was announced (about six months prior to its formal abolition in June 1980) companies were able to borrow on bank loans rather than bank acceptances and this reintermediation swelled the money supply figures. The high interest rates, exchange rate overshooting and reduced international competitiveness led to a severe recession and companies were forced to finance their increased borrowing requirement by bank overdrafts and loans. The 'supply side' effect of a rapid growth in lending for house purchase by the banks may also have increased aggregate advances.

Again it appeared that the interest rate mechanism working via the demand for bank advances was rather slow and uncertain in its effect. In part, because of the apparent failure of the FOF approach and the resurgence of interest in monetary base control (MBC), the Bank of England introduced its 'new measures' in August 1981.

8.2.4 *The new measures, 1981*

The new measures can be interpreted as a move *towards* MBC or as a refinement of the FOF approach and we discuss both of these aspects. The main changes introduced are (Bank of England, 1980, 1981b, 1982a):

1 Abolition of the $12\frac{1}{2}$ per cent reserve assets ratio[7] and a reduction of the $1\frac{1}{2}$ per cent cash ratio to $\frac{1}{2}$ per cent.
2 Additional statistics on retail deposits (M2) are being collected and a series for the monetary base M0 (cash plus banks operational deposits)[8] has been published.
3 Intervention by the Bank of England at the short end of the market will take place mainly through the bill market rather than lending directly to the discount houses.[9] The Bank's operational aim would be to keep very short-term interest rates within unpublished 'bands' by broadly offsetting changes in net flows between the Bank of England and the banks.

The Bank recognizes that retail deposits could 'become the denominator of a cash ratio associated with a monetary base system' and that abolition of the mandatory $12\frac{1}{2}$ per cent reserve ratio will allow 'the authorities to monitor the development of the functional demand for cash balances' (that is reserve assets) by the banks (Bank of England, 1980, p. 428). The Bank no doubt remembers the difficulties in controlling M3 after the introduction of the CCC reforms and is anxious to 'monitor' the commercial banks behaviour in an attempt to prevent similar difficulties emerging if MBC should be introduced. The mandatory cash requirement of $\frac{1}{2}$ per cent is a tax levied to pay for the clearing services provided by the CB; it is not intended to be used for the purposes of monetary control since payments are based on 'deposits' held six months earlier.

A mandatory reserve requirement may be viewed as a tax on banks since it forces them to hold zero yielding assets in excess of their requirements as prudential profit maximizing institutions; the larger the mandatory requirement the larger the burden of the tax. Such a tax encourages non-taxed institutions, for example banks operating in the Eurosterling market to bid deposits away from UK banks because they can operate on finer margins (between lending and borrowing rates) as they do not have to pay the 'reserve tax'. Such 'disintermediation' would distort the money supply statistics of the UK banks particularly in the transition period immediately after the introduction of a mandatory MBC system. Some (for example Griffiths (1980)) argue that even with a high mandatory reserve requirement such disintermediation would only be a transitional problem. Once both the domestic and offshore banks had reached their equilibrium level of deposits any further changes in the monetary base would produce an ordered change in both domestic and Euro markets and the domestic money supply would give the correct monetary 'signals'. This argument is similar to the view that domestic non-bank financial intermediaries (for example building societies) do not 'distort' the information content of 'money' and is also obviously connected with the problems of how to define 'money'. A sceptic might take the view that the working of the Eurosterling market is somewhat imperfectly understood even in an equilibrium framework, and that even less is known about dynamic considerations such as the speed of adjustment to external changes. The possibility of such disintermediation cannot be ignored, but the abolition of the $12\frac{1}{2}$ per cent reserve ratio lowers the tax on domestic banks since they are now able to rearrange their liquid assets such as commercial and Treasury bills solely according to their own profit maximizing motives,[10] and this reduces the potential for disintermediation.

Advocates of MBC would argue that the abolition of the $12\frac{1}{2}$ per cent reserve ratio and the probable introduction of the cash base as the reserve base of the system minimizes the possibility of the banks bidding away reserve assets from the NBPS thus causing unpredictable short-run changes in the money multiplier.[11] It is argued that with the reserve base defined relatively narrowly as 'cash' the impact of the authorities funding operations at the short end of the market have a more predictable influence on the base. If, for example, Treasury bills held by the banks are included in the base, sales of bills to the banks leave the reserve base unchanged (balances at the Bank fall, Treasury bills' holdings rise by an equal amount) whilst sales to the NBPS reduce the reserve base (bankers' balances and deposits of the NBPS fall by equal amounts). Under a cash base system, however, a sale of Treasury bills to either the banks or the

NBPS unambiguously reduces the reserve base. Note, however, that if banks engage in liability management this argument in favour of a narrow definition of the base only holds if the authorities do not support the gilts market. In the face of a rise in interest rates and a loss of 'cash', the banks may raise their rate on wholesale deposits which may encourage switching from government debt to deposits by the NBPS and this alters the monetary base, if the authorities purchase the debt.

The decision to forego the announcement of minimum lending rate appears to be aimed at depoliticizing interest rate changes. Although the authorities may engineer interest rate changes they do not wish the general public to be overtly informed. Rises in MLR tend to be associated with rises in banks' base rates and building society mortgage rates and attract political odium. Non-announcement probably allows more frequent short-term changes in interest rates since it enables the authorities to (rightly or wrongly) claim that interest rates have risen due to 'market forces' beyond the control of the government and that falls are indirectly due to the 'success' of the government's policies. This change is important for understanding the 'political economy' of monetary control. But more important, it also implies that banks may quickly alter base rates in line with market interest rates thus avoiding adverse relative interest rate effects on bank advances. This may be very important in improving control over broad monetary aggregates by 'market means'.

Prior to the Bank's 'new measures', cash shortages in the money market were relieved by direct lending through the discount window when the discount houses were unable to cover the whole of the 'weekly' Treasury bill tender (as they were required to do). Lending at the discount window could be either at market rates or above (penal rate). Under the 'new measures', the discount houses, when facing a cash shortage, offer bills to the Bank at a particular rate. The Bank can either accept the bills or lend overnight through the discount window at an interest rate of its own choosing (for example penal rate) thus either validating the market rates offered by the discount houses or instigating a change in rates. Intervention in the bill market has, in principle, altered very little under the 'new measures'. The crucial factor for monetary control is the authorities' willingness to take positive action to create and maintain a cash shortage or alter interest rates. The 'new measures' indicated that more vigorous open market operations might take place at the short end of the market. However, at the long end of the market there has been little or no change and the authorities did not suggest a policy of selling gilts by auction, for example.

To summarize, the new measures are a cautious move to assess the possible practical implications of a move to full monetary base control but also improve control methods using interest rates. The authorities have not given specific targets for operational deposits but they now have more flexibility in influencing short rates. Flexibility of short rates, and the use of a penal interest rate in its dealings with the discount houses will allow the authorities to monitor and assess the degree of control that is possible over the monetary base and the banks' demand function for 'operational deposits'. The abolition of the $12\frac{1}{2}$ per cent reserve ratio is probably warranted on grounds of equity with other financial institutions, but also minimizes the possibility that monetary control would involve substantial disintermediation in offshore markets, whatever method of control is used.

The new measures are consistent with a move towards MBC, although so far the Bank in its operations has shown a desire to use interest rate control rather than a policy of targeting the base. This appears to arise because both the monetary aggregate and the exchange rate are taken as intermediate targets. Evidence for this move to include the exchange rate as an intermediate target is provided by the events at the end of 1982. At this time the growth in £M3 and PSL2 were within the target band of 7–11 per cent set in the March budget and there appeared to be no reason why, by November 1982, interest rates should be raised for reasons of monetary control. (The exception here was M1 which was growing in excess of 15 per cent per annum but although officially included in the 7–11 per cent target range was not thought to be of major concern.) In the middle of November the effective rate for sterling fell by about 4 per cent and UK market interest rates began to increase. The Bank accepted offers of bills (in bands 3 and 4)[12] on 18 November at rates up to $\frac{1}{4}$ per cent higher than previously, thus validating the increase in market rates. Despite a $\frac{1}{2}$ per cent cut in the Eurodollar rate (triggered by a cut in the federal reserve discount rate) the pound fell again on 25 and 26 November and three-month interbank rates rose sharply by over $\frac{3}{4}$ per cent to $9\frac{15}{16}$ per cent. The Bank was still accepting bills at an unchanged rate but this did not prevent one clearing bank raising its base rate by 1 per cent to 10 per cent. Shortly after this the Bank accepted bills at a 1 per cent higher rate of 10 per cent, and other clearing banks then followed with rises in base rates to between 10 and $10\frac{1}{4}$ per cent. Although sterling steadied somewhat it came under renewed pressure in January 1983. Again three-month interbank rates rose relatively gently up to 10 January reaching $10\frac{5}{8}$ per cent, but the next day rose sharply by over $\frac{1}{2}$ per cent to $11\frac{3}{16}$ per cent and base rates of 11 per cent were announced. The bank again accepted this market rise in its dealing in bills, and sterling stabilized. The Bank's actions in the bill market over this period clearly show its willingness to allow a rise in interest rates to support sterling even when the monetary targets are being met. This would not be possible if a monetary base target had to be met at all times.

In the first year after the introduction of the 'new measures', changes in the money multiplier (table 8.1) were greater than changes in the base. Substantial variations in both the cash ratio of the NBPS and the operational (reserve) deposits ratio of the banks were responsible for the movements in the money multiplier. After this initial period, variations in the money multiplier are somewhat less marked, but conceal substantial variations in the cash ratio of the NBPS (Trundle, 1982) and the reserve–deposits ratio of the banks, Presumably a move to full MBC would be a substantial regime switch and any behavioural relations would be subject to the celebrated Lucas critique (Lucas, 1976). This certainly appears to be the case in the US where both ratios exhibit marked instability after the introduction of 'non-borrowed reserves' targets (see section 8.3).

It appears that the Bank is able to use the new measures to implement or validate changes in short rates and the 'clearers' then respond by quickly altering

TABLE 8.1 The monetary base and the money multiplier

	£M3	Wide monetary base	Money multiplier	% change over previous 3 months	
				Cash–deposits ratio of NBPS	Banks' 'reserve- deposits' ratio
March 82	2.0	0.8	1.2	−0.6	−5.8
June 82	2.6	0.2	2.4	−2.8	−1.9
Sept 82	3.1	−0.2	3.3	−2.6	−10.2
Dec 82	1.7	1.4	0.4	−0.2	−2.0
March 83	3.2	1.9	1.3	−1.0	−4.0
June 83	4.0	1.6	2.3	−2.3	−4.0
Sept 83	1.4	1.3	0.1	−0.4	2.2
Dec 83	2.4	1.6	0.8	−0.7	−2.0
March 84	2.1	0.9	1.2	−2.2	4.5
June 84	3.4	1.5	1.8	−1.1	−7.8
Aug 84	1.7	1.1	0.6	−0.3	−3.5

After August 1982 figures for the wide monetary base are an average figure for the month. Prior to this, figures are for the 'make-up day'.
Data is seasonally adjusted.

Source: Financial Statistics and *Bank of England Quarterly Bulletin*.

base rates. On occasions the clearing banks, when faced with a change in their marginal cost of funds as market rates change (particularly in response to foreign interest rates and a weakening of sterling) will themselves move base rates prior to signals or intervention from the Bank. The new measures may therefore be seen as allowing more frequent interest rate changes. The consequences for sterling of such changes are fairly predictable in the short run but the response of the monetary aggregates remains uncertain. Uncertainty concerning the link between open market operations and changes in rates on wholesale deposits and bank advances has probably been reduced by the Bank's new operating procedures. However, although this means that the worst excesses of the post-CCC era will be avoided, control over a broad monetary aggregate will still be subject to considerable error because of the uncertainty over the response of bank advances to relative interest rates (Cuthbertson and Foster, 1982; Cuthbertson, 1985a).

8.3 MONETARY CONTROL IN THE US

Analysis of the US money supply process is usually presented in terms of the 'reserve ratio approach' outlined in section 7.3. However, we can analyse this model either under an interest rate target or a target for the monetary base.

Throughout most of the 1970s the US operated with some form of monetary target either for narrow money or broad money or both. In 1979 the authorities instituted a fairly rigid form of control over the reserve *base* of the banks and it is on this aspect that we concentrate.

Prior to 1972 the authorities attempted to achieve their monetary targets by using the federal funds rate (that is the rate on short-term assets that the federal reserve could influence by its open market operations) as their operational target variable. When the money supply moved outside its target range the proviso clause whereby the Fed could alter the federal funds rate came into play. After 1972, target bands were set for the reserve base of the banks although the interest rate target was given most weight. Control of the money supply was, in principle at least, to be instituted by altering the federal funds rate and 'sliding up and down' the demand for money function.

In October 1979 the Fed announced a dramatic shift in policy. The Federal Open Market Committee (FOMC) set tight target bands for the rate of growth of a number of monetary aggregates (both narrow and broad money) over the year ahead as well as interim target paths for the following two or three months ahead. The operational target chosen by the Fed to control its intermediate monetary target was not the monetary base but the level of *non-borrowed* reserves. We can analyse this control system by a slight modification of the identities in our monetary base model of section 7.3.2.

The 'sources' of total reserves (TR) are borrowed reserves (BR) and non-borrowed reserves (NBR). The former are reserve assets borrowed by the banks at the federal reserve discount window. The main source of NBR are the Fed's open market operations in short-term debt. The 'uses' for the banks' total reserves are to acquire required reserves (RR) while the remainder constitute excess reserves (ER)

$$TR \equiv BR + NBR \tag{8.6a}$$

$$\equiv RR + ER \tag{8.6b}$$

Rearranging these two identities we obtain an expression for RR

$$RR = NBR - (ER - BR) = NBR - FR \tag{8.7}$$

where FR are free reserves. If the required reserve *ratio* RR/D is b and the cash-deposit ratio of the NBPS is α then the money supply is given by

$$M = C_p + D = (1 + \alpha)D$$

$$= \left(\frac{1 + \alpha}{b}\right)(NBR - FR)$$

Free reserves consist of borrowed reserves and the excess reserves of the banks. If the discount rate charged by the Fed r_p is low then banks will increase BR and expand their earning assets such as loans to the NBPS and consequently deposits will rise. The opportunity cost of excess reserves is the interest foregone on non-reserve earning assets such as bonds and bank loans. If we denote this vector of interest rates as r then excess reserves depend negatively on r. Thus the higher is the yield differential $r - r_p$ the lower is the free reserve ratio and hence the higher is the money supply for a given level of NBR. The analysis therefore yields a similar money supply function as in equation (7.23) (section 7.3.2) but with NBR replacing the monetary base

$$M^s = f(r, r_p, \text{NBR}) \quad f_1, f_3 > 0, f_2 < 0 \tag{8.8}$$

We are now in a position to analyse how the Fed sets its operational target for the level of NBR. Given a desired path for nominal income and the (narrow) money supply, the equilibrium interest rate to achieve the latter may be obtained by inverting the demand for money function. The demand for cash by the NBPS is then determined by income and the 'equilibrium' interest rate calculated above. The level of bank deposits determines the level of *required* reserves. The discount rate and the known market rate of interest are used to calculate the desired level of free reserves. The target for NBR which is announced by the Fed is the sum of required reserves and free reserves.

There is a great deal of debate in the US concerning the most appropriate quantitative operating target for the Fed. The Fed could target its own security portfolio, total reserves or the monetary base instead of non-borrowed reserves. It could also, if it wished, return to an interest rate target. These potential targets are also interdependent and therefore in choosing one the Fed must forego the others. Whatever quantitative operating target is ultimately chosen it then remains to determine whether it is to be calculated with respect to the current, future or past level of deposits. In fact the Fed in 1979 chose a lagged reserve accounting procedure. Interesting though these issues may be we refrain from commenting on their relative merits which are well documented elsewhere (Bryant, 1983; Axilrod, 1982; Walsh, 1982; Santomero, 1983); space constraints force us to only discuss the operation of the immediate post-1979 system.[13] It is worth noting that the Fed can supplement its target for NBR, which it attempts to achieve primarily by open market operations (OMO) at the short end of the market, by changes in its discount rate and in the required reserve ratio.

Although taken at face value, the use of non-borrowed reserves as an operating target appears to be a very rigid form of control, the Fed has had a considerable amount of discretion. First, the Fed frequently began a new target period from whatever level the money supply had achieved in the previous target period, even if there had been some overshoot. This 'target drift' can be seen in figure 8.1. Second, several monetary aggregates were targeted but if one exceeded its target range, the Fed could cite the slow growth in the other aggregates as a reason for not altering NBR. In fact over the 1980–2 period narrow money, M1, was broadly within the target band, transactions balances M2 were at the upper end of the range whilst the broad monetary aggregate M3 was well above the target range. Third, the response to deviations from the monetary targets has been gradual and on the odd occasion (for example May 1980) interest rates have taken precedence over the non-borrowed reserves target. Although the monetary aggregates for M1 and M2 have been kept within their target bands, this has been at the expense of a higher level of nominal interest rates and a much increased volatility in interest rates (figure 8.2). As

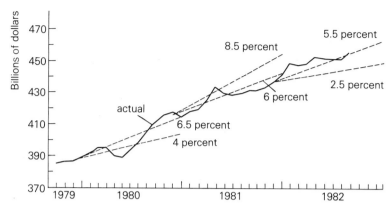

FIGURE 8.1   *M1 definition of the money stock: actual path and target cones, fall 1979 through summer 1981.*[a]

(Source: Bryant (1983))

[a] Seasonally adjusted monthly averages of daily data.

far as the ultimate targets of economic policy are concerned, the inflation rate has fallen since 1979 but so did real output.

What are the reasons for this mixed set of results in hitting the monetary targets? First, there appears to have been some instability in the demand for money function. There has been widespread use of assets that are close substitutes for M1 balances and that pay interest but are excluded from the definition of M1; for example, NOW accounts and savings accounts which allow automatic transfers to checking accounts (ATS accounts). There has been a growth in money market mutual funds and in repurchase agreements both of which provide close substitutes for transactions balances but also pay interest (Judd and Scadding, 1982). As we shall see in section 8.4 precise control of non-borrowed reserves does not totally insulate the equilibrium money supply from shifts in the demand for money function. A second reason for a somewhat poor performance is the instability in the demand for excess reserves by the banks and it appears that the demand for *borrowed* reserves from the discount window was also somewhat unpredictable (even after account is taken of the penalty surcharge imposed on heavy borrowers at various times over the period (Bryant, 1983).

Instability in the non-borrowed reserve *ratio* of the banks and variations in the level of non-borrowed reserves, the Feds operational target, lead to variations in M1. We can apportion the change in M1 between NBR and the *ratio* of non-borrowed reserves to M1, $k = M/\text{NBR}$. We have, approximately

$$\Delta M = \Delta k \times \text{NBR} + \Delta \text{NBR} \times k$$

The first term gives the change in M1 due to the change in the NBR ratio k and the second due to the change in the *level* of NBR. These two items are graphed

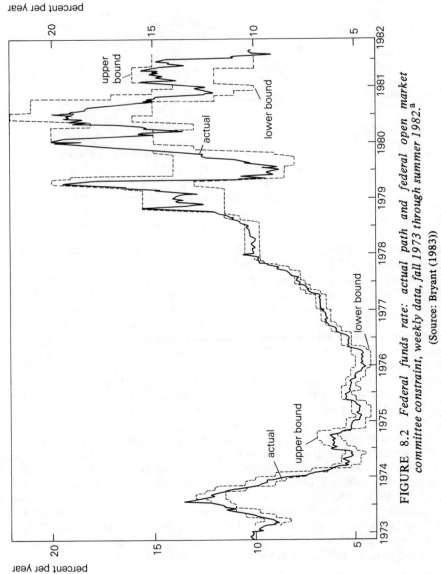

FIGURE 8.2 *Federal funds rate: actual path and federal open market committee constraint, weekly data, fall 1973 through summer 1982.*[a]

(Source: Bryant (1983))

[a] Weekly averages of daily data, not seasonally adjusted.

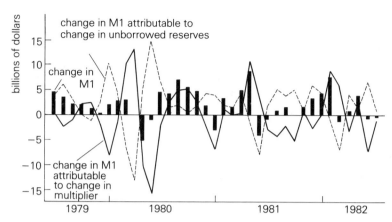

FIGURE 8.3 *Decomposition of changes in M1 with adjusted unborrowed reserves as 'high-powered money': June 1979 through June 1982.*
(Source: Bryant (1983))

in figure 8.3 and it is clear that changes in the 'money multiplier' k have as great an impact on M1 as changes in the level of NBR. So the change in the banks behavioural equations are not small relative to the policy actions of the Fed. Of course it is not the volatility of the reserve ratio of the banks that is ultimately of crucial importance but its unpredictability; however, we have already noted the latter.

For comparative purposes it is interesting to note that the impact on the UK money supply of changes in the money multiplier have frequently been as great as those due to changes in the monetary 'base' (figure 8.3) over the period since the introduction of the 'new measures' in 1981. Of course this may be the result of banks learning about the operation of the new system and need not necessarily imply unpredictability in the reserve ratios of the banks and the NBPS. However, both sets of figures refute the proposition that the reserve ratios do not vary greatly.

This concludes our brief analysis of the *practical* difficulties encountered when using interest rates and the FOF approach to control the money supply in the UK and the use of quantitative operating targets in the US. We now investigate some a priori considerations that determine the choice between an interest rate and a quantitative operating target.

8.4 INTEREST RATES VERSUS QUANTITATIVE OPERATING TARGETS

Our two case studies on the UK and US have provided insights into the practical problems involved in using either quantitative operational targets or interest rates to control the money supply. We now examine, in a more formal manner, the factors that influence the choice between these two regimes. We assume that the authorities only objective is to achieve its intermediate monetary target which we take to be narrow money (M1). This enables us to avoid the complications of a demand for money function that depends on relative interest rates; for M1 we need only one representative interest rate in the demand for money function. For similar reasons with M1 we can use our simplified money supply function of section 7.3.2 thus avoiding the complications of wholesale banks that engage in liability management. Even in this simple model of the money market, the choice between an interest rate target or a target for non-borrowed reserves (NBR)[14] is by no means straightforward. The choice is found to depend on the relative instability of the money supply and money demand functions and the slopes of these functions. Other things equal, the more unstable is the demand for money function relative to the supply function the more one tends to favour fixing the level of NBR rather than interest rates. It follows from this that if one knows the source of the disturbance one can choose the correct operating target to use; there may be times when a quantitative target is required and others when an interest rate target is most appropriate.

Note that we do not discuss the appropriate monetary operating target with respect to the authorities ultimate targets of policy (for example output and inflation) but only with respect to its intermediate target. Such considerations may give different answers to those provided by our more limited analysis here (Sellon and Teigen, 1982; Artis and Currie, 1981).

The model of the monetary sector we have in mind is given by the following equations, which are intentionally kept rather simple for ease of exposition (see Thornton (1982) for a more sophisticated model).

$$M^s = mr + b(\text{NBR}) + u \tag{8.9}$$

$$M^d = a_0 - ar + v \tag{8.10}$$

$$M^s = M^d \tag{8.11}$$

We have, for simplicity omitted the penal discount rate from the money supply function (equation (8.8)). The terms u and v represent stochastic shocks to the supply and demand functions with mean zero and variances σ_u^2, σ_v^2 respectively and covariance σ_{uv}. The model could easily be adapted to other quantitative operational targets such as control of the monetary base. Although the model we are using here has been derived in a monetary base framework it may be used to represent control via interest rates (appendix 8A).

The first point to note is that if the demand and supply functions contain no stochastic elements then either setting non-borrowed reserves at NBR_0 or fixing interest rates at r_0 (both achieved by open market operations) yields the monetary target M^* exactly (figure 8.4). There is no difference between the two operational targets (one is said to be the 'dual' of the other). A corollary of this is that when policy instruments can be adjusted in the light of new information, control of NBR appears to have little or no inherent superiority over interest rate control. Although figures for NBR and interest rates are available more speedily (daily) than those for the money supply (monthly) it is likely that the authorities would wish to wait at least several months before embarking on changes in *any* policy

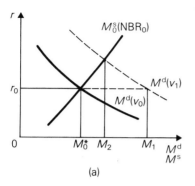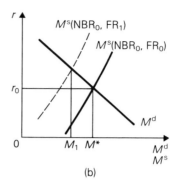

FIGURE 8.4 *NBR and interest rate targets; (a) shocks to the demand for money* ($v_0 > v_1$); *(b) shocks to the supply of money.*

instrument. A contingent rule whereby NBR were altered if the money supply exceeded its target value over a run of months, or alternatively interest rates were altered, would seem to be of equal usefulness; both depend upon the predictability of the response of the asset demand functions of the banks and the NBPS.

Thus the superiority claimed by advocates of MBC for targeting NBR rather than interest rates refers to that period of time before the authorities feel confident about altering *any* of its policy instruments. The choice of a fixed operational target is therefore concerned with a short time scale and hence with minimizing short-run fluctuations in the money supply. Longer run changes in the money supply may be equally well controlled under either of our two regimes.

8.4.1. *Fixing interest rates*

Under an operating target for interest rates, (free) reserves become endogenous and unexpected changes in them do not alter the money supply; (free) reserves are provided on demand at the going fixed interest rate. For example, given a stochastic increase in the demand for free reserves by the banks, they sell non-reserve assets such as short term debt on the open market. This tends to push up short term interest rates and therefore the authorities step in to purchase these assets, increasing the level of free reserves, hence the money supply remains at its target level M^*. In terms of figure 8.4b the money supply function shifts to the left as banks sell earnings assets and then returns to M^* as the authorities purchase these assets. On the other hand, under an interest rate operating target any stochastic shifts in the demand for money function are completely reflected in an overshoot or undershoot of the monetary target (figure 8.4a). An increase in the demand for money is accompanied by a sale of assets by the NBPS[15] and a potential increase in interest rates. The authorities again step in and purchase

TABLE 8.2   Alternative operational targets

Source of shock	Operational target	M^S error minimized when
Money demand	(a) NBR is appropriate operational target	(a) Money supply function inelastic and demand function elastic
	(b) Fix interest rate	(b) Error depends only on shift in demand function (σ_v)
Money supply	(a) Interest rate is appropriate target	(a) Zero error
	(b) Fix NBR	(b) Money supply function is elastic and money demand inelastic

these assets from the NBPS thus increasing NBR and the money supply (in figure 8.4(a) the money supply function is a horizontal line through r_0). Note that under an interest rate target, the error in hitting the monetary target depends only on v and is independent of the slopes of the supply and demand curves (appendix 8A).

8.4.2   *Fixed NBR*

Turning now to a target for NBR we see from figure 8.4(a) that if the demand function is unstable the deviation of the money supply from its target level $(M_2 - M^*)$ is less than when we fix interest rates. This arises because the increase in interest rates consequent on the shift in the demand for money does not bring forth an increase in NBR from the authorities. However, the rise in market interest rates does lead to a reduction in the desired level of free reserves by the banks so there is *some* increase in the money supply $M_0^* M_2$ above target. Notice that the overshoot is smaller the smaller the interest elasticity of free reserves (table 8.2). In the simple mechanical multiplier (section 7.3.1) the supply curve is completely inelastic (vertical) and the monetary target is met exactly in this case. It is also easy to see that for any given supply curve the overshoot is less the more elastic is the demand for money function. Thus under an NBR operating target the degree of overshoot (or undershoot) in the monetary target depends on the slopes of the supply and demand functions although when the source of instability is in the demand function the degree of over-shoot is always less than with an interest rate target.

Our final case is that of a shift in the money supply function under an NBR regime. Suppose there is a stochastic increase in the demand for free reserves by the banks. With a fixed level of NBR the banks sell non-reserve assets putting upward pressure on interest rates (figure 8.4(b)) and simultaneously reducing the money supply and the demand for money. There is an undershoot in the monetary target of $M^* - M_1$ which is greater the larger is the interest elasticity of the demand for money and the smaller is the interest elasticity of the supply of money. Thus the relative sizes of the elasticities to minimize fluctuations around the monetary target in this case are opposite to those required when the stochastic disturbances arise from the demand function. Of course under an interest rate target stochastic shocks to the money supply function do not lead to errors in meeting the monetary target. These alternatives are summarized in table 8.2.

So far we have neglected the role of the discount rate in the money supply function. In the US there has been a heated debate on the issue of the use of the discount rate as a penal rate under the post-1979 arrangements. The Fed decided not to link the discount rate to market rates. When monetary policy was tight and market interest rates high, this implied that the banks could expand their *borrowed* reserves at the discount window at a non-penal rate and hence support expansion of their balance sheets and the money supply, even though NBR were fixed by the Feds operating target. Critics suggested that the discount rate should be linked to market rates. Under this 'variable discount rate policy' the banks would not reduce their free reserves as much as they did under a fixed discount rate policy because the cost of borrowing from the Fed is higher. Hence the money supply function is steeper under a variable discount rate policy. (This is most easily seen by making the discount rate $r_p = \alpha r$ in our money supply function of equation (8.8) and this increases the value of m in equation (8.9).) The implications of a variable rate policy can be seen by reference to table 8.2. If the demand for money function is unstable the variable discount rate policy improves monetary control as compared with the fixed discount rate policy, under an NBR operating target. The converse applies if the money supply is unstable. If both functions are unstable the appropriate policy is indeterminate unless we know the covariances and slopes of the supply and demand functions. Under fixed interest rate policy the choice of a fixed or variable discount rate policy is of course immaterial.

8.4.3 *Summary*

The choice of the interest rate or NBR as the appropriate target depends upon the slopes of the supply and demand curves and their (relative) variances and covariances. Even in this simple model the assertion that the supply curve is more stable then the demand curve $(\sigma_u^2 < \sigma_v^2)$ does not *guarantee* the superiority of base control rather than control by interest rates since this also depends on the slopes of the two functions and the covariance between them (appendix 8A).

A more complete and realistic model which utilizes this stochastic framework is given by Bryant (1983) (for the US system, but it has wider applicability). What becomes immediately obvious are the tremendous informational requirements needed to apply the analysis. It may not be possible in a developing financial system to unambiguously say whether the demand or the supply of money function is more stable, especially if a particular form of control is to be applied for the first time (the Lucas critique again). In addition we may be uncertain about the size of the coefficients, rather than the (relative) sizes of the additive errors. Models with stochastic parameters are difficult to analyse and the informational requirements for choosing the appropriate operating target are even more severe (Driscoll and Ford, 1980; Turnovsky, 1977). Thus, in practice, the approach discussed provides little more than an appropriate framework for organizing ones thoughts. Ignoring the problems posed by the Lucas critique, then as more information about the relevant demand and supply functions becomes available the above analysis may be of more practical use. However, as we noted in section 3.3 on the mean-variance model the Lucas critique implies that the parameters of the supply and demand for money functions may alter under alternative monetary policy régimes. The validity of the above analysis which assumes invariant parameters is therefore considerably weakened.

8.5   SUMMARY: OPERATING TARGETS AND MONETARY CONTROL

The use of interest rates to control the growth of a broad monetary aggregate in the UK has undoubtedly met with considerable difficulties, most notably in the unpredictable behaviour of bank advances. The latter is in part caused by bank loans being increasingly used in the UK as a major source of company sector finance together with the banks' move towards liability rather than asset management. The changing short-run objectives of the banks and frequent 'regime changes' has also complicated matters.

The 'corset' succeeded in curtailing the banks competitive bidding for wholesale deposits but at a cost in terms of large scale disintermediation which distorted the monetary data. Under the 'new' measures introduced in the UK in 1981 the authorities still use the interest rate mechanism (supplemented in the medium term by changes in the PSBR) to control the monetary aggregates. Some of the more glaring difficulties encountered in the immediate post-CCC era are now being avoided as the banks appear to respond fairly quickly in adjusting their interest rate on loans to changes in market rates. However, control over broad monetary aggregates is still subject to fairly wide margins of error.

In the US the adoption of a quantitative operational target has also been beset by difficulties. Previously stable relationships such as the banks 'free' and 'borrowed' reserve ratios have exhibited large errors. It is becoming increasingly difficult to argue that this is because of a learning period by the banks, as the method has now been in use for some years. Expectations and the Lucas critique may provide part of the explanation for difficulties encountered, as might the Feds reluctance to charge a penal rate on borrowed reserves. Financial innovation in the range of near-monies provided by banks (which may or may not be a consequence of the introduction of quantitative operational targets) has distorted the targeted aggregates.

Turning from practical matters to the theoretical arguments for fixing interest rates or using a quantitative operating target, we noted that even in a very simple model the choice requires detailed knowledge of the *source* of disturbances in financial markets as well as the relative slopes of the supply and demand for money functions. The informational requirements are even more onerous if (as seems likely) the size of the relevant *parameters* are also uncertain.

In the remainder of this chapter we discuss the impact of structural changes in both domestic and offshore markets and draw some further implications on the usefulness of intermediate monetary targets.

8.6 FINANCIAL INNOVATION AND STRUCTURAL CHANGE

Hitherto we have noted the growing importance of monetary targets and briefly discussed methods of control in the US and the UK against a background of our knowledge of the theory of the financial firm. In our discussion of interest rate versus base control we highlighted the need to consider the behaviour of the whole of the banks balance sheet. In the longer term there is little to choose between the two methods of control on grounds of economic theory and in the short run the appropriate operating target depends upon ones view of the main source of disturbance in the money market. In the main our discussion has been within a framework where asset demand and supply functions are known (except for an additive stochastic error term). Our theories of the financial firm have largely been of the comparative static variety involving one period optimization of some objective function such as profits, sales or expected utility. In our discussion of two case studies in monetary control for the US and the UK, dynamic considerations entered the analysis in a relatively *ad hoc* manner. We now wish to continue with a discussion of dynamic effects in financial markets concentrating on financial innovation. Ultimately we shall be mainly interested in the implications of financial innovation for the control of monetary aggregates. With rapid structural change do the authorities need to re-define 'money', and is it still desirable or feasible to control any single monetary aggregate? We hope to throw some light on these key policy questions. We divide our discussion into those structural changes that affect domestic financial intermediaries and those that influence financial intermediation in foreign currencies and in offshore markets. The latter encompasses the behaviour of the Euromarkets.

8.6.1 *Domestic markets*

Goodhart (1984) has highlighted three main types of structural change in domestic markets. These comprise the switch to liability management in the 1970s, the continuing shift to variable rate lending on bank loans and the introduction of new payments systems for retail deposits. To a large extent these three elements are common to the banking systems in all industrialized countries, although the pace of change varies from country to country, with the US probably being the market 'leader'. Goodhart suggests that these structural changes have been facilitated by a relaxation of government controls on domestic banks (for example abandonment of interest rate cartels and direct controls on bank advances), improved technology (for example computers) and the existence of high and variable rates of inflation.

Liability management. We discussed this aspect with reference to the UK domestic banks but the trend to liability management has also taken place in other industrialized nations. Prior to the banks operating in the domestic whole-sale markets monetary control operated relatively smoothly via asset adjustment by the banks. Banks had a substantial cushion of government debt which could be sold in an attempt to obtain reserve assets acquired by the authorities as a result of their open market operations. A sale of government debt by the banks to the NBPS could lead to a multiple contraction in deposits. As the banks deposit rates were sticky a rise in the absolute level of interest rates due to tight monetary policy resulted in a change in relative interest rates in favour of government debt and hence a switch by the NBPS out of money into govern-ment debt. Narrow and broad money aggregates both tended to move together over this period.

Towards the end of the 1960s the proportion of public sector debt held in bank portfolios had fallen dramatically. For example in the UK the ratio fell from 60 per cent in 1949 to 12 per cent in 1970 and for the US commercial banks the comparable figures are 54 per cent and 23 per cent (Goodhart, 1984). By 1970 wholesale markets in domestic currencies had developed. Many domestic commercial banks had subsidiaries that operated in wholesale *Euromarkets* and they were therefore well equipped to take advantage of the emerging market in *domestic* wholesale deposits. Faced with a shortage of reserve assets and only moderate holdings of government debt the banks were reluctant to contract their profitable lending on bank advances to the private sector. They therefore bid for funds in the wholesale market pushing up wholesale deposit rates. The demand for broad money now responded to relative interest rates. The authorities can influence the absolute level of rates by open market operations but it has far less control over relative rates and the money supply, since the behaviour of the banks determines the rate on money. This is also reflected in the assets side of the banks balance sheet where advances to large companies depend on relative interest rates. We have discussed the difficulties in controlling bank advances with reference to the UK and do not repeat those arguments here. The move to liability management is now largely complete in a number of industrial countries and it seems unlikely that others will experience the acute difficulties encountered in the UK in the early 1970s.

The use of liability management has resulted in a negative relationship emerging between the annual rates of growth of broad and narrow money in the 1970s in the UK, Canada and Switzerland. For France and Japan, the correlation remains positive and Goodhart (1984) suggests that limitations on liability management in these countries due to the existence of credit ceilings may account for these results. The reason for the negative correlation is that the NBPS switches out of zero interest-bearing sight deposits as the absolute level of interest rates increases. However, if this is accompanied by a rise in wholesale deposit rates relative to rates on government debt (or an equal rise in these rates but a higher short-run 'own' elasticity on deposits) then the demand for broad money may rise as the absolute level of interest rates rise. (The more elaborate mechanisms in the Sprenkle–Miller model would also produce such a result.) These two monetary aggregates may therefore give conflicting information about the 'tightness' of the monetary stance.

Variable rate lending. We have already noted that retail banks undertake substantial positive maturity transformation. Risks are minimized because the banks operate the domestic payments mechanism and can therefore rely on funds returning to the bank. Prior to the advent of liability management they could also count on deposit rates and therefore the marginal cost of funds (neglecting real resource costs such as wages) being stable for fairly lengthy periods. Hence they could lend on long maturities at a fixed nominal loan rate. Faced with a low or predictable rate of inflation, the NBPS could be reasonably certain of the *real* cost of long-term borrowing from the banks. However, with high and variable rates of inflation which began in the 1970s in most European countries, the risks to fixed rate lending on long maturities became much higher.

On the demand side, borrowing long on a fixed nominal interest rate when inflation is high and variable will involve highly uncertain costs in real terms. On the other hand if short rates broadly reflect current inflation, the real cost of borrowing with a succession of short-term 'roll-over credits' is known with greater certainty. Increased use of such variable rate lending has probably reduced the interest sensitivity of bank loans since the timing of the borrowing matters less than for 'risky' long-term fixed interest loans.

Easy access to overdrafts, variable rate loans and substantial holdings of liquid assets by large companies may imply that they view these assets as close substitutes in meeting cash flow requirements. Companies may therefore be mainly concerned with their *net* liquidity position and separate demand functions for broad money and loans could be expected to be somewhat unstable. If it is net liquidity that influences company behaviour then targeting only *monetary* aggregates, may not achieve desired results.

One can also see why domestic banks that engage in the wholesale deposit market would favour a shift towards variable rate lending. If long-term fixed interest loans are supported by short-term wholesale deposits then a rise in the interest rate on the latter will squeeze bank profits. US saving and loan associations in the 1970s, German banks in 1978 and the UK commercial banks in the early 1970s suffered losses because of an element of longer-term fixed interest lending at a time of rising market rates on deposit liabilities. Although the increasing use of variable rate lending means that changes in the general level of interest rates will quickly be transmitted to the loan market this does not guarantee more accurate short-run control over broad money and credit because these respond to *relative* interest rates. It is the loan–deposit spread that is important. As banks become more competitive and efficient the spread between deposit and loan rates, which crudely speaking is the 'return to intermediation', is likely to narrow and hence the level of financial intermediation to increase. In the UK the demise of the long-term fixed interest market in debentures and preference shares is in part probably due to the increased attractiveness of variable rate lending by the banks and UK, companies are becoming increasingly reliant on the banking system as its major source of external finance. If so then curtailing the growth of the monetary aggregates may hinder long-term real investment.[16]

Improvements in payments technology. In the UK and other industrial countries improvements in payments technology include the use of computers in 'clearing' cheques; the use of automated teller machines to dispense cash and balance sheet information; increased use of credit cards and the implementation of electronic banking in the home, in retail outlets and between firms.

To the extent that such innovations reduce the real resource costs of banking (and shift the marginal cost curve to the right) the supply of banking intermediation will increase and deposits rise. If electronic banking reduces 'barriers to entry' for those wishing to provide retail deposit and checking services (for example one only requires automatic teller machines rather than expensive 'branches') the banking industry may experience new entrants that should be classified as institutions subject to monetary targets (for example entry of UK building societies into retail banking via its branch network).

Electronic banking will reduce the demand for retail deposits; persons as well as companies might only hold minimum overnight trading balances, any surplus funds being invested in 'overnight' interest bearing deposits. Widespread use of credit cards means that net liquidity rather than 'money' may provide the buffer stock for persons (as for companies). Broad monetary aggregates will become more sensitive to relative interest rates as the transactions costs of switching between 'money', other assets and credit falls. This may lead to further instability in existing demand for money and credit equations and suggests that net liquidity may provide a more stable asset demand function for the personal sector.

We noted in section 5.3 that 'financial innovation' in the provision of deposits (as distinct from the supply of credit) appears to have had an appreciable effect on the demand for narrow money in the US but not in other industrialized countries. If the extent of innovation experienced in the US is mirrored in other countries then greater instability in their narrow money aggregates may ensue. In the US the variety of accounts available to firms and persons and improved facilities for money transmission services for firms are too numerous to mention in detail here (Gambs, 1977; Judd and Scadding, 1981 and references therein). Essentially these 'new' accounts provide interest on money balances with varying penalty costs of moving balances into 'checking accounts' (for example security repurchase agreements (RPs) for firms and similar facilities in the form of money market mutual funds for persons). Improved money transmission services allow firms to transfer excess balances from local banks to 'money centre' banks ('concentration accounts') using wire transfers. 'Zero-balance accounts' allow a zero balance until the total volume of cheques for clearing is known, when funds can then be transferred into the 'checking account'.

One further issue which is worth mentioning in passing is that the payment of interest on retail deposits will reduce the bank's endowment profits and hence increase the riskiness of banks. The latter may require greater attention to prudential control and capital adequacy as banks become more competitive and operate on finer margins. There have been a number of banking crises in recent years, for example the insolvency of some secondary banks in the UK in 1974/75 and the foreign exchange losses of the Franklin bank in New York and the Herstatt bank in Cologne in 1974. The issue of prudential control has certainly become more important of late in a number of countries and has been applied to domestic banks as well as Eurobanking activities (see for example Bank of England (1983) for the UK and Johnston (1983a) for an account of proposals for prudential control in Euromarkets). Prudential controls are a form of tax on banks and if they are not applied uniformly they may lead to disintermediation. Having discussed the analytics of disintermediation with respect to the 'corset' in the UK, we refrain from dealing with the details of alternative arrangements for prudential control.

In summary, financial innovation in domestic asset and credit markets in most industrialized countries is proceeding apace and complicates the choice of an appropriate intermediate monetary target aggregate. The informational content of particular aggregates for the future course of inflation (or nominal income) is weakened and control methods may lead to disintermediation more easily than in the past.

8.7 OFFSHORE MARKETS

In the next few sections we analyse the behaviour of the Eurobanks and in the main we shall be interested in their implications for the conduct of domestic monetary policy. Three major areas of interest arise. First, are the Eurobanks capable of a multiple expansion of deposits and loans thus undermining domestic monetary policy? Second, although perhaps not increasing the total stock of assets, do the Eurobanks create 'liquidity' and hence influence domestic expenditure? Thirdly, do the Euromarkets increase the scope for disintermediation and thus distort the informational content of domestic monetary aggregates? These issues appear to be of increasing importance for small open economies that do not have exchange controls. In order to answer these questions we shall cover a wide range of issues rather quickly and therefore cannot provide a detailed analysis of each topic – further discussion is given in Johnston (1983a). We proceed as follows. First, we describe the main functions of the Eurobanks and then discuss the extent of credit creation in the Euromarket using two approaches: the simple credit multiplier and the portfolio approach, both of which we discussed in the previous chapter. On balance both approaches suggest that the deposit (or credit) multiplier of the Eurobanks is relatively small and perhaps not much in excess of unity.

Next we discuss the evidence on the degree of liquidity transformation (creation) in the Euromarkets. The evidence is mixed and suggests that although maturity transformation is not as great as in domestic retail banks, it is nevertheless substantial. In our final section on the Eurobanks we find that for economies without exchange controls, disintermediation may not be a serious problem as long as the authorities do not impose high mandatory reserve ratios on the domestic banking system. However, the latter constraint may limit the authorities ability to control the broad money supply. This applies *a fortiori* if diversification into foreign assets (and liabilities) increases in the future.

8.7.1 *Functions of the Eurobanks*

We have examined the reasons why agents hold assets of various types under the heading of the inventory, precautionary and risk-aversion models. Foreign currency deposits may be held for all of these reasons but the literature has tended to concentrate on the first two, both at a theoretical and empirical level. The demand for holdings of a particular foreign currency has been related to the level of trade between two countries, as trade between industrial countries is often invoiced in the currency of the exporting country. The risk-aversion model predicts asset diversification based on expected holding period yields and we briefly looked at empirical tests of this model for foreign currency holdings in section 5.6. However, none of these models tell us why foreign currency deposits are held in banks outside the country of denomination of the foreign currency. For example, why do UK residents hold dollar deposits in foreign banks located in London rather than in banks located in the US? We discuss this issue below after first giving a brief overview of the functions of Eurobanks.

Eurocurrency banking activities are conducted by banks in foreign currencies, that is, in currencies other than those in which the bank is located. Deposits and loans are given to 'host' residents and non-residents. The main operators in the Euromarket are the subsidiaries of well-known banks that also operate in their own country. For example the Bank of America and Credit Lyonnaise operating in London are Eurobanks. The market is not confined to Europe but most of the business is transacted through banks located there, particularly London which undertakes about 40 per cent of total Euro-business. The Euro-sterling market is part of the Eurocurrency market and consists of banks located outside the UK who deal in sterling denominated deposits and loans with both UK residents and non-residents. Eurosterling funds are therefore substitutes for bank deposits and loans held in UK banks. Similarly there exist Eurodeutschmark and Euroguilder deposits. Over three-quarters of Eurocurrency deposits of the NBPS are held in currencies other than their domestic currencies and over 90 per cent of loans to the NBPS are in foreign currencies, particularly the dollar which dominates the market.

The Eurobanks (EB) deal in the wholesale money markets acquiring large fixed term deposits and on-lending these as fixed term loans. Unlike domestic retail banks, stochastic cash drain is not a problem and they have less need to hold 'cash' as reserve assets. Matching of assets and liabilities enables them to hold a very small amount of reserve assets. They operate on very small margins between lending and borrowing rates which is one reason why they undertake considerable matching of assets and liabilities (table 8.3). As financial intermediaries they perform two major functions: liquidity transformation and reducing brokerage costs between ultimate borrowers and lenders. Unlike domestic retail banks their main function is in reducing brokerage costs. The Euromarket is a global one; an EB may channel funds from surplus units (for example OPEC) to deficit units (for example international firms or developing countries in balance of payments difficulties). However, a large proportion of EB business is interbank transactions. These interbank transactions involve 'liquidity smoothing', 'liquidity transfer', 'currency transfer' and 'global liquidity distribution' (Johnson, 1983a).

Liquidity smoothing occurs when one EB lends to another that is short of 'cash'; it is an interbank short term loan. Liquidity transfer enables the EB

TABLE 8.3 Maturity structure of claims and liabilities in non-sterling currencies, all UK-based Euro-banks* (21 November 1979)

Maturity	London interbank market		With banks abroad		Non-banks		Total		Certificates of deposit issued
	Claims†	Liabilities	Claims	Liabilities	Claims	Liabilities	Claims	Liabilities	
Less than 8 days	0.17	0.18	0.20	0.23	0.08	0.31	0.17	0.23	0.04
6 days–<1 month	0.19	0.19	0.17	0.18	0.09	0.22	0.15	0.19	0.16
1 month–<3 months	0.31	0.30	0.26	0.29	0.12	0.24	0.24	0.28	0.31
3 months–<6 months	0.22	0.22	0.18	0.19	0.10	0.14	0.17	0.19	0.22
6 months–<1 year	0.07	0.08	0.07	0.07	0.06	0.06	0.07	0.07	0.10
1 year–<3 years	0.02	0.03	0.05	0.02	0.14	0.02	0.07	0.02	0.13
3 years and over	0.01	0.01	0.06	0.01	0.42	0.02	0.13	0.01	0.04
All maturities	1.00	1.00	1.00	1.00	1.00	1.00	1.00	1.00	1.00
Total all maturities ($mn)	81 689	79 824	199 839	196 518	86 890	53 835	368 418	330 177	43 579
Net claims ($mn)	+1 865		+3 321		+33 055		+38 241		

* Figures as proportions of the total unless otherwise stated.
† Includes holdings of certificates of deposit and other negotiable paper issued.

Source: *Bank of England Quarterly Bulletin*, September 1980, table 14.

to spread any maturity mismatch across a number of banks and hence reduce risk. For example Eurobank A on receiving a three-month dollar deposit of $100m may lend a small fraction to a primary borrower for six months and on-lend the rest as a three-month (matching) deposit to another EB. Similarly if Eurobank A has a $100m loan demand on a six-month roll-over basis it may finance it initially with a three-month deposit from bank B. Bank B may obtain its funds by a one-month interbank loan from bank C. Such 'pyramiding' allows the EB to spread the maturity transformation amongst a number of banks in the system.

The EB use currency transfers to match the currency composition of their assets and liabilities. Suppose an EB received a three-month Eurosterling deposit but wished to lend in dollars. It could lend the Eurosterling deposit in the three-month interbank market and borrow dollars to finance its loan commitment. The alternative matching process is to use the Eurosterling deposit to purchase dollars in the spot foreign exchange market and simultaneously sell dollars for sterling in the three-month *forward* exchange market. At the end of three months the repayment of the dollar loan is used to pay for the sterling in the forward market transaction and the latter is available to repay the sterling deposit. Because of the efficiency of arbitrage, the cost of undertaking these two forms of currency matching are equal: the Eurosterling interest rate is equal to the Eurodollar rate plus the forward discount on sterling against the dollar.

All of the above functions could be undertaken by banks located in their own countries but directly communicating with overseas banks concerning currency transfer. Consideration of brokerage costs of intermediation have been put forward as a major reason why the offshore Euromarkets have developed; global liquidity *distribution* takes place via the EB because of their low transactions costs (Neihans and Hewson, 1976). Higher transactions costs between ultimate borrowers and ultimate lenders than through financial intermediaries provide a *raison d'être* for the latter as we saw in section 7.2 when discussing domestic intermediation. Banks located in different countries may have a surplus or deficit in different currencies due to the international trade and capital flows decisions of residents and non-residents. However, if the transactions costs of a direct transfer of funds between two peripheral banks are higher than in the Euromarket, then the peripheral banks will use the Eurobanks as intermediaries. It is the low transactions costs of the EBs that enable funds to be channelled from ultimate lender in country A to the peripheral bank in country A, who then on-lends the funds to the EB. The EB rechannels the funds to peripheral bank B who lends to an ultimate borrower in country B (or indeed, in country A). A currency swap may take place within the Euromarket before the funds are on-lent to peripheral bank B. For the Euromarket to be used at all, it may be shown that it is the *sum* of transactions costs of the ultimate borrowers, lenders and the intermediary that must be lower for transactions via the Euromarket, than via the bank located in the domestic market (Johnston, 1983a).

There are of course non-market reasons why the EB have flourished. Interest rate ceilings placed on domestic deposits in domestic banks, but not on deposits in offshore markets, leads to a switch of funds to EB. 'Regulation Q' in the US encouraged the growth in the Eurodollar market. High required reserve ratios on domestic banks impose a tax on these banks and reduce the after-tax profit margin on lending funds. EB usually do not have such reserve ratios imposed upon them are able to offer finer margins between borrowing and lending and therefore expand their balance sheets at the expense of domestic banks. We discuss this further in the next section on disintermediation. The risk of imposition of controls on international capital flows may also account for some of the growth in the EB. A UK investor for example, may prefer to hold French francs in an EB in London rather than in a bank located in France because of the risk of the imposition of exchange controls on the latter.

8.7.2   *Credit, liquidity and disintermediation*

There is a continuing debate concerning the ability of Eurobanks to expand their deposits and loans and therefore undermine domestic monetary policy. Another related issue is the ability of the Euromarkets to expand liquidity. The latter refers to the 'moneyness' of assets (and liabilities) and is thought to influence spending. The Euromarkets may also expand the total quantity of 'money' in the world economy and hence influence world output and prices.

As with the analysis of the purely domestic monetary system the issue of credit (or money) creation has been investigated using the credit multiplier approach and the portfolio (or 'new view') model. In general, empirical estimates of these models indicate that the Eurodollar multiplier is relatively low, perhaps just over unity and much smaller than that for domestic retail banks. Hence the ability of the Eurobanks to substantially expand the world money supply or thwart domestic monetary policy appears limited. Nevertheless the increasing use of the Eurodollar market as exchange controls are relaxed could alter the above conclusion.

Estimates of the liquidity creating potential of the Euromarket vary widely and one can merely make the general observation that the Eurobanks do undertake positive maturity transformation although not as much as domestic banks. But one view that does emerge is that the role of the Eurobanks may be to provide an efficient method of credit distribution rather than credit creation. On this view the Eurobanks pose much less of a problem for monetary control at the national or the global level.

The final area of concern for domestic monetary policy is the impact of legal reserve requirements on the ability of domestic banks to compete with the 'offshore' Eurobanks. There are two aspects to this question; equity or fairness and disintermediation. We shall ignore the former but we do analyse the ability of the offshore banks to expand at the expense of domestic banks and thus distort the domestic monetary aggregates.

Credit multiplier approach. The simple bank multiplier model of section 7.3.1 can be applied to Eurodollar deposit creation. A switch of funds from a UK bank to a Eurobank increases Eurodeposits. Assume the Eurobank holds its reserves as deposits at a US bank and on-lends the remainder of the funds to the non-bank sector. The ability of the Eurobank to undertake a multiple expansion of deposits then depends on the proportion of funds on-lent being redeposited. (The analogous concept in the domestic case is the size of the cash to deposit ratio.) The smaller the reserve ratio of the Eurobanks q and the larger the redeposit ratio b of the non-bank sector, the larger is the deposit multiplier. For an exogenous inflow into the eurobanks of ΔX the increase in Eurodeposits Δe is

$$\Delta e = \Delta X (1 + b(1 - q) + (b(1 - q))^2 + \ldots$$
$$= [1 - b(1 - q)]^{-1} \Delta X \qquad (8.12)$$

The model can be extended to the case where the expansion of Eurodollars has an impact on the US money supply. Unlike a switch of funds from a US bank to a Eurobank, a multiple expansion in Eurodollar deposits leads to an increase in the deposits of US banks, as the Eurobanks satisfy their increased demand for reserve assets held in US banks. US banks then have to hold additional required reserves with the Fed which reduces deposits in the US and hence the total size of the assets available to the Eurodollar market. In this 'three stage banking model' (Niehans and Hewson, 1976) the Eurodollar multiplier is reduced as compared with (8.12) above.

The role of central banks influences the size of the Eurodollar multiplier by affecting the redeposit ratio b. If central banks (other than the US central bank) are operating a fixed exchange rate policy then the Eurodollar deposits may end up as international reserves, as 'domestic recipients' of the Euro-deposits sell them to their central bank. The redeposit ratio of the central banks may be larger than that of the non-bank sector, if the central bank holds a substantial proportion of its foreign exchange reserves in the Euromarket.

Empirical estimates. Johnston (1983a) provides a survey of estimates of the Eurocurrency deposit multiplier. The desired reserve ratio q of the Eurobanks is thought to be rather small say of the order of one-thirtieth with the redeposit ratio b of the private sector of the order of one-eighth. Substituted in equation (8.12) above this gives a multiplier of about 1.1. With such a low value for q the size of the multiplier is dominated by the re-deposit ratio b. It is only when one assumes that central banks ultimately obtain the Eurodeposits and have a high propensity to redeposit funds that the multiplier reaches a maximum value of around 4. However, under floating exchange rates the accumulation of large foreign exchange reserves by central banks is severely curtailed and this probably means that the size of the Eurodollar multiplier is closer to the lower estimate given above.

Portfolio approach. The portfolio approach recognizes that the asset ratios will not be constant but will vary with interest rates. In principle, portfolio models can be very complex involving the supply and demand for a wide range of assets and liabilities. However, the essence of the model as applied to the Euromarket may be analysed by positing demand functions for domestic and Euro-loans and domestic and Euro-deposits (Niehans and Hewson, 1976). The private sector is assumed to switch deposits and loans between the two sectors based on relative interest rates and the distribution between the domestic and Eurobanks is determined by the solution of this simultaneous system. For example the 'domestic bank' may be a New York NY bank, the Eurobank may be situated in London and the currency involved, the dollar.

The supply of deposits by the private sector to the domestic market D and the Euromarket e depends on the domestic interest rate paid on deposits i and the rate on Eurodollar deposits r. Deposits in Euro-banks and domestic banks are assumed to be gross substitutes

$$D = D(i, r, W) \quad D_i, D_w > 0, D_r < 0$$

$$e = e(i, r, W) \quad e_r, e_w > 0, e_i < 0$$

where wealth W is defined as

$$W = D + e$$

The demand for loans in the domestic and Euromarket L and l respectively are also gross substitutes

$$L = L(i, r, W) \quad L_r, L_w > 0, L_i < 0$$

$$l = l(i, r, W) \quad l_r < 0, l_i, l_w > 0$$

The Eurobank holds its reserves r' at the domestic (NY) bank. If the reserve ratio of the Eurobank is q, then $r' = qe$. The reserves r' of the Eurobank are deposit liabilities of the domestic (NY) bank. Domestic banks hold reserves R (at the Fed) against domestic (dollar) deposits D and Eurodollar deposits of the Eurobank. If the domestic bank has a reserve ratio β then reserves held at the domestic central bank are

$$R = \beta(D + r')$$

From the deposit demand equations one can see that the division of a given stock of wealth between domestic deposits and Eurodeposits depends on their respective interest rates; hence so do the deposit multipliers. Deposits and loans are connected through the banks' budget constraint; reserves plus loans must equal deposits if the banks are to be in equilibrium. We therefore have two interdependent markets and we can solve for the equilibrium level of i and r in terms of the exogenous variables, namely the exogenous level of reserve assets of the domestic banks R (assumed to be controlled by the Fed) and the parameters of the supply and demand curves.

We can sketch the process that ensues when there is a switch of deposits from the domestic (US) economy to the Euromarket. The increase in the supply of Eurodeposits lowers the Eurodollar deposit and loan rates. The initial inflow of Eurodollars is therefore partly curtailed as the private sector then switches some funds back to the US where interest rates are for the moment unchanged. The Eurodollar multiplier is therefore initially less than one. However, the second round effects involve a fall in US deposit rates which in turn tends to induce a flow back into Eurodeposits. As always in these simultaneous equations models, the final configuration of equilibrium interest rates and level of deposit and loans depends on the coefficients of the model. Assuming gross substitutes, Niehans and Hewson find that the Eurodeposit multiplier is positive and is larger the higher the propensity to hold (redeposit) funds in the Euromarkets. However, it seems likely, in this model at least, that the Eurodeposit multiplier is less than unity. Of course if one introduces a wider range of asset choices including for example domestic bonds and Eurobonds the multiplier would take on a different value. However, even here it appears as if the Eurodollar multiplier is still likely to be small (Hewson and Sakakibara, 1976).

8.7.3   *Liquidity creation*

It appears from the above discussion that the Eurobanks do not, at present at least, have the capacity for a multiple expansion of deposits. Bank deposits may be considered as part of gross financial wealth. Expenditure decisions, for example consumption decisions in the life cycle hypothesis, are thought to depend on net wealth, that is assets less outstanding liabilities. Neglecting equity capital, banks do not create net wealth; the deposits of one member of the private sector are matched by liabilities in the form of loans. However, it is sometimes asserted that expenditure depends on net *liquid* assets, particularly when capital markets are imperfect (Flemming, 1973; Pissarides, 1978). If the Eurobanks engage in positive maturity transformation, the assets of the private sector will be of shorter maturity than their liabilities and hence they may create net liquidity.

Niehans and Hewson (1976) suggest a measure of net liquidity NL defined as

$$NL = \Sigma a_i(D_i - L_i)$$

where D_i and L_i are Eurodollar deposits and loans of maturity i respectively and a_i are weights. If assets and liabilities of the banks are matched for all maturity bands then NL would equal zero. They suggest that the weights should decline as their maturity dates increase (table 8.4). For UK based Eurobanks, assets and liabilities held in the interbank market are very nearly perfectly matched but loans to the NBPS tend to have a longer maturity date than deposits

TABLE   8.4   Weighting scheme for Euro assets and liabilities

Maturity Class	a_i
1. less than 8 days	0.9
2. 8 days–<1 month	0.8
3. 1 month–<3 months	0.7
4. 3 months–<6 months	0.6
5. 6 months–<1 year	0.4
6. 1 year–<3 years	0.2
7. 3 years and over	0.1

Source: Niehans and Hewson (1976).

(table 8.3) and applying the above formula one finds that the London based Eurobanks create about 25 cents of liquidity for every dollar deposited. This figure is much smaller than that obtained if the above formula were applied to domestic retail banks who undertake substantial maturity transformation. Hence taken at face value the Eurodollar market does not appear to create 'excessive liquidity' by comparison with domestic banks. However Johnston (1983a) argues that Niehans and Hewson's weights are inappropriate and suggests that from the NBPS point of view loans that have a long period to maturity ought to be given a high 'liquidity weighting' since these do not have to be repaid for some considerable time. Johnston's weighting scheme is shown in table 8.5 and when applied to the London Eurobanks (in 1979) indicates that they are creating about 50 cents per dollar of liquidity. Although high, this figure is still less than that for US banks operating in the US domestic market who undertake maturity transformation of around 80 cents per dollar. The degree of maturity transformation of London based Eurobanks is of the same order of magnitude as UK domestic non-clearing banks who engage in the wholesale deposit market in the domestic currency (sterling). (Thus Artis and Lewis (1981) conjecture that domestic wholesale banks operate in a similar way to Eurobanks.)

Callier (1983) argues that 'transcurrency intermediation' by Eurobanks implies that one cannot measure the degree of liquidity transformation merely by comparing the term to maturity (however weighted) of their assets and liabilities dominated in the Eurocurrency. For example, a US Eurobank may acquire a *one* month Eurodollar deposit and on-lend it as a *three* month sterling loan; clearly a case of maturity transformation. If the US Eurobank hedges to remove exchange risk it will purchase dollars in the three-month forward market. Its liabilities in dollars (the deposit) and its assets in dollars (the receipt of dollars in three months time) are of equal maturity. The maturity transformation has been a 'transcurrency' one.

Although the issues surrounding the quantitative measures of the degree of maturity transformation are ambiguous we can end by discussing the general principles of 'risk and return' that determine the degree to which the Eurobanks engage in maturity transformation. If the return to be obtained from two

TABLE 8.5 Alternative weighting structure for Euroassets and liabilities

Maturity class	Liabilities	Claims
Less than 8 days	1.0	−1.0
8 days–<1 month	0.5	−0.5
1 month–<3 months	0.2	−0.2
3 months–<6 months	0.1	−0.1
6 months–<1 year	−	−
1 year–<3 years	−0.2	0.2
3 years and over	−0.6	0.6

Source: Johnston (1983a).

three-month ('roll-over') loans is expected to be the same as that from a six-month loan, the bank would be indifferent and given a three-month deposit would lend short and undertake perfect matching. On the other hand if long-term rates are above short-term rates, positive maturity transformation becomes potentially profitable. However, if short-term deposit rates are higher than expected at the end of the three months, the bank could incur a loss as the marginal cost of funds exceeds the fixed six-month loan rate. Hence the volatility (variance) in interest rates will increase risk and limit the degree of maturity transformation. Competitive forces in the market will reduce the margin between lending and borrowing rates and such fine margins tend to reduce the degree of maturity transformation. (These observations are consistent with the predictions of the risk-aversion or mean-variance model of asset-liability choice which we elaborate in section 9.4 on the term structure of interest rates.)

8.7.4   *Euro-disintermediation*

The final area of Euromarket activity we wish to look at concerns the scope for disintermediation of funds from the domestic banking system to offshore banks. If the domestic currency and deposits at EBs are close substitutes from the point of view of the NBPS then disintermediation will distort the information content of domestic monetary aggregates. The analysis we shall apply is the same as that used to discuss the operation of the 'corset' in the UK (section 8.2) where required reserves ratios are viewed as a tax on the domestic banking system. After the abolition of exchange controls in the UK in 1979, UK residents could hold sterling in domestic banks or in the Eurosterling market. The former are within the definition of the targeted monetary aggregate but the latter are not.

If the required reserve ratio on domestic banks is q and the interest rate on domestic wholesale deposits is i then the marginal cost of one pounds worth of deposit funds to domestic banks is $(1 + q)i$. Without loss of generality we take the reserve ratio of Eurobanks to be zero and their marginal cost of funds is the interest rate on their deposits r. If domestic sterling deposits and Eurosterling deposits are *imperfect* substitutes then portfolio equilibrium will ensue at some interest differential $i - r$ (assuming no financial innovation that would alter the relative attractiveness of the two types of deposit). However, if the domestic central bank raises interest rates by undertaking open market operations, the marginal tax rate on domestic banks will increase (equation (8.3)); similarly, changes in the required reserve ratio affect the tax rate (for example the 'corset' may be considered as an example of a change in the required reserve ratio on marginal deposits). Under such circumstances the Eurosterling banks can increase their balance sheets by offering a finer margin between their lending and borrowing rates. UK firms then shift their sterling deposits to the Euro-market, reducing the UK money supply but holding an asset that may be a close substitute. The domestic money supply may therefore be a misleading indicator of the monetary stance. The latter problem may be more acute when the Euromarkets are undertaking substantial innovation in the provision of financial services, for example in attempting to attract smaller deposits into the Euro-market and diversifying their loan portfolios.

For the UK it is difficult to disentangle the separate effects of the corset and the abolition of exchange controls on the flow into Eurosterling and other Eurodeposits after 1979. In the US there was also a substantial shift into the Eurodollar market after the Fed introduced non-interest bearing required reserves as part of the move to money base control. However, at present with Eurodeposits amounting to about 4 per cent of national money stocks (Johnston, 1983a) the amount of disintermediation is relatively small and is certainly within most authorities' error margins for control of their domestic monetary aggregates. For small open economies like the UK that have recently relinquished exchange controls, the scope for influencing the domestic money supply without distortions requires the use of market measures and a competitive domestic banking system, with a low mandatory reserve requirement. The August 1981 'new measures' introduced by the Bank of England are consistent with this approach. However, as noted in section 7.5, Miller (1981) suggests that low mandatory reserve requirements on domestic banks implies that the absolute level of interest rates may have to rise substantially in order to curb excessive monetary growth, thus causing a fall in real output via exchange rate changes (Dornbusch overshooting) and the trade sector. Relaxation of monetary targets and the introduction of an exchange rate target may be useful in such circumstances.

8.8   SUMMARY: CREDIT AND MONETARY AGGREGATES

The pace of structural change in financial markets is now quite rapid. Broadly speaking the choice of a particular monetary aggregate as an intermediate target depends on the authorities' ability to control it and the existence of a predictable relationship between 'money' and the final objectives of economic policy, notably inflation. With innovation in financial markets, exactly what constitutes 'money' becomes problematic.

If the authorities' target narrow money (for example Switzerland and Canada) then large variations in bank lending and total deposits may ensue without violating the targeted aggregate. If a target for narrow money had been in force in the UK in 1980-1 the entry of the banks into the home loan market, which probably boosted the broad monetary aggregate, may not have been such a cause for concern. In Holland, Germany and France 'deposits' for long maturity periods are deemed 'non-monetary liabilities' and are not targeted. An increased demand for bank credit can be financed by bidding for such non-monetary liabilities. The supply of funds to industry via the banking system is not inhibited by monetary targets. With a broad monetary target, an increased demand for bank advances can only be met by the banks reducing their 'other' non-reserve assets and the scope for this is limited.

A switch of funds from the banks to the building societies (in the UK) would lead to government action if a monetary target were in force but not if a broad liquidity aggregate (such as PSL2 in the UK) is targeted. This definitional problem is likely to become more severe in the UK as building societies issue retail deposits (that a checking system) in competition with the banks and also bid for funds in the wholesale money markets.

The probable increased use of the Euromarkets also poses problems for the appropriate definition of 'money'. For example Eurosterling deposits held by UK residents and non-residents can be used to finance expenditures in the UK. Similarly Eurodollar deposits held by UK firms might facilitate increased spending in the UK. A multinational firm based in the UK might use a Eurodollar deposit to purchase primary imports and recoup the dollars when the final product is exported from the UK, thus averting any exchange risk.

Callier (1983) notes that by using Euromarkets and the forward market, domestic banks may expand credit in domestic currency without requiring additional reserves assets; thus possibly circumventing monetary control. Domestic banks are usually required to keep reserves with the central bank as a proportion of deposits in domestic currency but they are not allowed to keep net positions in foreign currency. However, domestic banks can raise foreign currency deposits through the Euromarkets and on-lend in domestic currency, avoiding exchange risk by a 'swap transaction'. A 'swap' is a simultaneous purchase (sale) of a currency and its sale (purchase) in the forward market. Thus a domestic bank may sell Eurocurrency spot, on-lend in domestic currency and simultaneously purchase foreign currency in the forward market (to repay the initial foreign currency Eurodeposit). The domestic bank does not hold a net position in foreign currency and also avoids holding low yield domestic reserve assets (since the initial deposit is in foreign currency).

To the extent that existing demand for money functions continue to forecast well it can be argued that the pace of structural change is not strong enough to warrant a change in the definition of 'money'. Considering the recent behaviour of demand for money functions for OECD countries (Boughton, 1979) this would appear to be a rather pious hope. Although the demand for narrow money appears to be reasonably stable (except in the US, recently), the demand for broad money is somewhat unstable. In part the above structural changes have led some monetary authorities to consider a wide range of monetary indicators rather than any single aggregate when deciding on policy action. For example in the UK the authorities have instituted target bands for narrow money (M1), broad money (£M3) and a liquidity aggregate (PSL2). Because of 'financial innovation' in the provision of interest bearing sight deposits, the narrow aggregate has recently (March 1984) been switched to the monetary base M0 (that is cash held by NBPS plus 'cash' reserves of banks) whilst £M3 remains as the broad targeted aggregate. The US has recently included Eurodollars held in the Carribean offshore market in its definition of transactions balances (M2). Some economic studies have indicated that a (complex) weighted average of various monetary aggregates may provide a more useful indicator of subsequent changes in money income and prices (Mills, 1983). The increased substitutability between money, near money, credit and offshore holdings of domestic and foreign currencies clearly creates problems in deciding on the appropriate monetary aggregates to target and suggests that a liquidity aggregate or a weighted average of a group of aggregates (for example Divisia aggregates) may be a more useful indicator of future changes in money income. However, the difficulty in controlling such a composite indicator may be more acute than controlling any single aggregate.

APPENDIX 8A   APPROPRIATE OPERATING TARGETS

The demand and supply functions are

$$M^s = mr + b \, \text{NBR} + u \qquad (8A.1)$$

$$M^d = a_0 - ar + v \qquad (8A.2)$$

$$M^d = M^s = M \qquad (8A.3)$$

Following Poole (1970) and Bryant (1983) the operational target for the interest rate r^* given the monetary target M^* is obtained by inverting the demand for money function

$$r^* = \frac{1}{a}(a_0 - M^*) \qquad (8A.4)$$

Substituting this back in the demand for money function and assuming equilibrium $M = M^d$ we have

$$M = M^* + v \qquad (8A.5)$$

$$V_r = \text{var}(M) = E(M - M^*)^2 = \sigma_v^2 \qquad (8A.6)$$

Hence the variance around the monetary target in the interest rate regime depends only on σ_v^2. The equilibrium interest rate and money stock using (8A.1)–(8A.3) are

$$r = (m + a)^{-1}(a_0 - b \, \text{NBR} + v - u) \qquad (8A.7)$$

$$M = \frac{ab}{m + a} \, \text{NBR} + \frac{ma_0}{m + a} + \frac{m}{m + a} v + \frac{a}{m + a} u \qquad (8A.8)$$

We choose the level of NBR so that for $v = u = 0$, $M = M^*$ hence under an NBR operating target

$$M = M^* + \frac{m}{m + a} v + \frac{a}{m + a} u \qquad (8A.9)$$

$$V_{\text{NBR}} = \text{var } M = \frac{m^2}{(m + a)^2} \sigma_v^2 + \frac{a^2}{(m + a)^2} \sigma_u^2 + \frac{2ma}{(m + a)^2} \sigma_{uv} \qquad (8A.10)$$

Thus the variance of M around the monetary target M^* in the NBR reserves regime V_{NBR} depends on the variances and covariances and the slopes of the supply and demand for money functions

$$\frac{V_{\text{NBR}}}{V_r} = (m + a)^{-2}\left(m^2 + a^2 \frac{\sigma_u^2}{\sigma_v^2} + 2ma \frac{\sigma_{uv}}{\sigma_v^2}\right) \qquad (8A.11)$$

It is obvious from the above expression that the variance under the NBR regime tends to be smaller than under the interest rate regime the smaller is (σ_u/σ_v) and if σ_{uv} is negative (that is the demand and supply shocks tend to shift the curves in opposite directions). Also $\sigma_u^2 < \sigma_v^2$, that is disturbances in the supply function are smaller than those in the demand function, does not guarantee the superiority of the NBR regime. To calculate conditions under which the latter holds (that is $V_{NBR}/V_r < 1$) we require information on σ_u^2, σ_v^2, σ_{uv} and the slope parameters a and m.

NOTES

1 The operations of the discount houses did cause some additional problems in controlling the money supply during the 1971–81 period but we ignore these (Zawadski, 1981).

2 See Artis (1978) and Tew (1978) for a useful analysis of this period.

3 Special deposits earned interest at rates close to those on reserve assets and hence the additional tax may not have been great. As they were not counted as part of liquid assets they were mainly used to mop up any excess bankers balances in the system arising from the PSBR and other factors. They can therefore be viewed as a substitute for open market sales of short assets to the NBPS.

4 Commercial bills eligible for discount at the Bank of England could be counted as reserve assets up to a maximum of 2 per cent of eligible liabilities (deposits).

5 There were three penalty zones. The proportion to be placed in special deposits increased from 5 per cent of interest bearing eligible liabilities (IBELS) for an overshoot up to 3 per cent of the ceiling to 50 per cent for an excess level of IBELS of over 5 per cent.

6 We can obtain an equivalent result by considering the marginal revenue of banks. Before the introduction of the SSD scheme one pounds worth of deposits earned $\beta r_R + (1 - \beta)r_A'$. Equating the latter with the marginal cost of one pounds worth of deposits r_m' and rearranging we have

$$r_A' = \frac{r_m'}{1 - \beta} - \frac{\beta}{1 - \beta} r_R = (1 + \beta)r_m' - \beta(1 + \beta)r_R$$

where we have used $1/(1 - \beta) \approx (1 + \beta)$. The above expression is equation (8.2) in the text. With the SSD scheme the marginal revenue earned is $\beta r_R + (1 - \beta - x)r_A'$ which when equated to marginal cost r_m' yields

$$\text{MR} = r_A' = (1 + \beta + x)r_m - \beta r_R(1 + \beta + x) = \text{MC}$$

which is equation (8.4) in the text. See Fama (1985) for a lucid account of the relationship between the rate on advances and CDs when 'information' is costly.

7 Consultations with each institution are to take place to establish adequate holdings of liquid assets for prudential reasons.

8 'Operational deposits' consist of till money and bankers balances at the Bank, excluding the $\frac{1}{2}$ per cent mandatory 'cash ratio deposits'; in short, 'free reserves'. Broadly speaking, M2 consists of the NBPS holdings of cash plus retail deposits held in banks and building societies.

9 Operations in the interbank market to alter 'cash' in the system are technically possible but would involve a diminished role for the discount houses and this the Bank does not appear to favour. Commercial bills rather than Treasury bills are now the main 'intervention assets'.

10 This view has to be modified to the extent of the undisclosed prudential requirements negotiated by the banks with the Bank of England and by their requirement to invest a minimum proportion of their assets in money market loans to the discount houses ('club money') (Bank of England, 1981b).

11 It is not obvious a priori that a wider aggregate is less stable than a narrow one and the empirical evidence on the banks' demand for various types of liquid asset does not unequivocally support a narrow aggregate (White, 1975; Parkin, 1970; Duck and Sheppard, 1978). The latter applies *a fortiori* when applied to a new system where 'cash' to the banks would be controlled for the first time in recent UK monetary history.

12 The maturity bands for bills are: band 1 = 1–14 days, band 2 = 15–33 days, band 3 = 34–63 days and band 4 = 64–91 days.

13 On 2 February 1984 the Fed moved to a *current* rather than a lagged NBR target. See Thornton (1982) for a formal analysis of the two approaches, while Meyer (1983) and the Federal Reserve Bank of St Louis (1984) provide a useful compendium on these issues.

14 For direct comparison with the US system post-1979 we use NBR as our quantitative target rather than the monetary base.

15 We are dealing with a comparative static system so that money balances cannot be obtained from new savings flows.

16 UK banks have also provided 'term-loans' of average maturity greater than seven years (Midland Bank, 1981) to industrial and commercial companies. This has, in part at least, filled the gap left after the fall in the market for fixed interest debt.

9

The Term Structure of Interest Rates

9.1 INTRODUCTION

In financial markets there exist a wide range of assets that an individual investor may hold. The term to maturity for the assets may vary from one day to infinity. Newly issued Treasury or commercial bills mature in 91 days, consols or perpetuities are never redeemed but pay a 'coupon' forever. Monetary policy often tends to impinge upon short rates in the first instance but investment, stockbuilding and consumption may depend upon long-term interest rates (for example on corporate bonds) as well as short rates. The interest rate transmission mechanism of monetary policy therefore depends crucially on the relationship between short and long rates of interest. Theories of the term structure attempt to model this relationship.

There are two broad approaches to modelling the term structure which we label the reduced form and structural approaches.[1] In the latter, explicit demand and supply functions are estimated and then solved for the equilibrium level of interest rates that clear the market; the relationship between long and short rates of interest then depends on the parameters and exogenous variables of these functions. In the reduced form approach the long rate is regressed directly on short rates (and other relevant 'exogenous' variables), and usually embodies a market clearing assumption. The two approaches are related and in some cases the reduced form equation used can be shown to be a special case of a particular structural model.

In section 9.2 we begin with an account of the various 'structural' models of the term structure relationship relating them to the asset demand functions discussed in previous chapters. Under certain restrictive assumptions we can show how reduced form models such as the expectations and liquidity preference hypotheses, discussed in section 9.3, may be derived from these structural models; this we do in section 9.4. We discuss reduced form models in the light of the efficient markets hypothesis (EMH) and rational expectations in section 9.5. Finally, we present a critique of the reduced form approach and a brief summary. Our analysis of models of the term structure provides an introduction to ways of building a more complete model of the financial sector, an issue we take up in the final chapter.

9.2 STRUCTURAL APPROACH

The structural approach may be applied using only the supply and demand curves for a single asset or by utilizing a (complete) set of asset demand and supply functions. We begin with the former.

In an unregulated market, the yield on a particular asset is determined by the intersection of the supply and demand curves for that asset and hence on the exogenous variables that impinge on supply and demand. Assume, for convenience, that the demand for a *long-term* asset depends upon the long rate R_L relative to current and expected short rates r^e and a set of exogenous variables X (for example wealth, transactions, lagged variables, etc.). If supply is exogenous, market clearing gives

$$\bar{S}_L = D_L = a_0 + a_1(R_L - r^e) + a_3 X \tag{9.1}$$

and the 'term structure' is given by the reduced form for R_L

$$R_L = \frac{1}{a_1}(\bar{S}_L - a_0 - a_3 X) + r^e \tag{9.2}$$

The relationship between the long rate and the current short rate (the 'term structure') is influenced by the exogenous supply of long term debt, the exogenous determinants of demand X and the determinants of the *expected* level of short rates. The coefficients a_i in the term structure equation (9.2) are determined by the theoretical model used to derive the asset demand functions. For example if the mean-variance model is used, the a_i depend on the variances and covariances of asset returns, and below we discuss this aspect further. We can extend this 'single market' model of the term structure by positing a supply function for the long-term asset that depends negatively on the long-term interest rate R_L and positively on current and expected short rates and on a set of exogenous supply variables. (Friedman (1979) estimates such a supply function for issues of long-term corporate bonds in the US and Holly (1980) provides a similar approach for the supply of UK local authority debt.) In this case equating supply and demand yields an equation of the form (9.2) but with S_L now representing the exogenous supply factors. (The coefficients on the RHS variables will of course, be composite demand *and* supply coefficients.)

There are problems in 'inverting' equations estimated under the assumption of endogenous supply and then calculating the interest rate consequences of an exogenous change in supply (see section 6.4 on buffer-stock monetarism) but we ignore them here.

We can extend the above approach to cover a wide range of assets and solve the whole system of equations for *all* the endogenous interest rates. The interdependent asset adjustment model of Christofides (1980) discussed in section 5.5 provides a simple model that embodies the main features of this approach. To take the simplest case, consider asset supplies to be exogenous. The long-run demand functions for 'shorts' S and 'longs' B are of the form[2]

$$S = S(R_L, R_S, Y, W) \tag{9.3}$$

TABLE 9.1   Long run solutions for interest rates

	Y	M	S	B
R_S	0.093	−0.118	0.090	0.042
R_L	0.090	−0.112	0.028	0.047

Source: Christofides (1980, p. 121).

$$B = B(R_L, R_S, Y, W) \tag{9.4}$$

where Y is income, wealth $W = S + M + B$ and M is money balances. These two equations may be solved for R_L and R_S as functions of income and the exogenous asset stocks. The resulting coefficients, given the estimated parameters of the demand functions from table 5.1, are given in table 9.1.

It can be seen that an increase in M has a more powerful effect on the short rate than the long rate and hence it can be used to 'twist' or shift the 'yield gap' $R_L - R_S$.

A test of the structural approach therefore requires estimation of 'sensible' asset demand and supply functions which are then solved for equilibrium interest rates. If this approach 'explains' movements in actual interest rates, the model is deemed a success.

In the structural approach the behaviour of long and short rates is determined by the coefficients and variables of the *estimated* asset demand and supply functions. Although there is no reason in principle why reduced form interest rate equations, consistent with the underlying demand and supply functions, could not be *directly* estimated; we would in general have less prior information (for example plausible demand elasticities) readily available with which to judge the results. (If *all* of the supply and demand equations are identified then this ceases to be a problem, the elasticities can be retrieved ('identified') in the reduced form.)

9.3   REDUCED FORM APPROACH

In the 'reduced form approach' we directly estimate the relationship between long and short rates. As we shall see this is equivalent to imposing *implicit* theoretical restrictions on the asset demand and supply functions. In a sense the reduced form approach involves equations that are special cases of those used in the structural approach. The models we consider under this heading include the expectations hypothesis, the liquidity preference hypothesis, the hedging and preferred habitat theories of the term structure.

9.3.1   *Expectations hypothesis*

The redemption yield R^N on a bond with N periods to maturity, paying a fixed coupon c per period (year), having a current market price p and a guaranteed redemption price of unity is defined as the solution of

$$p = \sum_{i=1}^{N} c(1 + R^N)^{-i} + (1 + R^N)^{-N} \tag{9.5}$$

R^N is therefore the constant average (annual) rate of return that equates the discounted stream of (coupon) 'receipts' with the current market price. With zero default risk, all bonds of maturity N should yield the same return, regardless of their issue date or coupon. Low coupon bonds must have low prices so that a capital gain accrues over the period to redemption; then the low coupon bond will yield a return R^N equal to that on a high coupon bond.

Meiselman (1962) proposed that risk aversion is not an important phenomenon and therefore long rates are determined solely by expected future short rates. £1 invested in a long-term bond with N periods (years) to maturity will yield a terminal wealth of $(1 + R^N)^N$ where R^N is the annual yield on the N period bond. An alternative choice for the investor is to purchase a 'one period bill' every year and reinvest the proceeds (including interest receipts). The current interest rate on the bill r_t is known with certainty at the time of purchase but the individual must form expectations using information available at time t, of future short-term rates ($E_t r_{t+j}$) in the subsequent $N-1$ periods. £1 invested in bills yields an expected terminal wealth of $(1 + r_t)(1 + E_t r_{t+1}) \ldots (1 + E_t r_{t+N-1})$. If agents quickly (and costlessly) switch between longs and shorts to elimintate profitable opportunities, and are only interested in expected returns (that is risk neutral) then the market will be in equilibrium when

$$(1 + R^N)^N = (1 + r_t)(1 + E_t r_{t+1}) \ldots (1 + E_t r_{t+N-1}) \tag{9.6}$$

Taking logs of both sides and noting that $\log((1 + x) \approx x, |x| < 1$, we obtain the 'fundamental equation' (Begg, 1984) of bond pricing

$$R^N = \frac{1}{N}(r_t + E_t r_{t+1} + E_t r_{t+N-1}) \tag{9.7}$$

The relationship between the yield on bonds of different maturities thus depends on expectations about future short-term rates. The yield curve shows the relationship between the (current) yields on bonds of different maturities (that is for different values of N). If $E_t r_{t+j} = r_t$ for all j, then the N period bond yield R^N will equal the current short rate. The yield curve is a horizontal line. If short-term rates are expected to increase, then 'longer bond rates' (that is N large) will be above the rates on shorter dated bonds, the yield curve will be upward sloping as in figure 9.1 (the converse applies here, of course).

The pure expectations hypothesis therefore assumes (a) agents are aware of profitable opportunities and are 'risk neutral', (b) they act quickly on this information to instantaneously equate expected holding period yields on assets of differing maturities. The agent maximizes expected return by immediately switching into that asset that yields the highest expected return given his (fixed) holding period: he is a 'plunger'. Equilibrium asset holdings are indeterminate; there is no well-defined demand function.

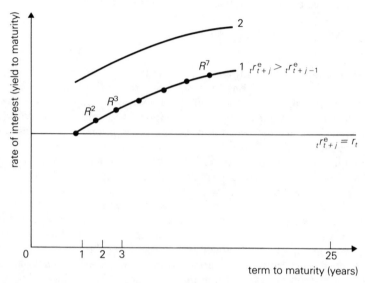

FIGURE 9.1   *Yield curves: For the yield curve marked 1 short rates are expected to be higher in the future. Yield curve 2 has a higher* absolute *level of* all *short rates (but future rates are expected to be higher than current rates as in curve 1).*

9.3.2   *Liquidity preference hypothesis*

Here, the agent is risk averse and the 'risk premium' is thought to increase as the term to maturity increases (Hicks, 1939). The latter will certainly be the case if investors are concerned with real returns and successive future short rates fully reflect actual future rates of inflation. Under these circumstances, choice of an N period long period long bond means that all deviations of *ex post* inflation in the future will result in changes in the *real* yield to be earned on the bond.

In equation (9.7), to each expected short rate one may add a positive risk premium, although in practice this is usually proxied by a *single* risk premium variable added to the equation. The liquidity preference theory gives no indication of what type of asset demand equations or degree of portfolio diversification is possible. For example, if the liquidity premium depends (monotonically) on the term to maturity, the individual will still switch from 'shorts' to 'longs' whenever the return on the latter (including the risk premium) exceeds the return on the former. The degree of diversification is indeterminate and each agent is a 'plunger' as in the expectations hypothesis. If the liquidity premium varies with the amount of the 'risky' asset held, then this merely complicates but does not enlighten us concerning the underlying asset demand and supply equations.

9.3.3 *Other theories*

The hedging theory of the term structure assumes infinite risk aversion in the sense that investors only buy bonds whose maturity matches their desired holding period; expectations are irrelevant and the shape of the yield curve is determined by the supply and demand at each maturity.

The preferred habitat theory of Modigliani and Sutch (1966, 1967) takes an agnostic view of the risk premium. Risk premiums may vary for a wide variety of reasons such as different holding periods, commitments, etc. The only restriction is that bonds which mature at dates close together should be reasonably close substitutes and have similar risk premiums. The question of the determinants of risk premiums is, therefore, side-stepped by comparing assets within the same 'habitat' (that is between N and $N + j$ years to maturity where j is small).

In the above theories, the determinants of the risk premiums are left rather vague, and precise testing of the theories therefore becomes difficult. Some researchers have assumed that the risk premium depends on the maturity composition of the debt. The latter variable (for example proportion of 'longs' in total assets) is usually added to the basic expectations equation (9.7) in an *ad hoc* manner, without recourse to the underlying demand and supply functions. Tests of the expectations hypothesis, using past rates of interest to proxy expected future rates in equation (9.7), usually give a reasonable fit since both series are highly trended (but the results may be prone to the spurious regression problem, appendix A). There have also been attempts to model the risk premium (for example by the variance of capital gains on risky assets (Rowan and O'Brian, 1970) but with rather limited success.

9.4 STRUCTURAL AND REDUCED FORM MODELS: A COMPARISON

We now return to a simple 'single market' structural model (Buse, 1975) to investigate in more detail the possible determinants of the *coefficients* in the term structure equations of the reduced form approach. Let us suppose that individual's determine their asset *shares* $\alpha_i = (A_i/W)$ (rather than the absolute amount of assets A_i) according to the mean-variance model. Using the notation of section 3.3.3 assume a one period horizon and that '2' is the safe asset; we have[3]

$$\Pi = \alpha_1 R_1 + \alpha_2 r_2 \tag{9.8}$$

$$\sigma_\pi^2 = \text{var}(\Pi) = (\alpha_1 \sigma_1)^2 \tag{9.9}$$

choosing α_1 and α_2 to maximize the Lagrangian L

$$L = \Pi^e - \frac{c}{2} \sigma_\pi^2 + \lambda(\alpha_1 + \alpha_2 - 1)$$

$$L = \alpha_1 R_1^e + \alpha_2 r_2 - \frac{c}{2} (\alpha_1 \sigma_1)^2 + \lambda(\alpha_1 + \alpha_2 - 1) \tag{9.10}$$

where c is the coefficient of absolute risk aversion, we obtain the asset demand function for the risky asset (share)

$$\alpha_1^d = \frac{(R_1^e - r_2)}{c\sigma_1^2} \tag{9.11}$$

Now assuming a regime where α_1 is exogenous, market clearing gives the term structure equation

$$r_1 - r_2 = -g_1^e + \alpha_1 c\sigma_1^2 \tag{9.12}$$

We have separated out R_1^e into the running yield r_1 and the expected capital gain g_1^e. The long–short interest rate differential $(r_1 - r_2)$ therefore depends on the uncertainty surrounding the variability in the price of the risky asset σ_1^2, the coefficient of absolute risk aversion c, the exogenous share of the long asset in the portfolio α_1 and the expected capital gain g_1^e. We can now draw some implications from this simple model and demonstrate the close association between the reduced form and structural approaches. First, if there is no risk aversion $(c = 0)$ the expected returns R_1^e and r_2 are equalized and the equation reduces to the pure expectations theory for a one period horizon. The latter also follows when investors hold 'Keynesian' point expectations with certainty $(\sigma_1^2 = 0)$. The liquidity preference theory suggests that long rates should lie above short rates and this is prediced by the above equation when c and σ_1^2 are greater than zero. The share of the long asset in the portfolio is often included when testing the preferred habitat theory, as a proxy for the risk premium on assets in different (but 'close') habitats.

It is perhaps worth noting that equation (9.12) has elements in common with equation (9.2) discussed earlier. In fact if we let $a_1 = 1/(c\sigma_1^2)$, $R_L = R_1 + g^e$ and $r^e = r_2$ and somewhat cavalierly $S_L = \alpha_1$, the two equations differ only by the term in exogenous variables $(1/a_1)(-a_0 - a_3 X)$. But if c or σ_1^2 approach zero then $a_1 \to \infty$ and from (9.2) we see that the long rate equals the (expected) short rate and the exogenous variables 'drop out' of the equation. The expectations hypothesis thus assumes 'longs' and 'shorts' are perfect substitutes, $a_1 = \infty$. The latter in the mean variance framework requires zero risk aversion $(c = 0)$ or zero perceived risk $(\sigma_1^2 = 0)$ and the assumption that the expected utility from terminal wealth is the only argument in the objective function.

We cannot push the simple model of equation (9.12) too far. It merely shows that if agents are risk neutral, or do not perceive risk, then expected returns on different assets over the (fixed) holding period will be equalized; the latter is the basis of the expectations hypothesis. Similarly, the risk premium may be related to the variances (and covariances) on asset returns and the degree of risk aversion. Since latter items may change over time and under different (monetary policy) regimes, we would not expect risk premiums to remain constant.

9.4.1   *Policy implications*

If the pure expectations theory is correct, then there is a clear link between the current short rate and the long rate. When expected short rates are determined entirely by past rates, then the government can use monetary policy to alter current short rates and use the term structure equation to predict the behaviour of long rates. If the risk premium is non-zero and depends upon variables within the authorities' control (for example the maturity structure of the debt), the authorities may be able to manipulate short rates while keeping long rates constant (that is 'bend' or 'twist' the yield curve). This may be useful, for example, if the authorities wish to use short rates to influence capital flows and long rates to stimulate investment. However, the application of the efficient markets hypothesis (and rational expectations) to these reduced form models of the term structure negates these policy conclusions and it is to this we now turn.

9.5   THE EFFICIENT MARKETS HYPOTHESIS

The efficient markets hypothesis (EMH) predates the rational expectations hypothesis (REH) but both are closely interrelated. We could discuss the application of the REH to the term structure of interest rates without invoking the EMH but as the latter is frequently referred to in the literature we briefly discuss it here. The EMH, when applied to the term structure, appears to show that the long rate of interest is influenced only by its previous value (and possibly a risk premium). However, Begg's (1984) critique suggests that the EMH implies that the change in the long rate depends on the longs–shorts differential.

The EMH assumes that asset markets are 'efficient', together with an assumption of how prices are determined in the market (for example instantaneous market clearing). The EMH is therefore a joint assumption about market behaviour and the formation of expectations. We need to define an 'efficient market'.

Formally a market is said to be 'efficient' when prices fully and instantaneously reflect all available relevant information so that opportunities for supernormal profits are continuously eliminated. If agents use all available information in an 'efficient market' they must form their expectations according to the REH. Otherwise supernormal profits could arise by exploiting systematic forecasting errors. An 'efficient market' has low transactions costs, low costs of collecting and processing information, perfectly flexible prices and no impediments to voluntary exchange. (At the risk of introducing too much terminology it is worth noting that an 'efficient market' requires fewer restrictive assumptions than is required for a 'perfect market'. The latter has to be 'efficient' but also requires agents to be price takers in perfect competition.)

One aspect of the EMH (embodying as it does the REH), which is particularly useful in empirical work, is that it provides a fairly simple method of proxying expectational variables by observables. However, because the EMH is a joint hypothesis, rejection of the hypothesis by the data does not indicate whether it is RE or our model of the behaviour of the market which is incorrect.

9.5.1   *EMH and the yield curve*

Modigliani and Shiller (1973) in an elegant article apply the EMH to the liquidity preference hypothesis. For expositional purposes we drastically simplify the model. Actual future short-term interest rates are assumed to be generated by an (autoregressive) chain rule of forecasting. Applying the REH, *expected* rates will be determined using the equation

$$r_{t+1} = a_1 r_t + a_2 r_{t-1} + u_{t+1} \tag{9.13}$$

Thus, for example, $E_t r_{t+2}$ is given by

$$E_t r_{t+2} = a_1 (E_t r_{t+1}) + a_2 E_t r_t + E_t u_{t+1} \tag{9.14}$$

$$= a_1 (a_1 r_t + a_2 r_{t-1}) + a_2 r_t = (a_1^2 + a_2) r_t + a_1 a_2 r_{t-1} \tag{9.15}$$

where we have used the fact that r_t and r_{t-1} are known at time t and therefore $E_t r_{t-j} = r_{t-j} (j \geqslant 0)$. RE forecast errors u_{t+1} are random, with mean zero (that is $E_t u_{t+j} = 0, j \geqslant 0$), constant variance and independent of any other available information at time t. Additional lags in (9.13) would give additional lags in r_t for the expectations terms $E_t r_{t+j}$, but otherwise the analysis follows our simplified model. For simplicity, assume a three period long bond, and an additive risk premium δ_t and assume the bond market is 'efficient'

$$R_t^3 = \tfrac{1}{3}(r_t + E_t r_{t+1} + E_t r_{t+2}) + \delta_t \tag{9.16}$$

Using the RE chain rule

$$R_t^3 = \tfrac{1}{3}[r_t + (a_1 r_t + a_2 r_{t-1}) + (a_1^2 + a_2) r_t + a_1 a_2 r_{t-1}] + \delta_t \tag{9.17}$$

$$R_t^3 = \tfrac{1}{3}[(1 + a_1 + a_1^2 + a_2) r_t + (a_2 + a_1 a_2) r_{t-1})] + \delta_t \tag{9.18}$$

$$R_t^3 = c_0 r_t + c_1 r_{t-1} + \delta_t \tag{9.19}$$

Thus the liquidity preference hypothesis plus the EMH indicates that long rates are a weighted average of past short rates with the weights reflecting the expectations generating coefficients a_j. δ_t is modelled by the recent volatility of short rates and a regression equation (9.19) yields estimates of c_0 and c_1. Modigliani and Shiller determine expected nominal rates ($E_t r_{t+j}$) by using separate autoregressive equations for the real rate and expected inflation and allow high order lags in the respective autoregressive forecasting equations. They used a data sample for the USA from 1955–71 on the grounds that after 1971 government policy changes would have altered the expectations generating equations (the Lucas critique).

Modigliani and Shiller find that the $\hat{c}_i$ are statistically significant along with the risk premium variable, and the equation fits the data well. They provide a consistency test of the RE hypothesis. The a_i in equation (9.13) may be estimated directly; these may then be used to calculate the c_i terms (for example $c_1 = \hat{a}_2(1 + \hat{a}_1)/3$) and may be checked against the freely estimated $\hat{c}_i$ terms in equation (9.19). The two estimates are very similar, thus lending support to the EMH for the bond market.

9.5.2 Random walk hypothesis

Under RE and clearing markets, the current period long-term bond rate R^N (for large N) may be shown to be a random walk, that is equal to its own lagged value (plus a random error term). Lagging equation (9.7) one period, and subtracting the resulting equation from equation (9.7), we obtain

$$R_t^N - R_{t-1}^N = \frac{1}{N}[(r_t - E_{t-1}r_t) + (E_t r_{t+1} - E_{t-1}r_{t+1}) + \ldots +]$$

$$+ \frac{1}{N}[(E_t r_{t+N-1} - r_{t-1})] + \delta_t^N - \delta_{t-1}^N \tag{9.20}$$

Providing r_t is forecast using RE, then the forecast error $(r_t - E_{t-1}r_t)$ and the revisions to expectations $(E_t r_{t+j} - E_{t-1}r_{t+j})$ are zero mean independent random variables. For large N (and finite value for $E_t r_{t+N-1}$) the term in the second bracket is negligible. Also, if the change in the risk premium is not systematic over time, then the right-hand side of (9.20) may be represented by a random error ϵ_t with $E_{t-1}\epsilon_t = 0$ (and ϵ_t independent of any information I_{t-1} available at time $t - 1$ or earlier, $E(\epsilon_t/I_{t-1}) = 0$. Hence

$$R_t^N = R_{t-1}^N + \epsilon_t \tag{9.21}$$

This result is not in conflict with Modigliani and Shiller, where R^N depends upon expected short rates. In the random walk model, R_{t-1}^N already contains all the information about such rates; if it did not, unexploited opportunities for profit would exist. The evidence in favour of the random walk hypothesis is mixed. Pesando (1978) and Sargent (1976, 1979a) find evidence in favour, Shiller (1979) finds the converse; however, econometric problems in small samples can be acute (Evans and Savin, 1981).

Shiller's counter-evidence for the UK and US consists of:

1　Equation (9.7) suggests that the long rate ought to move slowly since it is a weighted average of future short rates. Using *actual* future short rates as RE proxies for expected rates, Shiller generates an R_t^N series from (9.7) which does *not* track the actual movement in R_t^N at all closely.

2　$(R_t^N - R_{t-1}^N)$ is not independent (in a regression context) of past changes in $(R_{t-1}^N - r_{t-1})$ and also depends upon a constant term. (Begg (1982) interprets these effects as proxying a variable risk premium due to uncertainty about inflation, thus preserving the 'EMH plus variable risk premium' interpretation.)

There is independent evidence on the validity of the REH in the bond market using survey data on expectations. Friedman (1980a) uses survey data on professional forecasters *predictions* concerning future interest rates $E_{t-1}r_t$. A test of unbiasedness and 'full information' (orthogonality) aspects of REH may be obtained using a regression of the form

$$r_t = a + b(E_{t-1}r_t) + cI_{t-1} + u_t \tag{9.22}$$

where I_{t-1} are a set of variables known at time $t - 1$. Under the assumption of RE, we expect $\hat{a} = \hat{c} = 0$, $\hat{b} = 1$ (and u_t to be independent of all information dated at time $t - 1$ or earlier). Friedman's study rather decisively rejects these aspects of the RE hypothesis.

If the random walk hypothesis (with a zero risk premium) holds, the authorities can only influence the current long rate by instigating 'surprises' (which affect u_t), such as a sudden unexpected sale of long term debt; this clearly limits the authorities ability to influence long rates. Confirmation of the random walk hypothesis suggests that (a) agents use all available information to form expectation; (b) agents are risk neutral and act to eliminate profitable opportunities and quickly produce equilibrium in the market. In short, the efficient markets hypothesis holds.

9.6 CRITICISMS OF THE REDUCED FORM APPROACH

In a recent article Begg (1984) has provided a severe criticism of the 'fundamental' term structure equation (9.7) used in the various reduced form approaches to the term structure, including the random walk hypothesis. His argument is that the fundamental equation is incorrect except for the rather unrealistic cases where either coupon payments are zero (that is a pure discount bond) or when the short rate of interest is expected to remain constant over the maturity horizon of the bond. The equation is incorrect because it assumes that coupon payments can be instantaneously reinvested throughout the life of the bond at the rate R^N, and this is only true if the short rate is expected to remain constant.

A simple proof that the redemption yield formula of equation (9.5) (from which we obtain (9.6) and (9.7)) assumes that the coupon c is reinvested at a rate R^N may be obtained for the *two period* horizon. Assuming a zero redemption price and yield to maturity R

$$p = c(1 + R)^{-1} + c(1 + R)^{-2} \tag{9.23}$$

The terminal value T in two years time of p invested at a constant rate R is $p(1 + R)^2$. Multiplying the RHS of (9.23) by $(1 + R)^2$ we obtain an equivalent expression for the terminal value

$$T = c(1 + R) + c \tag{9.24}$$

from which it is clear that the formula for R in the 'fundamental equation' (9.7) assumes that the coupon c paid at the end of the first year is reinvested at a rate R.

Turning now to the fundamental bond pricing equation (9.6) (and without loss of generality assuming perfect foresight) we see that the RHS of this expression assumes that earnings are reinvested at the going (short-term) interest rate *at that date*. But we know that the LHS assumes coupon payments are reinvested at a rate R^N. Thus the fundamental equation can only be correct either when coupon payments are zero (and the issue of reinvestment does not arise) or when all short rates r_{t+i} are equal to the constant value R^N. The random walk hypothesis relies on the 'fundamental equation' and hence is, generally, an incorrect characterization of bond market equilibrium. Begg demonstrates this with a simple example using figure 9.2. Here short rates are perfectly foreseen and expected to remain constant after t^* and hence by the fundamental equation the redemption yield R at t^* on a perpetuity is also equal to r^*. In the random walk model there are no foreseen changes in redemption yields $R = R_{-1} + u$, and therefore the redemption yield at time t must also equal r^*. Thus the

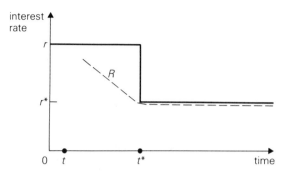

FIGURE 9.2   *Perfect foresight path for R.*

fundamental equation together with the random walk (RE) hypothesis predict that, on average, the perpetuity yields r^* between t and t^*. But under such circumstances it is inconceivable that investors would hold any perpetuities since they can obtain a higher return r on current short assets! The random walk hypothesis therefore does not characterize a situation of equilibrium.

Begg presents a solution to the above problem by suggesting that we formulate our equilibrium condition in terms of a single period return (as in the Buse model above) thus side-stepping the issue of reinvesting the coupon payments. For example, for a perpetuity, the single period return is the running yield (c/p) plus the (expected) capital gain dp/p and this is equated with the current short rate, r

$$\frac{dp}{p} + \frac{c}{p} = r \tag{9.25}$$

Substituting for p from the formula for the redemption yield on a perpetuity $p = c/R$, we have

$$\frac{dR}{R} = R - r \tag{9.26}$$

In the case of the simple perfectly foreseen path for r in figure 9.2 the equilibrium path for R given by the first-order difference equation (9.26), is indicated by the dotted line. Between t and t^*, using (9.26), we see that R_t is falling since R_t is less than r but reaches r^* at t^*. The running yield plus the capital gain equals r throughout the period t to t^*. Thus if it is anticipated that short rates will change in the future, bond yields and bond prices will not follow a random walk. Begg notes that the reason the random walk model for long-term bonds has reasonable empirical support is that short rates broadly follow a random walk and according to equation (9.26) long rates are related to short rates.

9.7 SUMMARY

We have identified two broad approaches to modelling the term structure of interest rates: the structural and the reduced form approach. In the structural approach the supply and demand curves for assets are estimated and solved for the equilibrium interest rates. The latter are determined by the exogenous variables in the system such as income and outstanding asset stocks. The relationship between long and short rates is then seen to be the outcome of the interaction of the forces of supply and demand in these interdependent markets. The various reduced form approaches look directly at the relationship between long and short rates and usually invoke the EMH. Expected holding period yields are equalized but with RE the coefficients linking the long rate with past short rates depends on the parameters that determine expectations about future short rates. This has a fairly strong policy implication. For example if the authorities change their monetary policy regime from one where interest rates are held constant to one where the monetary base is targeted, then the expectations coefficients will change. In this case expectations about future interest rates may not continue to be determined by past rates but by the degree of overshoot in the target for the base. The term structure equation may therefore appear unstable and hence the authorities cannot manipulate short rates and expect to obtain a predictable effect on long rates. This proposition manifests itself in the random walk model of the long rate where the authorities can only influence the latter by 'surprises' such as an unexpected sale or purchase of long-term debt. However, all may not be lost. For minor shifts in operating practice, the relationship may be stable; ultimately the importance of the Lucas critique is an empirical matter. Far more serious is Begg's critique of the whole reduced form approach which suggests that it may be more useful to model the term structure by the 'structural approach'.

By examining the theories of the term structure we have implicitly begun to outline a model of the financial sector. Market determined interest rates and associated equilibrium quantities may be determined by the 'intersection' of the appropriate supply and demand curves. These interest rates may then determine others that are fixed by institutions such as the bank lending rate, for example. We might use an unrestricted term structure equation to model the relationship between long rates and short rates although modelling the risk premium and allowing for regime changes could prove problematic. We discuss these issues further in the next chapter.

NOTES

1 Friedman (1977) labels these approaches 'unrestricted' (that is reduced form) and 'restricted' (that is structural).
2 The demand for money function is not independent of these two equations and may be calculated from the budget constraint $W = M + B + S$.

3 Buse (1975) presents a slightly more general model than this. The expected *real* return per £ invested is

$$\Pi^e = \alpha_1 R_1^e + \alpha_2 r_2 - \dot{p}^e$$

where $\dot{p}^e$ is the one-period ahead expected inflation rate and $R_1^e = r_1 + g_1^e$. Thus $\sigma_\pi^2 = \alpha_1^2 \sigma_1^2 + \sigma_p^2 - 2\alpha_1 \sigma_{1p}$. Choosing α_1 (and α_2) to maximize the Lagrangian yields

$$\alpha_1 = \frac{R_1^e - r_2}{c\sigma_1^2} + \frac{\sigma_{1p}}{\sigma_1^2}$$

and therefore

$$r_1 - r_2 = -g_1^e + c\sigma_1^2 \alpha_1 - c\sigma_{1p}$$

The term structure (and the demand equation for α_1) therefore depends on an additional term, which includes the covariance between inflation and the return on the risky asset σ_{1p}. The latter provides another element that determines the 'risk premium'. Buse for the UK, 1963(1)–1972(4), finds some support that the long rate on government debt minus the short rate depends on expected capital gains (proxied by lagged capital gains) and the share of risky assets in the portfolio α_1.

10

Financial Models and Complete Macromodels

10.1 INTRODUCTION

In previous chapters we have discussed the importance of asset demand functions in the transmission mechanisms of monetary and fiscal policy, and issues surrounding the control of the money supply. These aspects all feature prominently in this chapter but from a slightly different standpoint. We hope to compare the analytic approaches already discussed with 'real world' models. We concentrate on two interrelated areas: financial models and 'complete' macromodels. We assume that 'complete' models are designed to analyse the outcome of different policies on the authorities' (ultimate) policy targets which we take to be inflation and real output.

Real world financial models may be divided into three broad groups: reduced form, money market and portfolio models. The first describes the economy in terms of a few reduced form equations linking policy instruments to policy targets. Money market models concentrate on the supply and demand for money while the portfolio approach considers the interaction between a number of financial markets. In the first half of the chapter we discuss each of these in turn drawing heavily on material presented in earlier chapters.

Having explained the structure of some 'real world' financial models we consider 'complete' models that also embody a real sector. This enables us to examine the interaction between the financial and real sectors of the economy. In particular we investigate the transmission mechanisms of monetary and fiscal policy and hence the neutrality and crowding out debates. These issues are discussed with reference to 'buffer-stock disequilibrium', neo-Keynesian, rational expectations and reduced form, 'real world' models. Finally we present a brief summary and some thoughts on areas for further research.

Models of the financial sector and 'complete' models of the macroeconomy are extremely varied, often complex and those that are used continuously for forecasting are frequently altered. Also it is sometimes difficult to ascertain (from published sources) the exact comparative properties one is interested in. For these reasons we present a schematic outline of the approaches adopted, with particular models used purely as examples. It follows that we shall present a simplified, although not we hope a misleading account; the reader should in no way consider our presentation as being a definitive account of these models; we use them for illustrative purposes only.

10.2 FINANCIAL MODELS

In chapter 1 we noted that the main transmission mechanisms of monetary policy are (a) the influence of interest rates and the money supply on the exchange rate and hence via competitiveness on output and prices, (b) the direct effect of the money supply or interest rates on real expenditures and via the Phillips curve on inflation, (c) the effect of changes in the money supply on wealth and hence on (consumers') expenditure. As a minimum, we therefore require our 'financial model' to determine the money supply and interest rates. We now consider, in turn, the reduced form, the money market and the portfolio approach.

10.2.1   *The reduced form approach*

The reduced form approach collapses the monetary sector into a very small number of equations usually directly linking assumed policy instruments to a particular monetary variable. For example in some models the link between the budget deficit (or PSBR) and the broad monetary aggregate (for example £M3) is encapsulated in a single equation (see for example the Liverpool model of Minford et al. (1980)).

In a rather extreme form of the reduced form approach it is assumed that the money supply is controlled by the authorities and hence it is not modelled at all. 'Inverting' an interest inelastic demand for money function then gives the money multiplier relationship – that is the vertical LM curve. If the demand for money function is assumed to be interest elastic (IS–LM model) and the long-run supply curve vertical, the model yields a reduced form for a closed economy in which money income depends on the money supply and some measure of the fiscal stance. This approach has been adopted by the Federal Reserve Bank of St Louis for the US economy; fiscal and monetary policy have short-run effects on output but in the long run there is complete crowding out and money is 'neutral'. Thus the reduced form approach to the *financial* sector tends to lead to a reduced form 'complete' model whereby policy instruments are directly linked to the governments policy targets; we discuss this approach further in the section on 'complete' models.

10.2.2   *The money market approach*

The money market approach provides an explicit model of the supply and demand for money but largely neglects other assets. The monetary base model of the money supply process is particularly amenable to this type of approach and forms a key element in the monetary sectors of a number of US models. If banks do not bid for wholesale deposits then this provides a useful account of the determination of the supply of money.

Simplifying somewhat, we know from chapter 8 that the money supply function for retail banks may be written

$$M^s = f(\text{NBR}, r) \quad f_1, f_2 > 0 \tag{10.1}$$

where NBR are non-borrowed reserves and are assumed to be controlled by the authorities; r is a market determined interest rate. Given a normal demand function for *narrow* money that depends only on a single opportunity cost variable r and income, equilibrium in the money market determines the money stock and the interest rate (for a given level of income). With the addition of the IS curve and the Phillips curve the equilibrium level of output and prices are also determined as in the textbook **AD–AS** approach. The simplicity of this approach is lost when either the demand or supply function for money is assumed to depend on more than one interest rate, for example the own rate on money and the rate on long-term debt. We then require a model of how banks influence the own rate and how the authorities intervene in the market for government debt. This leads to the portfolio approach.

10.2.3   *The portfolio approach*

The main characteristic of this approach is the recognition that demand and supply decisions for a whole range of assets are likely to be made simultaneously so that a *set* of interest rates is determined in the market. However, it is accepted that some rates of interest may be set by the authorities (for example the rate on Treasury bills) and others by rules of thumb in oligopolistic markets (for example banks' base rates on lending in the 1950s and 1960s in the UK). Also long rates may be determined by a term structure relationship as discussed in the previous chapter. In some variants of the portfolio approach the demand function for (broad) money may not be explicitly modelled but derived as the residual item in the balance sheet. However, note that this does not imply that the demand for money function is indeterminate, in fact, it is determined by all the variables that influence the other items in the balance sheet (see section 3.4 on interdependent asset demands). Thus portfolio models as described here tend to be rather eclectic. As an example of this approach we present a simplified account of a version of the HM Treasury model of the UK monetary sector (Spencer and Mowl, 1978).

In the HM Treasury model the broad monetary aggregate £M3 is not explicitly modelled but is derived as the sum of certificates of deposit (the residual of the banks' balance sheet), time deposits (the residual of the private sector balance sheet) and retail deposits (that is M1). The latter is explicitly modelled as a demand determined variable. One may conveniently view the choices to be made by the private sector as a decision tree (figure 10.1), although all financial decisions on the different 'branches' of the tree will be made over a very short time period. First the private sector's net wealth is given from the real sector of the model as the difference between income and expenditure. The private sector then decides on the allocation of this between long-term government debt, liquid assets and bank advances according to demand functions that are determined by relative interest rates, wealth and activity variables. Liquid assets consist of parallel money market assets (PMMA) (for example local authority deposits and certificates of deposit), retail and time deposits. It is assumed that the two parallel money market assets are considered as perfect substitutes by the NBPS; therefore there exists a well-defined demand function only for the

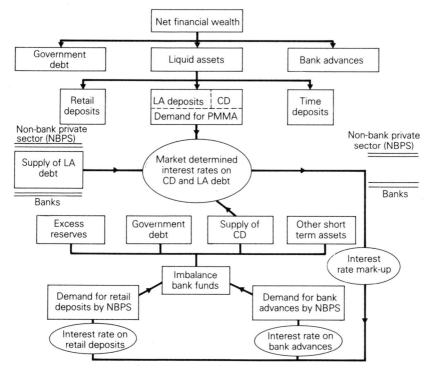

FIGURE 10.1   *Decision framework in a portfolio model.*

two assets *taken together*. Retail deposits are demand determined and time deposits are the residual item in the 'liquid assets' balance sheet.

The banks are assumed to set time deposit, retail deposit and bank lending rates in line with market determined short rates. At these predetermined interest rates the inflow of funds in the form of retail and time deposits may not match the outflow of funds as bank advances (and reserve assets), all of which are demand determined.[1] For example a deficit may be met either by 'asset management' that is by selling bank assets such as commercial bills or long-term debt or by liability management, that is by bidding for certificates of deposit. It is at this point that supply side considerations enter into the determination of the money stock. The banks' choice between asset or liability management is determined by the relative cost (that is interest rates adjusted for the 'reserve tax') of the two options; we therefore have a supply function for certificates of deposit (Spencer, 1984). The supply of local authority debt, the other component of 'parallel money' is largely determined by the financing requirements of local authorities. Hence the total supply of parallel money market assets can be equated with the private sector's demand function to yield an equilibrium stock and interest rate on certificates of deposit. £M3 is then determined as the sum of retail, time and certificates of deposit (here we ignore cash which is demand determined).

The demand function for broad money is therefore implicit and depends on the interaction of several other asset demand functions of the banks and the private sector. If we simulate the financial model with step changes in the level of output, the price level and interest rates, we can ascertain the implicit elasticities of the demand for broad money. In the HM Treasury model the long-run price level elasticity of £M3 is unity, the real income elasticity is about 0.5 and the elasticity with respect to the long rate is about (minus) 3 – all of which are plausible.

The HM Treasury model is clearly eclectic; some interest rates and associated asset stocks are determined by market clearing relationships and some (for example bank advances rate) are determined as a mark-up on other rates, with the associated asset stocks being demand determined. The real and monetary sectors are totally integrated when the 'complete' model is used for simulation. For example, interest rates that are determined in the financial sector influence output in the real sector (IS curve) and the price level (via the Phillips curve); output and prices cause further changes in asset demands and interest rates. Hence a simultaneous solution for interest rates, asset stocks, expenditure and prices is obtained in the 'complete' model.

In portfolio models the government budget constraint is usually explicit and therefore the authorities have the option of influencing the money supply by changes in the budget deficit, by changes in interest rates, by open market operations and by intervention in the foreign exchange market. From the above schematic outline it should be obvious that the authorities' control over the (broad) money supply is very indirect and depends on the complex interaction of a number of asset demand and supply functions.

10.3   COMPLETE MODELS

'Complete' models allow one to analyse the crowding-out and neutrality proposi-tions. The form of the asset demand functions embedded in the models determine, in part, the short-run impact of monetary and fiscal policy on real output and prices. We examine these issues first, within the framework of a 'buffer-stock' model. Next we analyse the impact of monetary policy in a neo-Keynesian and a rational expectations (RE) model and then assess the extent of crowding out in such models. We briefly look at evidence on neutrality and crowding out in reduced form studies before presenting a brief summary of our main conclusions.

10.3.1   *Buffer-stock disequilibrium models BSDM*

BSDM are 'complete' models which explain both monetary and real variables. The essential feature of BSDM is the role of disequilibrium between the supply and demand for money in influencing prices and expenditure. Disequilibria in *real* variables particularly the level of stocks (of goods) may also influence price changes and other real variables but we ignore this aspect here.

The title we have chosen to describe this approach is by no means entirely satisfactory. Disequilibrium models discussed under this heading must not be confused with the 'fix-price quantity constrained' disequilibrium models (Cuddington et al., 1984) where markets may not clear even in the 'long run'. In BSDMs the emphasis is usually on *short-run* disequilibria. The determination of the level of output in the *long run* in these BSDM models can in principle be as varied as one wishes, ranging from a neo-classical model to a neo-Keynesian upward sloping supply function.

Equations of the following form frequently appear in BSDM

$$Y - Y_{-1} = a(Y^* - Y_{-1}) + b(M - M^d) \tag{10.2a}$$

$$P - P_{-1} = cZ + d(M - M^d) \tag{10.2b}$$

The variables are all in logarithms, Y is a real expenditure variable, Y^* is the desired (long-run) value of Y, M is the money supply, M^d is the desired long-run demand for money, P is the price level and Z is a set of 'other variables' (for example excess demand, price expectations) that influence the rate of inflation. Expenditure thus partially adjusts to its own disequilibrium and any disequilibrium in the money market.[2] The short-run division of the money supply between output and price changes is then heavily dependent on the size of the monetary disequilibrium coefficients in the price and expenditure functions.

To make the model operational, Y^* might, for example, be determined by income and (real) interest rates (as in the simple IS curve) and M^d by a 'conventional' long-run demand for money function with the price level, output and interest rates as independent variables

$$M^d = a_0 + a_1 Y - a_2 R \tag{10.2c}$$

In BSDMs the money supply M is often determined by the flow of funds approach; the money supply is the outcome of the PSBR less debt sales to the private sector plus bank advances, where the latter two asset demands might be primarily demand determined (Davidson, 1984; Jonson and Trevor, 1979). Sometimes the money supply process is not modelled but treated as exogenous (Laidler and Bentley, 1983).

If the money disequilibrium term appears in more than one equation (as above) then the equation system (10.2a)–(10.2c) involves cross-equation restrictions on the parameters a_i of the long-run money demand function. Estimation of the system of equations yields an estimate of the parameters of the long-run demand for money function which may be assessed against ones priors and estimates obtained from direct estimation of the demand for money as in chapter 5. (A test of the cross-equation restrictions provides a further test of the model, as do outside sample forecasts.)

A BSDM is used by the Federal Reserve Bank of Australia for analysis and forecasting (Jonson and Trevor, 1979). Output in the long run is independent of aggregate demand (that is a vertical long-run supply curve) but in the short run is heavily influenced by monetary disequilibrium, as are prices. It appears that the monetary disequilibrium term has a stronger effect on prices relative to that on output and the model therefore predicts that a tight monetary policy reduces inflation at little cost in terms of a temporary loss in output. Jonson (1976) presents a BSDM for the UK, and the Bank of England has experimented with models of this type but has not used them in their main forecasting exercises (Hilliard, 1980, Currie, 1982). A recent example of this type of model for the UK, which appears to be reasonably robust empirically, is given by Davidson (1984). In Davidson's model disequilibrium money affects a wide range of real and nominal variables including the exchange rate, the current balance, bond holdings and bank advances as well as output and prices. Models along similar lines have been estimated for the UK and Canada under fixed exchange rates (Laidler and O'Shea, 1980; Laidler et al., 1983) and for the US (Laidler and Bentley, 1983).

One question that springs to mind is how the BSDM approach relates to reaults from 'conventional' demand for money functions of chapter 5, the 'disequilibrium money' approach of section 6.3 and the single equation buffer-stock approach of section 6.4. The 'conventional approach' assumes that the aggregate money supply reacts passively to changes in the arguments of the demand for money function. Clearly this is an unreasonable assumption when monetary targets are in operation but even when the authorities have an interest rate policy, the money supply may move independently of changes in money demand. Changes in bank advances and the PSBR are obvious sources of independent changes in the money supply, and Brunner and Meltzers' (1976) credit market hypothesis, whereby an increase in the demand for capital goods leads to an independent increase in the money supply, is also relevant here. When the money supply moves independently of the demand for money then the arguments of the demand for money adjust to re-establish equilibrium in the money market. Most observers would agree that *all* the arguments are likely to alter simultaneously. However, in single equation studies of the demand for money the best one can do is to use *one* of the arguments as the dependent variable and include the money supply as an independent variable. Artis and Lewis (1976) chose the interest rate as being the variable most likely to exhibit most of the adjustment, but Laidler (1980), for example, has used real output. In these 'inverted' demand for money functions, estimates of the relevant elasticities of money demand may differ substantially from those obtained in the 'conventional approach' where money is the dependent variable. We argued in section 6.4 that these differences could be due in part to econometric problems (for example errors in variables) but equally they could reflect the fact that causation runs predominantly from money to interest rates, output and prices. Since we have little a priori information on the 'true' direction of causation, and little clear evidence from causality tests (Goodhart et al., 1976; Schwert, 1983; Sims, 1972; Friedman, 1977), these two approaches provide a range of alternative estimates of the elasticities of the demand for money.

The Carr–Darby approach (section 6.4) indicates that when money supply shocks are added to a conventional short-run demand for money function a large proportion of the excess (strictly unanticipated) money is initially held as money balances. This is not necessarily in conflict with the broad conclusions of the BSDMs above since the latter provide a mechanism whereby this 'excess' money is slowly dissipated in changes in prices, output and interest rates.

Thus 'complete' BSDMs may be viewed as complementary to the Carr-Darby approach, and more general than merely inverting the demand for money function, since 'complete' BSDMs allow monetary disequilibrium to influence a whole range of expenditure (and asset) decisions. A problem with 'complete' BSDMs is that the parameters of the demand for money function are conditional on the rest of the model being correctly specified; any misspecification in other parts of the model will lead to incorrect estimates of the demand for money function. However, the BSDMs do provide an explicit quantified model of why conventional demand functions may exhibit 'instability' when money supply shocks are large and why 'implausibly' long adjustment lags are found in empirical estimates of these equations. A comprehensive synthesis of these alternative approaches to estimating the parameters of the demand for money function has yet to emerge and although the BSD approach has its critics (White, 1981) it is certainly an approach worth pursuing.

10.3.2   *Money and prices in a neo-Keynesian (NK) model*

We know from our analytic models of chapter 1 that, in an NK model, the impact over time of the money supply on prices and output depends on the form of the demand for money function including lag responses. The transmission mechanism also depends on behaviour in the expenditure sector and the labour market. We now wish to present some illustrative results on this issue using a version of the HM Treasury model. We use the latter because detailed results are readily available and, as it is a model of a small open economy, the transmission mechanisms are more diverse than for a closed economy. In many respects the structural equations of the HM Treasury model are similar to those in the Dornbusch (1976) 'overshooting' model, but because there is less than perfect capital mobility (and because the current account also influences the exchange rate), overshooting in the exchange rate need not necessarily occur. However, a key difference between the two models is in the modelling of expectations: the Dornbusch model assumes (Muth) RE whereas the simulations of the Treasury model below do not.

In the Treasury model the demand for money is proportional to the price level and there is a vertical long-run PEAPC; taken together this ensures the 'neutrality' of money in the long run. The vertical PEAPC is derived from a vertical Phillips curve for wages and a cost mark-up equation for prices. The exchange rate has a direct effect on prices working via import costs. The IS curve is downward sloping because of interest elastic (investment) expenditures and there are wealth effects in the consumption function.[3] Wealth effects are also present in the (implicit) demand for money function.

The exchange rate plays a key role in the transmission mechanism. Under floating exchange rates the latter moves to clear the current and capital account. In the short run, exchange rate movements are dominated by short-term capital flows while over the longer term the current account is the predominant influence. As in the Dornbusch (KAM) model the (logarithm of the) long-run equilibrium exchange rate $\bar{s}$ (domestic per unit of foreign currency) is influenced by (the logarithm of) relative money supplies $m - m^*$ (although relative prices also have a 25 per cent weight). The expected change in the exchange rate $s^e - s$ partially adjusts to the difference between the actual and equilibrium rate $\bar{s} - s$ (although short-run extrapolative expectations are also incorporated). The desired stock of domestic assets held by foreigners (net of foreign assets held by domestic residents) K^* is determined by (a) the uncovered return, that is by the domestic–foreign interest differential $r - r^*$, and (b) the expected change in the exchange rate. If we assume partial adjustment then capital flows into the domestic economy are given by

$$\Delta K = \gamma(K^* - K_{-1})$$
$$= g(r - r^* - s^e + s, K_{-1}) \tag{10.3}$$

We also have

$$s^e - s = g_0(\bar{s} - s) = g_0(m - m^* - s) \tag{10.4}$$

Substituting (10.4) in (10.3) and assuming equilibrium in the capital account $\Delta K = 0$ we obtain after some rearrangement

$$s = f(\overset{(+)}{m - m^*}, \overset{(+)}{r^* - r}, K_{-1}) \tag{10.5}$$

Hence in broad terms the current spot rate is determined by relative interest rates (the uncovered differential) and relative money supplies in the short run.

A reduction in the money supply. We consider the consequences of two methods for reducing the money supply: a cut in government expenditure and a rise in short-term domestic interest rates by open market operations (table 10.1). In each case the chosen policy instrument is continuously adjusted to ensure the (broad) money supply is 1 per cent lower than in the 'base run'.

The cut in government expenditure (with interest rates held constant) leads to fall in output and downward pressure on wages and prices via the PEAPC. The reduction in the money supply via the government budget constraint has a direct influence on the long-run exchange rate which appreciates leading to an appreciation in the actual rate. The latter has an adverse effect on the trade balance but this is more than offset in the short run by the improvement in domestic inflation and hence competitiveness due to the deflationary policy. The current account therefore improves and the exchange rate appreciates even further to clear the overall payments position. The exchange rate overshoots in the first three years (table 10.1). The turn-round in real output from year 5 is primarily due to the positive wealth effect on consumption as prices fall. It should be clear from table 10.1 that the short-run cost in terms of lost output of achieving lower inflation is quite severe. Also even after nine years neither real output nor the price level has settled down to its long-run equilibrium value.

Reducing the money supply by raising interest rates has a relatively slow feed-through to the price level but with minimal adverse effects on real output. The latter arises because of the long lags on competitiveness in the trade equations and the rather inelastic IS curve. The rise in domestic interest rates requires an

TABLE 10.1   The effects of a 1 per cent reduction in £M3 using alternative
policy instruments: HM Treasury model[1]

Policy instruments	Year	GDP	Price level (GDP deflator)	Effective exchange rate[2]
Government expenditure	1	−0.6	−0.1	1.2
on goods and services	3	−0.1	−1.1	1.5
	5	0.3	−1.5	0.9
	7	0.5	−1.6	0.7
	9	0.4	−1.2	0.6
Interest rates	1	−0.1	−0.1	1.1
	3	−0.1	−0.4	0.8
	5	0.0	−0.6	0.6
	7	0.1	−0.7	0.4
	9	0.2	−0.9	−0.2

[1] Figures are percentage differences from the 'base run'.
[2] A positive value indicates an appreciation of sterling.

Source: Richardson (1981).

appreciation of spot exchange rate to maintain capital account equilibrium
(equation (10.5)). Higher interest rates reduce bank advances and the money
supply. The latter leads directly to a rise in the equilibrium spot rate, an appreciation in the actual spot rate and hence downward pressure on prices as
described above.

Naturally the above results are sensitive to the parameter values used in the
model, particularly the response of capital flows and the strength of the inflation-
unemployment link in the Phillips curve. There are no rational expectations
elements in this version of the HM Treasury model, and by way of a contrast
we outline the results of a similar exercise using the Liverpool RE model of
the UK economy.

10.3.3   Money and prices in an RE model

The key elements in the Liverpool model (Minford and Peel, 1983) comprise
fairly conventional IS and LM curves (with wealth effects) and perfect capital
mobility (the uncovered arbitrage condition is assumed to hold). The supply
function is of the Sargent–Wallace (SW) type but a 'one-off' price 'surprise'
leads to changes in output over several periods. (A lagged dependent variable is
included.) The supply function contains an additional term in the real exchange
rate to represent increased profit margins in the non-traded sector when import
prices (costs) are low. The Liverpool model is similar to the Dornbusch overshooting model since both use (Muth) RE and the uncovered interest parity
condition. Both models imply supply side crowding out (although the supply
functions are different – the Dornbusch model has a 'conventional' vertical

long-run Phillips curve). The slope of the SW supply function in the Liverpool model is rather crucial for the dynamics of the results obtained; the price 'surprise' needs to be large to obtain a relatively small change in real output.

Consider an *unanticipated* reduction in the money supply. The aggregate demand (AD) curve shifts to the left and output and prices fall along the short-run supply curve. Interest rates rise as the LM curve shifts to the left and hence the uncovered interest parity relationship leads to a 'jump' in the exchange rate. There is a deterioration in price competitiveness and hence output. However, in the first year the reduction in output from a 1 per cent cut in the money supply is quite mild at about 0.1 per cent while the effect on prices at about 0.8 per cent is strong. The exchange rate overshoots and in subsequent years the output loss is quickly attenuated. Hence this particular RE model gives a very different time profile for output and prices to that obtained in the non-RE HM Treasury model. The assumption of RE appears to have shortened the time horizon needed to reach long-run equilibrium after a monetary squeeze.

10.3.4   *Crowding out in neo-Keynesian and RE models*

We discussed two categories of crowding out of a fiscal stimulus in our analytic discussion in chapter 1, these being 'financial' and 'physical' crowding out. The former refers to crowding out that results purely on the demand side and the latter due to supply side decisions. Financial crowding out in a fix-price closed economy may result from a completely inelastic demand for money function (vertical LM curve) or an infinite interest elasticity of expenditures (horizontal IS curve). When we add wealth effects and the government budget constraint to the fix-price model, bond financed deficits (or mixed money-bond finance) *may* lead to instability and extreme crowding out. Physical crowding out ensues if we have a neo-classical supply curve and if fiscal policy does not influence the supply and demand curves for labour. In an RE model with flexible prices (that is a new classical model) physical crowding out takes place if we have a Sargent–Wallace 'surprise' supply function.

For a small open economy we examined, in chapter 1, crowding out under flexible exchange rates in the Mundell–Fleming and Dornbusch models. The Mundell–Fleming model ignores the wealth effects, exchange rate expectations and the price level is constant. The impact of fiscal policy depends on the degree of capital mobility. With perfect capital mobility (horizontal BB curve) fiscal policy is completely crowded out but with low capital mobility (near vertical BB curve) there is 'crowding in'. The reason for these different outcomes arises because in the former case the exchange rate appreciates, net trade falls and offsets the expansionary fiscal stimulus whereas in the latter case the converse applies (Artis 1984).

We can add inflation and wealth effects to the Mundell–Fleming model. The addition of a wages version of the PEAPC curve (and a price equation) allows demand effects to feed directly into wages and hence prices. If, as is highly likely, a change in the nominal exchange rate affects domestic inflation, then any fiscal stimulus will result in additional demand side effects working via price competitiveness and a change in net trade. Also, an increase in inflation may trigger off wealth effects. *Real* wealth may fall putting downward pressure on consumers' expenditure and upward pressure on interest rates (as the wealth induced increase in the demand for money shifts the LM curve to the left) with the latter leading to a fall in investment demand. To the extent that nominal rates of interest increase in line with inflation then capital losses on long-term debt may lead to a fall in consumption (for example Peseran and Evans (1984) for the UK and Modigliani (1975) for the US). This augmented Mundell-Flemming model may be described as broadly neo-Keynesian. The HM Treasury model of the UK economy embodies the above transmission mechanisms but also includes endogenous expectations about the exchange rate. Below we again take a version of the HM Treasury model to provide illustrative results on crowding out in a neo-Keynesian framework.

The Dornbusch model, with less than perfect capital mobility, resembles the above neo-Keynesian model with one crucial difference: the former assumes (Muth) RE in the money and foreign exchange markets. Below we take the Liverpool model of the UK economy as an example of a small open economy RE model.

Neo-Keynesian model. Simulation results of a version of the HM Treasury model (Mowl, 1980) under alternative assumptions are given in table 10.2. With a constant exchange rate, earnings and interest rates (that is horizontal LM curve) there is no crowding out of fiscal policy (column (1)). When earnings are endogenized and determined by a PEAPC there is partial crowding out as

TABLE 10.2   Reduction in government expenditure (on goods) of 0.5 per cent of GDP in the 'base run': HM Treasury model[1]

Assumptions	*(1)*	*(2)*	*(3)*	*(4)*
Earnings	fixed	endog.[2]	endog.	endog.
Exchange rate	fixed	fixed	float	float
Interest rates	fixed	fixed	fixed	endog.
Money supply	accom.[2]	accom.	accom.	fixed
Effects on				
(a) Output Q1	0.4	0.4	0.4	0.4
Q8	0.6	0.5	0.7	0.4
Q16	0.5	0.3	0.7	0.1
(b) Consumer price level Q1	0.0	0.0	0.0	0.0
Q8	0.0	0.2	0.5	0.3
Q16	0.0	0.5	1.5	0.7

[1] Figures in the table are percentage changes from the 'base'. All simulations include an 'anticipatory adjustment to interest rates (see text).
[2] accom., accommodating monetary policy; endog., behavioural equation used.

Source: Mowl (1980).

higher inflation leads to lower consumption (wealth effects) a loss in price competitiveness and a lower volume of net trade (column (2)).

Under floating exchange rates but with interest rates still fixed (that is mixed money-bonds financing) there is 'crowding in' (column (3)). The increase in the money supply required to finance (part) of the budget deficit leads directly to a fall in the long-run equilibrium exchange rate and hence in the current spot exchange rate. The latter leads directly to an increase in inflation via import prices, but on balance, competitiveness improves and net trade expands. The expansionary effects of the latter are offset somewhat by the inflation induced wealth effects on consumption but the net effect on output is positive. (Thus the model incorporates elements of the Mundell–Fleming approach but with the addition of price determination and wealth effects.)

There is a rather dramatic change when the interest rate becomes endogenous and the money supply is held constant (that is pure bond finance). An *ad hoc* adjustment to interest rates is made to (crudely) model anticipatory expectations effects in the term structure equation (as RE effects are not explicitly modelled). An increase in government expenditure is expected to lead to a rise in interest rates in the future (IS curve to the right with a fixed LM curve). Anticipating this rise and consequent capital loss, agents might sell 'risky' assets today. But this pushes up interest rates *today*. In the 'fixed' money supply simulation an *ad hoc* adjustment bringing interest rate changes eight quarters forward is adopted. (Fair, 1979 using a US neo-Keynesian model, does this in a fully Muth-rational way (Muth, 1961).)

After an increase in government expenditure the rise in interest rates required to hold the money supply constant leads to a capital inflow which tends to push up the exchange rate. On the other hand the trade deficit tends to lead to a depreciation. However, the net effect is a strong appreciation (of 3 per cent in the effective exchange rate by the fourth year). The latter leads to a deterioration in price competitiveness and a fall in net trade. Higher interest rates have a direct effect on investment expenditure and negative wealth effects, caused by higher prices, tend to depress consumption. The net result is that there is nearly complete crowding out by the end of the fourth year (column (4)). Note that 'crowding out' is a mixture of financial (or demand side) and supply side crowding out (via the Phillips curve). Thus under floating rates and a tight monetary policy substantial crowding out occurs.

Other models. The results on crowding out from US models under bond financed deficits appear to be somewhat mixed (Choudry, 1976). The MPS, St Louis and Wharton models appear to exhibit crowding out while (these vintages of) the DRI and Brookings models do not (table 10.3). It is impossible to ascertain whether these results arise primarily from financial or physical crowding out.

The Liverpool RE model of the UK economy exhibits crowding out about four years after an unanticipated permanent change in the fiscal policy stance (Minford and Peel, 1983). This is a physical crowding out via the SW supply function. The reason for the delayed crowding out effect is that price 'surprises' consequent on the increase in government expenditure exhibit 'persistence' effects on the supply of output.

TABLE 10.3   Crowding out in US models under bond financed deficits:
real GDP multipliers

Quarters	Brookings	DRI	MPS	Wharton mk III	St Louis
1	1.8	1.4	1.2	1.3	0.5
4	2.8	1.6	2.2	2.0	0.5
8	2.7	0.9	2.2	2.4	−0.2
16	2.0	0.3	−0.5	2.4	−0.2
36	1.0	2.7	−	−1.9	−

Source: Choudry (1976).

10.3.5 *Reduced form models, 'neutrality' and crowding out*

Reduced form models which use prices, real output or nominal income as
the dependent variable, and the money supply and some measure of the fiscal
stance as independent variables, have been used to investigate the crowding out
issue and the neutrality proposition. (viz. the St Louis model referred to above).
Some favour this approach because they feel that the money supply affects a
very wide range of asset yields some of which are difficult to measure (for
example the implicit yield on durables). Hence it may be more useful to look
at the relationship between money and the variables of interest directly. This
reduced form approach may capture all of the small changes in relative yields
and all other channels of monetary influence that may be omitted in large scale
models. The results for the US, on balance, tend to support full crowding out
and the neutrality proposition. For the UK the evidence on both these counts
seems less strong (see Thompson (1984) for a concise survey, Wren-Lewis
(1984) and Holly and Longbottom (1982) for recent UK evidence and Batten
and Thornton (1984) for recent US evidence).

There are acute problems with the reduced form approach. First, the Lucas
critique applies *a fortiori* since the parameters to be estimated are convolutions
of all the structural parameters of the economy. Second, a 'good fit' may be
due to reverse causality. For example a rise in the price level (say due to oil
prices) leads to an increase in the demand for money. If the authorities are
operating a fixed interest rate policy or we have an open economy under fixed
exchange rates, then there will be an 'accommodating' change in the money
supply. This reverse causality may also give rise to biased parameter estimates
(Desai, 1981). Finally, if counter-cyclical fiscal policy is successful, we would
not expect to see any correlation between output and the fiscal policy variable.

Causality tests have been used to assess whether money causes prices (or
nominal income) rather than the other way round. Results are mixed both for
the US and UK (see Desai (1981) for a recent survey). However Tobin (1970)
shows that turning points in the growth in money may lead turning points
in the growth in nominal income in a 'Keynesian' model where money is demand
determined. Also, in RE models, anticipated changes in monetary policy can
lead to changes in endogenous variables such as money income before the

actual change in the money supply takes place. Hence results from causality tests are open to a number of interpretations.

10.4 SUMMARY

There is considerable diversity in models of the financial sector and their interaction with the real sector. Approaches range from single equation reduced forms to complex structural models. The RE approach incorporates a radically different view of the adjustment to equilibrium than more conventional neo-Keynesian models. It is now widely accepted that money is neutral in the long run but the time scale over which real effects are present is still a controversial issue. The degree of crowding out depends crucially on the type of exchange rate regime and monetary policy in operation; in general, evidence on the extent of crowding out is conflicting.

10.5 FINAL THOUGHTS

In this section we provide some reflections on the material covered in the book and discuss areas for future research. Although the bulk of this text has dealt with the supply and demand for money, we have also discussed some wider issues of monetary models and monetary policy. On the positive side, we probably know more about how the economy has worked in the past and are more aware of pitfalls that may befall policy makers in the future. The Lucas critique has highlighted the importance of the interaction between government policy, the behaviour of the private sector and the 'credibility' of government pronouncements; this aspect is rapidly being given a more rigorous analysis by applying the theory of games (Miller, 1984; Miller and Salmon, 1984a, 1984b; Backus and Driffill, 1984). The role of expectations particularly in financial markets, and the importance of distinguishing between the effects of anticipated and unanticipated policy responses will undoubtedly form an important area of future research. Explicit modelling of expectations will soon become commonplace in large scale econometric models; behavioural equations with forward looking variables will replace some of those previously based purely on backward looking expectations schemes (as in the adaptive expectations hypothesis).

With unemployment as an important policy issue and perhaps the inflation problem receding into the background, then more attention will be directed towards models that incorporate 'sticky price' assumptions in labour and goods markets with financial markets conforming to the RE hypothesis. In such a New Keynesian type of approach there could also be a role for a 'buffer-stock disequilibrium' effect as part of an explanation of the transmission mechanism. Whilst one can detect some convergence of views in the general macroeconomic debate, nevertheless the gap between the NC and other schools remains substantial. Solow quoting the philosopher Frank Ramsey (Klamer, 1984) sums this up by noting that conversations between rival schools are often of the form 'I went to Grantchester today'. 'That is funny, I didn't'.

A stable demand function for money depending on a limited set of independent variables is a necessary condition for money to exert a predictable influence on the economy. Since the authorities do not directly control the 'money supply', a model of the money supply process is required. Most of the material in this book has been directed towards examining these two issues from a theoretical and empirical standpoint.

Our theories of money demand fall into two main categories: transactions models and asset or portfolio models. The theories indicate the appropriate arguments to include in the demand function for money (and other assets) together with a priori restrictions on parameters. Although our theories usually yield 'partial models' that deal with a particular motive for holding money, this is not necessarily a drawback. A given theory may be applicable to a specific set of agents or institutions (and we may legitimately be able to invoke the 'separability' argument). However, data limitations do frequently prevent a strict test of a particular theory. For example only a 'composite model' involving a number of different theories may be legitimately applied to *aggregate* data on broad money. Two further problems are then likely to arise. First, we need to model the adjustment process and, second, to model any 'unobservables' such as expectations variables. We therefore simultaneously test a set of hypotheses and not just our 'static equilibrium' theory. This is the Duhem-Quine thesis (Cross, 1982). Rejection of the model then implies a rejection of either the static equilibrium theory or the auxiliary hypotheses but it is impossible to say which. It is perhaps not surprising that alternative views can coexist simultaneously.

We have noted that the mean-variance model is particularly tractable and has been used to explain a wide range of asset demand functions. The inventory model is frequently invoked in applied work although the relationship between the level of transactions and the demand for money is, according to our analysis, likely to be rather complex. The precautionary models have not been prevalent in the applied literature because of the difficulty in measuring the variability of net cash inflows.

Despite the formidable problems noted above, empirical work has provided considerable insights into the determinants of asset demands and reasons why temporal instability might arise. Taking the demand for money for example, empirical work in the US has highlighted the importance of financial innovation in shifting the demand function for narrow money (M1) while in the UK the 1970s' data provides evidence on the importance of shocks to the money supply when interpreting movements in the demand for broad money (£M3). The UK evidence suggests that the adjustment process in the money market depends on the direction of causation between money and the arguments of the demand for money function. Research into 'buffer-stock money' is a direct consequence of this insight. The impact of financial innovation on the demand for money and the role of money as a buffer stock are areas that are likely to be vigorously pursued by researchers in the future, thus demonstrating that new avenues in research are just as likely to be sparked off by 'empirical anomalies' as by new theories (Kuhn, 1962). Another promising area of applied research on the demand for money that has only recently come to the fore is the use of Divisia aggregates. Here it is recognized that the various items that constitute 'money' are not perfect substitutes and hence a weighted aggregate (weighted by the contribution of each item to 'money services') is more appropriate than simply adding the separate items together as in the official statistics. This approach is unlikely to be a panacea but it does appear to improve the empirical performance of broad money aggregates (Barnett et al., 1984).

Even if one accepts that sharply defined tests of a particular theory of the demand for money are unlikely, given data limitations, nevertheless important empirical questions remain. The importance of wealth in asset demand functions still needs further investigation especially in view of its importance in the wider macroeconomic debate over the budget constraint and crowding out. The RE 'revolution' has meant that far more attention will be devoted to measuring expectations variables and 'risk'. Both variables occur in the mean-variance model of asset demands and in models of the term structure. The RE hypothesis allows one to measure the variance of returns and this may provide an adequate proxy for 'risk' (Friedman and Roley, 1979b; Engle et al., 1983). In future research we can also expect to see forward looking variables (particularly expected income) in the demand for various liquid assets. In small open economies especially those that have removed all capital controls, the substitutability between domestic and foreign assets needs further investigation and here expectations about changes in the exchange rate may be modelled using the RE hypothesis. This work has important implications for the transmission of monetary policy via the exchange rate.

Our analysis of the determination of the supply of money has concentrated on those models of the financial firm that appear helpful in understanding problems of monetary control in the US and UK, although such problems are not confined to these two countries. (Other issues in this area such as the relationship between market structure and performance, the appropriate liability and capital structure for banks are surveyed by Baltensberger (1980) and Santomero (1984)). The insights gained from a recognition that the banking firm does not decide on its long-run portfolio allocation independently of other factors such as real resource costs are considerable, nevertheless empirical implementation of general models of the banking firm are conspicuous by their absence. Thus although our knowledge of the money supply process may be helped by further developments in the theory of the financial firm, it must be recognized that the rapid pace of financial innovation both in domestic and 'offshore' markets may make the successful empirical implementation of these models even more problematic in the future. Our lack of empirical evidence in this area poses problems for the use of either a narrow or broad monetary aggregate as an intermediate policy target. If Divisia aggregates provide greater informational content about the future course of the economy and hence are more useful as intermediate targets, the problem of control by market means remains acute. These problems will no doubt sharpen the controversy over the choice between interest rates and (the various variants of) base control as operating targets. In small open economies the exchange rate and monetary policy are inextricably linked. The use of the exchange rate as an intermediate target is therefore important (Artis and Currie, 1981) and the implications of greater international co-operation over exchange rate movements (Blanchard and Summers, 1984) will no doubt receive further attention.

The importance of the Lucas critique when analysing alternative monetary policy regimes cannot be overstressed. Policy changes that alter perceptions about the variance of asset returns may alter the parameters of the banks (and NBPS) asset demand functions. Hence the impact of monetary policy on financial variables such as interest rates (and the exchange rate) becomes more difficult to assess. More research in this area is likely to be forthcoming.

In testing asset demand functions there has been somewhat of a dichotomy between the empirical approach recently adopted in the UK and common practice elsewhere. For example most current empirical work in the US uses the first-order partial adjustment model whereas in the UK the error feedback and autoregressive distributed lag EF-ADL models are more prevalent. The latter is however beginning to appear in the US literature (Gordon, 1984). The EF-ADL approach and the 'general to specific' modelling strategy does not of course, solve all our estimation problems but it does avoid some pitfalls caused by commencing the investigation with a very restrictive lag structure. Until we obtain a sound theoretic basis for the adjustment mechanisms in asset demand functions there is likely to be continued emphasis on the ADL approach and systems estimation utilizing the interdependent asset adjustment framework.

We have not discussed the 'identification problem' since most empirical work on the demand for assets ignores the problem. However, the reader should be aware that the conditions required to identify the demand for money are assumed by some to be 'formidable' (Cooley and LeRoy, 1981). If one accepts the latter view, estimation of a structural demand function is impossible. (For a general discussion of this problem see Sims (1980)). Cooley and LeRoy also argue that because researchers only present their 'best results', which inevitably 'confirm' their theory, then 'empirical' results are likely to reflect the a priori beliefs of the researchers rather than the sample information. The latter problem is likely to become less acute in the future as we may see a move away from merely testing one theory against the data, towards much more rigorous model evaluation procedures. The encompassing principle whereby a theory should explain why other researchers reached the conclusions they did, given that the proposed model is true (Hendry, 1983; Hendry and Richard, 1982; Mizon, 1984) is likely to be more widely adopted. Given the paucity of data with which most economists usually work, the importance of rigorous testing cannot be overstressed. Recently there have been useful advances in this area and these seem set to continue.

The reader would be correct in assuming that, even given the progress that has been made, there is still a yawning gap between our relatively sophisticated theories of the demand for money (and other assets) and our rather crude attempts at testing these theories. There is still disagreement about the appropriate arguments of the demand function and there appears to be some instability in the demand for narrow money in the US and the demand for broad money in the UK. Asset demand functions for the banks are also subject to instability. We can only conclude that this casts doubt on the authorities' ability to control monetary aggregates at all precisely, and that the latter have a predictable effect on the economy. However, our understanding of the difficulties involved in the successful implementation of monetary policy is now much improved and that should militate against wrongful acceptance of simple solutions to a complex and changing problem.

We have no doubt that economics should be classified as a science. The methodology is scientific, following as it does the deductive approach. In testing our theories we also use scientific methods although we do not have the advantage of laboratory experiments. We also have a difficult problem in that our 'policy experiments' may alter the structure of the system (for example the Lucas critique) – although this is not unheard of in the natural sciences (for example Heisenberg's uncertainty principle in quantum mechanics). We hope that the sheer ingenuity of the economics profession has percolated through to the reader. However, it would be incorrect to say that this has led to any diminution in the degree of controversy surrounding particular views. The evidence is rarely decisive and a priori considerations play an important part in assessing different theories. While one may quibble about the arcane nature of some economic theories, one can only hope that progress is being made. We have attempted to convince the reader that this is indeed the case in the limited areas of monetary economics discussed in this text.

NOTES

1 In this version of the HM Treasury model, bank advances to the personal sector are determined by a disequilibrium model. Actual advances are a weighted average of the 'notional' supply and demand curves.
2 Loosely speaking equations like (10.2) may be viewed as a generalization of the interdependent asset adjustment model to include real assets.
3 In the HM Treasury model the 'wealth effect' on consumption is merely the 'inflation loss' on money fixed assets. At high rates of inflation the purchasing power of money fixed assets declines and people increase their saving to rebuild their assets. Hence consumption and inflation are negatively related (Bean, 1978). The mechanism here is therefore different from that which is obtained by including the *level* of real wealth directly in the consumption function. We largely gloss over these differences in this chapter.

Appendix A

Econometric modelling of aggregate time series data

A.1 INTRODUCTION

Several important topics in econometrics are relevant to an understanding of applied work that has recently appeared in the literature. In this appendix we present a highly selective introductory account of some of these issues. This will enable the non-specialists in this area to understand more fully the theoretical basis of some of the empirical issues discussed in chapter 5. More importantly perhaps, the material below will help the reader to interpret the recent empirical work in journal articles.

In what follows it is assumed that the reader is familiar with alternative estimation methods such as ordinary least squares (OLS) generalized least squares (GLS) and instrumental variables (IV) estimators such as two stage least squares (2SLS) at least at an elementary level. Some knowledge of the properties of estimators such as unbiasedness and consistency is also assumed. The identification problem (in simultaneous systems), is not discussed, not because we feel that it is unimportant but because (unfortunately) it is not a central issue in most applied work. The issues discussed may be summed up under three broad headings: short-run dynamics, autocorrelation and the 'general to specific' modelling strategy. Although we deal with each issue separately there are common themes running through all three areas. It is probably true to say that these issues have had their main impact on empirical work in the UK and Europe rather than elsewhere and are still subject to debate and controversy.

In principle we should like one model to be superior to all others in all respects; in practice this rarely if ever occurs and the 'best model' then consists of a weighted average of attributes with 'weights' chosen by the researcher to reflect his subjective view of the relative importance of the various elements. Under such conditions applied econometrics becomes something of an art rather than a science; acceptability is in the eye of the beholder. Hendry (1983) provides a lucid account of the criteria used in model evaluation.

We begin, in section A.2, with a discussion of the spurious regression problem. As the name suggests this concerns the conditions under which one may obtain a spuriously good within-sample 'fit' for an equation although the variables are statistically independent. It turns out that one way of detecting this problem is the presence of serial correlation in the residuals of the equation. This leads us naturally into a discussion of the treatment of autocorrelation and common factors.

In a series of recent articles it has been shown that it is not sufficient to apply a GLS estimator in the presence of serial correlation in the *residuals*. *Error* autocorrelation implies implicit non-linear restrictions between the parameters of the equation and the validity of these restrictions must be tested *before* one can accept the GLS estimates of the parameters as valid. Early studies of asset demand functions frequently ignore this problem which may result in 'incorrect' inferences and parameter estimates. The non-linear restrictions implicit in autocorrelation are known as common factors. Autocorrelation reduces the number of parameters to be estimated and therefore improves the 'efficiency' of the estimates. In this limited sense autocorrelation is a 'convenient simplification' and not a 'nuisance'.

The above approach to autocorrelation suggests that it may be advantageous to start an empirical investigation with a very general ADL model and sequentially 'test down' to produce a parsimonious representation which nevertheless retains the a priori theoretical model as its long-run solution. Autocorrelated errors and the associated common factors provide one method of applying the 'general to specific' modelling strategy. This analysis enables us to clarify the interconnections between autocorrelation, the ADL model and the dynamics of asset demand functions discussed in chapter 5.

In section A.4 we demonstrate how 'errors in variables' may lead to an erroneous acceptance of a lagged response in a structural behavioural equation. Again, we saw in chapter 5 that this may be a problem when 'badly measured variables' such as wealth and the 'expected return' are used in asset demand functions.

In chapter 5 we noted that an unrestricted ADL model could be reduced to a more parsimonious 'error feedback equation' EFE. The latter may be solved for the static and 'dynamic' long-run equilibrium and compared with the underlying theoretical model. This provides a second example of the 'general to specific' modelling strategy. Starting from a general unrestricted ADL model in the levels of the variables we can rearrange the variables to produce sensible decision variables (for example by differencing, by using 'ratio terms' or by excluding statistically insignificant variables). In this way we again reduce the number of parameters to be estimated and if the restrictions imposed on the variables are accepted by the data we obtain an acceptable parsimonious equation.

In section A.6 we present some 'reparameterizations' that are frequently used and also discuss the derivation and testing of static and dynamic equilibrium effects.

We remind the reader that we can only deal with these recent advances in a fairly cursory manner but the issues merit attention because they are central to an understanding of the recent empirical literature. The topics discussed are still subject to clarification and debate and hence a full understanding requires a study of the source material.

A.2   SPURIOUS REGRESSION

Although the spurious regression problem has been known for some considerable time (Yule, 1926) it became widely known to applied economists through a series of papers by Granger and Newbold (1974, 1977). If statistically *independent* series are highly trended then a regression equation between such series will exhibit a spuriously good fit[1] in terms of $\bar{R}^2$. The reason is that trended series are non-stationary and hence do not yield well-behaved test statistics. (For example the statistical distribution of $\bar{R}^2$ is bi-modal when the data series are non-stationary.) The (best linear) unbiased (BLUE) properties of the OLS estimator rely on the assumption that the errors are a stationary white noise series and in particular that $Eu_t = 0$. The simple model $Y_t = a + bX_t + u_t$ where Y_t and X_t are tended implies $Y_t = u_t + \alpha$ under the null-hypothesis H_0; $b = 0$. Hence u_t has the (time series) property of Y_t and is non-stationary, resulting in misleading values for $\bar{R}^2$, t- and F-statistics.

A 'time series' solution to avoid the spurious regression problem is to difference all the data series until stationarity ensues. u_t is then a linear combination of stationary variables and is therefore also a stationary series. However, as discussed in the next section, differencing loses all long-run information in the data and also, may not be a valid restriction. An alternative solution to the spurious regression problem is to ensure that there is no serial correlation in the error term.

Granger and Newbold find that in the 'levels equation' the 'spurious regression' frequently exhibits serial correlation in the residuals, but correct (that is low) $\bar{R}^2$ are obtained in the levels regressions with random residuals. This is intuitively plausible since the properties of the test statistics depend upon the errors being stationary. It is possible that the trend in Y_t is explained by the trend in bX_t and u_t is stationary (Y_t and X_t are co-integrable (Granger, 1983; Hendry and Ericsson, 1983)). Thus it appears that we may minimize the possibility of accepting a spurious relationship in equations in the levels of trended variables provided the equation does not suffer from serial correlation in the errors. The correct treatment for serial correlation is therefore of paramount importance and it is to this we now turn.

A.3 SYSTEMATIC DYNAMICS, ERROR DYNAMICS, COMMON FACTORS AND AUTOCORRELATION

In this section we discuss certain problems posed by serial correlation and its relation to lagged responses. Lagged variables may appear in asset demand functions because of adjustment and expectations lags. However, serial correlation in the *residuals* of an equation may often be removed by adding additional lagged variables. It is important, particularly for policy analysis to determine whether estimated lags are due to 'true' lagged adjustment or merely due to the statistical properties of the *residuals*. Our analysis provides a methodology for distinguishing between 'true' (adjustment) lags and (apparent) lag effects introduced due to serially correlated residuals.

We begin by demonstrating that autocorrelation in the (true) errors implies non-linear restrictions (or 'common factors') between parameters. Early studies of asset demand functions do not usually test the validity of these restrictions but if they do not hold, biased and inconsistent estimators ensue. Next we discuss the response of applied researchers to the presence of *residual* serial correlation and argue that the addition of lagged variables may not always provide the most judicious approach to this problem. Finally, we briefly discuss the notion that, from a purely *statistical* point of view, autocorrelation is a 'convenient simplification' rather than a nuisance in that it reduces the number of parameters to be estimated. This is one aspect of the 'general to specific' modelling strategy. However, applied economists have often eschewed this common factor approach because it introduces a non-white noise error term and the latter is usually in conflict with the *theoretical* behavioural model.

A.3.1   *Autocorrelation and common factors*

To demonstrate the issues involved consider a simplified demand for money function with *instantaneous* adjustment, which has an error term subject to first order autocorrelation

$$M_t = m_y Y_t + u_t \tag{A.1}$$

$$u_t = \rho u_{t-1} + \epsilon_t \quad \text{or} \quad u_t = (1 - \rho L)^{-1} \epsilon_t \tag{A.2}$$

with $-1 < \rho < 1$ and ϵ_t is 'white noise'.

Substituting (A.2) in (A.1) and multiplying through by $(1 - \rho L)$

$$(1 - \rho L) M_t = m_y (1 - \rho L) Y_t + \epsilon_t \tag{A.3}$$

or

$$M_t = \rho M_{t-1} + m_y Y_t - \rho m_y Y_{t-1} + \epsilon_t \tag{A.4}$$

$$M_t = c_0 M_{t-1} + c_1 Y_t + c_2 Y_{t-1} + \epsilon_t \tag{A.5}$$

where the values of c_i are the estimated coefficients and if (A.1) and (A.2) are 'true' then $c_0 = \rho$, $c_1 = m_y$ and $c_2 = -\rho m_y$.

If the instantaneous adjustment model is the 'true' structural model but there is autocorrelation in the *error* terms then there is an implicit non-linear restriction namely $c_2/c_1 = -c_0$ between the *estimated* coefficients in equation (A.5). The validity of the non-linear restriction can be tested by comparing the error sums of squares in the restricted equation (A.3) with that in the unrestricted equation using a likelihood ratio test (Hendry and Mizon, 1978).

In much of the early empirical work, researchers who detected evidence of *residual* serial correlation in the static structural model (A.1) proceeded to 'correct' for autocorrection.

The 'Cochrane–Orcutt' equation (A.3) *imposes* the non-linear restriction, but we need to *test* for the validity of the restriction. If the Cochrane–Orcutt *estimate* of m_y in equation (A.3) is statistically insignificant or unacceptable on a priori grounds (for example of the wrong sign) this may be a consequence of invalidly imposing the non-linear restriction implicit in the assumption of autocorrelation; the 'true' value of m_y may not be statistically insignificant. Put another way, the invalid imposition of the non-linear restriction biases the estimate of the parameter m_y.

To summarize the argument so far. If the structural model (A.1) is assumed to have autocorrelation in the (true) errors then the first task of the researcher is to test for the validity of the implicit non-linear restrictions. Only if the restrictions hold can one then test for the statistical signficance of ρ and m_y. Failure to test for the validity of the non-linear restriction may produce biased estimates of the structural parameters.

Let us briefly present some further technical jargon. Equation (A.3) shows that autocorrelation implies a common term ('factor') $(1 - \rho L)$ in the lag polynomials on M and Y. If the non-linear restriction in (A.3) holds then we will have separated out the error dynamics (that is the value of ρ in $u_t = \rho u_{t-1} + \epsilon$) from the systematic dynamics (m_y) in (A.1) – which are of zero order in this simple example.

The above discussion prompts the question of what the applied researcher can do if the common factor restriction is rejected. A reasonable, though not exhaustive set of options might be as follows.

1 Assume that the *residual* autocorrelation in the structural equation is due to a more complex error structure (for example low order ARMA model) and re-estimate the structural equation subject to this new hypothesis about the error terms.[2]
2 Add 'new' independent variables to the structural model or try different functional forms in an attempt to proxy the *residual* serial correlation by a different maintained hypothesis.
3 Re-estimate over shorter sample periods to see if the serial correlation is caused by a (sharp) structural break in the relationship.
4 Include additional lags in the dependent and independent variables but without restricting the parameters of the equation.

Each of the above options provides a very different view of the underlying structural model. The first option preserves the assumption that (A.1) is the true structural model and there are no adjustment lags. The second approach essentially implies a 'new' structural equation, the third suggests instability in the parameters over time and the fourth introduces a lagged response of M to changes in Y. The ease in adopting item 4 and the fact that it does not imply a 'new' *long-run* static equilibrium solution for M has led numerous researchers to assume that *residual* serial correlation in the structural equation (A.1) is the result of mis-specified dynamics. Equation (A.5), without parameter restrictions, is adopted as the new maintained hypothesis. Clearly whilst this procedure may remove residual serial correlation and provide a better fit than the initial 'instantaneous' equation (A.1), it may not reveal the true model.[3] Ideally one should try a number of the above approaches and compare the statistical results obtained.

Thus the usual response to the existence of *residual* serial correlation that is not *error autocorrelation* (that is the common factor restrictions do not hold) has been to add additional lagged variables. Researchers have assumed a more complex lag response, whilst maintaining the initial long-run static equilibrium equation given by 'economic theory' (as represented by equation (A.1) in our simple example). This is a typical pragmatic solution adopted by applied researchers. In its defence one can say that it is probably better than imposing an invalid common factor restriction (that is running a Cochrane–Orcutt type regression to obtain an estimate of m_y) and preserves the initial long-run maintained hypothesis given by economic theory. The weakness of this pragmatic approach is that the more complex lag structure may be merely providing a poor proxy for other variables that have been incorrectly omitted. (Outside sample forecast tests may provide some check on the latter possibility. If included lagged variables and excluded 'true' variables move differently outside of the sample period of estimation the estimated equation will forecast badly.)

A.3.2   *Autocorrelation as a simplification not a nuisance*

Most applied economists, before the appearance of a series of papers by Hendry and others (Hendry, 1979; Mizon, 1977; Mizon and Hendry, 1980) viewed autocorrelation as a nuisance; it required 'sophisticated' econometric techniques and left part of the model (that is the autocorrelation coefficient ρ) unexplained by economic factors. Hendry and co-workers argue that autocorrelation is not a nuisance but a 'convenient simplification' since it reduces the number of parameters to be estimated and hence increases the 'efficiency' of the parameter estimates. The Hendry thesis also provides a particular modelling strategy known as the 'general to specific' approach. (We shall return to the latter in a different guise when discussing 'reparameterization'.)

If we start with a general (autoregressive) distributed lag ADL model with M_t depending upon $M_{t-1}, \ldots, M_{t-j}, \ldots, Y, \ldots, Y_{t-j}$ then it is possible to simplify the model in two obvious ways. In the first stage we can sequentially drop higher order lags M_{t-j} and Y_{t-j} until statistical tests indicate we can go no further. Second, we can test for *error* autocorrelation (that is common factors). The latter reduces the number of lags on *each* variable by one at each stage, with a 'cost' in terms of estimating only one additional parameter ρ. We thus obtain more 'efficient' estimates of the remaining parameters; the gain in efficiency is greater the larger the number of *different* independent variables.

For example a maintained hypothesis with four lags in M and Y might be reduced in the first stage to three lags on these variables,[4] leaving seven parameters $b_0, \ldots, b_6$ (that is excluding the estimate of σ^2) to be estimated

$$M_t = b_0 Y_t + b_1 Y_{t-1} + b_2 Y_{t-2} + b_3 Y_{t-3} + b_4 M_{t-1} + b_5 M_{t-2}$$
$$+ b_6 M_{t-3} + u_t \tag{A.6}$$

However, if there are two common factors in the lag coefficients $b_0, \ldots, b_6$ the above model can be reduced to

$$M_t = a_0 Y_t + a_1 Y_{t-1} + a_2 M_{t-1} + u_t \tag{A.7}$$

$$u_t = \rho_1 u_{t-1} + \rho_2 u_{t-2} + \epsilon_t \quad (\epsilon_t \text{ is white noise}) \tag{A.8}$$

and we need only estimate five parameters ρ_1, ρ_2, a_0, a_1, a_2, rather than seven. Hence error autocorrelation is a 'convenient simplification'.[5]

Applied economists, as opposed to applied econometricians have been a little reluctant to embrace the second 'autocorrelation' stage of the above methodology. This is because, in general, 'economic theory' suggests that white noise errors are appropriate. Hence applied economists have often embraced (A.6) which has 'white noise' errors (and for which OLS provides consistent estimators as long as the independent variables are independent of the errors) rather than equations (A.7) and (A.8), which provide consistent *and* asymptotically efficient estimators.

This may not be too serious an aberration. The applied economist is trading off 'theory' (that is white noise errors) against statistical purity (that is consistent *and* asymptotically efficient estimators). Equation (A.7) provides a different lag response to that of equation (A.6). But if the freely estimated coefficients in the latter *closely* obey the common factor restrictions, the lag response will be very similar in the two equations.[6]

A.3.3   *Levels versus differences and autocorrelation*

There has been a rather fierce debate in the literature recently between the so-called 'time-series' modellers and 'econometric' modellers (Williams, 1978). The former argue that when the data in levels of the variables is highly trended (as in the case for many aggregate time series) the regression should be run on differenced variables only. Differencing of the variables induces a property known as stationarity in the data series. The normal statistical tests only apply if the error term is stationary. Obviously if only differenced variables are used we cannot obtain a solution for the levels of the variables, even though it is the latter on which economic theory usually provides testable a priori restrictions. There has been a counter-attack to this view recently, and, for example, Hendry and Mizon (1978) argue that (a) the difference model may be tested as a special case of the ADL model, and (b) the difference model may be interpreted as a common factor in the lag polynomial (that is error autocorrelation).

Consider, for example the ADL model

$$M_t = \phi_0 Y_t + \phi_1 Y_{t-1} + \gamma M_{t-1} + \epsilon_t \tag{A.9}$$

with ϵ_t white noise. We may 'reparameterize' this equation to yield the equivalent equation

$$\Delta M_t = \phi_0 \Delta Y_t + (\phi_0 + \phi_1) Y_{t-1} + (\gamma - 1) M_{t-1} + \epsilon_t \tag{A.10}$$

If the difference equation

$$\Delta M_t = \phi_0 \Delta Y_t + v_t \tag{A.11}$$

where v_t is white noise, is the true model then $\phi_0 + \phi_1 = \gamma - 1 = 0$ in equation (A.10). Furthermore if (A.11) is true and v_t is white noise then so is ϵ_t in (A.10) (since the coefficients on Y_{t-1} and M_{t-1} are both zero). Hence an F-test (or likelihood ratio test) of the joint hypothesis $\phi_0 + \phi_1 = \gamma - 1 = 0$ is a valid test for the difference model. The latter is thus a special case of the ADL model.

Consider now an alternative method of testing for a 'difference model'. A slightly different reparameterization of the ADL model (A.9) yields

$$(1 - \gamma L) M_t = \phi_0 \left[1 + \frac{\phi_0}{\phi_1} L \right] Y_t + \epsilon_t \tag{A.12}$$

If the difference model is the true model then $\phi_0 = -\phi_1$ and $\gamma = 1$, hence our ADL model reduces to

$$(1 - L) M_t = \phi_0 (1 - L) Y_t + \epsilon_t \tag{A.13}$$

From equation (A.13) we see that there is a common factor of $(1-L)$. Hence starting from the unrestricted ADL model (A.9), a test of the difference model is a test of the joint hypothesis (a) that there is a common factor (that is non-linear restriction) in the lag polynomial of the form $(1 - \rho L)$ and (b) that the common factor or autocorrelation coefficient ρ is unity. We are able to test both of these hypotheses sequentially and hence test the empirical validity of a difference formulation against the more general ADL model (A.9).

Both the above methods of testing the empirical validity of a difference formulation are equally valid and provide a further example of the 'general to specific' research methodology. A researcher who *starts* from an equation purely in differences of the variables would be unlikely to detect a long-run relationship between the levels of the variables as in (A.9) or equivalently (A.10). However, the reader should note that the approach outlined here is still a contentious issue (Williams, 1978).

A.3.4 *Summary*

If we begin our empirical investigation with a general autoregressive distributed lag ADL, equation (for example with a maximum lag of four periods using quarterly data), this has several advantages:

1 We start with an equation that is consistent with the long-run static equili-brium given by economic theory.
2 It allows us to drop insignificant high order lags and then test for common factors to produce more efficient parameter estimates.
3 It allows us to maintain the high order lags but with white noise errors thus allowing the use of OLS to produce consistent estimators of the parameters (we ignore other sources of inconsistent estimators here).
4 The high order ADL equation allows a flexible response of the dependent variable to changes in each independent variable and the response can be determined by the data, rather than imposed at the outset.
5 ADL allows us to minimize the possibility of omitted variables bias, due to omitted lagged variables.
6 The partial adjustment and adaptive expectations hypothesis can be obtained as special cases (that is are 'nested' within the general ADL model).

A researcher who has few a priori views about the lag response may therefore avoid several statistical pitfalls by starting with a general ADL model that yields a static long-run equilibrium solution consistent with economic theory and then sequentially simplifying the equation (that is 'testing down') by dropping insignificant high order lags or incorporating valid common factors. This 'general to specific approach', it is argued, avoids *imposing* untested and therefore possibly invalid restrictions on the lag response at the beginning of the estimation search. Not surprisingly perhaps, this modelling strategy has been adopted in a number of recent single equation empirical studies of asset demand functions which we reported in chapter 5. Finally, those who find this 'general to specific' methodology appealing may find a discussion of the method, applied to a *system* of equations (for UK Building Societies), given by Hendry and Anderson (1984).

A.4 ERRORS IN VARIABLES AND LAGGED ADJUSTMENT

'Errors in variables' may lead to instability in the coefficients of the demand for money and may also lead to an erroneous acceptance of lag effects. Errors in measuring the *independent* variables of an equation causes biased and inconsistent OLS parameter estimates (Koutsoyiannis, 1977; Grether and Madala, 1973).

If errors of measurement vary over time, then this may manifest itself in parameter instability. The latter is easily seen in the following simple model, where M_t is money balances and r_t^e is the expected return on bonds (including the expected capital gain)

$$M_t = -\beta r_t^e + u_t \tag{A.14}$$

Assume (A.14) is the true model but r^e is measured as the actual return r_t rather than the expected return. Assuming unbiased expectations

$$r_t = r_t^e + v_t \tag{A.15}$$

where v_t is a white noise measurement error (independent of u_t). Substituting (A.15) in (A.14), we have

$$M_t = -\beta r_t + \beta v_t + u_t = -\beta r_t + w_t \tag{A.16}$$

where $w_t = \beta v_t + u_t$. An OLS regression of M_t on r_t yields a biased estimate of β because r_t and w_t are correlated (as w_t depends on v_t which is correlated with r_t)

$$E\hat{\beta} = -\beta + E\left[\frac{\Sigma r_t w_t}{\Sigma r_t^2}\right] \tag{A.17}$$

Since $E[\cdot] \neq 0$, $\hat{\beta}$ is a biased (and inconsistent) estimator of the true parameter β. If the correlation between r_t and v_t varies over time, as, for example, when the authorities move from a policy of pegging interest rates, to one of controlling money supply by changes in r_t, then the OLS estimator $\hat{\beta}$ may appear to be unstable.

Consider now the possibility that 'errors in variables' may lead to acceptance of 'lag effects' when none are present in the true model. Suppose the measurement error v_t is autocorrelated, that is $v_t = \epsilon_t/(1 - \rho L)$ where ϵ_t is white noise. Repeating the above exercise where M_t reacts *instantaneously* to r_t^e and substituting for v_t in (A.16), we have

$$(1 - \rho L) M_t = -\beta[(1 - \rho L) r_t - \epsilon_t] + (1 - \rho L) u_t \tag{A.18}$$

$$M_t = -\beta r_t + \rho \beta r_{t-1} + \rho M_{t-1} + w_t' \tag{A.19}$$

where $w_t' = (\beta \epsilon_t + u_t - \rho u_{t-1})$. Hence the 'true' instantaneous adjustment model (A.14) plus an autocorrelated measurement error results in an equation that contains a lagged dependent variable and is consistent with an ADL or EFE (as r_t and r_{t-1} may be reparameterized as $-\beta \Delta r_t$ and $\beta(\rho - 1)r_{t-1}$). Estimation of equation (A.19) without the common factor restriction imposed may result in a lagged adjustment model being accepted, whereas the 'true' model contains no lagged adjustment of money to the *expected* return. Clearly, this highlights the need to model expectations carefully. Instrumental variables estimation could be applied to r_t^e in (A.14) to provide a consistent estimate of the true parameter β. However, in much applied work it is *assumed* that the interest rate rather than the *expected* return is the appropriate variable. In section 5.4 we discussed the above problem in terms of measurement error in data on financial wealth (Grice and Bennett, 1984).

A.5 GENERAL TO SPECIFIC MODELLING: REPARAMETERIZATION

Extraction of common factors (autocorrelated errors) simplifies an equation but an alternative simplification procedure frequently used is reparameterization (usually of an ADL model). One can reparameterize an equation in a vast number of equivalent ways but here we concentrate on the EFE, the partial adjustment, adaptive expectation, static and difference models, as ('nested') special cases of the ADL model. The reader might like to bear in mind that a reparameterized but *unrestricted* equation yields no new information about the dynamic and long-run properties of the initial ADL equation in the *levels* of the variables. One cannot get something for nothing. However, the reparameterized equation is often so arranged that 'hypotheses of interest' (for example unit income elasticity) may be more easily obtained. Of course if valid restrictions are imposed on either the reparameterized or ADL levels equations then a 'new' restricted model may emerge as superior to the initial unrestricted model.

We begin by reparameterizing a simple ADL model to yield an EFE. The ADL model in logarithms is

$$y_t = \gamma y_{t-1} + \alpha_0 x_t + \alpha_1 x_{t-1} + b + u_t \tag{A.20}$$

which may be reparameterized as follows

$$\Delta y_t = (\gamma - 1) y_{t-1} + \alpha_0 \Delta x_t + (\alpha_0 + \alpha_1) x_{t-1} + b + u_t$$

$$\Delta y_t = (\gamma - 1)(y_{t-1} - x_{t-1}) + \alpha_0 \Delta x_t + (\alpha_0 + \alpha_1 + \gamma - 1) x_{t-1} + b + u_t$$

$$\Delta y_t = c_0 (y - x)_{t-1} + c_1 \Delta x_t + c_2 x_{t-1} + b + u_t \tag{A.21}$$

Equation (A.21) is of the error feedback variety with the change in y depending upon the change in x, and an equilibrium error feedback term $(y - x)_{t-1}$. Estimates of c_0, c_1 and c_2, obtained from equation (A.21) may be solved to yield implicit estimates of γ, α_0, α_1 (for example $c_1 = \alpha_0$). The latter are exactly the same as those obtained by running regression (A.20) – as are the standard errors of the coefficients and the equation standard errors.

The long run static equilibrium solution for the ADL equation (A.20) is $y = [(\alpha_0 + \alpha_1)/(1 - \gamma)] x + b/(1 - \gamma)$. We now assert that a hypothesis of interest is that this elasticity is unity. This restriction may be tested by comparing the error sum of squares in the ADL equation with those in an equation with the restriction imposed and using an F or likelihood ratio statistic. However, an equivalent test is easily obtained using the reparameterized EFE. A unit elasticity implies $\alpha_0 + \alpha_1 = 1 - \gamma$ and hence $c_2 = 0$. A t-test on c_2 is sufficient to test the unit elasticity restriction. (Of course in this case $t^2 = F$, where F refers to the above F-test.) Similarly a test of a difference relationship is provided by a joint test $c_0 = c_2 = 0$ and requires an F-test using the EFE.[7] A test of the partial adjustment or adaptive expectations model (ignoring restrictions on the error terms) is most easily accomplished in the ADL model and is a t-test of $\alpha_1 = 0$; in the EFE (A.21) an F-test of $c_2 = c_0 + c_1$ is required.

The reader would be quite right in being sceptical of the usefulness of the EFE if its only advantage was in performing t-tests rather than the equivalent F-tests. Other advantages claimed for the EFE approach are as follows.

1 The sensitivity of the crucial static *'long-run'* parameters c_0 and c_2 to changes in the data period and addition of new variables are more easily 'eyeballed' in the EFE formulation.
2 In *small samples*, it appears that the OLS parameter estimates of the EFE may provide better estimates of the true structural parameters (in terms of a lower small sample bias) than the unrestricted ADL model. Davidson et al. (1978) provide Monte Carlo evidence on this for a simple EFE).
3 Error feedback equations are consistent with one period quadratic cost minimization 'models' of adjustment lags (section 4.2). In section 6.4.3 we show that the EFE may also be consistent with forward looking expectations models.
4 If one has a prior belief that the change in y depends upon the change in x (as well as other variables) then the EFE is a natural representation of this view. Compared with levels of trended variables y_{t-1}, x_t the terms in Δx_t are likely to be only weakly correlated with other incorrectly excluded variables. Hence the coefficient c_1 should be relatively free from omitted variables bias (recall that omitted variables bias is zero if included and excluded variables are uncorrelated with each other). The point estimate c_1 should therefore be more robust to specification changes than the coefficients of the 'levels variables' (for example $c_2 x_{t-1}$). In practice the t-statistics on 'difference terms' also tend to be relatively invariant to specification changes. But we cannot infer this a priori since the t-statistics alter with the standard error of the equation and the intercorrelations between *all* the independent variables.

It can be seen that the EFE utilizes the 'time series approach' by reparameterizing some variables as differences while also retaining the variables that determine the long run static equilibrium solution, namely $(y - x)_{t-1}$ and x_{t-1}.

One further point on estimation needs to be made. If the EFE contains a constant term (that is a column of 'ones') and the term $(y - x)_{t-1}$ does not vary greatly in the data, then the two series will be collinear and c_0 and b will have high standard errors. Davidson et al. (1978) point out that under such circumstances putting $b = 0$, will not (usually) affect the long-run equilibrium solution, whereas $c_0 = 0$ does so. Hence they suggest dropping the constant term, if anything, in these circumstances (Monte Carlo experiments also indicate that wrongly accepting H_0. $c_0 = 0$ may often occur in small samples (Davidson et al., 1978; Hendry and von Ungern Sternberg, 1983).

In a more general ADL model with longer lags $y_t = \beta(L) y_t + \alpha(L) x_t$, the type of reparameterizations and restrictions that occur are (a) dropping high order lags; (b) 'smoothing', that is if a subset of coefficients are equal, the variables are reparameterized as $\alpha(x_t + x_{t-1} + x_{t-2})$ etc; (c) differencing, that is if a subset of coefficients sum to zero, the variables are reparameterized as a difference; for example if for the set of variables $\alpha_0 x_t + \alpha_1 x_{t-1} + \alpha_2 x_{t-2}$ we have $\alpha_0 + \alpha_1 + \alpha_2 = 0$, this may be reparameterized as $\gamma_0 \Delta x_t + \gamma_1 \Delta x_{t-1}$; (d) a unit elasticity involves a reparameterization as $\Delta y = \delta (y - x)_{t-j}$ and terms in $\Delta y_{t-j}, \Delta x_{t-j}$ but *no* terms in the 'levels' of the variables.

The reparameterizations in (b) and (c) may be repeated. For example $\gamma_0 \Delta x_t + \gamma_1 \Delta x_{t-1}$ may be rewritten equivalently as $\lambda_0(\Delta x_t - \Delta x_{t-1}) + \lambda_1 \Delta x_{t-1}$ where $\lambda_0 = \gamma_0$ and $\lambda_1 = (\gamma_0 + \gamma_1)$. If $\gamma_0 + \gamma_1 = 0$ then we can accept the restriction that only the acceleration in x is statistically significant (that is the term $\lambda_0(\Delta x_t - \Delta x_{t-1})$).

These reparameterizations allow restrictions on parameters to be easily tested and may reduce the number of parameters to be estimated; there is a trade-off between increased efficiency of the estimators and possible omitted variables bias. The restrictions are tested sequentially and the final equation is a data acceptable simplification of the maintained hypothesis.[4]

In practical applications of the ADL 'general to specific' methodology, the initial ADL equation is chosen to be as unrestricted as possible. However, with a limited data set the so-called unrestricted equation will usually contain some restrictions (for example potentially important variables omitted). After 'testing down', these restrictions may be released, for example, by adding 'new' variables as more degrees of freedom are then available. This destroys the purity of the testing down procedure (and the calculation of the overall significance level of the test) but non-nested tests (Davidson and MacKinnon, 1981) are available to compare the different models that ensue.

A.5.2 *Static and dynamic equilibrium*

The ADL equation and its special cases (for example EFE, partial adjustment) may be solved for the static and dynamic equilibrium. The former is usually expected to be consistent with the economic theory that underlies the equation. However, economic theory rarely gives any indication about the appropriate relationship between the *level* of the variable of interest (for example real money balances) and the *rate of growth* of the independent variables (for example the rate of growth in real income). It has been noted that 'growth effects' in estimated ADL–EFE equations may be quite large (see section 5.2) and should be subject to statistical tests. We deal with two issues here: (a) the calculation of growth equilibria, and (b) statistical tests for zero growth effects. We arbitrarily choose to solve the unrestricted EFE (A.21) but the method can easily be applied to the ADL equation (A.20) to yield the same answer.

For our first-order difference equation (A.21) to be dynamically stable we require $|1 + c_0| < 1$ or $-2 < c_0 < 0$; hence c_0 is negative. In *static* equilibrium all growth terms are zero by definition and (A.21) gives

$$0 = c_0(y - x) + c_2 x + b \tag{A.22}$$

$$y = \left(\frac{c_0 - c_2}{c_0}\right) x - \frac{b}{c_0} \tag{A.23}$$

Hence the EFE has an elasticity with respect to x that is greater than, equal to or less than unity depending upon whether c_2 is greater than, equal to or less than zero.

In a 'dynamic equilibrium' where y grows at a constant rate g, we have $y_t = y_{t-j} + jg$, and similarly for x if it grows at a rate g_1. Substituting these expressions in the EFE (note that $\Delta x_{t-j} = g_1$ for all j) and rearranging we obtain

$$c_0 y_t = (c_0 - c_2) x_t + g(1 + c_0) - g_1(c_0 + c_1 - c_2) - b \tag{A.24}$$

Differencing (A.23) or (A.24) and noting that $\Delta g = 0$ we obtain

$$g = ((c_0 - c_2)/c_0) g_1$$

and substituting this in (A.24) we obtain after some further manipulation

$$y_t = \frac{c_0 - c_2}{c_0} x_t + \frac{c_0(1 - c_1) - c_2}{c_0^2} g_1 - \frac{b}{c_0} \tag{A.25}$$

Thus, in general, the relationship between y and x depends on the rate of growth in x.

An interesting special case of (A.25) occurs when there is a unit elasticity in static equilibrium between y and x, that is $c_2 = 0$, and

$$y_t - x_t = g_1 \frac{1 - c_1}{c_0} - \frac{b}{c_0} \tag{A.26}$$

Now c_0 must be negative in order that the first order difference equation (A.21) in y be dynamically stable. Therefore if c_1 is less than unity the ratio Y/X (or in logarithms, $y - x$) depends negatively on the rate of growth in X. For example if Y is real money balances and X is real income then the money–income ratio is lower, the higher the rate of growth in real income. A negative growth effect occurs when the impact effect of x_t, that is c_1, is *less than* the long-run effect of unity. Such undershooting also gives rise to a negative growth effect in the more general equation (A.21).

Negative growth effects may also occur in more general ADL equations. For example in the unrestricted EFE (A.21) a non-zero growth effect occurs unless $c_2 = c_0(1 - c_1)$, as may be seen from (A.25).

Although our economic theories usually give no indication of the dynamic relationship between variables, some might find these growth effects implausible.

It is worth noting that negative growth effects are nothing more than the 'persistent underprediction' noted in section 4.2 in connection with the partial adjustment model. Both are manifestations of the same phenomenon, namely monotonic adjustment in first order difference equations.

In principle we can test for the presence of growth effects quite easily. For example in the ADL-EFE equation (A.21) we noted that a zero growth effect requires the non-linear restriction $c_2 = c_0(1 - c_1)$ to hold. A comparison of the residual sum of squares RSS in the unrestricted ADL-EFE equation (A.21) with the RSS from an equation with the restriction imposed (using an F or LR statistic) provides a valid test procedure.

We may be able to accept the hypothesis of zero growth effects. Alternatively if we accept the unrestricted ADL-EFE (A.21) as the true model then we must also accept the implicit growth effects. However, even in the latter case we may take the view that algebraically solving the estimated equation under a constant rate of growth assumption is likely to yield 'unrealistic' results since the data set on which the equation is estimated is vastly different (see also, section 4.4.3). Here we are eschewing the possibility of constant parameters under a constant rate of growth assumption. This is a form of Lucas critique.

A.5.1 *Summary*

Beginning one's empirical investigation with an unrestricted ADL model reduces the possibility of 'omitted variables bias' due to the omission of lagged variables. It also tends to remove any residual serial correlation. Reparameterization of the unrestricted ADL model into sensible decision variables may allow certain hypotheses of interest to be easily tested. Differenced variables are likely to have robust parameter estimates since such variables are usually not highly correlated with other included and possible omitted (relevant) variables. 'Growth effects' may be easily tested in this framework. There is some, as yet rather weak, evidence that the EF approach may provide a slightly increased probability of correctly identifying the 'long-run' relationship between variables.

A.6 CONCLUSIONS

We have found that some recent themes in the econometrics literature are interconnected. Serial correlation in the residuals of a regression in the levels of trended variables is indicative of a spurious relationship. Correction for error autocorrelation requires a test of the implicit common factor restriction(s) before an assessment of the statistical properties of the parameters can be entertained. The question of the choice between an equation purely in differences of the variables and an equation containing some 'levels' variables may be tested using the common factor approach to autocorrelation. Alternatively an unrestricted ADL equation which is reparameterized into levels and difference terms may provide a direct test of the validity of a purely 'differenced relationship'.

Although not a panacea, there are advantages in beginning an empirical investigation with an unrestricted ADL equation if one has only weak priors concerning lag responses. One can then sequentially simplify the equation to produce a parsimonious equation that is consistent with the equilibrium theory. This 'general to specific' modelling strategy may be implemented either by extracting common factors or by simplifying the equation using sensible reparameterizations of the variables.

NOTES

1 To demonstrate this in the simplest case, Granger and Newbold (1974) *generate* two independent data series

$$Y_t = a_0 + a_1 Y_{t-1} + v_t \qquad (1)$$

and

$$X_t = b_0 + b_1 X_{t-1} + w_t \qquad (2)$$

where a_0, a_1, b_0, b_1 are chosen by the researcher (e.g. $a_0 = b_0 = 0, a_1 = b_1 = 1$; independent random walks). v_t and w_t are then drawn successively from two 'tables' of *independent* random numbers. With starting values Y_0 and X_0 and a series of random drawings v_t and w_t, two artificial and (independent) data series Y_t and X_t are constructed using (1) and (2). These are then used in a regression $Y_t = a + bX_t$. This may be repeated for different data sets generated using 'new' v_t and w_t values, giving a distribution of values for $\hat{a}, \hat{b}, \bar{R}^2$, etc. This is a Monte Carlo experiment.

2 The autoregressive part of the ARMA error model will again imply implicit non-linear restrictions. A purely moving average error added to the structural equation does not involve 'common factors'.

3 This procedure does not guarantee the removal of residual serial correlation as the latter may be caused by a complex ARMA model which cannot be adequately proxied by lagged values alone. For similar reasons additional lagged variables (or some subset of them) may not improve the 'fit' of the equation, however, in practice some improvement in 'fit' often results.

4 If the significance level of each individual restriction is ϵ then the significance level for the set of k restrictions is $(1 - \epsilon)^k$ at most (Mizon and Hendry, 1980).

5 The greater the number of different independent variables the greater the 'efficiency' gain from error autocorrelation. For example if equation (A.6) also contained terms in the current period and three lags of wealth W, then equation (A.7) would only contain W_t and W_{t-1}. There is an *additional* efficiency gain in not having to estimate the coefficients on W_{t-2}, W_{t-3}.

6 We can demonstrate this with our simple instantaneous adjustment model. Suppose the true model is

$$M_t = c_1 Y_t + \frac{\epsilon_t}{1 - \rho L} \qquad (3)$$

but the applied researcher accepts the *unrestricted* model

$$M_t = c_0 M_{t-1} + c_1 Y_t + c_2 Y_{t-1} \qquad (4)$$

The response of M_t to a unit step change in Y_t is c_1 in period t. In period $t+1$

$$\Delta M_{t+1} = c_0 \Delta M_t + c_1 \Delta Y_{t+1} + c_2 \Delta Y_t = c_0 c_1 + c_2$$

However, if (3) is the true model, we know that $c_2 = -c_0 c_1$ and therefore $\Delta M_{t+1} \approx 0$ in equation (4). The true model (3) (implicitly) *imposes* the restriction, and $\Delta M_{t+1} = 0$ always. In equation (4) the restriction is not *imposed* but should hold approximately if (3) is true; the closer the approximation the closer is the time response of (4) to that in the 'instantaneous' true model. A word of warning: if c_0 is close to unity as is usually the case, and c_1 and c_2 are poorly determined, the *estimates* of the c_i in equation (4) may give an incorrect *lag* response of M to a change in Y.

7   This is also equivalent to a test of a common factor ρ with a unit root.

References

Akerlof, G. A. (1970) The market for lemons: qualitative uncertainty and the market mechanism. *Quarterly Journal of Economics*, **84**, 488–500.

Akerlof, G. A. (1979) Irving Fisher on his head: the consequences of constant target-threshold monitoring of money holdings. *Quarterly Journal of Economics*, May, 169–8.

Akerlof, G. A. and Milbourne, D. (1980) The short-run demand for money. *Economic Journal*, **90** (360), 885–900.

Anderson, G. J. and Blundell, R. W. (1982) Estimation and hypothesis testing in dynamic singular equation systems. *Econometrica*, **50** (6), 1559–71.

Arango, S. and Nadiri, M. I. (1981) Demand for money in open economies. *Journal of Monetary Economics*, **7** (1), 69–83.

Artis, M. J. (1978) Monetary policy – part II. In F. Blackaby (ed.), *British Economic Policy 1960-74*. Cambridge: Cambridge University Press.

Artis, M. J. (1984) *Macroeconomics*, Oxford, Oxford University Press.

Artis, M. J. and Currie, D. A. (1981) Monetary targets and the exchange rate: a case for conditional targets. In W. Eltis and P. N. Sinclair (eds), The Money Supply and the Exchange Rate, *Oxford Economic Papers, Special Supplement*, **33**, July.

Artis, M. J. and Cuthbertson, K. (1985) The demand for M1: a forward looking buffer stock model, National Institute of Economic and Social Research, Discussion Paper.

Artis, M. J. and Lewis, M. K. (1976) The demand for money in the UK 1963-73. *The Manchester School*, **44**, 147–81.

Artis, M. J. and Lewis, M. K. (1981) *Monetary Control in the UK*. Oxford: Philip Allan.

Artis, M. J. and Lewis, M. K. (1984) How unstable is the demand for money in the United Kingdom? *Economica*, **51**, 473–6.

Axilrod, S. H. (1982) Monetary policy, money supply and the Federal Reserve's operating procedures. *Federal Reserve Bulletin*, January, 13–24.

Azariadis, C. (1975) Implicit contracts and underemployment equilibria. *Journal of Political Economy*, **83**, 1183–201.

Backus, D. K. and Driffill, E. J. (1985) Inflation and reputation. American Economic Review, forthcoming.

Baltensperger, E. (1972) Economies of scale, firm size and concentration in banking. *Journal of Money, Credit and Banking*, **4** (3), 467–88.

Baltensperger, E. (1980) Alternative approaches to the theory of the banking firm. *Journal of Monetary Economics*, **6**, 1–37.

Bank of England (1980) Methods of monetary control. *Bank of England Quarterly Bulletin*, **20** (4), 428–29.

Bank of England (1981a) *Bank of England Quarterly Bulletin*, **21** (3), 326–38.

Bank of England (1981b) Monetary control – provisions. *Bank of England Quarterly Bulletin*, **21** (3), 347–50.

Bank of England (1982a) The role of the Bank of England in the money market. *Bank of England Quarterly Bulletin*, **22** (1), 86–94.

Bank of England (1982b) The supplementary special deposits scheme. *Bank of England Quarterly Bulletin*, **22** (1), 74–85.

Bank of England (1983) The nature and implications of financial innovation. *Bank of England Quarterly Bulletin*, **23** (3), 358–76.

Bank of England (1984) *Bank of England Quarterly Bulletin*,

Barnett, W. A., Offenbacher, E. K. and Spindt, P. A. (1984). The new Divisia monetary aggregates. *Journal of Political Economy*, **92** (6), 1049–85.

Barratt, C. R. and Walters, A. A. (1966) The stability of Keynesian and money multipliers in the UK. *Review of Economics and Statistics*, **48**, 395–405.

Barro, R. J. (1970) Inflation, the payments period and the demand for money. *Journal of Political Economy*, **78** (6), 1228–63.

Barro, R. J. (1974) Are government bonds net wealth? *Journal of Political Economy*, **82**, 1095–117.

Barro, R. J. (1976) Integral constraints and aggregation in an inventory model of money demand. *Journal of Finance*, **31** (1), 77–88.

Barro, R. J. and Fischer, S. (1976) Recent developments in monetary theory. *Journal of Monetary Economics*, **2**, 133–67.

Barro, R. J. and Santomero, A. J. (1972) Household money holdings and the demand deposit rate. *Journal of Money, Credit and Banking*, **4**, 397–413.

Batchelor, R. (1981) Aggregate expectations under stable laws. *Journal of Econometrics*, **16**, 199–210.

Batten, D. S. and Thornton, D. L. (1984) How robust are the policy conclusions of the St Louis equation? Some further evidence. *Federal Reserve Bank of St Louis Review*, **66** (6), 26–31.

Baumol, W. J. (1952) The transactions demand for cash: an inventory theoretic approach. *Quarterly Journal of Economics*, **66**, 545–56.

Bean, C. R. (1978) The determination of consumers' expenditure in the UK. *Government Economic Service Working Paper*, 4.

Begg, D. K. H. (1982) *The Rational Expectations Revolution in Macroeconomics: Theories and Evidence*, Philip Allan, Oxford.

Begg, D. K. H. (1982) Rational expectations, wage rigidity and involuntary unemployment. A particular theory, *Oxford Economic Papers*, **34** (2), 23–47.

Begg, D. K. H. (1984) Rational expectations and bond pricing: modelling the term structure with and without certainty equivalence. *Economic Journal Supplement*, Conference Papers, **94**, 45–57.

Berndt, E. R., McCurdy, T. H. and Rose, D. E. (1980) On testing theories of financial intermediary portfolio selection. *Review of Economic Studies*, **47**, 861–73.

Bewley, R. A. (1981) The portfolio behaviour of the London clearing banks 1963–71. *Manchester School*, 191–210.

Bilson, J. F. O. (1978) The monetary approach to the exchange rate: some empirical evidence. *IMF Staff Papers*, **25** (1), 48–75.

Blanchard, O. J. (1981) Output, the stock market and interest rates. *American Economic Review*, **71**, 132–43.

Blanchard, O. J. and Summers, L. H. (1984) Perspectives on high world real interest rates. *Brookings Papers on Economic Activity*, **2**, 273–324.

Blinder, A. S. and Solow, R. (1973) Does fiscal policy matter? *Journal of Public Economics*, **2**, 319–37.

Blundell-Wignall, A., Rondoni, M. and Ziegelschmidt, H. (1984). The demand for money and velocity in major OECD countries. *OECD Economics and Statistics Department, Working paper*, No. 13, February.

Boughton, J. M. (1979) Demand for money in the major OECD countries. *OECD Economic Outlook, Occasional Studies*, January.

Boughton, J. M. (1981) Recent instability of the demand for money: an international perspective. *Southern Economic Journal*, 47 (3), 579–97.

Bowden, R. (1978) Specification, estimation and inference for models of markets in disequilibrium. *International Economic Review*, 19, 711–26.

Box, G. E. P. and Pierce, D. A. (1970) Distribution of residual autocorrelations in autoregressive-integrated moving average time series models. *Journal of the American Statistical Association*, 65, 1509–26.

Brainard, W. C. and Tobin, J. (1968) Econometric models: their problems and usefulness: pitfalls in financial model building. *American Economic Review*, 58, 2.

Bronfenbrenner, M. and Mayer, T. (1960) Liquidity functions in the American economy. *Econometrica*, 28, 810–34.

Brooks, S., Cuthbertson, K. and Mayes, D. (1985) *The Exchange Rate Environment*. London: Croom Helm, to be published.

Brunner, K. and Meltzer, A. H. (1964) Some further evidence on supply and demand functions for money. *Journal of Finance*, 19, 240–83.

Brunner, K. and Meltzer, A. H. (1972) Friedman's monetary theory. *Journal of Political Economy*, 80, 951–77.

Brunner, K. and Meltzer, A. (1976) An aggregative theory for a closed economy. In J. L. Stein (ed.), *Monetarism*, Amsterdam: North Holland, 60–103.

Bryant, R. C. (1983) *Controlling Money: the Federal Reserve and its critics*, Washington D.C., Brookings Institution.

Buiter, W. H. (1980) Monetary, financial and fiscal policies under rational expectations. *IMF Staff Papers*, 27 (4), 785–813.

Buiter, W. H. (1981) The superiority of contingent rules over fixed rules in models with rational expectations. *Economic Journal*, 91, 647–70.

Buiter, W. H. and Armstrong, C. A. (1978) A didactic note on the transactions demand for money and behaviour towards risk. *Journal of Money, Credit and Banking*, 10 (4), 529–38.

Buiter, W. H. and Tobin, J. (1979) Debt neutrality: a brief review of doctrine and evidence, in G. M. von Furstenberg (ed.), *Social Security versus Private Savings*, Cambridge, Mass.

Buse, A. (1975) Testing a simple portfolio model of interest rates. *Oxford Economic Papers*, 27, 82–94.

Callier, P. (1983) Eurobanks and liquidity creation: a broader perspective. *Weltwirtschaftliches Archiv*, 119 (2), 314–25.

Carlson, J. A. and Parkin, J. M. (1975) Inflation expectations. *Economica*, 42, 123–38.

Carr, J. and Darby, M. J. (1981) The role of money supply shocks in the short-run demand for money. *Journal of Monetary Economics*, 8 (2), 183–200.

Chang, W. W., Hamberg, D. and Hirata, J. (1983) Liquidity preference as behaviour toward risk in a demand for short term securities – not money. *American Economic Review*, 73, 420–7.

Chang, W. W., Hamberg, D. and Hirata, J. (1984) On liquidity preference – again: reply. *American Economic Review*, 74 (4), 812–13.

Choudry, N. N. (1976) Integration of fiscal and monetary sectors in econometric models: a survey of theoretical issues and empirical findings. *IMF Staff Papers*, 23 (2), 395–440.

Chow, G. C. (1984) *Econometrics*, London, McGraw-Hill.

Christofides, L. N. (1976) Quadratic costs and multi-asset partial adjustment equations. *Applied Economics*, 8, 4.

Christofides, L. N. (1980) An empirical analysis of bond markets and their implications for the term structure of interest rates. *Manchester School*, June, 111–24.

Cooley, T. and LeRoy, S. (1981) Identification and estimation of money demand. *American Economic Review*, 71, 825–44.

Cooley, T. F. and Prescott, E. C. (1973) Systematic variation models varying parameter regression: a theory and some applications, *Annals of Economic and Social Measurement*, 4, 463–73.

Courakis, A. S. (1975) Testing theories of Discount House portfolio selection. *Review of Economic Studies*, 42, 643–8.

Cross, R. (1982) The Duhem–Quine thesis, Lakatos and the appraisal of theories in macroeconomics. *Economic Journal*, 92, 320–40.

Cuddington, J. T. (1983) Currency substitution, capital mobility and money demand. *Journal of International Money and Finance*, 2 (2), 111–35.

Cuddington, J. T., Johansson, P. O. and Lofgren, K. G. (1984) *Disequilibrium Macroeconomics in Open Economies*, Oxford: Basil Blackwell.

Cummins, J. D. and Outreville, J. F. (1984) The portfolio behaviour of pension funds in the US: an econometric analysis of changes since the new regulation of 1974. *Applied Economics*, 16, 687–701.

Currie, D. (1981) Some long-run features of dynamic time series models. *Economic Journal*, 91, 714–15.

Currie, D. (1982) The long-run properties of the Bank of England's small model of the UK economy. *Applied Economics*, 14, 63–72.

Cuthbertson, K. (1983) The monetary sector. In A Britton (ed.), *Output Inflation and Employment*, London, Heinemann.

Cuthbertson, K. (1985a) Bank lending to UK industrial and commercial companies. *Oxford Bulletin of Economics and Statistics*, 42 (2), 91–118.

Cuthbertson, K. (1985b) Monetary anticipations and the demand for money. National Intitute of Economic and Social Research, Discussion Paper.

Cuthbertson, K. (1985c) Price expectations and lags in the demand for money. *Scottish Journal of Political Economy*, to be published.

Cuthbertson, K. and Foster, N. (1982) Bank lending to industrial and commercial companies in three models of the UK economy. *National Institute Economic Review*, 102, 63–77.

Cuthbertson, K. and Taylor, M. P. (1985a) Monetary anticipations and the demand for money: results for the UK using the Kalman filter, National Institute of Economic and Social Research Discussion Paper.

Cuthbertson, K. and Taylor, M. P. (1985b) A forward looking buffer stock model of the demand for M1: results for the UK using the Kalman filter, National Institute of Economic and Social Research, Discussion Paper.

Darby, M. R. (1972) The allocation of transitory income among consumer assets. *American Economic Review*, 62, 928–41.

Davidson, J. (1984) Money disequilibrium: an approach to modelling monetary phenomena in the UK. London School of Economics, mimeo.

Davidson, J. E. H., Hendry, D. F., Srba, F. and Yeo, S. (1978) Econometric modelling of the aggregate time series relationship between consumers' expenditure and income in the UK. *Economic Journal*, 88 (4), 661–91.

Davidson, R. and MacKinnon, J. G. (1981) Several tests for model specification in the presence of alternative hypotheses. *Econometrica*, 49 (3), 781–93.

Davidson, R. and MacKinnon, J. G. Some non-nested hypothesis tests and the relations among them. *Review of Economic Studies*, XLIX, 551–65.

Deaton, A. and Muellbauer, J. (1980) *Economics and Consumer Behaviour.* Cambridge: Cambridge University Press.

Desai, M. (1981) *Testing Monetarism*, London: F. Pinter.

Dornbusch, R. (1976) Expectations and exchange rate dynamics. *Journal of Political Economy*, **84** (6), 1161–76.

Driscoll, M. J. and Ford, J. L. (1980) The stability of the demand for money function and the predictability of the effects of monetary policy. *Economic Journal*, **90** (360), 867–84.

Duck, N. W. and Sheppard, D. K. (1978) A proposal for the control of the UK money supply. *Economic Journal*, **88**, 1–17.

Engle, R. F., Lilien, D. M. and Robins, R. P. (1983) Estimating time varying risk premia in the term structure. University of California, San Diego, Discussion Paper.

Evans, N. E. and Savin, G. B. A. (1981) Testing for unit roots: I. *Econometrica*, **49**, 753–77.

Fair, R. C. (1979) An analysis of a macroeconometric model with rational expectations in the bond and stock markets. *American Economic Review*, **69**, 539–52.

Fair, R. C. and Jaffe, D. M. (1972) Methods of estimation for markets in disequilibria. *Econometrica*, **40** (3), 497–514.

Fama, E. F. (1985) What's different about banks? *Journal of Monetary Economics*, **15** (1), 29–39.

Federal Reserve Bank of St Louis (1984) *Financial Innovations*, Boston: Kluwer Nijhoft.

Feige, E. (1967) Expectations and adjustments in the monetary sector. *American Economic Review*, **57**, 462–73.

Feige, E. L. and Parkin, J. M. (1971) The optimal quantity of money bonds, commodity inventories and capital. *American Economic Review*, **61** (3), 335–49.

Feige, E. and Pierce, D. K. (1976) Economically rational price expectations. *Journal of Political Economy*, **84** (3), 499–522.

Figlewski, S. and Wachtel, P. (1981) The formation of inflationary expectations. *Review of Economics and Statistics*, **58**, 1–10.

Fisher, I. (1911) *The Purchasing Power of Money*, New York: Macmillan.

Fleming, J. M. (1962) Domestic financial policies under fixed and under floating exchange rates. *International Monetary Fund Staff Papers*, **9**, 369–79.

Flemming, J. S. (1973) The consumption function when capital markets are imperfect: the permanent income hypothesis reconsidered. *Oxford Economic Papers*, **25**, 160–72.

Flemming, J. S. (1976) *Inflation*, Oxford: Oxford University Press.

Foster, J. and Gregory, M. (1977) Inflationary expectations: the use of qualitative survey data. *Applied Economics*, **9** (4), 319–29.

Frenkel, J. A. and Rodriguez, C. A. (1982) Exchange rate dynamics and the overshooting hypothesis. *IMF Staff Papers*, **29** (1), 1–30.

Fried, J. and Howitt, P. (1980) Credit rationing and implicit contract theory. *Journal of Money, Credit and Banking*, **12** (3), 471–87.

Friedman, B. M. (1977) Financial flow variables and the short-run determination of long-term interest rates. *Journal of Political Economy*, **85** (4), 661–89.

Friedman, B. M. (1979) Substitution and expectation effects on long-term borrowing behaviour and long-term interest rates. *Journal of Money, Credit and Banking,* **11** (2), 131–50.

Friedman, B. M. (1980a) Survey evidence on the rationality of interest rate expectations. *Journal of Monetary Economics,* **6** (4), 453–466.

Friedman, B. M. (1980b) Price inflation, portfolio choice and nominal interest rates. *American Economic Review,* **70** (1), 32–48.

Friedman, B. M. and Roley, V. V. (1979a) A note on the derivation of linear homogeneous asset demand function. *Harvard University, Discussion Paper,* 703, April.

Friedman, B. M. and Roley, V. V. (1979b) Investors' portfolio behaviour under alternative models of long-term interest rate expectations: unitary, rational or autoregressive. *Econometrica,* **47** (6), 1475–97.

Friedman, M. (1956) The quantity theory of money: a restatement. In M. Friedman (ed.), *Studies in the Quantity Theory of Money,* Chicago: University of Chicago Press.

Friedman, M. (1968) The role of monetary policy. *American Economic Review,* **58**, 1–17.

Friedman, M. (1980) *Memoranda on Monetary Control,* Treasury and Civil Service Committee, session 1979–80, vol. 1, HC720, London, HMSO.

Friedman, M. and Schwartz, A. J. (1982) *Monetary Trends in the United States and the United Kingdom: Their Relationship to Income, Prices and Interest Rates 1867–1975,* Chicago, University of Chicago Press.

Gambs, C. M. (1977) Money – a changing concept in a changing world. *Federal Reserve Bank of Kansas City Review,* January.

Godfrey, L. G. (1978a) Testing for higher order serial correlation when the regressors include lagged dependent variables. *Econometrica,* **46** (6), 1303–10.

Godfrey, L. G. (1978b) Testing against general autoregressive and moving average error models when the regressors include lagged dependent variables. *Econometrica,* **46** (6), 1293–1302.

Goldfeld, S. M. (1973) The demand for money revisited. *Brookings Papers on Economic Activity,* **3**, 577–638.

Goldfeld, S. M. (1976) The case of the missing money. *Brookings Papers on Economic Activity,* **3**, 683–730.

Goodhart, C. A. E. (1984) *Monetary Theory and Practice: The UK Experience,* London: Macmillan.

Goodhart, C. A. E., Gowland, D. and Williams, D. (1976) Money, income and causality: the UK experience. *American Economic Review,* **66**, 417–23.

Gordon, R. J. (1984) The short-run demand for money: a reconsideration. *Journal of Money Credit and Banking,* XVI, 4, 403–34.

Granger, C. W. J. (1966) The typical spectral shape of an economic variable. *Econometrica,* **34** (1), 150–61.

Granger, C. W. J. (1983) Co-integrability of economic time series and the error correction mechanism. University of California Discussion Paper.

Granger, C. W. J. and Newbold, P. (1974) Spurious regressions in econometrics. *Journal of Econometrics,* **12** (2), 111–20.

Granger, C. W. J. and Newbold, P. (1977) *Forecasting Economic Time Series,* London: Academic Press.

Grether, D. M. and Maddala, G. S. (1973) Errors in variables and serially correlated disturbances in distributed lag models. *Econometrica,* **41** (2), 225–62.

Grice, J. and Bennett, A. (1984) Wealth and the demand for £M3 in the United Kingdom 1963–1978. *Manchester School,* **52** (3), 239–71.

Griffiths, B. (1979) The reform of monetary control in the United Kingdom. *Annual Monetary Review no. 1,* October, Centre for Banking and International Finance, The City University.

Griffiths, B. (1980) Base control: the next steps. *Annual Monetary Review no. 2*, December, Centre for Banking and International Finance, The City University.

Grossman, H. I. and Policano, A. J. (1975) Money balances, commodity inventories and inflationary expectations. *Journal of Political Economy*, **83** (6), 1093–1112.

Gurley, J. G. and Shaw, E. S. (1960) *Money in a Theory of Finance*, Washington: Brookings Institution.

Haache, G. (1974) The demand for money in the UK: experience since 1971. *Bank of England Quarterly Bulletin*, **14** (3), 284–305.

Hafer, R. W. and Hein, S. E. (1979) Evidence on the temporal stability of the demand for money relationship in the United States. *Federal Reserve Bank of St Louis Review*, **61** (2), 3–14.

Hall, S. G., Henry, S. G. B. and Wren-Lewis, S. (1984) Manufacturing stocks and forward looking expectations in the UK. *National Institute of Economic and Social Research, Discussion Paper*, 64.

Hamberger, M. J. (1966) The demand for money by households, money substitutes and monetary policy. *Journal of Political Economy*, **74**, 600–23.

Hamberger, M. J. (1977) The demand for money in an open economy: Germany and the UK. *Journal of Monetary Economics*, **3** (1), 25–40.

Hamberger, M. J. (1980) The demand for money in the United States: a comment. In K. Brunner and A. Meltzer (eds), *On the State of Macroeconomics*, Carnegie Rochester Conference Series, 12, 273–85.

Hansen, L. P. and Sargent, T. J. (1982) Instrumental variables procedures for estimating linear rational expectations models. *Journal of Monetary Economics*, **9**, 263–96.

Harvey, A. C. (1981) *The Econometric Analysis of Time Series*, Oxford: Philip Allan.

Hendry, D. and Mizon, G. (1978) Serial correlation as a convenient simplification, not a nuisance: a comment on a study of the demand for money by the Bank of England. *Economic Journal*, **88**, 549–563.

Hendry, D. F. (1977) On the time series approach to econometric model building. In C. A. Sims (ed.), *New Methods in Business Cycle Research*, Federal Reserve Bank of Minneapolis.

Hendry, D. F. (1979) Predictive failure and econometric modelling in macroeconomics: the transactions demand for money. In P. Ormerod (ed.), *Economic Modelling*, London: Heinemann.

Hayashi, F. and Sims, C. (1983) Nearly efficient estimation of time series models with predetermined but not exogenous instruments. *Econometrica*, **51** (3), 783–98.

Hendry, D. F. (1983) Econometric modelling: the consumption function in retrospect. *Scottish Journal of Political Economy*, **30** (3), 193–220.

Hendry, D. F. and Anderson, G. (1984) An econometric model of United Kingdom Building Societies. *Oxford Bulletin of Economics and Statistics*, **46** (3), 185–210.

Hendry, D. F. and Ericsson, N. R. (1983) Assertion without empirical basis: an econometric appraisal of Friedman and Schwartz' 'Monetary trends in ... the United Kingdom'. *Bank of England, Panel of Academic Consultants, Panel Paper*, No. 22, October.

Hendry, D. F. and Richard, J. F. (1982) On the formulation of empirical models in dynamic econometrics. *Journal of Econometrics*, **20**, 3–33.

Hendry, D. F. and von Ungern Sternberg, T. (1983) Liquidity and inflation effects on consumers' expenditure. In A. Deaton (ed.), *Essays in the Theory and Measurement of Consumers' Behaviour*,

Hendry, D. F., Pagan, A. R. and Sargan, J. D. (1984) Dynamic specification. In Z. Griliches and M. Intrilligator (eds), *Handbook of Econometrics*, vol. 2, Amsterdam, North Holland.

Hesselman, L. (1983) The macroeconomic role of relative price variability in the USA and the UK. *Applied Economics*, 15 (2), 225–33.

Hewson, J. and Sakakibara, E. (1976) A general equilibrium approach to the Eurodollar market. *Journal of Money, Credit and Banking*, 8 (3), 297–323.

Hey, J. D. (1979) *Uncertainty in Microeconomics*, Oxford: Martin Robertson.

Hicks, J. R. (1939) *Value and Capital*, Oxford: Clarendon Press.

Hilliard, B. C. (1980) The Bank of England, small monetary model: recent developments and simulation properties. *Bank of England, Discussion Paper*, 13, November.

Holly, S. (1980) The role of expectations in the determination of the maturity structure of the supply of bonds. *London Business School, Economic Forecasting Unit, Discussion Paper*, 82.

Holly, S. and Longbottom, A. (1982) The empirical relationship between the money stock and the price level in the United Kingdom. *Bulletin of Economic Research*, 34 (1), 17–42.

Honohan, P. (1980) Testing a standard theory of portfolio selection. *Oxford Bulletin of Economics and Statistics*, 42 (1), 17–35.

Johnston, R. B. (1983a) *The Economics of the Euromarket*, London: Macmillan.

Johnston, R. B. (1983b) A disequilibrium monetary model of the UK economy. HM Treasury, mimeo.

Johnston, R. B. (1984) The demand for non-interest bearing money in the UK. *Government Economic Service Working Paper*, No. 66.

Jonson, P. D. (1976) Money and economic activity in the open economy: the United Kingdom. *Journal of Political Economy*, 84, 979–1012.

Jonson, P. D. and Trevor, R. (1979) Monetary rules: a preliminary analysis. *Reserve Bank of Australia, Discussion Paper*, 7903.

Judd, J. P. and Scadding, J. D. (1981) Liability management, bank loans and deposit 'market' disequilibrium. *Federal Reserve Bank of San Francisco Review*, 21–43.

Judd, J. and Scadding, T. (1982) The search for a stable demand for money function. *Journal of Economic Literature*, 20 (3), 993–1023.

Kannianien, V. and Tarkka, J. (1983) The demand for money: microfoundations for the shock-absorber approach. University of Helsinki, mimeo.

Karni, E. (1974) The value of time and the demand for money. *Journal of Money, Credit and Banking*, 6, 45–64.

Kennan, J. (1979) The estimation of partial adjustment models with rational expectations. *Econometrica*, 47 (6), 1441–55.

Keynes, J. M. (1936) *The General Theory of Employment, Interest and Money*, London: Macmillan.

King, R. E. (1981) Monetary information and monetary neutrality. *Journal of Monetary Economics*, 7, 195–206.

Kiviet, J. F. (1981) On the rigor of some specification tests for modelling dynamic relationships. Paper presented to Amsterdam Conference of the Econometric Society.

Klamer, A. (1984) *The New Classical Macroeconomics*. Brighton, England: Wheatsheaf Books.

Klein, B. (1974a) The competitive supply of money. *Journal of Money, Credit and Banking*, **6**, 423–54.

Klein, B. (1974b) Competitive interest payments on bank deposits and the long-run demand for money. *American Economic Review*, **64**, 931–49.

Klein, L. R. (1969) Estimation of interdependent systems in macroeconomics. *Econometrica*, **37**, 171–92.

Klein, M. A. (1971) A theory of the banking firm. *Journal of Money, Credit and Banking*, **3**, 205–18.

Koutsoyiannis, A. (1977) *Theory of Econometrics*, 2nd edn. London: Macmillan.

Koutsoyiannis, A. (1982) *Non-Price Decision: The Firm in a Modern Context*. London: Macmillan.

Kuhn, T. (1962) *The Structure of Scientific Revolutions*. Chicago: University of Chicago Press.

Laffont, J. J. and Garcia, R. (1977) Disequilibrium econometrics for business loans. *Econometrica*, **45** (5), 1187–204.

Laidler, D. E. W. (1966) The role of interest rates and the demand for money – some empirical evidence. *Journal of Political Economy*, **74**, 545–55.

Laidler, D. E. W. (1971) The influence of money on economic activity: a survey of some current problems. In G. Clayton, J. C. Gilbert and R. Sedgwick (eds), *Monetary Theory and Policy in the 1970s*, Oxford: Oxford University Press.

Laidler, D. E. W. (1973) Expectations, adjustment and the dynamic response of income to policy changes. *Journal of Money, Credit and Banking*, **4**, 157–72.

Laidler, D. E. W. (1977) *The Demand for Money: Theories and Evidence*, 2nd edn, New York: Dun-Donnelly.

Laidler, D. E. W. (1980) The demand for money in the United States – yet again. In K. Brunner and A. Meltzer (eds), *On the State of Macroeconomics*, Carnegie-Rochester Conference Series on Public Policy, vol. 12, Spring.

Laidler, D. E. W. (1982) *Monetarist Perspectives*, Oxford: Philip Allan.

Laidler, D. E. W. (1983) The buffer-stock notion in monetary economics. *Economic Journal*, **94** (Supplement), 17–33.

Laidler, D. E. W. and Bentley, B. (1983) A small macro-model of the post-war United States. *The Manchester School*, **51** (4), 317–40.

Laidler, D. E. W. and O'Shea, P. (1980) An empirical macromodel of an open economy under fixed exchange rates: the UK, 1954–70. *Economica*, **47**, 141–58.

Laidler, D. E. W. and Parkin, J. M. (1970) The demand for money in the United Kingdom 1956–1967: some preliminary estimates. *Manchester School*, **38**, 187–208.

Laidler, D. E. W., Bentley, B., Johnson, D. and Johnson, S. T. (1983) A small macroeconomic model of an open economy: the case of Canada. In E. Claasen and P. Salin (eds), *Recent Issues in the Theory of Flexible Exchange Rates*, Amsterdam: North Holland.

Langohr, H. (1981) Banks borrowing from the Central Bank and reserve position doctrine: Belgium 1960–1973. *Journal of Monetary Economics*, **7**, 107–24.

Laumas, G. S. (1978) A test of the stability of the demand for money. *Scottish Journal of Political Economy*, **25** (3), 239–51.

Lee, T. H. (1967) Alternative interest rates and the demand for money, the empirical evidence. *American Economic Review*, **57**, 1168–81.

Lee, T. H. (1969) Alternative interest rates and the demand for money – reply. *American Economic Review*, **59**, 412–17.

Levacic, R. and Rebmann, A. (1982) *Macroeconomics: An Introduction to Keynesian–Neo Classical Controversies*. London: Macmillan.

Llewellyn, D. T., Dennis, G., Hall, M. and Nellis, J. (1982) *The Framework of UK Monetary Policy*. London: Heinemann,

Lomax, R. and Mowl, C. J. (1978) Balance of payments flows and the monetary aggregates in the United Kingdom. *HM Treasury, Working Paper*, No. 5.

Lucas, R. E. Jnr (1976) Econometric policy evaluation: a critique in The Phillips curve and labour markers. *Carnegie-Rochester Conference Series on Public Policy*, **1**, 19–46.

McCallum, B. T. (1976) Rational expectations and the estimation of econometric models: an alternative procedure. *International Economic Review*, **17**, 484–90.

McCallum, B. T. (1980) Rational expectations and macroeconomic stabilisation policy: an overview. *Journal of Money, Credit and Banking*, **12** (4), 716–46.

McKenzie, G. and Thomas, S. (1984) Currency substitution, monetary policy and international banking, University of Southampton, Discussion Paper.

MacKinnon, J. G. and Milbourne, R. D. (1984) Monetary anticipations and the demand for money. *Journal of Monetary Economics*, **13**, 263–74.

Masson, P. R. (1978) Structural models of the demand for bonds and the term structure of interest rates. *Economica*, **45**, 363–77.

Meiselman, D. (1962) *The Term Structure of Interest Rates*, Oxford: Clarendon Press.

Melton, W. C. and Roley, V. V. (1981) Imperfect asset elasticities and financial model building. *Journal of Econometrics*, **15**, 139–54.

Meltzer, A. H. (1963) The demand for money: the evidence from the time series. *Journal of Political Economy*, **71**, 219–46.

Meyer, L. H. (1983) *Improving Money Stock Control*. Federal Reserve Bank of St Louis, Policy Conference Series, Boston: Kluwer Nijhoff.

Meyer, P. A. and Neri, J. A. (1975) A Keynes–Friedman money demand function. *American Economic Review*, **65**, 610–23.

Midland Bank (1981) Bank lending in a changing environment – a response to recent criticisms. *Midland Bank Review*, Autumn-Winter, 17–22.

Milbourne, R. (1983), Optimal money holding under uncertainty, *International Economic Review*, **24** (3), 685–98.

Milbourne, R., Buckholtz, P. and Wasan, M. T. (1983) A theoretical derivation of the functional form of short run money holdings. *Review of Economic Studies*, **L**, 531–41.

Miller, M. (1981) Monetary control in the UK. *Cambridge Journal of Economics*, **5**, 71–9.

Miller, M. (1984) Government, unions and stagflation in the UK. *National Institute Economic Review*, **109**, 68–72.

Miller, M. and Orr, D. (1966) A model of the demand for money by firms. *Quarterly Journal of Economics*, **80**, 414–35.

Miller, M. and Orr, D. (1968) The demand for money by firms: extension of analytic results. *Journal of Finance*, **23**, 735–59.

Miller, M. and Salmon, M. (1984a) Dynamic games and the time inconsistency of optimal policy in open economies. *Centre for Economic Policy Research, Discussion Paper*, 27, August.

Miller, M. and Salmon, M. (1984b) Policy co-ordination and dynamic games. Department of Economics, Warwick University, mimeo.

Mills, T. C. (1978) The functional form of the UK demand for money. *Applied Statistics*, **27** (1), 52–7.

Mills, T. C. (1983) The information content of the UK monetary components and aggregates. *Bulletin of Economic Research*, **35** (1), 25–46.

Minford, A. P. L. and Peel, D. A. (1982) The Phillips curve and rational expectations. *Weltwirtschaftliches Archiv*, **118**, 456–78.

Minford, P. and Peel, D. (1983) *Rational Expectations and the New Macroeconomics*. Oxford: Martin Robertson.

Minford, P., Brech, M. and Matthews, K. (1980) A rational expectations model of the UK under floating exchange rates. *European Economic Review*, **14** (2), 189–220.

Mishkin, F. S. (1983) *A Rational Expectations Approach to Macroeconometrics*, Chicago: Chicago University Press.

Mizon, G. E. (1977) Model selection procedures. In M. J. Artis and A. R. Nobay (eds), *Studies in Modern Economic Analysis*, Oxford: Basil Blackwell.

Mizon, G. E. (1984) The encompassing approach in econometrics. In D. F. Hendry and K. F. Wallis (eds), *Econometrics and Quantitative Economics*, Oxford: Basil Blackwell.

Mizon, G. E. and Hendry, D. F. (1980) An empirical application and Monte Carlo analysis of tests of dynamic specification. *Review of Economic Studies*, **47** (1), 21–46.

Modigliani, F. (1975) The channels of monetary policy in the Federal Reserve – MIT – Pen, econometric model of the US. In G. Renton (ed.), *Modelling the Economy*, London: Heinemann.

Modigliani, F. and Shiller, R. J. (1973) Inflation, rational expectations and the term structure of interest rates. *Economica*, **40**, 41–3.

Modigliani, F. and Sutch, R. (1966) Innovations in interest rate policy. *American Economic Review, Papers and Proceedings*, **56**, 178–97.

Modigliani, F. and Sutch, R. (1967) Debt management and the term structure of interest rates. *Journal of Political Economy*, **75**, 569–88.

Monti, M. (1971) A theoretical model of the bank behaviour and its implications for monetary policy. *L'Industria Revista di Economica Politica*, **2**, 165–91.

Mowl, C. (1980) Simulations on the Treasury model. *Government Economic Service Working Paper*, no. 34, HM Treasury.

Muellbauer, J. and Portes, R. (1978) Macroeconomic models with quantity rationing. *Economic Journal*, **88**, 788–821.

Mundell, R. A. (1960) The monetary dynamics of adjustment under fixed and flexible exchange rates. *Quarterly Journal of Economics*.

Mundell, R. A. (1963) Capital mobility and stabilisation policy under fixed and flexible exchange rates. *Canadian Journal of Economics and Political Science*, **29**, 475–85.

Muth, J. F. (1960) Optimal properties of exponentially weighted forecasts. Reprinted in R. E. Lucas Jnr and T. J. Sargent (eds), (1981) *Rational Expectations and Econometric Practice*, London: George Allen and Unwin.

Muth, J. F. (1961) Rational expectations and the theory of price movements. *Journal of Political Economy*, **29** (6). Reprinted in R. E. Lucas Jnr and T. J. Sargent (eds), (1981), *Rational Expectations and Econometric Practice*, London: George Allen and Unwin.

Nickell, S. J. (1985) Error correction, partial adjustment and all that; an expositary note. *Oxford Bulletin of Economics and Statistics*, **47** (2), 119–30.

Niehans, J. (1978) *The Theory of Money*, Baltimore, MD: John Hopkins University Press.

Niehans, J. and Hewson, J. (1976) The Eurodollar market and monetary theory. *Journal of Money, Credit and Banking*, **8** (1), 1027.

OECD (1979) Demand for money in major OECD countries. *OECD Economic Outlook, Occasional Studies*, January.

Oxley, L. T. (1983) The functional form of the UK demand for 'broad' money, 1963–1979. *Scottish Journal of Political Economy*, **30** (1), 69–74.

Pagan, A. (1984) Econometric issues in the analysis of regressions with generated regressors. *International Economic Review*, **25** (1), 221–48.

Parkin, J. M. (1970) Discount House, portfolio and debt selection. *Review of Economic Studies*, **37** (4), 469–97.

Parkin, J. M. (1978) A comparison of alternative techniques of monetary control under rational expectations. *The Manchester School*, **46** (3), 252–87.

Parkin, J. M., Grey, M. R. and Barrett, R. J. (1970) The portfolio behaviour of commercial banks. In K. Hilton and D. F. Heathfield (eds), *The Econometric Study of the United Kingdom*, London: Macmillan.

Parks, R. W. (1978) Inflation and relative price variability. *Journal of Political Economy*, **86**, 79–95.

Pesando, J. E. (1978) On the efficiency of the bond market: some Canadian evidence. *Journal of Political Economy*, **86**, 1057–76.

Pesaran, M. H. (1981) Identification of rational expectations models. *Journal of Econometrics*, **16**, 3753–98.

Pesaran, M. H. and Evans, R. A. (1984) Inflation, capital gains and UK personal savings: 1953–1981. *Economic Journal*, **94**, 237–57.

Phlips, L. (1974) *Applied Consumption Analysis*, Amsterdam: North Holland.

Pissarides, C. A. (1978) Liquidity considerations in the theory of consumption. *Quarterly Journal of Economics*, **82**, 279–96.

Poole, W. (1970) Optimal choice of monetary policy instruments in a simple stochastic macro model. *Quarterly Journal of Economics*, **84** (2), 197–216.

Price, L. D. (1972) The demand for money in the UK: a further investigation. *Bank of England Quarterly Bulletin*, **12** (1), 43–55.

Richardson, P. (1981) Money and prices: a simulation study using the Treasury macroeconomic model. *Government Economic Service Working Paper*, No. 41, March.

Richter, R. and Teigen, R. L. (1982) Commercial bank behavior and monetary policy in an open economy; West Germany 1960–1980. *Journal of Monetary Economics*, **10** (3), 383–406.

Rowan, D. C. and O'Brien, R. J. (1970) Expectations, interest rate structure and debt policy. In K. Hilton and D. Heathfield (eds), *The Economic Study of the United Kingdon*, London: Macmillan.

Salmon, M. (1982) Error correction mechanisms. *Economic Journal*, **92**, 615–29.

Santomero, A. M. (1974) A model of the demand for money by households. *Journal of Finance*, **29** (1), 89–102.

Santomero, A. M. (1983) Controlling monetary aggregates; the discount window. *Journal of Finance*, **38** (3), 827–43.

Santomero, A. M. (1984) Modelling the banking firm. *Journal of Money, Credit and Banking*, **16** (4), 576–602.

Santomero, A. M. and Seater, J. J. (1981) Partial adjustment in the demand for money: theory and empirics. *American Economic Review*, **71**, 566–78.

Sargan, J. D. (1958) The estimation of economic relationships using instrumental variables. *Econometrica*, **36**, 393–413.

Sargent, T. J. (1971) A note on the 'accelerationist' controversy. *Journal of Money, Credit and Banking*, 8. Reprinted in R. E. Lucas and T. J. Sargent (eds), (1981), *Rational Expectations and Econometric Practice*, London: George Allen and Unwin.

Sargent, T. J. (1976) A classical macroeconomic model of the United States. *Journal of Political Economy*, **84**, 207–38.

Sargent, T. J. (1979a) A note on the maximum likelihood estimation of the rational expectations model of the term structure. *Journal of Political Economy*, **5**, 133–43.

Sargent, T. J. (1979b) *Macroeconomic Theory*, London: Academic Press.

Savage, D. (1978) The monetary sector of the NIESR model: preliminary results. *National Institute of Economic and Social Research, Discussion Paper*, No. 23.

Schwert, G. W. (1983) Tests of casuality: the message in the innovations. In K. Brunner and A. Meltzer (eds), *Theory, Policy Institutions*, Carnegie-Rochester Series on Public Policy, Amsterdam: North Holland.

Sellon, G. H. Jnr and Teigen, R. L. (1982) The choice of short-run targets for monetary policy, Parts I and II. In *Issues in Monetary Policy II*, Federal Reserve Bank of Kansas City.

Sheffrin, S. M. (1983) *Rational Expectations*, Cambridge: Cambridge University Press.

Shiller, R. J. (1979) The volatility of long-term interest rates and expectations models of the term structure. *Journal of Political Economy*, **87**, 1190–219.

Sims, C. A. (1972) Money income and causality. *American Economic Review*, **62**, 540–52.

Sims, C. A. (1980) Macroeconomics and reality, *Econometrica*,

Sinclair, P. J. N. (1983) *The Foundations of Macroeconomics and Monetary Theory*, Oxford: Oxford University Press.

Slovin, M. B. and Sushka, M. E. (1983) A model of the commercial loan rate. *Journal of Finance*, **38** (5), 1583–96.

Smith, S. G. (1975) Pitfalls in financial model building: a clarification. *American Economic Review*, **65**, 510–16.

Smith, G. (1978) Dynamic models of portfolio behaviour: comment on Purvis. *American Economic Review*, **68**, 410–16.

Smith, G. (1980) Further evidence on the value of a priori information. *Journal of Finance*, **35** (1), 181–89.

Smith, G. (1981) The systematic specification of a full prior covariance matrix for asset demand equations. *Quarterly Journal of Economics*, 317–38.

Smith, S. G. snd Brainard, W. (1976) The value of a priori information in estimating a financial model. *Journal of Finance*, **31** (5), 1299–322.

Smith, S. G. and Brainard, W. (1982) A disequilibrium model of savings and loan associations. *Journal of Finance*, **37** (5), 1277–293.

Spencer, P. D. (1981) A model of the demand for British Government stocks by non-bank residents 1967–77. *Economic Journal*, **91** (364), 938–60.

Spencer, P. D. (1984) Precautionary and speculative aspects of the behaviour of banks in the UK under competition and credit control 1972-80. *Economic Journal*, **94** (375), 554–68.

Spencer, P. D. and Mowl, C. (1978) A financial sector for the Treasury model. *Government Economic Service Working Paper*, No. 17, December.

Spitzer, J. J. (1976) The demand for money, the liquidity trap and functional forms. *International Economic Review*, **17**, 220–7.

Spitzer, J. J. (1977) A simultaneous equations system of money demand and supply using generalised functional forms. *Journal of Econometrics*, **5**, 117–28.

Sprenkle, C. M. (1966) Large economic units, banks and the transactions demand for money. *Quarterly Journal of Economics*, **80**, 436–42.

Sprenkle, C. M. (1969) The uselessness of transactions demand models. *Journal of Finance*, **4**, 835–47.

Sprenkle, C. M. (1972) On the observed transactions demand for money. *Manchester School*, **40** (3), 261–67.

Sprenkle, C. M. (1974) An overdue note on some 'Ancient but Popular' literature. *Journal of Finance*, **29**, 1577–80.

Sprenkle, C. M. (1984) On liquidity preference again: comment. *American Economic Review*, **74** (4), 809–11.

Sprenkle, C. M. and Miller, M. H. (1980) The precautionary demand for narrow and broad money. *Economica*, **47**, 407–21.

Starleaf, D. R. (1970) The specification of money demand–supply models which involve the use of distribution lags. *Journal of Finance*, **25** (4), 743–60.

Stiglitz, J. E. (1972) Portfolio allocation with many risky assets. In G. P. Szegö and K. Shell (eds), *Mathematical Methods in Investment and Finance*, London: North Holland.

Taylor, J. B. (1979) Staggered wage setting in a macroeconomic model. *American Economic Review, Papers and Proceedings*, **69**, 1–8–13.

Taylor, J. B. (1980) Aggregate dynamics and staggered contracts. *Journal of Political Economy*, **88**, 1–23.

Teigen, R. (1964) Demand and supply functions for money in the United States. *Econometrica*, **32** (4), 477–509.

Tew, B. (1978) Monetary policy – part I. In F. Blackaby (ed.), *British Economic Policy 1960–74*, Cambridge: Cambridge University Press.

Tobin, J. (1980) *Asset Accumulation and Economic Activity*, Oxford: Basil Blackwell.

Thompson, W. N. (1984) Money in UK macromodels. In Demery et al. (eds), *Macroeconomics*, London: Longman.

Thornton, D. L. (1982) Simple analytics of the money supply process and monetary control. *Federal Reserve Bank of St Louis Review*, **64** (8), 22–39.

Tobin, J. (1956) The interest elasticity of transactions demand for cash. *Review of Economics and Statistics*, **38**, 241–47.

Tobin, J. (1963) Commercial banks as creators of money. In D. Carson (ed.), *Banking and Monetary Studies*, Homewood, IL: Irwin.

Tobin, J. (1970) Money and income: post hoc ergo propter hoc. *Quarterly Journal of Economics*, **84**, 301–17.

Trundle, J. M. (1982) Recent changes in the use of cash. *Bank of England Quarterly Bulletin*, **22** (4), 519–29.

Tucker, D. (1966) Dynamic income adjustment to money supply changes, *American Economic Review*, **56**, 433–49.

Turnovsky, S. J. (1977) *Macroeconomic Analysis and Stabilisation Policy*. Cambridge: Cambridge University Press.

Wallis, K. F. (1980) Econometric implications of the rational expectations hypothesis. *Econometrica*, **48** (1), 49–73.

Walsh, C. E. (1982) The effects of alternative operating procedures on economic and financial relationships. In *Monetary Policy Issues in the 1980s*, Symposium sponsored by Federal Reserve Bank of Kansas City.

Walsh, C. E. (1984) Interest rate volatility and monetary policy. *Journal of Money, Credit and Banking*, **16** (2), 133–50.

Wessels, R. E. (1982) The supply and use of central bank advance facilities. *Journal of Monetary Economics*, **10** (1), 89–100.

Weiss, L. (1980) The role for active monetary policy in a rational expectations model. *Journal of Political Economy*, 2, 221–33.

Whalen, E. L. (1966) A rationalisation of the precautionary demand for cash. *Quarterly Journal of Economics*, May.

White, W. H. (1981) The case for and against disequilibrium money. *IMF Staff Papers*, 2813, 534–72.

White, W. R. (1975) Some econometric models of deposit bank portfolio behaviour in the UK 1963–70. In G. Renton (ed.), *Modelling the Economy*, London: Heinemann.

Wickens, M. R. (1982) The efficient estimation of econometric models with rational expectations. *Review of Economic Studies*, XLIX, 55–67.

Williams, D. (1978) Estimating in levels or first differences: a defence of the method used for certain demand for money equations. *Economic Journal*, 88, 564–8.

Wills, H. R. (1982) The simple economics of bank regulation. *Economica*, 49, 249–59.

Wilson, H. (1980) *Report of the Committee to Review the Functioning of Financial Institutions*, Cmnd 7937, HM Stationery Office.

Wren-Lewis, S. (1984) Omitted variables in equations relating prices to money. *Applied Economics*, 16, 483–96.

Yule, G. U. (1926) Why do we sometimes get nonsense correlations between time series? A study in sampling and the nature of time series. *Journal of the Royal Statistical Society*, 89, 1–64.

Zawadzki, K. K. F. (1981) *Competition and Credit Control*, Oxford: Basil Blackwell.

Zellner, A. (1962) An efficient method of estimating seemingly unrelated regressions and tests for aggregation bias. *Journal of the American Statistical Association*, 57, 348–68.

Author Index

Subject Index